AF333230

Painters, Patrons, and Identity

Painters, Patrons,

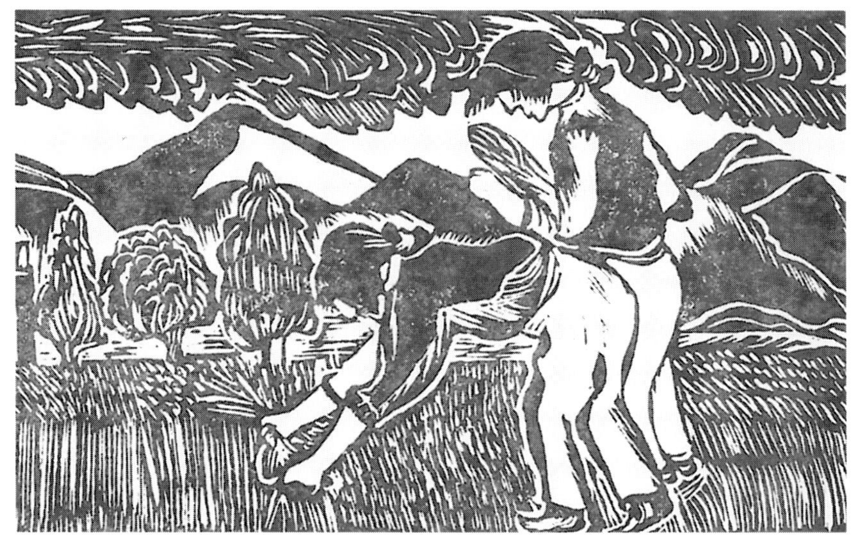

ESSAYS IN NATIVE AMERICAN ART

and Identity

to Honor J. J. Brody

Edited by Joyce M. Szabo

University of New Mexico Press · Albuquerque

© 2001 by Joyce M. Szabo
All rights reserved.
First Edition

Library of Congress Cataloging-in-Publication Data:
    Painters, patrons, and identity : essays in Native American art to honor
J. J. Brody / edited by Joyce M. Szabo—1st ed.
        p.   cm.
    Includes bibliographical references and index.
    ISBN 0-8263-2025-2 (cloth : alk. paper)
        1. Indian art—North America.   2. Indian artists—North America.
3. Brody, J. J.   I. Szabo, Joyce M.   II. Brody, J. J.
E98.A7   P28   2001
704.03'97—dc21   00-009017

Frontispiece: Juan Pino, Tesuque Pueblo. Untitled *[Harvesting Grain],* n.d., linoleum block print, 4⅜ in. x 8⅛ in. School of American Research, cat. no. IAF.P149.

Table of Contents

Acknowledgments　　　*vii*

List of Figures　　　*ix*

List of Color Plates　　　*xiii*
Color Plates follow page 114

Introduction　　　*1*
Joyce M. Szabo

Chapter 1
Toys, Models, Collectibles: Miniature Tipis in the Reservation Era　　　*9*
Adrianne A. Santina

Chapter 2
Identity Recovered: Portrait of a Northern Arapaho Quillworker　　　*33*
Marsha C. Bol

Chapter 3
From General Souvenir to Personal Memento: Fort Marion
Drawings and the Significance of Books　　　*49*
Joyce M. Szabo

Chapter 4
Social Power and the Men's Northern Traditional Powwow
Clothing Style　　　*71*
Aaron Fry

Chapter 5
Juan Pino, Pueblo Printmaker   *95*
RUTH LaNORE

Chapter 6
Indian Identity and Evaluating the Past: Bonita Wa Wa Calachaw
Nuñez, an Indian Princess Painter   *119*
KATHLEEN E. ASH-MILBY

Chapter 7
The Hunt for Identity in Clarence Monegar's Wildlife Paintings   *141*
SAMUEL E. WATSON III

Chapter 8
Made in Japan with the Exception of Two: Native American and
Appalachian Arts Come of Age   *163*
JOY L. GRITTON

Chapter 9
Picturing Sovereignty: Landscape in Contemporary Native
American Art   *187*
KATE MORRIS

Chapter 10
Rock Art and the Shape of Landscape   *211*
H. DENISE SMITH

Chapter 11
Chief Blankets on the Middle Missouri: Navajo Artists and
Their Patrons   *241*
GRETA J. MURPHY

Chapter 12
"Walking in Strange Gardens": Early Floral Design in the
Columbia River Plateau   *263*
STEVEN LeROY GRAFE

Bibliography   *281*

Index   *299*

Acknowledgments

Many people deserve heartfelt thanks for their parts in making this volume possible. Naomi and Arthur Rosenberg were extremely generous in providing funding to assist in the reproduction of the color plates included here. Dana Asbury at the University of New Mexico Press was a very patient editor working with this novice volume editor. Dana's initial enthusiasm for a festschrift in honor of Jerry Brody allowed the dream to become a reality. Copy editors and designers, including Amy Elder and Deborah Flynn Post, worked diligently to smooth the flaws in the manuscript and to work the visual magic they do so well.

List of Figures

Frontispiece Juan Pino, Tesuque Pueblo. Untitled [*Harvesting Grain*], n.d.

1.1	Sarcee, Miniature Tipi, 1905.	14
1.2	Cover, Tipi, Model, n.d.	17
1.3	Plains, Miniature Tipi, n.d.	19
1.4	Sioux(?), Miniature Tipi, 1900.	21
1.5	Cheyenne, Miniature Tipi, 1902–4.	24
2.1	Fire Wood, "Small Red Painted Robe."	37
2.2	Fire Wood, "Eagle Design Robe."	38
2.3	Fire Wood, "Lean Back."	39
2.4	Northern Arapaho, Quilled Cradle.	41
3.1	Bear's Heart, Southern Cheyenne, *Courting Scene.*	51
3.2	Making Medicine, Southern Cheyenne, *Indian Prisoners at Fort Marion Being Photographed.*	56
3.3	Bear's Heart, Southern Cheyenne, *Drawn by Himself.*	60
3.4	Wohaw, Kiowa, Untitled, 1882.	65
4.1	Deer toe "bells," 1998.	79
4.2	Northern Traditional bustle, 1996.	82
4.3	Wayne Cleland (Anishnabe), 1997.	85
4.4	Contemporary soldier hat, 1996.	87
5.1	Juan Pino, Tesuque Pueblo, Untitled *[Man and Two Deer]*, n.d.	98

5.2   Lorencito *[sic]* Pino, Tesuque Pueblo, Jar, ca. 1930.   *100*

5.3   *"Happy New Year" Card, 1929–1930, to Olive Rush from Marguerite and Charles Kassler.*   *102*

5.4   Juan Pino, Tesuque Pueblo, Untitled *[Pueblo Scene with Two Burros and Walking Man]*, n.d.   *105*

5.5   Juan Pino, Tesuque Pueblo, Untitled *[Pueblo Scene with Man in Overalls]*, n.d.   *107*

5.6   Gustave Baumann, *July*, 1912.   *108*

5.7   Gustave Baumann, *Excavated Area of the Aztec Ruin*, 1917.   *110*

6.1   Bonita Wa Wa Calachaw Nuñez, Untitled, n.d.   *120*

6.2   Wa Wa Chaw and her husband, Manuel Nuñez, from about 1910.   *122*

6.3   Käthe Kollwitz, *The Sacrifice* (*Das Opfer*), 1922–23.   *129*

6.4   Bonita Wa Wa Calachaw Nuñez. . . . *Her Memory*, n.d.   *130*

6.5   Bonita Wa Wa Calachaw Nuñez, Untitled, n.d.   *131*

6.6   Bonita Wa Wa Calachaw Nuñez, Detail of Untitled, n.d.   *133*

7.1   Clarence Monegar, *Feeding Grouse*, 1943.   *145*

7.2   Clarence Monegar, *S. H. Van Gorden*, 1938.   *147*

7.3   Clarence Monegar, Untitled, 1940.   *148*

7.4   Clarence Monegar, *Scout*, 1940.   *150*

7.5   Clarence Monegar, *Buck in the Snow*, 1942.   *152*

8.1   Chair Workers Preparing Seats and a Model Dining Room Arrangement Showing Modern Applications of Appalachian Arts.   *177*

9.1   Kay WalkingStick, *Venere Alpina*, 1997.   *196*

9.2   Hachivi Edgar Heap of Birds, *Neuf,* 1991–92.   *201*

10.1   Map of Abo Pueblo and Vicinity.   *212*

10.2   Map Showing All Loci Recorded at Abo Pueblo.   *220*

10.3   Early Puebloan Rock Art Loci, Abo.   *228*

10.4   Late Puebloan Rock Art Loci, Abo.   *229*

10.5   Late or Historic Puebloan Rock Art Loci, Abo.   *230*

10.6   Historic Rock Art Loci, Abo.   *231*

10.7   Locus ET4 (computer enhanced).   *232*

10.8   Locus AL (computer enhanced).   *233*

10.9   Athapaskan Rock Art Loci, Abo.   *235*

10.10   Comparison of Late/Historic, Historic, and Athapaskan Panels, Abo.   *236*

11.1   Navajo First-Phase Chief Blanket, ca. 1800–1850.   *246*

11.2   Navajo Second-Phase Chief Blanket, ca. 1860–70.   *247*

11.3   Navajo Third-Phase Chief Blanket, ca. 1860–70.   *248*

11.4   Courting Blanket, Lakota, ca. 1890.   *249*

11.5   Parfleche, Crow or Wind River Shoshoni, ca. 1850–1900.   *250*

11.6   Edna Kash Kash (Cayuse-Umatilla) and a Navajo First-Phase Chief Blanket to which an intermontane-style blanket strip was added.   *251*

11.7   Map Showing the Protohistoric Middle Missouri, Pacific-Plateau, and Southwest Trade Systems.   *254*

12.1   "Oregon Rose" Quilt, 1851.   *267*

12.2   Tish Kamiakin wearing a woven coverlet, ca. 1864.   *268*

12.3   *Half-breed Child in Cradle with Indian Ornamental Trappings,* 1860–61.   *270*

12.4   Nez Perce Miniature Double Saddlebag, collected 1866–69.   *272*

12.5   Nez Perce Man's Coat, collected 1877.   *274*

12.6   Nez Perce Woman's Leggings, before 1883.   *276*

12.7   Nez Perce Cradle, before 1883.   *277*

List of Color Plates
(following page 114)

1   Plains, Miniature Tipi, n.d.

2   Sioux, Miniature Tipi, 1880–1900.

3   Buzzard, Southern Cheyenne, *At Home.*

4   Bear's Heart, Southern Cheyenne, *Self-Portrait.*

5   Old-style bustle, ca. 1993.

6   Northern Traditional bustle, 1995.

7   Bonita Wa Wa Calachaw Nuñez, Untitled, n.d.

8   Bonita Wa Wa Calachaw Nuñez, *Birth of a Baby,* before 1959.

9   Clarence Monegar, Untitled, n.d.

10   Clarence Monegar. *Running Deer,* 1942.

11   T. C. Cannon. *Made in Japan with Exception of One,* 1966.

12   James Lavadour, *Nest of Suns,* 1998.

13   George Longfish, *The End of the Innocence,* 1991–92.

14   Yakama Double Saddle Pouch, collected 1876.

15   Colville Gloves, collected 1878–79.

"*I*ndian Painters and White Patrons," a dissertation written by Jacob Jerome Brody in 1970 for the completion of his doctoral degree in art history at the University of New Mexico, has had far-reaching effects. Published by the University of New Mexico Press in the following year, *Indian Painters and White Patrons* was greeted with acclaim by some and criticism by others. In the volume, Brody took what was the first hard look at the system of outside patronage that had encouraged Native American painting in the early years of the twentieth century and that continues to do so even today. His lack of romanticism, his focused art historical investigation of issues, and his clear writing style made the work immediately accessible to varied audiences. It remains the essential beginning point for today's ongoing explorations of the diversity and history of Native American painting for outside audiences.[1]

The book was criticized for what some perceived as its presentation of Native artists blindly following what others dictated; nothing could be further from the truth. Brody's dissertation and the subsequent book brought to light some of the complex issues that worked together to encourage Native American painting, most prominently in the Southwest. In hindsight, some of the practices of the early twentieth century, judged in later twentieth-century terms, seem obviously racist and restrictive. What Brody brought to his examination is what any good art historian needs to bring, a suggestion of how the era during which something occurred affected the actions of people. As various writers would unfortunately do after him, judgment has often been passed without such considerations.

Just as it is doubtful that Jerry Brody envisioned the reception his first book would have, so he undoubtedly did not foresee what the granting of his Ph.D. would do for the University of New Mexico. With his 1970 degree, Jerry became the first Ph.D.

recipient in the university's newly established doctoral program in art history. Since that time countless students have entered the program to obtain both master's and doctoral degrees.

When the Department of Art and Art History originally decided to add a graduate program in art history, they did so with clear ideas about what they could provide to the already overpopulated world of art history programs. Determining to only offer advanced study in areas they could do well and, in most cases, uniquely given their location, they did not develop programs in Greek and Roman art or Renaissance painting; instead they looked to the history and cultures of the Southwest. Photography, a strong component of the university's studio program, was an unmistakable focus; the history of photography, a new and as of then-unusual field of study, offered the department an opportunity to excel. The history of modern art and the history of architecture were also obvious choices given the importance of New Mexico to various aspects of modernism and the connection of the Department of Art, subsequently renamed the Department of Art and Art History, to the university's School of Architecture. American art, both as a component of each of these areas and as a field uniquely its own, was a fourth component. The rich Spanish heritage of the region made Spanish colonial art history a definite addition as was the pre-Columbian art and architecture of Meso and South America. Native American art history was not only a clear choice, one in which the department could make an important contribution and potentially expand the boundaries of more traditional art history, but also the area in which the first Ph.D. was granted.

The year 2000 will receive a great deal of attention for many reasons, but the Department of Art and Art History at the University of New Mexico adds a focus uniquely its own; this is the thirtieth anniversary of the founding of its doctoral program in art history and, consequently, the thirtieth anniversary of J. J. Brody's Ph.D. in Native American art history. What to this day remains one of the very few programs in the nation to offer both master's and doctoral programs in Native American art history celebrates its continued existence and honors its initial recipient, the man who prodded the program into being.

After the publication of *Indian Painters and White Patrons,* Jerry continued his work as a curator at the Maxwell Museum of Anthropology at UNM, a position he had had since 1962, and held a faculty appointment in anthropology from 1965 to 1985. In 1972 he became the director of the Maxwell; he continued as director until 1985 while simultaneously becoming a professor in the Department of Art and Art History. When he stepped down as director of the Maxwell, he turned his attention to full-time teaching in art and art history until his retirement in 1989.

Given his close association with museums and his dedication to teaching not only

Native American art history but also museum studies, Jerry Brody has curated many exhibitions over the years, both before and after his "retirement." Among the most important of those exhibitions were *Between Traditions: Navajo Weaving from 1880 to 1920* (Maxwell, 1976), *Myth, Metaphor, and Mimbreno Art* (Maxwell, 1977), *The Chaco Phenomenon* (Maxwell, 1983), *Beauty from the Earth* (University Museum, University of Pennsylvania, 1990), *A Bridge across Cultures: Pueblo Painters in Santa Fe, 1910–1932* (Wheelwright Museum of the American Indian, 1992), *To Touch the Past: The Painted Pottery of the Mimbres People* (Weisman Art Museum, 1996), and *Better Than the Picture of the Camera: Early Twentieth-Century Pueblo Indian Painting* (University Art Museum, University of New Mexico, 1998).

His publications, of course, did not stop with that first book. Jerry has published various monographs and exhibition catalogues, many since his retirement. These include *Between Traditions: Navajo Weaving, 1880–1920* (1976), *Mimbres Painted Pottery* (1977), *The Chaco Phenomenon* (1983), *Beauty from the Earth* (1990), *The Anasazi* (1990), *Anasazi and Pueblo Painting* (1991), and *Pueblo Indian Painting: Tradition and Modernism in New Mexico, 1900–1930* (1997).

These are only the major volumes. Essays and articles abound and continue to question long-held assumptions about various aspects of Native American art. Particularly important essays include "The Rhetoric of Formalism: Interpreting Anasazi Architecture" (1997), "Kachina Images in American Art: The Way of the Doll" (1994), "In Our Own Time: Anasazi and Pueblo Pottery in the Twentieth Century and Beyond" (1991), "Changing Perceptions of North American Indian Art" (1990), "Site Use, Pictorial Space, and Subject Matter in Late Prehistoric and Early Historic Rio Grande Pueblo Art" (1989), "Tradition, Transition, and Transformation in American Indian Art" (1987), "The Mimbres People: Belief in Life and Continuity" (1984), "Pueblo Fine Arts" (1979), "The Creative Consumer: Survival, Revival, and Invention in Southwest Indian Arts" (1977), and "In Advance of the Readymade: Kiva Murals and Navajo Dry Paintings" (1974). Each of these exhibitions, monographs, and essays has expanded knowledge concerning a wide variety of art forms while simultaneously raising questions that have encouraged further investigation. There is a school of thought that holds that anything published, or even presented in a formal paper, that does not promote discussion is a failure; Jerry Brody has never failed to stimulate debate.

The idea of a festschrift, a volume of essays offered in honor of an individual, has a long history in academic scholarship, yet such volumes have become rare in recent years. This volume is a true celebration of a scholar and his contributions to date; it is not a memorial celebrating the completion of anything, for Jerry Brody's work continues at an even greater pace, if that is possible, than it has in previous years. While some people retire to play golf, Jerry retired to pursue research and writing.

Jerry's work continues in other ways perhaps not as immediately visible to those not closely connected to the Department of Art and Art History at the University of New Mexico. Here he established a legacy that remains unbroken. Each of the contributors to this volume has, or will have by the time of publication, received a graduate degree in Native American art history from UNM and has studied with Jerry. Some of the authors, Marsha C. Bol, Joy L. Gritton, and Joyce M. Szabo, received their degrees during the time Jerry taught in the department, and he served as the chair of their committees on studies directing dissertations and theses on various aspects of Native American art. Other writers represent a slightly younger generation of students who came after Jerry had retired but retained emeritus status and taught the occasional class. He also conducted an intensive summer seminar at the School of American Research in Santa Fe, which UNM students enrolled in the graduate program in Native American art history were privileged to attend and for which they received course credit; from this 1992 seminar came the subjects for various master's theses, two of which, those by Greta J. Murphy and Ruth LaNore, are explored in chapters in this volume. While not investigating topics they dealt with during that summer seminar, Steven LeRoy Grafe, H. Denise Smith, Kate Morris, Kathleen E. Ash-Milby, and Samuel E. Watson III have provided chapters that suggest the kinds of research skills they honed during those summer sessions at the School of American Research. The newest members of the department to contribute essays, Adrianne A. Santina and Aaron Fry, have both studied with Jerry and have benefited greatly from that opportunity.

The range of topics explored in this anthology and the approaches taken to the problems examined reflect the kind of academic inquiry that Jerry Brody demands of himself and inspires in others. Even though he is a noted expert on Native art of the Southwest, both archaeological and historic, two of the first three doctoral students to complete their studies under his direction wrote their dissertations on Plains topics. Marsha C. Bol here continues her focus on Plains women's art of the reservation era by exploring references in Cleaver Warden's 1904–5 field notes to art produced by Fire Wood, a northern Arapaho woman. It is rare that Plains women artists are known by name from this era, and Bol's essay brings to light long-overlooked information that adds greatly to our understanding of the roles women played within their community, using their art to both honor and safeguard family members. Joyce M. Szabo also continues her study of a kind of art more frequently associated with Plains men as she examines two books of drawings created by southern Plains warriors incarcerated at Fort Marion in Saint Augustine, Florida, between 1875 and 1878. While such drawings have received great attention, the small autograph books Szabo discusses appear to be unique, filled with work by many artists, and seemingly created as tokens of friendship for people to whom the artists grew attached during their three-year exile. Thus her essay questions the different purposes for which drawings were made by Fort Marion prisoners and the differences between art as souvenir, personalized memento, and gift.

Adrianne A. Santina also explores the world of small-scale works created by Plains artists; she offers the first in-depth art historical examination of miniature tipis from the reservation period. Using these as an avenue to learn more about Cheyenne and Arapaho concepts of architecture and community space while simultaneously investigating the roles of toys, models, and collectibles, Santina examines the allure of the miniature for both creator and user. Aaron Fry's discussion of powwow clothing brings us to the present day as he not only establishes the historical precedents for powwow clothing but also examines its roles not simply in affirming Native identity in the contemporary world but also in actively creating identities in response to both internal and external factors. Fry demands that investigations of Native American art include what he terms rigorous theoretical analysis, an analysis he effectively provides for men's Northern Traditional-style powwow clothing.

Many of the writers here explore various aspects of modern Native American art, and each owes his or her beginning interest in this area to Jerry Brody's groundbreaking work. Three of these authors investigate artists who have received little, if any, attention. Ruth LaNore began her study of the images of the Tesuque printmaker Juan Pino during her summer seminar at the School of American Research, and it grew into an important examination, a rediscovery of an artist comparatively well known during the early years of the twentieth century to the Euro-American artists who filled Santa Fe but whose work, since then seen as far too influenced by those very non-Native artists, has disappeared from view. Perhaps LaNore's study will allow Pino to reclaim his position in the history of Native American art. Kathleen Ash-Milby also explores the work of another little-known Native American painter, Bonita Wa Wa Calachaw Nuñez. Born to a Luiseño mother, Nuñez was adopted by a wealthy Euro-American suffragist and her brother and subsequently raised in New York. Largely a self-taught artist, Nuñez is one of many Native American women from the early years of the twentieth century who were seen or marketed as "Indian princesses." The contradictory pulls of her life as a Native woman raised in Anglo society are strong in the paintings she left at her death in 1972, and Ash-Milby brings many of those issues to light.

Samuel E. Watson III looks at another Native American painter, Charles Monegar (1910–68). Of Hochunk or Winnebago heritage, Monegar created two distinct bodies of work, one an evocation of his Native heritage; the other, more successful in its day, distinctive renditions of hunting scenes and animal life. Like Wa Wa Calachaw Nuñez's, Monegar's work reflects the contradictory nature of the artist's life. Watson not only explores those issues but places Monegar's work firmly within the context of 1930s and 1940s American regionalism at large. Such a view of Native artists as part of regionalist aesthetics is one Jerry Brody has long advocated.

The opposition of modern and what for many has been termed "traditional" has been at the core of much debate concerning Native American art in the twentieth century, and Joy L. Gritton examines these paired issues through parallels she perceives in the way in which Native American arts and those created by Appalachian artists have been seen by outside patrons. Gritton, like Brody, investigates questions of continuity, or the lack thereof, and form, content, and function in the face of outsider interventions and the way these arts have been adapted to "modern applications."

Kate Morris also expands beyond the study of a single artist to suggest the ways in which various Native artists use their work to explore issues of sovereignty through references to landscape or the lack thereof. Tying the longevity of landscape imagery to early paintings by Mimbres artists who, according to Brody, "drew the world around them as they conceived it . . . animals, mythical creatures, abstractions of mountains, clouds, and plants as they saw, remembered and imagined them," Morris examines how contemporary artists such as George Longfish, Emmi Whitehorse, and Truman Lowe have continued not only to draw the world as they conceive it but also to transform their representations into statements that are simultaneously personal and political.[2]

Two contributors to the current volume investigate aspects of the Southwest that have been and continue to be of great interest to Brody: rock art and Navajo weaving. H. Denise Smith's examination of rock art at Abo in midcentral New Mexico and its use to create and define space is an innovative application of new technologies and theoretical discussions; it carries a view of the importance of landscape and its marking for both personal and political reasons back from the current day to the archaeological past. Layers of meaning are suggested when rock art is seen not only to heighten a sense of place and indicate a center but also to mark boundaries and suggest limits. Abo was a place of contact and exchange between the Southwest and the Plains, a contact that continues in many ways to the current day. Greta J. Murphy views another aspect of the far-too-little-explored connections between those two regions by examining Navajo textiles and their linkage to Plains aesthetics. Focusing specifically on the type of blanket generally known as the chief blanket for its appeal to and use by Plains chiefs, Murphy's essay directly acknowledges Jerry Brody not only through its subtitle, "Navajo Artists and Their Patrons," but also through its insistent exploration of a nineteenth-century practice that took into account the desires of the patron in a long-established exchange system.

Finally, Steven LeRoy Grafe takes Jerry's lead in tackling a long-held assumption in the history of art created by Native American artists of the Plateau region, which has invariably been attributed to the influence of Native people from the Great Lakes region entering the Plateau with fur trappers. Grafe amasses in-depth support and relies on well-documented works of art to argue that floral beadwork became a part of the Plateau aesthetic through the continuous and varied influences that came with non-Native people into the region. From Spode china to floral quilts, Grafe establishes a strong case for continuously "walking in strange gardens" of floral imagery in nineteenth-century Plateau art.

The twelve essays collected here are varied in specific subject but united in their unrelenting pursuit of answers to perplexing questions. As Jerry Brody invariably told, and continues to tell, graduate students, there are two reasons to publish something—one, to get new information out into the world and, second, but no less important, to promote discussion. The assembled writers provide essays for those reasons but also add a third—to honor through a festschrift the contributions of a great teacher and scholar. Such a volume of collected essays might be seen as an old-fashioned tribute, but it is one that carries a contemporary spirit of active exploration of issues that have no simple answers. Jerry Brody does not allow either himself or his students to settle for the easy solution to anything. None of the writers here nor the man they honor will ever change their attitude about this basic tenet of art historical investigation.

Joyce M. Szabo
Albuquerque
January 2000

Notes

1. See the discussion of the impact of *Indian Painters and White Patrons* in Margaret Dubin, "Sanctioned Scribes: How Critics and Historians Write the Native American Art World," in *Native American Art in the Twentieth Century*, ed. W. Jackson Rushing III (London and New York: Routledge, 1999), 149–166.

2. J. J. Brody and Rina Swentzell, *To Touch the Past: The Painted Pottery of the Mimbres People* (New York: Hudson Hills Press, 1996), 11.

CHAPTER 1

TOYS, MODELS, COLLECTIBLES

Miniature Tipis in the Reservation Era

ADRIANNE A. SANTINA

Tipis, portable houses created by nomadic Plains Indians, highlight major features of the worldview and social organization of varied Plains cultures. In many groups, men painted the exteriors of tipi covers to depict their acts of bravery in battle or their visionary experiences. Women decorated their tipis by creating beaded or quilled disks, rectangular banners, and dangles. Such objects were made and attached to the tipi cover during ritual activities and contributed to the sacred nature of the lodge. While tipis were one of the preferred house forms of Plains groups from the sixteenth century onward, relatively few made before the twentieth century exist today. This dearth of material evidence creates difficulties in understanding tipis, their ornamentation, and the ways they expressed cultural beliefs, aesthetic values, and individual creativity.

Information about tipis and their exterior decoration may nevertheless be found in miniature and small-scale tipis made in the late nineteenth and early twentieth centuries (plate 1). These objects exist in much larger numbers than their full-size counterparts.[1] Some miniature and toy tipis have been identified as actual re-creations of larger ones. One scholar states that "toy tipis were often replicas of a full-size tipi and bore similar decoration." Likewise, Crow woman Pretty Shield told her biographer, Frank Linderman, that as a child she had a small tipi that was a replica of her aunt's. Pretty Shield described her lodge as follows: "I had a little tepee [lodge] that I pitched whenever my aunt pitched hers. It was made exactly like my aunt's, had the same number of poles, only of course my tepee was very small."[2] Toy and small-scale tipis are a potentially rich resource for information on full-size tipis, as they could be post-factum models of specific lodges. In addition, miniature and toy tipis often bear beaded or quilled decorations. Many of these ornaments show the same shape and placement on the miniature as on full-size lodges, indicating a definite connection to full-size tipis. Surprisingly, however, miniature tipis as a genre unto themselves have not been widely studied and are rarely discussed as viable secondary documents relating to full-size tipis. Only John Ewers and Nancy Fagin, both of whom examine model tipis commissioned by ethnologist James Mooney, attempt to reconcile the appearance of the model tipis to the full-size ones. In each of their analyses, the model tipis were viewed as valuable sources of information concerning the painting of visionary experiences on tipi covers.[3]

Full-size tipi covers are primary sources in a study of Plains architecture and its attendant meanings, but many of these primary documents no longer exist. An evaluation of the viability of miniature tipis as secondary documents, sources once-removed yet definitely related to the primary object, is undertaken in an attempt to determine how they relate to their full-size counterparts. Two important questions to consider are, why miniature tipis were created and why, and by whom, such tipis were collected. One reason for the making of miniature and model tipis was for use as toys within the groups themselves. Among Plains people such as the Cheyenne and Lakota, toys often took the form of small-scale reproductions of everyday and house-hold objects. Girls, for instance, played with miniature tipis, dolls, and cradles made for them by their mothers and grandmothers, while boys, predictably, played with miniature bows and arrows. Toy tipis could range in size from less than a foot tall to several feet tall, large enough for the girl to actually pitch the lodge. Often the children would create their own "mimic camp" in which girls would pretend to be mothers, and the boys, their able-bodied sons and husbands.[4] The toys were meant to familiarize the children with the activities they would undertake later in life. Because some toy tipis were small-scale re-creations of full-size lodges while others were not, their meanings and associations can vary. By their very nature, toys can cross categories, creating a "continuing tension between, on the one hand, the notion of the plaything and, on the other, a notion of the miniature replica."[5] This tension, in fact, can lead to misattributions of miniature tipis as toys and vice versa. Toy tipis, then, carry one set of meanings in their context as toys and another in the context of museum and private collections.

At the end of the nineteenth and beginning of the twentieth centuries, anthropologists and other scholars visited Plains Indian reservations for the purpose of conducting firsthand research before such groups became acculturated to American Christian society. James Mooney, in his studies of Kiowa and Cheyenne heraldry, recorded tipi designs and had many of these replicated on models. Clark Wissler, an anthropologist from the American Museum of Natural History, also attempted to obtain models and full-size tipis. In a letter written while he was at the Pine Ridge Reservation in South Dakota, Wissler asks his superior, Franz Boas, if he ought to collect a full-size tipi for the museum. Miniature tipis were also available, as Wissler indicates: "I can get little ones made and painted by an old Indian who used to decorate tippis *[sic]*."[6] It was not uncommon for anthropologists to commission model tipis as miniature copies of actual ones to study and display in a museum setting. This reduced the effort associated with collecting, transporting, preserving, and exhibiting a full-size tipi. It is also worth noting that Mooney and Wissler appeared to be more interested in collecting and studying painted tipis than those that carried beaded or quilled items—ornamentation made by women. While many reasons may account for this seeming lack of concern, one most certainly is that the informants and artists who worked for the anthropologists were male. This lacuna in the Mooney collections further indicates the need to look to other miniature tipis for examples of exterior lodge decoration.[7]

While miniature and model tipis were made as toys for children and as cultural specimens for anthropologists, they exist in large enough numbers to indicate another reason for their creation. Certainly not every miniature tipi currently in a museum collection was made for an anthropologist. Many miniature tipis show features that were definitely not included on their larger counterparts, such as beading around the base. This type of decorative addition suggests that miniature tipis were not always conceived as replicas but as collectibles to sell to non-Indians. Anthropologists who commissioned miniature tipis and other objects often guided the Indian artists who worked for them.[8] Objects that were made for sale to less knowledgeable outsiders, however, show features uncommon on full-size lodges because the artists were not under the supervision of anthropologists. As scholars had shown an interest in purchasing miniature or model tipis, it seems reasonable that the making of these continued as collectibles for non-Indian visitors to reservations and surrounding areas.[9] Unfortunately, many miniature tipis have poor provenance, so any assertion as to why they were made must remain in the realm of speculation.

In scholarly literature discussing miniature tipis, the terms "miniature" and "model" are often used interchangeably. "Miniature," as the more general term, is also the most common. It implies that the object shows a much-reduced scale in comparison to the original. Given that full-size tipis were often more than ten feet tall, the use of the term "miniature" is appropriate in describing these smaller ones. The exceptions are the small-scale play tipis that children could actually enter. While the practical aspects of the term "miniature" are clear, the theoretical ones are less so and have undergone significant analysis. Susan Stewart's examination of the miniature in Euro-American literature and culture determines that miniatures act as agents to focus nostalgic reveries regarding childhood and cultural others. Stewart offers an indication of how a miniature can function for its audience, which is particularly relevant, as most miniature tipis in museum collections seem to have been made for non-Indians. According to Stewart, "the miniature offers a world clearly limited in space but frozen and thereby both particularized and generalized in time—particularized in that the miniature concentrates upon the single instance and not the abstract rule, but generalized in that that instance comes to transcend, to stand for, a spectrum of other instances."[10] Such a characterization of the miniature is appropriate for this discussion, as individual miniature tipis focus attention on themselves as unique objects. At the same time, miniature tipis can also carry a variety of associations, including a specific full-size lodge, a tribal style of making or ornamenting tipis, and the artistic and economic goals of the artist. Such varied connotations are what allow miniature tipis to slide between categories—toy, model, collectible—in the first place, complicating matters regarding their relation to full-size tipis.

"Model," the other term commonly used to categorize miniature tipis, carries a greater degree of specificity than "miniature"; it refers to a specific building or structure. Nonetheless, models form an ambiguous genre that splinters into several subcategories. One of these, the "reconstruction model," bears directly on this examination. A "reconstruction model" is made after a building has been completely destroyed and serves as a re-creation, in miniature scale, of the original structure. This type of model appears in museum displays at institutions such as the American Museum of Natural History and the Field Museum of Natural History. Some tipi models, those comprising the Mooney collections for example, fit this category. Most others, because they do not refer to specific tipis, are best considered in the realm of "symbolic models." These types of models may appear as two- or three-dimensional depictions of buildings. Such renderings are not completely accurate re-creations of larger structures, but they can provide good information on selected features, such as ornamentation or design systems.[11] Miniature tipis that are symbolic models, then, can still be useful as secondary documents, offering information on certain elements of full-size tipis.

Miniature Tipis with Painted Vision-Inspired Imagery

Full-size tipis with imagery originating in a vision or dream were rare in Plains groups. Among the Kiowa, for example, only one-fifth of all tipis in use before the reservation era carried vision-inspired designs.[12] Most tipis bore quilled or beaded ornaments, or had no exterior decoration at all. Painting a lodge with vision-derived imagery was a privilege reserved only for those who received a design during a personal visionary experience. Because the designs expressed the substance of the vision while also playing vital roles in the manifestation of the visionary's powers, lodges and other vision-derived objects were treated with "care and attention." They were only to be used in conjunction with certain ritual movements, prayers, and songs.[13] Such prescriptions explain the rarity of painted tipis, while the visual dynamism of the lodge covers themselves accounts for the desire of outsiders to document these objects, in full-size and miniature replicas.

The James Mooney collections of Kiowa and Cheyenne tipi models show painted depictions of vision-inspired imagery on their exteriors. Both these collections were made for the same purpose: to re-create in miniature actual nineteenth-century pre-reservation encampments. Model tipis were painted by Kiowa and Cheyenne artists between 1891 and 1904 under the guidance of Mooney, who collected tipi and shield designs from both groups. In each collection, the models have, for the most part, been related to specific lodges that were in use before the reservation era.[14]

In working with the Kiowa and Cheyenne tipi models, scholars are aided by the extensive documentation surrounding these objects. Groundbreaking studies in these areas, such as those by Ewers and Fagin, establish the reliability of these specific models as important secondary sources relating to full-size tipis. Because the provenance of each of these models is known and Mooney's field notes are available, these models have been proven to be accurate re-creations.[15] In fact, Fagin concludes her analysis of the Cheyenne models by stating that the designs on them "do not appear to be new creations of early twentieth-century Indian artists or of their informants and compare favorably with the surviving historic sources."[16] Unfortunately, for a large percentage of the remaining miniature and model tipis, such documentation does not exist, creating the necessity of looking at other features of the objects, such as their shape and attendant design elements, to determine their viability as secondary sources.

In addition to the Mooney model tipis, small-scale play tipis made for children were, occasionally, painted with vision-derived motifs. Two different photographs by Edward Curtis depict Piegan girls standing in front of small-scale tipis, each of which is covered with vision-inspired paintings. Given the sacred meanings of visionary scenes painted on lodges, it may seem odd that a child's play tipi would have carried such imagery. However, among the Blackfoot, a favored child, or *minípoka*, might have received a play tipi with visionary scenes painted by a patron. In some cases, the child "borrowed" the design for the life of the play-lodge; in others, a medicine bundle was included with the lodge and the tipi design was the child's to use as long as she pleased. In spite of their seemingly anomalous nature, these two play-size lodges pictured by Curtis re-create, on a child's scale, designs on full-size tipis.[17]

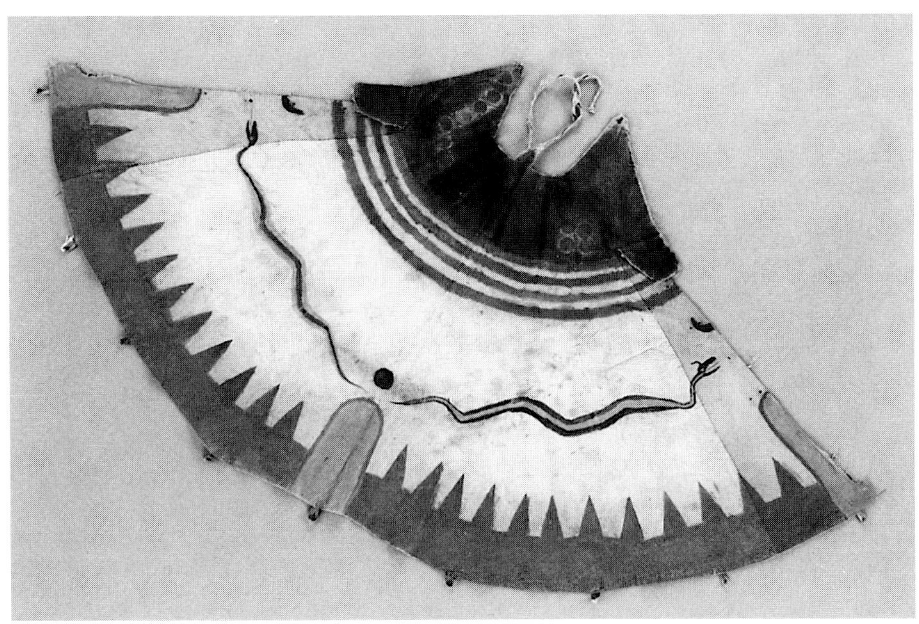

Although the miniature tipis with vision-inspired imagery discussed here have proven to be valuable secondary sources for full-size lodge covers, this does not mean that all miniature tipis with visionary scenes are reliable. Even anthropologists were not always successful in obtaining miniature tipis that accurately replicated a specific full-size one. For example, Pliny Earle Goddard, an anthropologist who served as a curator for the American Museum of Natural History, collected several beautiful miniature tipis from the Sarcee that show vision-inspired paintings on their exteriors. Within this group is a miniature lodge cover divided into three horizontal sections (fig. 1.1). A painted orange band with orange triangles encircles the base of the lodge. Two snakes appear in the middle section, each facing the door. Orange lines separate the middle from the upper section, while the smoke flap area is painted black with blue circles. The motifs depicted on this miniature tipi and their organization on the cover are consistent with the appearances of painted lodges on the northern Plains.[18]

Once Goddard received this tipi, he realized it had no connection to any lodge cover made by the Sarcee in the past. In Goddard's inventory describing the objects he collected, he says of this tipi: "The Sarcee never had a tent like this (I was told differently when the arrangement was made)."[19] Interestingly, Goddard relates that the imagery for this lodge originated in the dream of an old woman, not a man, as was customary. The individual who made this miniature tipi was aware that outsiders wanted "authentic" items produced by Native Americans. Although the painted designs may have originated in a vision, Goddard was unable to confirm that this lodge was a reconstruction model.[20] As a symbolic model, this tipi provides a good indication of motifs and compositional arrangements on northern Plains lodge covers. Certain aspects of its shape, such as the holes in the smoke flaps and comparatively wide space between the flaps, also show consistencies with full-size lodges on the northern Plains.

Miniature Tipis with Battle Imagery

Miniature tipis with painted combat scenes routinely appear within the genre. Full-size lodges with battle imagery were painted by a warrior or group of warriors after they proved their bravery in battle.[21] Combat scenes, painted to commemorate and to publicly announce a warrior's deeds, were pictured most often on buffalo hides in the pre-reservation era and less frequently on other surfaces, such as lodge covers.

Two model tipis in the Mooney collections, one Kiowa and one Cheyenne, have battle scenes on their covers. Perhaps the most well documented of these is the Kiowa Tipi with Battle Pictures, given to Kiowa chief Little Bluff by Sleeping Bear, a Cheyenne chief, in the 1840s.[22] When Sleeping Bear gave the lodge to Little Bluff, it was already painted to show yellow horizontal stripes on the southern side and Cheyenne battle imagery on the northern side.[23] Little Bluff added his own embellishments to the tipi, among them black stripes between the yellow ones on the southern side and twenty tomahawks on the northern side. Charley Buffalo, a relation of one of the owners of the full-size lodge, painted the model to reproduce the horizontal stripes and battle images. The events depicted on the model are "imaginary." According to Kiowa traditions, an artist could not depict another man's battle deeds without that man's permission. Charley Buffalo likely acted within the confines of Kiowa values when he painted fictitious events on the model, as he could not secure permission from the individuals whose deeds appeared on the original cover.[24] In pre-reservation battle paintings, however, it was uncommon for a warrior-artist to paint an event that had not occurred.[25]

The model shows seven scenes of hand-to-hand combat between Kiowa warriors, U.S. soldiers, and other Plains men. Although the actions depicted are imaginary,

Charley Buffalo nonetheless was careful to include details found in battle imagery, such as shields, headdresses, and even painting on the horse's body. One element of the painting, however, is inconsistent with depictions of battle scenes on full-size lodges. While the size of the tipi has been miniaturized, the figures have not been reduced to the same scale. Full-size lodge covers averaged eighteen to twenty feet in height; on those with battle imagery, the figures would range from six to twelve inches tall.[26] These dimensions allowed warrior-artists to depict many figures on a lodge that together would comprise well over seven scenes. The change in scale is highlighted by the full-size re-creation of the Tipi with Battle Pictures made by Dixon Palmer in 1973 after Charley Buffalo's model. Palmer's re-creation, depicting only the seven scenes, portrays the figures in a much larger scale than on earlier full-size lodge covers.[27]

Because of the discrepancies in size of figures, number of scenes depicted, and contents of the events illustrated, this model of the Tipi with Battle Pictures is an incomplete reproduction of the full-size one it attempts to replicate. This does not mean that Charley Buffalo's model is not a good secondary source for the original full-size one. The model of the Tipi with Battle Pictures can provide information on specific elements, such as the overall design and perhaps some details on the figures. Nonetheless, the differences indicate that the gap between the secondary and the primary source, in this case, is wider than with the Mooney tipis carrying vision-inspired imagery. The model of the Tipi with Battle Pictures also illustrates that within the genre of model tipis, artists did not feel bound to reproduce exactly the painting on a specific full-size tipi.

Other miniature tipis with battle scenes show the divergence in scale from full-size lodges and simultaneously stem from the traditions of Plains painting. A miniature tipi made of leather at the Denver Art Museum depicts three primary battle scenes with the same warrior shown in each (fig. 1.2). Fifteen calumets with red pipe bowls appear over the combat scenes, while directly above the calumets is a band of horseshoes. Finally, the upper section is separated from the lower by horizontal red and blue stripes. The main figure is identifiable by his elaborate hairstyle and accouterments, including feathers in his hair, a red "scarf" about his neck, and a shield with feathers. Such elements indicate that this warrior, and therefore the likely artist, is Sioux. Two of the large opponents, with their hair drawn up in pompadours, are probably Crow warriors.[28]

While it is difficult to determine if the events pictured on this tipi actually occurred or if they are fictitious, the actions depicted fit within the tradition of representational painting on the Plains. For example, events such as the firing of guns are indicated as blasts emanating from the gun barrels in the scene on the southern side. In addition, some elements, including the calumets, horseshoes, and wound marks,

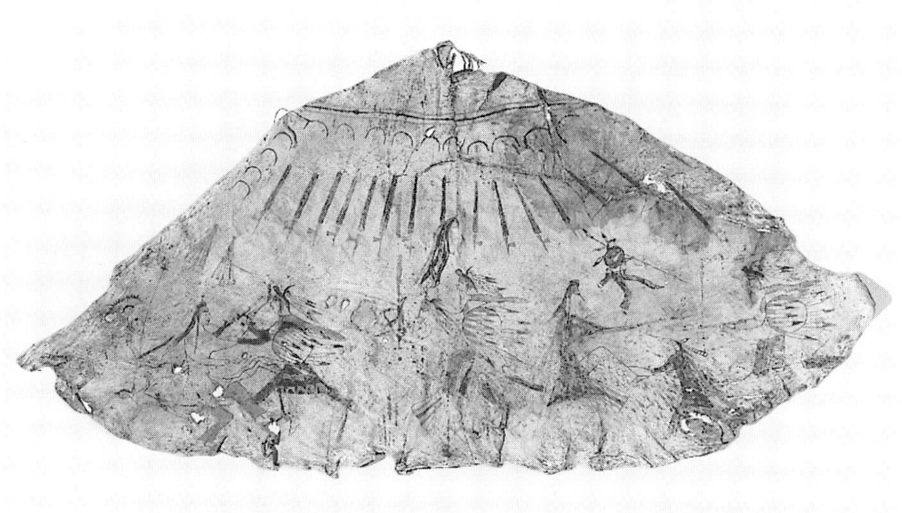

may be symbolic references to successes accomplished in battle. Calumets are depicted on pre-reservation era objects made by the Mandan as references to war parties led. Among the Mandan, horseshoes denote that a warrior had a horse shot from beneath him, and the wound marks refer to battle injuries.[29] The paintings on this miniature tipi fall well within the context of battle imagery on the Plains. But the lack of cultural affiliation for the object makes a definitive reading of this tipi impossible.

Elements of this miniature lodge cover show divergences from full-size tipis with painted imagery. Perhaps the most glaring instance of the differences is in its shape; the miniature re-creates the general outline of a tipi but it omits smoke flaps, a hallmark, even a defining element, of tipis.[30] Moreover, the scale of the figures in relation to the cover is again not evocative of that on a full-size tipi. These figures would be much larger, indeed immense comparatively speaking, if this miniature were reproduced in full-size dimensions. While it clearly refers to and evokes tipis, this miniature strays from some of the conventions associated with full-size tipis and the depiction of battle imagery on their exteriors. The omission of the smoke flaps in particular suggests that this object was conceived, first and foremost, as a canvas for battle scenes, as opposed to a replica of a specific lodge depicting these same events.

Other miniature tipis extend even further beyond the conventions associated with tipi decoration and hide painting. A miniature tipi in the collection of the American Museum of Natural History shows a two-part composition divided by vertical lines running down the back of the lodge (plate 1). On the northern side are two pairs of warriors engaged in hand-to-hand combat. The southern side depicts four animals: a bear, a pronghorn, an elk, and a buffalo. A broad green stripe at the bottom provides a ground line for the figures and the upper area, including the smoke flaps, is also colored green. Further framing the two scenes are vertical rows of circles with painted feathers stemming from them. Similarly, a row of decorative motifs of triangles with feathers runs across the top of each scene.

Some aspects of the painting on this tipi stem from earlier battle imagery, as in the man adorned with a warbonnet touching his opponent with a gun. In the other scene, one warrior fires his gun at his enemy; the event is indicated by the blast marks at the end of the barrel. The inclusion of the animals, however, is perplexing in light of the history of hide painting and ledger art. None of the four animals show a relation to the battle scenes on the other side. In fact, the animals themselves are not engaged in any sort of activity and do not interact with each other. In short, there is no "scene" with a narrative depicted on the southern side. Instead of specifying a story involving these animals, the artist simply presents them, as if merely stating that these creatures exist on the Plains. Each of the animals has qualities that are important in Plains societies, such as the life-giving element of the buffalo and the speed of the prong-horn. Inasmuch, they can appear in vision-inspired or hunting scenes. If the former is the case however, this tipi would be unprecedented in combining visionary and battle experiences on one lodge. The southern side most likely does not refer to a visionary experience but originates in the changes that occurred in representational painting in the late nineteenth century. Some ledger-style drawings, for example, picture flocks of birds and other animals indigenous to the Plains.[31]

Like several of the miniature lodge covers examined here, this miniature tipi carries some features that refer to full-size tipis, most notably the shape, the compositional arrangement of the painted elements, and the attached dangles. These traits combined with the anomalous ones make this miniature lodge cover representative of full-size lodges in general and simultaneously indicative of the changes in painting traditions on the Plains. The space between the primary and secondary sources, as exemplified by this miniature lodge cover, continues to widen.

Miniature Tipis with Hunting and Ceremonial Scenes

Miniature lodge covers with images of hunting scenes and ceremonial activities demonstrate divergences from full-size ones because of the subject matter of the paintings.

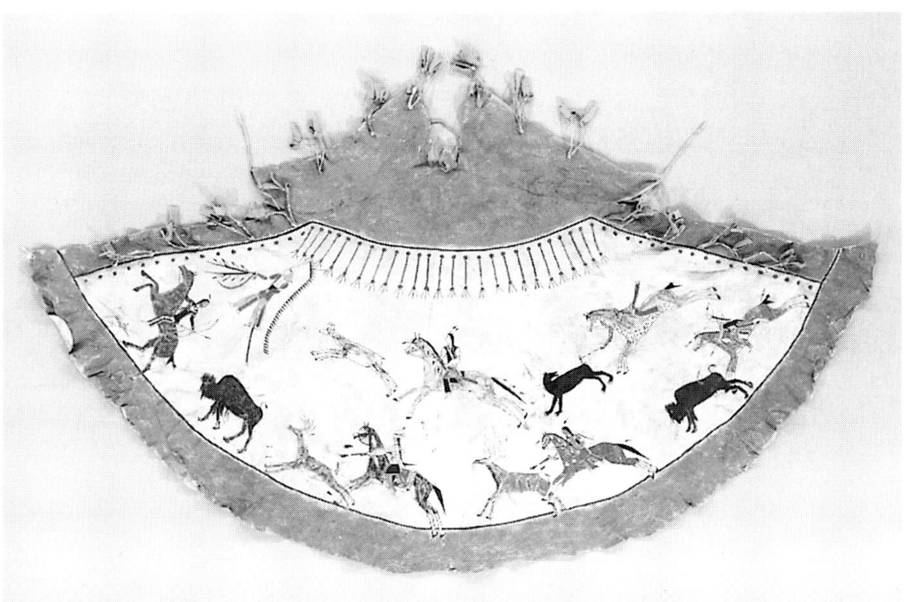

One miniature tipi, for example, depicts seven warriors engaged in a hunt (fig. 1.3). In this scene, unlike most others of the same subject, the warriors hunt a variety of animals, not one specific type. Two men chase after wounded buffalo; two more pursue a deer and elk, while above them others chase a bighorn ram and a bear. The men use several types of weapons including guns, bows and arrows, and even a tomahawk. These varied motifs, both in the weapons and animals depicted, refer to the hunt in general but do not necessarily reference specific events. Like the miniature tipi with four different animals (plate 1), the painting on this lodge cover illustrates the various animals hunted, in addition to the major methods of hunting on the Plains. In doing so, it demonstrates the elasticity of conventions associated with painting and miniature tipi-making in the reservation era. The painting is, in fact, far-removed from images depicted on full-size tipis. As Evan Maurer notes, a hunting scene such as this would not have appeared on a full-size lodge. Inasmuch, this miniature tipi was likely made for outside sale.[32] Again, the artist's canvas has taken on the form of the tipi in miniature, evoking tipis via its shape and attached dangles.

This tipi, then, is best described as a symbolic model; it gives some information about tipis, in the smoke flaps and dangles, while other aspects, such as the painting, do not.

Changes that occurred in hide painting and ledger art in the reservation era are made manifest on this miniature lodge cover and those bearing battle imagery. The depiction of combat and hunting scenes by male artists in ledger art has been characterized as nostalgic referencing of the pre-reservation era. In her study of ledger art, Joyce Szabo describes the possible motivation for creating representational images: "Men now in reservation environments, stripped of their traditional avenues to power, deprived of many important rituals, dispossessed of hunting grounds and the once mighty buffalo, looked to the past in reminiscent illustrations recounting the glory of yesterday. Buffalo could still fill ledger pages and brave warriors could still count coup over fallen enemies."[33] Szabo's words, while specifically referring to ledger art, are nonetheless applicable here. The artists who painted battle and hunting scenes on miniature tipis were clearly aware of the changing of painting customs on the Plains and used the "canvas" of the miniature tipi to engage in similar nostalgic evocations of pre-reservation life.[34] Such imagery was also attractive to the outside audience hungry for references to the pre-reservation lifestyles of Plains peoples. Certainly, the depiction of hunting and combat scenes on a miniature tipi made that object all the more alluring to non-Indians.

In addition to showing imagery of hunting and warfare on the Plains, miniature tipis carried portrayals of ceremonies and dances. A miniature tipi at the State Historical Society of North Dakota shows a buffalo hunt, an immature golden eagle with wings outstretched, and male dancers accompanied by a drum group (fig. 1.4).[35] Although noteworthy because such subject matter would not have appeared on full-size lodges, this miniature tipi is especially interesting because it bears similarities to hide robes painted by the Shoshone artist Cadzi Cody.[36] Congruencies between one of Cadzi Cody's robes and the miniature tipi include the buffalo hunt complete with mounted warriors, some of whose horses are being charged and gored by buffalo.[37] The dancers perform a Shoshone Wolf Dance and are dressed virtually identically; they wear hair roaches with feathers, breast plates made of hairpipes, and leggings with fringe or tassels. In each drum group the men raise one hand as they provide the accompaniment for the dancers. Formal similarities abound in the bodies of the dancers, horses, and buffalo. For instance, the thin arms and legs of the men, with their feet only outlined. Of course, neither object is a perfect reflection of the other. The eagle on the miniature tipi is absent from the robe, and the dance ground on the robe contains an American flag, a motif not appearing on the tipi.

Cadzi Cody depicted this scene and others similar to it on a variety of robes and at least one miniature tipi made explicitly for sale to Euro-American tourists. He in-

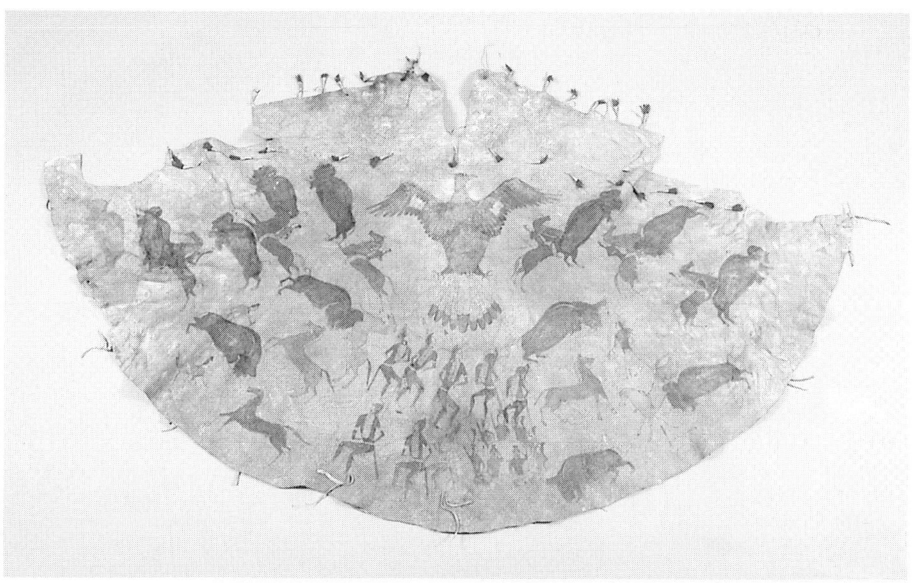

cluded the buffalo hunt to "make the painting more salable to white tourists visiting the reservation to observe the Sun Dance."[38] The presence of other details also appears to be motivated by a desire to make the object attractive to outsiders. For example, on some robes Cadzi Cody replaced the flagpole with a Sun Dance pole to reference the midsummer world renewal ceremony well known to non-Indians, even though the dancers wear Wolf Dance clothing. In this way, the artist "acknowledged that strict accuracy was less important than images that emphasized otherness."[39] That Cadzi Cody created these works for outsiders is further indicated by the use of stencils on the buffalo's bodies to increase the quantity of items painted. Given that Cadzi Cody made numerous copies of this scene, and that there are many stylistic and compositional similarities between the dancers and buffalo on both the tipi and robe, it is highly likely that Cadzi Cody painted the miniature tipi as well. As he was content to replace the flagpole with the Sun Dance pole, it is logical that the eagle appears as another of these interchangeable motifs. Cadzi Cody was clearly aware that his prospective customers wanted images that evoked Plains culture and beliefs, and the bird with wings outstretched served this purpose. Although this tipi was collected in North Dakota and has been identified as Sioux, the similarities between it and works by the Shoshone artist Cadzi Cody suggest that he was the painter, if not the maker of the tipi.[40]

Here, then, is an instance of an even greater departure from actual-size tipis than seen on any of the other miniature lodge covers examined here. The imagery painted on robes made explicitly for outsiders was directly transferred to miniature tipis. In addition to the easing of conventions involved in narrative paintings on hide and drawings on paper, those associated with tipis also became more fluid as Plains peoples were forced to abandon tipis as their primary dwellings. The concern for making objects palatable to outsiders permeated ledger-style art and various objects made by other Native American groups.[41] In her study of miniature souvenirs made by Woodlands Indians, Ruth Phillips notes that "in response to the expectations of consumers, Native artists represented themselves in an increasingly stereotypical manner, repetitively showing Indians involved in a very limited number of activities related to warfare, hunting or camping in the wild."[42] Although the scenes depicted on the miniature tipis extend beyond these parameters, they do so only marginally. As artists were increasingly motivated to make miniature tipis desirable for sale to outsiders, the miniatures moved farther away from being specific models of full-size tipis. It seems that the shape of the Plains artist's "canvas" became less and less related to the imagery painted on it during the reservation era. Many miniature tipis, by not referencing a specific full-size lodge, allude to the idea of the tipi in only general terms.

Miniature Tipis with Beaded or Quilled Decoration

Beaded and quilled ornamentation also appears on miniature tipis, sometimes accompanying painted imagery. Full-size lodge covers, in fact, bore beaded or quilled decoration more frequently than painted vision-inspired or battle imagery. In many Plains groups, such as the Cheyenne and Arapaho, women who participated in quilling or beading societies created disks and rectangular or trapezoidal banners for lodge covers. These were then affixed to the lodge in a special ceremony performed for that occasion. Although miniature lodge covers carrying beaded or quilled attachments were less aggressively collected by anthropologists than those with painted imagery, full-size tipis with such ornamentation nevertheless had symbolic meanings and attested to the abilities of their makers. Among the Cheyenne, for instance, quilled ornaments on lodge covers referred to the cardinal directions. Likewise, among the northern Cheyenne, creating quilled decorations for a lodge was considered the most important task any member of a quilling society could complete.[43]

The Mooney collection of Cheyenne model tipis contains one that bears only quilled decoration (fig. 1.5). Quilled dangles with three "legs" each run down the front on both sides of the tipi's opening. In addition, yellow yarn and small deer hooves are attached alongside these dangles. At the back, just underneath the smokehole, is a rectangular banner with short dangles suspended from the bottom. On both the northern and southern sides of the cover are two long, quilled attachments that have a quilled loop at the bottom. Locks of hair are fastened to the cover near these dangles and to the pockets on the smoke flaps.[44] Full-size tipis carried dangles with the three-part division, deer toes, and the long hair attachments on the smoke flaps. Additionally, rectangular banners were often attached to Cheyenne lodges at the back, although disks were also used.[45] These decorations coincide, for the most part, with descriptions of Cheyenne lodge ornamentation. Differences are manifest in the scale of the dangles on the front; on a full-size lodge, the dangles would be much smaller in relation to the lodge and would appear in twice as many numbers. Such divergences can be attributed to the limitations of the media, as the quilled dangles would be virtually minuscule and the deer toes impossibly small if reduced to the same scale as the miniature tipi cover. Nonetheless, the banner at the back shows the same proportions as those on full-size lodges. The differences, then, are minor and do not detract from the usefulness of this miniature tipi as a secondary source for lodge decorations.

Other miniature tipis with beadwork ornaments do not closely follow the conventions, either stylistic or practical, associated with decorating a tipi with beaded or quilled objects. Many miniature tipis have four beaded disks affixed to the midsection and a rectangular banner at the back like full-size tipis, but they carry additional ornamentation that would not have been placed on the larger ones. For example, several miniature tipis are beaded around the smoke flaps and base, and others have completely beaded pockets on the smoke flaps.[46] Such details, clearly impractical for full-size lodge covers, add a sense of delicacy to the miniature tipi covers; the sparkling beads lend to the objects a precious quality, like that of a jewel. Finally, these additions indicate that miniature tipis with beadwork were, like the painted ones, not always conceived as accurate replicas of full-size tipis. These elements suggest that many such miniature tipis were designed to appeal to non-Indian buyers.

In addition to directly repeating beadwork designs found on full-size tipis, miniature lodge covers carried anomalous features. One Sioux miniature tipi cover dating to the late nineteenth century shows beaded elk dreamers and an elk, quilled rosettes and dangles, and painted figures (plate 2). Because of its rich imagery and varied media, this tipi embodies the most difficult and provocative issues relating to miniature tipis. The most surprising aspect of the tipi is the beaded depiction of the elk dreamers with their patron animal. Associated with the visionary epistemé, elks and elk dreamers were included in vision-inspired themes or imagery that could appear on

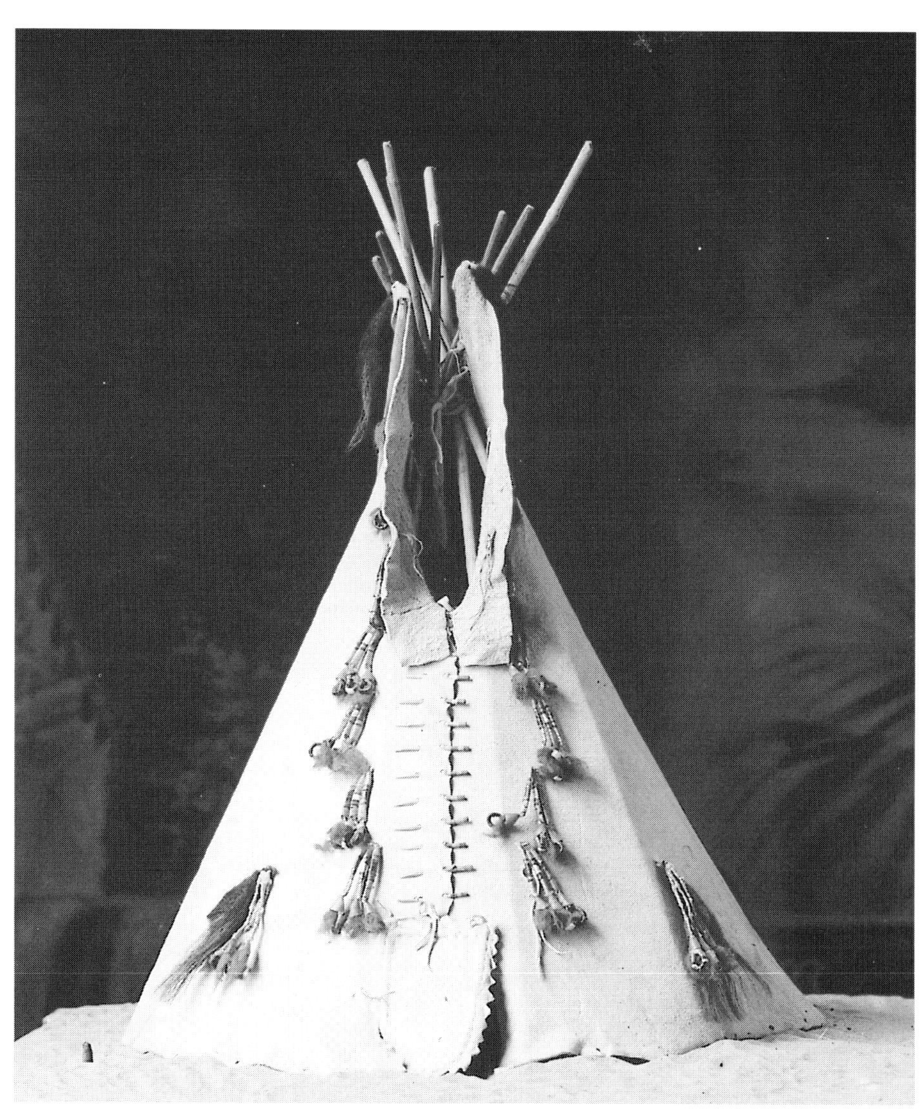

FIGURE 1.5
Cheyenne, Miniature Tipi, 1902–4. Hide, quills,
deer toes, yarn. Field Museum of Natural History,
Chicago, IL. Neg. No. CSA 27079.

tipis.[47] In this case, however, they are shown in beadwork, a medium that would not have been employed to depict such figures on a full-size lodge. As beadwork was an art form primarily used by women, the appearance of these figures in that medium is especially perplexing in light of the painted imagery on the tipi, which includes a mounted warrior wearing a warbonnet.[48] Because this miniature tipi mixes media and imagery in an unprecedented way, how the figures should be read is unclear. Should the warrior depicted on the side of the lodge be viewed as one of the elk dreamers at the back? Conversely, because a woman likely completed the beadwork, it may be that the artist herself was a member of the elk dreamers and the images speak to her experience. Another explanation for the appearance of seemingly incongruous imagery and media on this miniature tipi is that the figures were not meant to be read according to pre-reservation ideals. Throughout the late nineteenth century, women created beaded depictions of elk dreamers on a variety of objects from clothing to bags. Perhaps such images were included on the miniature lodge cover to increase its salability to outsiders.[49]

In the context of reservation-era art in which artistic conventions loosened, this miniature tipi adds an important note. In the context of full-size lodges, however, it remains a problematic secondary source. The major elements of the tipi, such as its shape, quilled rosettes, painted imagery, and beadwork, had important places within the genre of full-size tipis. While all these elements are present on this lodge cover, they differ from their previous uses and appearances on the larger tipis. For example, quilled disks were commonly placed on tipis just beneath the smokehole. However, two quilled disks were attached to this tipi at the back, and one overlaps the other, a feature uncommon on full-size tipis. Moreover, the depiction of human and animal figures in beadwork did not appear on larger tipis. The combination of all these elements creates an object that does not give information about Sioux culture by re-creating a full-size tipi but that instead speaks volumes about changes in Sioux art and culture in the late nineteenth century.

Miniature Tipis as Romantic Evocations of Plains Culture

Each of the miniature tipis examined in this study offers, to varying degrees, information on full-size tipis. Some, the Mooney tipis for example, show strong correlations to their full-size counterparts. Others, however, demonstrate many divergences from full-size lodges and reference the larger ones in general ways, mainly through their shape. The determination of whether miniature tipis are reliable secondary sources for a study of full-size tipis must, then, proceed on a case by case basis. Although the provenance of many miniature tipis is unknown, their viability as secondary documents can be determined through other means including their shape and exterior decoration. Each group of miniature lodge covers discussed here, from those with painted vision-inspired imagery to those with beaded decoration, includes examples with anomalous features. This, in turn, indicates that no single type of exterior ornamentation placed on a miniature tipi renders that object, a priori, more reliable than others with different decoration.

Miniature tipis create a distinct and varied genre. As such, they can be considered in light of Susan Stewart's comments quoted at the beginning of this essay. Stewart's categorization of the miniature as displaying both particularized and generalized features is relevant for miniature tipis. Because miniatures do not have to exactly replicate a larger object, they are unique objects in their own right. This is what allows some miniature tipis to bear no connection to full-size lodges and what Plains artists capitalized on when making miniature tipis for sale as collectibles to non-Indians. Simultaneously, miniature tipis also function in broader terms to evoke full-size tipis in both specific and general ways. On a more expanded level, miniature tipis reflect the changes in art-making within Plains groups during the nineteenth and twentieth centuries. Finally, they reference a way of life no longer available to Plains peoples.

Through their capacity to carry both specific and generalized associations, miniature tipis can be important secondary sources for full-size ones. Some miniature tipis are closely related to their larger counterparts. In these instances, the space between the full-size and the miniature lodge, or the primary and the secondary document, is relatively narrow. Indeed, when dealing with primary documents that no longer exist, the secondary sources are most useful when the gap between them and their corresponding primary sources is as small as possible. As many miniature lodge covers do not refer to a specific tipi but instead to the concept of the tipi, the space between these and their corresponding primary documents is relatively wide. Miniature tipis that demonstrate a great distance from full-size lodges may be useful secondary sources in a limited fashion. The relationship between the larger tipis and miniatures in this category is less clear and more difficult to define. These objects may be most useful when viewed as primary sources unto themselves, offering information on Plains artistic practices and the expectations of non-Indian consumers of Indian-manufactured items during the reservation era.

In spite of the incongruities between many miniature and full-size lodge covers, the miniatures remain appealing items for non-Indian viewers. The allure of miniatures to a Euro-American audience has been categorized by Susan Stewart: "Whereas speech unfolds in time, the miniature unfolds in space. The observer is offered a transcendent and simultaneous view of the miniature, yet is trapped outside the possibility of a lived reality of the miniature. Hence the nostalgic desire to present the lower classes, peasant life, or the cultural other within a timeless and uncontaminable miniature form."[50] Many miniature tipis were made in the era succeeding the Plains Indian wars, when Plains peoples were forced to abandon their nomadic tipi-dwelling existence. While forced acculturation was believed to be the only way to ensure the survival of Native Americans, their previous lifestyle was simultaneously viewed by Euro-Americans through a romanticized lens. Tipis and other objects, such as war-bonnets, came to be symbols par excellence of Plains Indian lifestyles. For outsiders, miniature tipis evoke the golden age of Plains peoples and effectively freeze these groups in the past. Miniature tipis, by referencing this past reality, serve as alluring and seductive re-creations of a life totally inaccessible, yet desirable, to Euro-Americans.

This is not to say that every miniature tipi, regardless of its status as a secondary source for full-size tipis, functions only to summon romantic associations with the larger tipis. Indeed, the artists who created miniature tipis often took advantage of the space between these and full-size ones to make an object neither directly connected to full-size lodges nor totally divorced from them. These unique objects embody the concept of intertextuality as defined by Mieke Bal and Norman Bryson: "By reusing forms taken from earlier works, an artist also takes along the text out of which the borrowed element is broken away, while also constructing a new text with the debris."[51] Plains Indian artists working during the reservation era enjoyed a loosening of conventions affiliated with varied art forms and created objects that had not previously existed within Plains groups. These artists often took motifs from other art forms and used them in new contexts so that a miniature tipi could show beaded elk dreamers or a painted depiction of Shoshone Wolf Dancers. Miniature tipis can carry many meanings, depending on their exterior decoration. However, they all share at least one meaning—the association with the *concept* of the tipi, if not a specific full-size one. Some artists, as indicated by Bal and Bryson, may not have wanted to foreground all the meanings associated with a borrowed motif, but that motif nevertheless alludes to its previous context. The constant evocation of the tipi likely accounts for the allure of miniature tipis to an outside audience but was not necessarily the goal of all artists who created miniature tipis.

Notes

I thank Joyce M. Szabo and Brian Winkenweder for their guidance in writing this essay. Also, I owe thanks to Kara Kudzma of the Denver Art Museum and Mark Halvorson of the State Historical Society of North Dakota for their gracious assistance during my visits to those institutions. The research for this essay was supported by a grant from the Henry Luce Foundation.

1. My research indicates that there are more than one hundred miniature, model, and toy tipis in museums and private collections in the United States. By contrast, there are fewer than half this number of full-size tipis available for study in similar circumstances.

2. Norman Bancroft-Hunt, *The Indians of the Great Plains* (Norman: University of Oklahoma Press, 1981), 51.

As Pretty Shield was raised by her aunt, the play lodge was a replica of her aunt's. Frank B. Linderman, *Pretty Shield, Medicine Woman of the Crows* (Lincoln: University of Nebraska Press, 1972), 27.

3. See John C. Ewers, *Murals in the Round: Painted Tipis of the Kiowa and Kiowa-Apache Indians* (Washington D.C.: Smithsonian Institution Press, 1978), and Nancy L. Fagin, "The James Mooney Collection of Cheyenne Tipi Models at Field Museum of Natural History," *Plains Anthropologist* 33 (1988): 261–78.

4. See, for example, George Bird Grinnell, *The Cheyenne Indians: Their History and Ways of Life,* vol. 1 (New Haven: Yale University Press, 1923; reprint, Lincoln: University of Nebraska Press, 1972), 110.

5. Dan Fleming, *Powerplay: Toys as Popular Culture* (Manchester and New York: Manchester University Press, 1996), 147.

6. Clark Wissler to Franz Boas, 3 August, 1902, Accession File, 1902–72, American Museum of Natural History. Scholars also had objects made for reasons other than displays. During his fieldwork on the Pine Ridge Reservation in the 1930s, Erik Erikson, cultural anthropologist and clinical psychologist, studied modes of play within Lakota culture. Erikson recalls that "the women of the camp made small tepees, wagons, and dolls for me in order to demonstrate what they had played with as children"; Erikson, *Childhood and Society* (New York and London: W. W. Norton, 1950), 142.

7. Only one of the eighteen Cheyenne tipi models at the Field Museum of Natural History carries quilled ornamentation.

8. John C. Ewers, "Plains Indian Artists and Anthropologists: A Fruitful Collaboration," *American Indian Art Magazine* 9 (winter 1983): 49.

9. Evan M. Maurer cites the Mooney collections as stimulating the interest of outsiders in miniature tipis as collectibles; Maurer, *Visions of the People: A Pictorial History of Plains Indian Life* (Minneapolis: Minneapolis Institute of Arts, 1992), 249.

10. Susan Stewart, *On Longing: Narratives of the Miniature, the Gigantic, the Souvenir, the Collection* (Durham, N.C.: Duke University Press, 1993), 66–69, 48.

11. *Dictionary of Art,* s.v. "Architectural Model."

12. Ewers, *Murals in the Round,* 8.

13. Lee Irwin, *The Dream Seekers: Native American Visionary Traditions of the Great Plains* (Norman: University of Oklahoma Press, 1994), 211–12.

14. The Kiowa collection was intended to reproduce their Sun Dance camp circle from 1867; Ewers, *Murals in the Round,* 10. The Cheyenne models were re-creations of lodges pitched in their 1874 Sun Dance circle; Fagin, "The James Mooney Collection of Cheyenne Tipi Models," 262. Some of the Cheyenne models were painted by Kiowa artists. See Fagin's article for a discussion of this issue.

15. See, for example, Imre Nagy's study of Lame Bull's spiritual oeuvre, which includes one of the Cheyenne models made for Mooney; Nagy, "Lame Bull, the Cheyenne Medicine Man," *American Indian Art Magazine* 23 (winter 1997): 70–83; and Nagy, " 'The Black Came Over the Sun . . .' Lame Bull's Spiritual Oeuvre," *Irodalom-és Művészettörténeti Tanulmányok, Studia Historiae Literarum et Artium 1* (Szeged: Móra Ferenc Müzeum, 1997): 59–93.

16. Fagin, "The James Mooney Collection of Cheyenne Tipi Models," 277.

17. Edward S. Curtis, *The North American Indian,* vol. 6 (1911; reprint, New York: Johnson

Reprint 1970), facing page 64; and Curtis, *The North American Indian,* vol. 18 (1928; reprint, New York: Johnson Reprint, 1970), facing page 106. Paul Raczka, "Minípoka: Children of Plenty," *American Indian Art Magazine* 5 (summer 1979): 64–65. I am indebted to Steven L. Grafe, whose generous assistance helped solve the problems posed by the Curtis photographs referenced here.

18. See, for example, Clark Wissler's description of painted Blackfoot lodges; Wissler, "Ceremonial Bundles of the Blackfoot Indians," *Anthropological Papers of the American Museum of Natural History* 7 (1912): 240–41.

19. Pliny Earle Goddard, catalog of specimens purchased on the Sarcee Reserve, July and August 1905, Accession File, 1905–44, American Museum of Natural History.

20. I am not suggesting that the design for this lodge did not come from the vision of an old woman. Indeed, there are examples of Plains Indian women having visions of painted lodges. In addition, there are a number of circumstances that could account for this tipi. The old woman may have had Blackfoot friends or relatives whose lodges may have inspired her vision. Nonetheless, Goddard clearly states that this tipi did not have a full-size counterpart among the Sarcee. For an account of a woman who had a vision of a painted lodge, see George A. Dorsey and Alfred L. Kroeber, *Traditions of the Arapaho,* Field Columbian Museum Anthropological Series, vol. 5, no. 81 (Chicago: Field Columbian Museum, 1903), 136–39. Interestingly, the Arapaho woman decided not to make the lodge from her vision.

21. See, for example, the Lakota canvas tipi dating to the mid-1880s at the Denver Art Museum (accession no. 1963.271) or the E. B. Fiske photo showing two Lakota tipis with battle imagery (neg. no. 5530, State Historical Society of North Dakota). The latter tipi is published in Peter Nabokov and Robert Easton, *Native American Architecture* (Oxford: Oxford University Press, 1989), 151.

22. These two tipis, the Kiowa Tipi with Battle Pictures and the Cheyenne lodge owned by Pocked Nose, bear strong similarities. Most observations in the formal analysis of the Tipi with Battle Pictures may be applied to Pocked Nose's lodge. Because of this, only the Kiowa lodge is examined here. For a discussion of Pocked Nose's lodge, see Fagin, "The James Mooney Collection of Cheyenne Tipi Models," 270. In addition to Mooney's studies on the Tipi with Battle Pictures, see Ewers, *Murals in the Round,* 14–17, and Candace S. Greene and Thomas D. Drescher, "The Tipi with Battle Pictures: The Kiowa Tradition of Intangible Property Rights," *Trademark Reporter* 84 (1994): 418–33.

23. Tipis were pitched with their openings to the east; the sides of the cover are referenced according to the cardinal directions they would face.

24. Greene and Drescher, "The Tipi with Battle Pictures," 422, 425–26; Ewers, *Murals in the Round,* 16.

25. Joyce M. Szabo, "Howling Wolf: An Autobiography of a Plains Warrior-Artist," *Allen Memorial Art Museum Bulletin* 46 (1994): 7.

26. Of course, tipi covers vary in size, from twelve feet in height for a small lodge to well over twenty feet for a large one.

27. Dixon Palmer's re-creation of this tipi is published in Miles Libhart and Rosemary Ellison, *Painted Tipis by Contemporary Plains Indian Artists* (Anadarko, Okla.: Oklahoma Indian Arts and Crafts Cooperative, 1973), 23.

28. The Denver Art Museum's computerized listing of objects states that the tipi is Sioux but that this identification is "uncertain."

29. These symbols appear on a dress painted to depict the battle exploits of the Mandan warriors Lean Bear and Red White Buffalo; Maurer, *Visions of the People,* 222–23.

30. According to Ted Brasser tipis are differentiated from other conical lodges by their having smoke flaps and not being a true cone but a tilted one; Brasser, "The Tipi as an Element in the Emergence of Historic Plains Indian Nomadism," *Plains Anthropologist* 27 (1982): 309.

31. See the drawings by Making Medicine and Black Hawk illustrated in Janet Catherine Berlo,

ed., *Plains Indian Drawings, 1865–1935: Pages from a Visual History* (New York: Harry N. Abrams in association with the American Federation of Arts and the Drawing Center, 1996), 136, 189.

32. Maurer, *Visions of the People,* 249.

33. Joyce M. Szabo, *Howling Wolf and the History of Ledger Art* (Albuquerque: University of New Mexico Press, 1994), 43.

34. Unfortunately, space limitations prevent the inclusion and examination of several other miniature tipis that show similar traits. Among these are two miniature tipis in the collection of the State Historical Society of North Dakota, catalog nos. 671 and 86.234.116; the latter is also known as Wise Spirit's tipi. In addition, a toy tipi in the collection of Charles and Valerie Diker merits inclusion in this category. This tipi appears in Allen Wardwell, ed., *Native Paths: American Indian Art from the Collection of Charles and Valerie Diker* (New York: Metropolitan Museum of Art, 1998), frontispiece and page 30.

35. The computerized notes on this tipi at the State Historical Society of North Dakota list this bird as a turkey vulture, but the markings on the wings and tail feathers are clearly those of the immature golden eagle.

36. The notes at the State Historical Society of North Dakota indicate that the design on this tipi was copied from the Washakie Sun Dance robes. Washakie was Cadzi Cody's father and the two created works together; Edwin L. Wade, ed., *The Arts of the North American Indian: Native Traditions in Evolution* (New York: Hudson Hills Press, 1986), 103. Because many paintings similar to that on the miniature tipi are attributed to Cadzi Cody only, I discuss this lodge in reference to Cadzi Cody's work. Another robe with a design comparable to those discussed here is at the Heritage Plantation of Sandwich, Massachusetts, no. 1980.3.1. See Maurer, *Visions of the People,* 252.

37. This robe is at the Denver Art Museum (accession no. 1947.268). It is pictured in Richard Conn, *Circles of the World: Traditional Art of the Plains Indians* (Denver: Denver Art Museum, 1989), 122.

38. Maurer, *Visions of the People,* 252. The miniature tipi bearing Cadzi Cody's work is published in Richard Conn, *Native American Art in the Denver Art Museum* (Denver: Denver Art Museum, 1979), 141.

39. Louise Lincoln, "The Social Construction of Plains Art, 1875–1915," in Maurer, *Visions of the People,* 51–52.

40. It has been suggested that the images on this tipi were merely copied from the Washakie Sun Dance robes. As tourism on the Plains to view ceremonials increased, objects such as miniature tipis and robes could easily make their way from one place to another. While it is possible that the maker of the tipi simply copied Cadzi Cody's design, the similarities between the two objects and Cadzi Cody's clear use of stencils strongly support the claim that he painted this miniature lodge cover.

41. Szabo, *Howling Wolf and the History of Ledger Art,* 27.

42. Ruth B. Phillips, "Souvenirs from North America: The Miniature as Image of Woodlands Indian Life," *American Indian Art Magazine* 14 (summer 1989): 60.

43. Grinnell, *The Cheyenne Indians,* vol. 1, 163, 165.

44. Ibid., 235.

45. Alfred L. Kroeber, *The Arapaho* (1902, 1904, 1907; reprint, Lincoln: University of Nebraska Press, 1983), 63.

46. See, for example, the miniature lodge pictured in Bancroft-Hunt, *The Indians of the Great Plains,* 51. In addition, a miniature tipi at the State Historical Society of North Dakota (catalog no. 456) shows beadwork around the flaps and at the base. It also has some pictographic images burned into the sides, but these are exceedingly difficult to read. Another miniature lodge cover at the State Historical Society of North Dakota (catalog no. 14346) shows beaded smoke flap pockets.

47. Alice Fletcher, "The Elk Mystery or Festival, Ogallala Sioux," *Sixteenth and Seventeenth Annual Reports of the Trustees of the Peabody Museum of American Archaeology and Ethnology* 3 (1884):

282. Fletcher notes that the tipi used by the Elk Dreamer Society shows a painted elk above the door. The phrase "visionary epistemé" comes from Lee Irwin's study of Plains Indian religion, *The Dream Seekers.*

48. Another image is painted on the lodge on the other side of the entrance, but it is very light and virtually indecipherable.

49. For examples of beaded work created by women, see the vest and bag pictured in Maurer, *Visions of the People,* 133–34. Interestingly, miniature tipis made explicitly for sale to museums show further incongruities in media and design. For example, a miniature lodge cover at the Oklahoma Historical Society (catalog no. 3381) has disks around the middle with feathers hanging down and a rectangular banner at the back. These designs, however, are entirely painted, not beaded or quilled.

50. Stewart, *On Longing,* 66.

51. Mieke Bal and Norman Bryson, "Semiotics and Art History," *Art Bulletin* 73 (June 1991): 207.

Chapter 2

Identity Recovered

Portrait of a Northern Arapaho Quillworker

MARSHA C. BOL

While museum collections hold thousands, perhaps even millions, of specimens of artwork made by Plains Indian women during the nineteenth and early twentieth centuries, the museum shelves are noticeably silent about the identity of these artists and their creative intentions. As these objects were removed from their home environment, a process concurrently reenacted throughout the colonial collecting world, they were generally severed from their connection to maker and meaning. Thus when Cleaver Warden, an Arapaho who was employed as a field-worker among his own people, wrote of the specific artistic accomplishments of a named northern Arapaho woman, he was recording an exceptional document in the history of Plains Indian art.[1] In his field notebook from 1904–5, he noted:

> Fire Wood, an old woman of Northern Arapaho, Wyoming began to quill cradles, tepees, robes and various other articles when she was fifteen (15) years old. This inducement to work was encouraged by her own parents to keep her home surroundings and honor her kindred. All the old women began to notice her skill and good memory, that they would invited *[sic]* her over to notable gatherings of old women. After she got married, her occupation continued, reaching her mark to 60 assorted Baby cradles, 14 Buffalo Robes, 5 ornamental tepees[,] 10 Robes (Calf's)[,] 1 Lean Buffalo Back. Of course she had made [more] than 5 tepees of the standard degrees.
>
> When Bird Woman[,] mother of Fire Wood, died 10 years ago, her Tepee Bag laid *[sic]* idle, until two years afterwards, the latter [Fire Wood] by payment of articles to elder women, took possession of the Woman's Bag. (Tepee)

She was instructed [in] the manner of handling of contents and also method of consecration upon others.[2]

In these few paragraphs Warden summarized the artistic history of this prolific quillworker. Embedded within these paragraphs he provided substantive information about one woman's artistic life within her society at the turn of the twentieth century. Fire Wood began quilling seriously at age fifteen. By that time she was already showing signs of a special talent, quilling cradles, tipis, robes, and other things, thereby attracting the attention of the old women. Among the northern Arapaho, notice by elder women was of particular significance. Elders, both female and male, were (and still are) the ritual authorities and the keepers of the sacred knowledge in their society, which ordered its world by age hierarchy. During their lifetime men moved through a series of age-graded societies, or lodges, until they reached the highest place in the age structure held by the seven Water-Sprinkling Old Men. As young men they first joined the Kit Fox society, advancing as they aged through successive societies. With each advance new members were instructed in additional sacred knowledge, gained access to progressive supernatural aid in warfare, received the right to wear society regalia, and assumed increasing responsibilities for the welfare of the camp. Initiation and ritual activities of all the age-structured societies was supervised by the elder men who acted as ceremonial grandfathers, making the regalia for the younger men, instructing the initiates, and directing the ceremonies.

Although women did not have an equivalent series of societies through which to advance, they, too, received ritual guidance and instruction from the old women who held authority over the most sacred types of quillwork production. Whenever any one of four kinds of quill-embroidered work was being undertaken, one of the seven elderly women, who each owned a sacred quillworking bundle, had to be in attendance to supervise the quillwork production. These four types of work were the making of cradles, robes, tipi ornaments, and the hide blanket that draped over the backrest, sometimes referred to as a pillow or a lean back.[3] Apparently the elder women exercised no ritual control over other types of quilled objects, such as moccasins, shirts, dresses, leggings, or bags, which, therefore, likely comprised a class of secular quillwork. Women made these items independently and whenever they pleased, with no requirement for ritual supervision during their production.

The ritualized forms of quillwork—cradles, robes, tipi ornaments, and backrest robes—are all objects that contained or demarcated boundaries for the human body or, in the case of the tipi, the communal body. These four types of quillwork also shared certain common circumstances.[4] First, a woman made these items not for herself but as highly valued gifts to be bestowed on a relative to strengthen kinship ties and to "honor her kindred" as Fire Wood was encouraged to do by her parents. Second, most frequently she made these gifts for male relatives, particularly for those with whom she had a respect relationship, which would include her brothers and male cousins who were like brothers to her.[5] Third, she made these objects to fulfill a vow, which she pledged in public, that the recipient of her gift would additionally receive blessings from the supernatural powers.

Cleaver Warden recorded Fire Wood's explanations of the circumstances surrounding her creation of eight quilled robes and one backrest blanket, including colored pencil drawings of each in his field notebook.[6] Fire Wood's stated purposes for her robemaking clearly demonstrate that central Plains women's art was an important social mechanism for maintaining and solidifying kinship relationships. The majority of the robes she made were for her male kin, especially her brothers and cousins. For example, Warden says in his notes regarding his drawing of one of Fire Wood's robes, entitled "Double Headed Green Robe for man": "This robe was made for Wallowing Bull by Fire Wood, cousin, who received a good pony. This gift was to show the ties of relationship."[7] Furthermore, Fire Wood made many of her robes as a *vow* on behalf of one of her close relatives. As Warden says of the "Ear Robe:"

This Ear Robe was made by Fire Wood for her brother, Bird's Head some years ago. Because Bird's Head went away on warpath, she made a vow publicly that the Robe would be made, so that he might be spared and return in triumph and glory over an enemy.

Shortly, after the brother's days were being numbered on [the] bone handle of [her] Rawhide scraper, Fire Wood then proceeded with the said robe. Surely, the brother returned as a good warrior having struck an enemy in a severest battle.

Upon the arrival of him parading into camp circle, she went & met him, placed said robe, and kissed him as a token of love and respect.[8]

On the social level Fire Wood conveyed significant messages with this gift of a robe to her brother. When he returned to camp, she publicly met him during the parade and bestowed upon him the robe and with it the honor it conveyed in the presence of their community. In her role as his sister, she publicly honored her brother, which, in turn, demonstrated that he held the respect of an important relative. In a society where individual status and prestige were greatly desired and could be accumulated by a public display of sanctioned deeds, this sisterly act created admiration and added both to his stature and that of his family in the community. On a spiritual level Fire Wood, in placing the pledged robe on her brother's shoulders,

demonstrated the efficacy of her vow in ensuring her brother's safe, indeed trium-
phant, return from battle. This passage also offers an alternate meaning for the
markings on the handles of women's elk antler scraping tools, markings that have
generally been believed to indicate a count of the number of hides or similar work
completed by the female owner.[9] In Fire Wood's case, she used the marks to keep a
tally of the number of days her brother was away with his war party.

Fire Wood vowed and made two more robes for her brother, Bird's Head, when he
went to war. Warden wrote: "In order that [her] brother might be spared in expedition (warpath) she went to work faithfully and had it looked as in the drawing. The
party soon spied the enemy, and fought them in which Bird's Head captured a fine
horse and upon the receipt of said robe, presented the animal to sister, who went
about cheering and praising him publicly." Another of these robes, according to
Warden "was vowed and in time made by Fire Wood . . . for her brother. This act was a
token of love and respect and a bright future" (fig. 2.1).[10]

Fire Wood created her quillwork pieces as a pledge for the recipient's protection
from harm and for a "bright future," implying a long life. Two other robes she made
were in fulfillment of a vow for a patient's recovery from illness. Warden again
recorded: "This robe [was] made by Fire Wood (woman) for 'Sitting Bird in Sight'
when sick in bed. The man got well and he gave a good pony to old woman for good
deeds." A second robe was made for Fire Wood's brother's son, another important
male relative (fig. 2.2). In the sketchbook Warden noted: "Bird's Head [son] was taken
sick one day (some years ago) that his [Bird's Head] sister (Fire Wood) vowed to make
an Eagle Design Robe in order that he may recover. Fire Wood then at once selected a
good size and well shaped hide, had it marked out. In a course of time, she completed
it and presented it to her own brother['s son], who in meantime had completely
recovered."[11]

Fire Wood and Warden have added to our understanding of the purposes of these
quilled pieces. Their record demonstrates that a woman's vow coupled with its artistic
enactment was an action intended to increase the recipient's longevity, whether a
warrior going into battle or a patient recovering from illness, giving us insights into
Arapaho women's purposes embedded in certain of their creations. Several examples
suggest that it was not the completed object itself but, rather, the vow followed by the
ritual action of quillwork that influenced the desired outcome. Bird's Head's son
recovered from his illness once Fire Wood made her vow and began the quillworking
process. He did not receive the robe until some later time, when he was already
recovered.[12]

Fire Wood did not undertake her quill embroidery alone. The initial and most
critical step in the process was to invite one of the seven old women to direct the

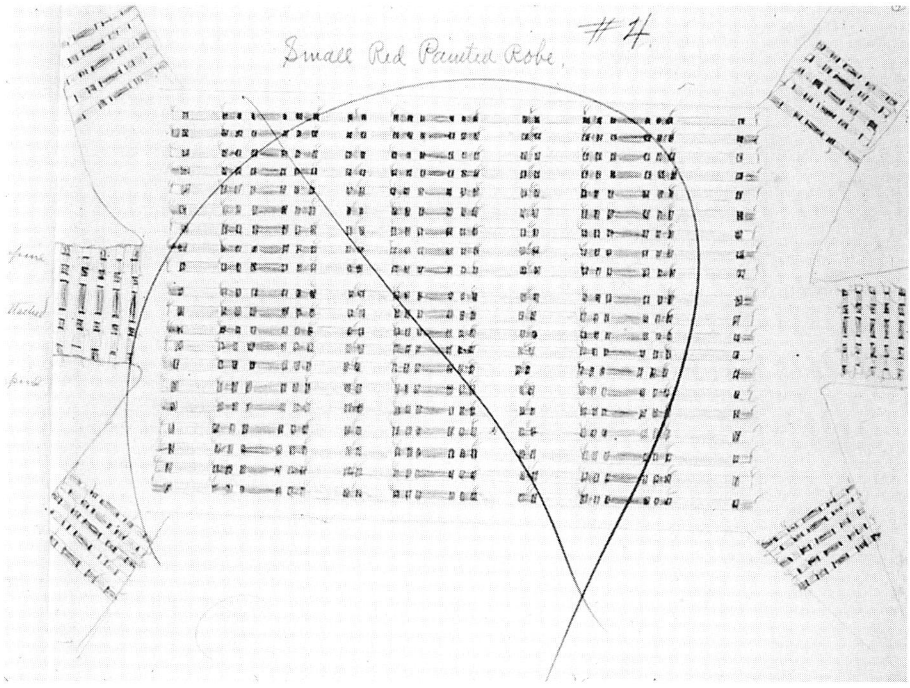

FIGURE 2.1
Fire Wood, "Small Red Painted Robe." Fire Wood made this robe with twenty horizontal lines of quillwork for her brother, Bird's Head. Even though Warden called the robe "painted," there is no evidence of painted decoration. Warden says in his sketchbook notes: "Remember that all colored lines on said robe are in porcupine quill." The Field Museum. Neg. No. A113855, photo by John Weinstein.

quillworking. As the elder woman guided and instructed the younger, the elder was conferring her knowledge, her access to spiritual power, and her capacity for long life on the intended recipient of the robe. Jeffrey Anderson has proposed that "having achieved longevity is symbolic in Arapaho conceptions of having lived in a 'good way' and received blessings from above. . . . If one has lived a long life, then one has proper knowledge and the power to go with it to ensure long life for others. When elders pass on some knowledge or object to younger persons, the capacity to promote long life for the recipient is carried with it."[13]

Two other Fire Wood pieces sketched by Warden further amplify the concept of

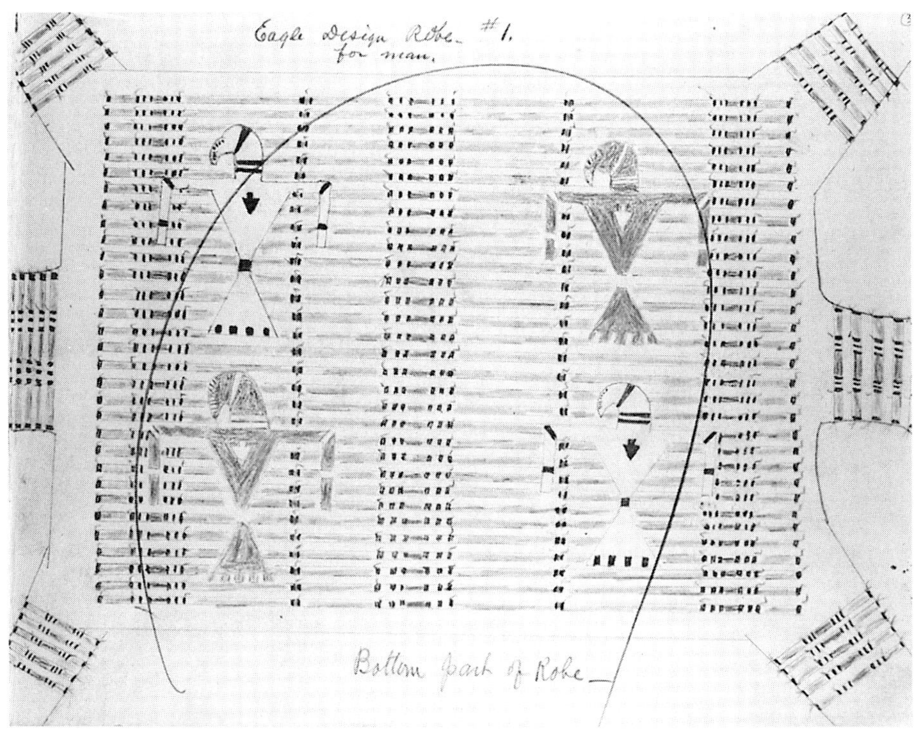

FIGURE 2.2

Fire Wood, "Eagle Design Robe." This robe was
made by Fire Wood for her brother's son when he
was taken ill. According to Warden's sketchbook
notes: "There should be 40 horizontal lines [of
quillwork] on [the] robe." Two of the eagles were
embroidered in red quills, and the other two in
undyed white quills. The Field Museum. Neg. No.
A113854, photo by John Weinstein.

making a pledge with the intention of bestowing protection. "The Legged Rattle
Robe was vowed and in time completed while Fire Wood (the maker) was visiting the
Sioux Indians, to give away on her return. This was done in order that family might
be preserved during [her] absence." In this instance Fire Wood made a vow that she
would quill a robe in order to protect her family while she was absent. Warden gave no
further details to explicate the circumstances of this event. Presumably Fire Wood
sought to ensure the safety or "preservation" of more than one person when she said
her "family." Thus it appears that the making of the vow and the act of quilling the

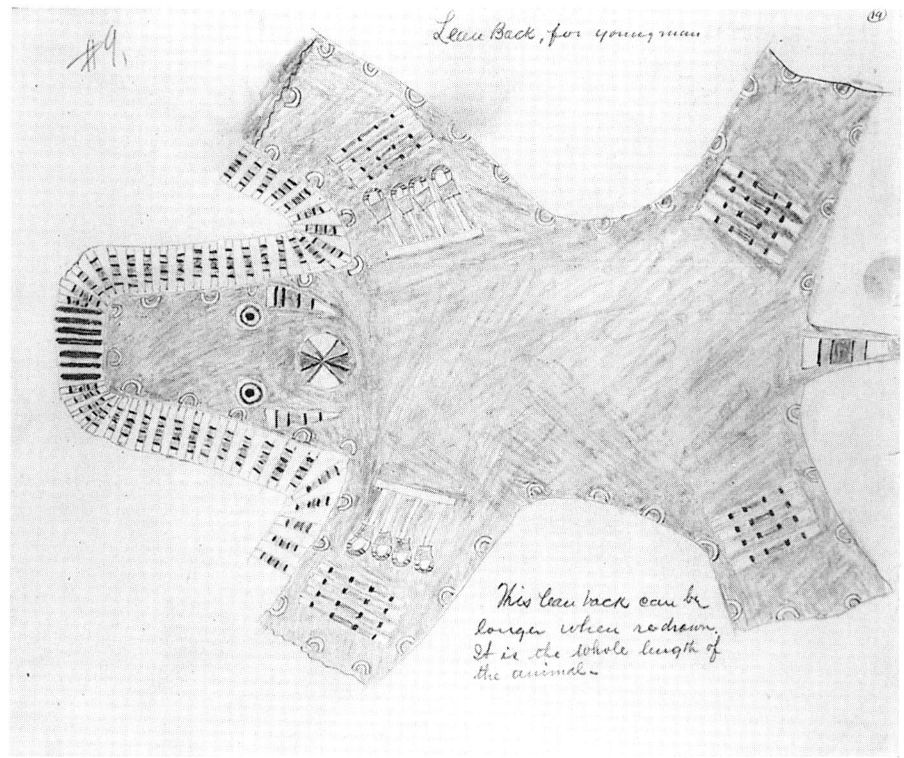

FIGURE 2.3

Fire Wood, "Lean Back." This robe was meant to be draped over the top of a backrest tripod. As Warden explains in his sketchbook, "This lean back [is] suspended through a nostril to a tripod of [the] bed." Fire Wood made this robe for her son's homecoming from Carlisle Industrial Indian School in the early 1880s. Warden describes the robe: "There should be 100 colored [white, yellow, and red quills, marked with dark] 'bars' from shoulders to each [side] of chin of robe." The Field Museum. Neg. No. A113856, photo by John Weinstein.

robe were what was necessary for the vow's fulfillment, since, in this case, the finished robe was intended to be given away.[14]

The last drawing in Cleaver Warden's sketchbook of Fire Wood's work is a backrest blanket for use in a tipi (fig. 2.3). Warden noted: "This Buffalo Lean Back was vowed and in time completed by Fire Wood, Northern Arapaho, old woman, Wyoming, for her son, Wm. Shakespeare. This young man had just returned from school and to show her deep love and honor, she made it as it appeared on Drawing Book." Fire Wood's son, William Shakespeare, was sent to Carlisle Indian Industrial School in 1881 and undoubtedly knew Cleaver Warden, who was also attending the school between 1880 and 1887.[15] It is notable that Fire Wood pledged to quill a piece in order to confer protection on her son from a new and different kind of threat rather than the more usual war party for which she had completed robes for her brother. In the early years of, first, Carlisle Indian School and then other boarding schools, Indian children faced dangers they had never before confronted. Many students sickened and died, ending their term far away from home in the school cemetery. Shakespeare, in writing a letter many years later to the Carlisle School superintendent, said: "The reason I left the school so soon is I were *[sic]* in very ill health."[16] Fire Wood took action to protect her son using the methods she knew best, applying these to new circumstances. She honored her son with the backrest when he returned home not from a war party but from boarding school outside the Arapaho world. In so doing she continued to apply her art in support of the basic traditional Arapaho values of honoring and validating the successful returnee while at the same time aiding in his recovery from illness.

In addition to the backrest and buffalo robes, Warden recorded that Fire Wood made "60 assorted Baby cradles." Every northern Arapaho newborn received a cradle. No cradle was reused for another baby. Once the baby outgrew it, the cradle was dismantled. Although Warden made no sketches of Fire Wood's cradles, northern Arapaho quillwork on cradles did not vary greatly. In general a six-inch diameter quilled disk or rosette, closely resembling those made as tipi ornaments, was stitched on the top of the cradle's hood in a position over the child's head. A banding of quillwork also encircled the cradle opening (fig. 2.4). Alfred L. Kroeber, who conducted field research on Arapaho arts between 1899 and 1901, described the process of cradlemaking:

> If a man is married, his sister may want to make a cradle for his child. She provides food for a number of old people, shows them her materials, and asks how she is to make the cradle. The old people tell her how to make it, and show her the designs with which it is to be decorated. Then they all pray in turn that the child's cradle may be made perfectly, and that it may be for the good of the child. After the woman has finished the cradle, she repeats her invitation to the old people. Then the child is put into the cradle and taken to its father. He receives it, and makes a gift to the maker.[17]

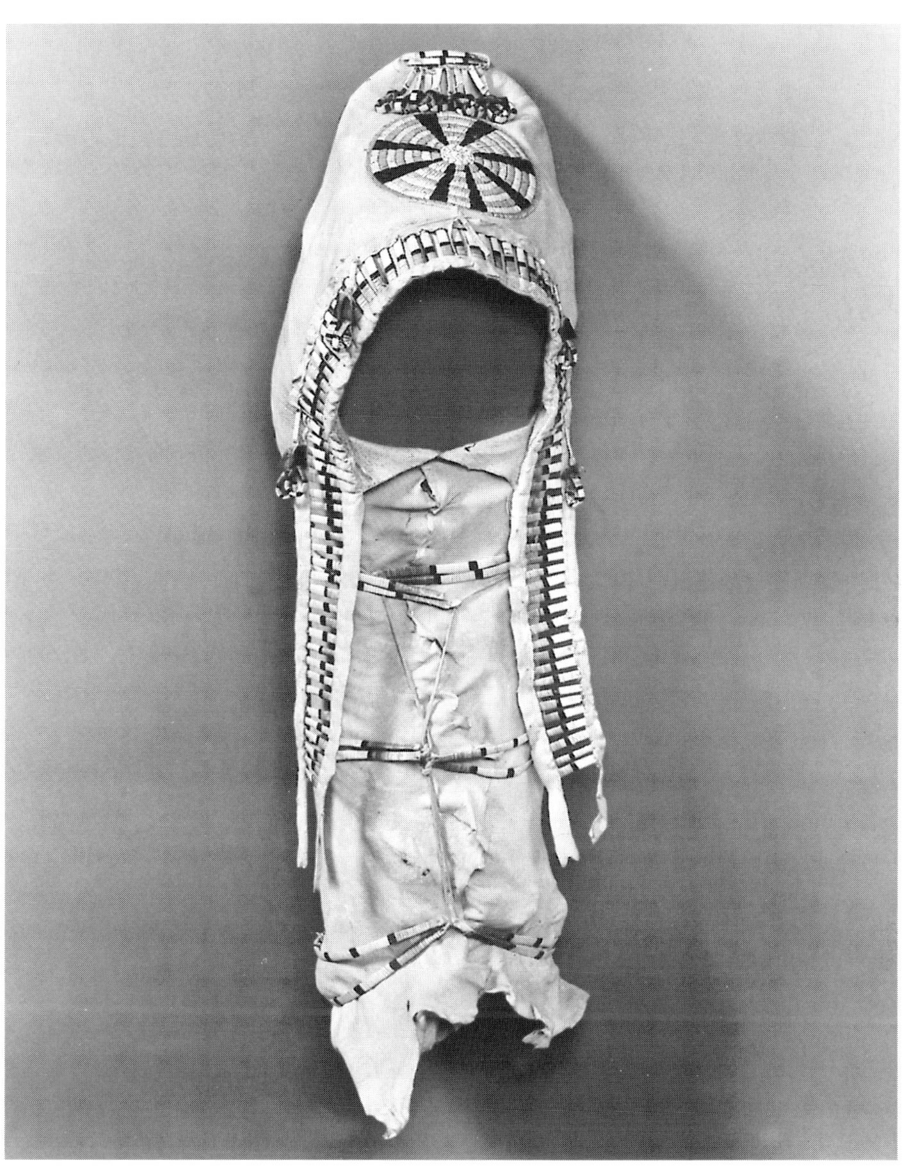

FIGURE 2.4
Northern Arapaho, Quilled Cradle. Every northern
Arapaho baby received a cradle. On top of the
cradle's hood was stitched a quilled disk, and a band
of quillwork encircled the cradle opening. Denver
Art Museum, 1939.336.

The ritual cradlemaking process parallels that of robemaking and also tipi ornamentation. When Sister M. Inez Hilger conducted fieldwork among the northern Arapaho in the 1930s and 1940s, collecting material for her work on Arapaho child life, one of her Arapaho consultants, in discussing making a cradle, pointed out: "When we built a tipi, the same thing was done." Sisters made cradles for their brothers' children. If a sister was not available, then another female relative of the father sponsored the cradle. Surely Fire Wood did not have sixty brothers, but she undoubtedly had a great number of male relatives whose children received cradles under her sponsorship.[18]

The maker invited one or more of the elder women who owned sacred bags to instruct and supervise her quill embroidery. It was important that no mistakes be made.[19] Kroeber noted that the goal was a perfectly made cradle. As Ann Wolf, a recognized ceremonial leader in cradlemaking, told Hilger:

> "When I decided to make a cradle for her [Yellow Plume's] daughter, I asked two of my great-grandmothers to show me how to make it. I brought buckskin and rawhide and quills to her. I had to sit for many days working on the quills, my great-grandmother directing me." The disk over the head of the child was always to be 10 successive rings of quill work, counting the center piece as one. No measurements of diameter or circumference were followed; only rings were counted. All rings were alike in width. The band which was attached over the face of the child and which reached down the sides of the cradle cover was to have 100 crossbars of quill work.[20]

In the cradlemaking context, quillwork was a ritual act that, if performed perfectly, could bring the blessings of long life and good fortune. Perfection in execution was viewed as evidence of possessing supernatural power. Arapaho women, when supervised by the old ones who had access to the extra-human, were temporarily endowed with the capability to perfectly construct a cradle, thus showering supernatural blessings upon the child. Likewise, if the quillwork was done incorrectly, harm and misfortune might follow.[21] On the occasion of making a cradle, the goal, as Kroeber said, was "for the good of the child," in other words for those things most important for a newborn baby—good health and long life. At this critical time a vulnerable newborn particularly needed protection. Once again the oversight of the old women with their capability to confer long life to the child, coupled with the process of producing the quillwork in the correct way, ensured the safekeeping and longevity of the child. Likely this same necessity to quill the piece perfectly, which could only be achieved under the ritual guidance of the elder women, also applied to the other types of ritual quillwork, that is, robes, backrests, and tipi ornaments. Robes and backrests were also made at critical times, when the prospective recipient was in danger from outside threats or illness.

When the child outgrew the cradle, it was ritually dismantled. Ann Wolf described the process: "Whenever I tore up a cradle, I prayed. I prayed to God and the old ladies who started the making of the cradles and to all to whom the old Indians used to pray, . . . telling them that the baby was big now and didn't need the cradle any more; that we were thankful that the cradle had done its service. Then I tore the cradle apart and saved the quill work as a keepsake."[22]

Fire Wood earned the right to become one of the Seven Old Women who owned the seven sacred bags and supervised the quillworking of the younger women. As Warden stated:

> When Bird Woman[,] mother of Fire Wood, died 10 years ago [ca. 1894], her Tepee Bag laid *[sic]* idle, until two years afterwards, the latter [Fire Wood] by payment of articles to elder women, took possession of the Woman's Bag. (Tepee)
>
> She was instructed [in] the manner of handling of contents and also [the] method of consecration upon others.[23]

According to Jeffrey Anderson, the Arapaho life cycle was more protracted than in ungraded Plains tribal systems. It was not until the mature years in life that an Arapaho adult could be considered ready to receive the most sacred knowledge of the tribe, and then "only when the prerequisite knowledge had been acquired and people acted in the appropriate ways would senior generations pass on knowledge." Fire Wood, by her lengthy list of quillworking accomplishments, had evidently earned the right to own one of the sacred bags, thereby receiving the sacred knowledge necessary to instruct others in the quilling of robes, cradles, tipis, and backrests. She had been guided by the elder women for most of her life in the correct ways to produce these objects.[24]

The story of Fire Wood's quilled work breaks the constricted boundaries of recorded information about Plains women's art. Her story reveals that northern Arapaho women were hard at work ensuring the spiritual safekeeping resulting in the actual physical protection of family and tribal members. The women artists particularly focused on those persons most at risk: newborns, the sick, and young men going off to war or to boarding school. Through the medium of quillwork, northern Arapaho women sought the instruction of powerful, knowledgeable elder women who guided them to produce perfectly made quillwork in the correct way. In so doing these women artists were confident in the knowledge that they were contributing to the well-being of their community at a spiritual level beyond the day-to-day practical matters of food preparation and construction of warm clothing.[25]

Why did Cleaver Warden choose to memorialize Fire Wood's achievements? Nowhere else in his field notes did he identify other artists, male or female, whose work he collected nor did he record their histories. In fact there has long been a gaping hole when it comes to recorded information about Plains women artists both in general and more specifically about individual artists. In large part this can be accounted for because most field-workers were male. Their documentation interests tended toward the more flamboyant Plains male pursuits of warfare, religion, and politics. Also, most male researchers were non-Indians. It was improper and inappropriate for them to spend large amounts of time with women of the tribe.[26]

Cleaver Warden, on the other hand, was Arapaho. He was conducting fieldwork in his own society and spoke the language fluently. Warden attended Carlisle Indian School with Fire Wood's son, William Shakespeare, and was probably acquainted with the family. All this gave Warden access to Fire Wood and knowledge of her prominence as a quillworker. It also prepared him to recognize the significance of an extraordinary occurrence. Cleaver Warden experienced a vision while observing Fire Wood at work.

> When I was watching Fire Wood, doing quill work, her face and head were decorated with yellow paint. . . .
>
> Whether by constantly eyeing the design or disk and glanced *[sic]* at her suddenly caused the strange vision, I could not say, but even viewing other objects seemed to picture out alike. That is, there were rays of those colored disks on every thing in [the] tepee. . . . Since I have had trouble with indigestion I thought then it was the cause of the visions.
>
> About an hour afterwards, I asked Fire Wood if she uses or wears any kind of paint when she quills and [she] told me in a solemn way that at times she adorned herself in yellow paint but never told any one of the blessing.[27]

Perhaps as a recipient of this vision Warden was prompted to single out Fire Wood's artistic history to record.

Notes

The Carnegie Museum of Natural History's Department of Anthropology supported the research for this chapter when I was an associate curator of anthropology. Janice Klein, Field Museum registrar, who shot working photos of Warden's sketchbook, greatly assisted my research.

1. Cleaver Warden, "Symbolism on various Kinds of Buffalo Robes Lean Backs & etc.—of Northern Arapahoe. Wyoming," bound notebook, n.d., 4–5, A-1, Box 1, G. A. Dorsey and Cleaver Warden Arapaho Notes, Field Museum of Natural History Anthropology Archives, Chicago. Cleaver Warden was a southern Arapaho man who worked for years on behalf of both George Dorsey, as chairman of the Department of Anthropology at the Field Museum, and Alfred L. Kroeber. Warden acted as an interpreter for both Dorsey and Kroeber when they were in the field during their research trips among the southern and northern Arapaho people from about 1899 to 1907. Much of Warden's investigations for Dorsey recorded information about the various age-related societies and their ceremonies. An equally significant part of his mission was to collect cultural objects, both those used in the various societies and in traditional daily life, which he purchased directly from their Arapaho owners.

Warden likely came to these two anthropologists' attention because he could speak, read, and write English. Born in 1867 Cleaver Warden was part of a group of Arapaho and Cheyenne children from Oklahoma who were sent to Carlisle Indian Industrial School in Pennsylvania in 1880 shortly after the school's opening (1879). He remained until 1887 when he finally returned home to Oklahoma fully proficient in spoken and written English.

For additional information on Warden, see Marsha C. Bol, "Collecting Symbolism among the Arapaho: George A. Dorsey and C. Warden, Indian," in *The Great Southwest of the Fred Harvey Company and the Santa Fe Railway,* ed. Marta Weigle and Barbara A. Babcock (Phoenix: Heard Museum, 1996), 110–24.

2. This notebook and its accompanying sketchbook are undated. From Warden's correspondence (November 8, 1904–February 25, 1905) with George Dorsey, it seems most likely the notebooks originated with the November 1904–February 1905 field trip Warden made to Wyoming.

3. Arapaho women could become members of a single women's society, the women's Buffalo Lodge. Although the Buffalo Lodge had elements of the male age-structured societies, women did not advance through a series of societies like men. For a description of this hide backrest blanket, see Alfred L. Kroeber, *The Arapaho* (1902, 1904, 1907; reprint, Lincoln: University of Nebraska Press, 1983), 65–66.

4. Jeffrey Dale Anderson, "Northern Arapaho Knowledge and Life Movement," Ph.D. diss., University of Chicago, 1994, 201, 189.

5. As Sister M. Inez Hilger points out: "All cousins 'to the nth degree' were brothers and sisters. . . . At the onset of puberty, . . . both boys and girls were taught to be reserved in each other's presence. They were taught to respect each other. It was then that they began to realize that they were brothers and sisters, and that they were different. When puberty was reached, brothers and sisters no longer spoke to each other unless it was absolutely necessary, and then only in a quiet respectful way, the sister keeping her eyes cast down"; Hilger, *Arapaho Child Life and Its Cultural Background,* Smithsonian Institution, Bureau of American Ethnology Bulletin 148 (Washington, D.C.: Government Printing Office, 1952): 68,

6. Cleaver Warden, Book 4 (bound sketchbook), no date, A-1, Box–1, G. A. Dorsey and Cleaver Warden Arapaho Notes, Field Museum of Natural History Anthropology Archives, Chicago. The whereabouts of the actual robes and backrest is unknown. All these pieces of Fire Wood's work are known only from Warden's drawings and field notes. Some of his drawings are entitled "painted" robe although the majority of the appliqué is quillwork according to his descriptions.

7. Warden, Notebook, 22–23.

8. Ibid., 24–25.

9. Kroeber gives two interpretations for the scratches on scrapers: "The elk-horn scrapers are usually marked with a number of parallel scratches or lines, which are a record of the ages of the children of the woman who owns the scraper. One woman kept count of the number of hides she had dressed with her instrument. Twenty-six scratches denoted so many buffalo-skins"; Kroeber, *Arapaho,* 26,29. See also Hilger, *Arapaho Child Life,* 87–88.

10. Warden, Notebook, 29, 11–12. Warden also describes this robe in his sketchbook, n.p., saying: "The robe in opposite page was vowed and made by Fire Wood, of Arapaho Agcy, Wyoming, for her brother, Bird's Head. This act towards a *dear brother* was for a good luck in life & etc. Sometime afterwards, the brother went out on warpath, fought and captured a horse from Utes some years ago, and presented [to] her." The italicized words "dear" and "brother" (underlined in the original) are especially significant, emphasizing the importance of the brother-sister relationship.

11. Warden, Sketchbook, n.p.

12. Alice Marriott, in her 1937 study "The Trade Guild of the Southern Cheyenne Women," also found that members of southern Cheyenne women's sewing guilds undertook their projects in fulfillment of a vow; Marriott, *Bulletin of the Oklahoma Anthropological Society* 4 (April 1956): 19–27. Marriott said of the southern Cheyenne women's sewing guild, "the sacred character of the article ceases to exist as soon as the work is completed," 26.

13. Anderson, "Northern Arapaho Knowledge," 134, 184. Marriott, "Trade Guild," 26, noted that in the southern Cheyenne women's sewing guild "tipi-makers are said to have been longer-lived than other women. . . . The conferring of longevity by the making of tipis and walls was felt to be one of the most important advantages gained by membership in the guild."

14. Warden, Notebook, 19–20. Warden says, further, "When she [Fire Wood] did return to tribe, Bird Woman from Oklahoma, planning to return got it by special request for a friend," 20.

15. Ibid., 30–31. Beginning at age sixteen, War Bonnet, renamed William Shakespeare at boarding school, spent three years at Carlisle Indian School. Like Cleaver Warden, Shakespeare also used his education to serve his tribe as an interpreter, and he is credited with having introduced the peyote religion to the northern Arapaho people from the southern Arapaho. For more about William Shakespeare, see Loretta Fowler, "Oral Historian or Ethnologist?: The Career of Bill Shakespeare," in *American Indian Intellectuals,* ed. Margot Liberty (Saint Paul: West Publishing, 1978), 228–29; Fowler, *Arapahoe Politics, 1851–1978: Symbols in Crises of Authority* (Lincoln: University of Nebraska Press, 1982), 73–74, 96, 99, 111, 125; and Virginia Cole Trenholm, *The Arapahoes, Our People* (Norman: University of Oklahoma Press, 1986), 281, 296.

16. Fowler, "Oral Historian or Ethnologist?" 228.

17. Kroeber, *Arapaho,* 16.

18. Hilger, *Arapaho Child Life,* 37. See also Kroeber, *Arapaho,* 64–65. Hilger says, "Always it was a relative of the man who did so [sponsored a cradle]," 35.

19. Hilger, *Arapaho Child Life,* 35.

20. Ibid., 36.

21. Ruth Phillips has noted the connection between perfection and extra-human powers among Great Lakes women artists. See Phillips, "Great Lakes Textiles: Meaning and Value in Women's Art," in *On the Border: Native American Weaving Traditions of the Great Lakes and Prairie* (Moorhead, Minn.: Plains Art Museum, 1990), 5. Anderson, "Northern Arapaho Knowledge," 129, applies this concept to storytelling.

22. Hilger, *Arapaho Child Life,* 38.

23. Warden, Notebook, 4–5. Kroeber, *Arapaho,* 30–33, recorded an account at the turn of the century from an elder woman about her ceremony to receive one of the sacred bags.

24. Anderson, "Northern Arapaho Knowledge," 116, 122, 134.

25. The accession notes for an Arapaho object (no. 3179–314) in the collections of the Carnegie Museum of Natural History collected by Warden further demonstrate this protective purpose of quillworkers as revealed in an Arapaho story: "See the story of Big Owl or Ghost who carried off the fretful boy, then his mother finally saved him by skillfulness of quilled work, etc."

26. See Bol, "Collecting Symbolism among the Arapaho," 112–20, for more information on Warden's collecting techniques. Frank B. Linderman noted in his biography of Pretty-Shield: "Throughout forty-six years in Montana I have had much to do with its several Indian tribes, and

yet have never, until now, talked for ten consecutive minutes directly to an old Indian woman. I have found Indian women diffident, and so self-effacing that acquaintance with them is next to impossible. Even when Indian women have sometimes acted as my interpreters while gathering tribal legends they remained strangers to me"; Linderman, *Pretty-Shield, Medicine Woman of the Crows* (1932; reprint, Lincoln: University of Nebraska Press, 1972), 9.

27. Warden, Notebook, 32–33.

From General Souvenir to Personal Memento

Fort Marion Drawings and the Significance of Books

JOYCE M. SZABO

*T*he last struggle of the southern Plains people for control of their buffalo ranges and homelands resulted in the military conquest of the area in 1875 and the subsequent enforcement of the reservation system.[1] As a means of ensuring the newly won peace, the War Department sent the supposedly worst offenders in the recent wars to an eastern prison far from their respective tribes. Thirty-three Cheyennes, twenty-seven Kiowas, nine Comanches, two Arapahoes, and one Caddo were selected for exile to Fort Marion in Saint Augustine, Florida, where they remained under the care of Lt. Richard H. Pratt for three years, from May 1875 to April 1878.[2]

Pratt requested and was granted leeway in his treatment of the hostages, and he encouraged the men to use their time as constructively as possible under the circumstances. Several women from the town, including Pratt's wife, volunteered as teachers and soon many of the prisoners were learning to read and write. The exiled Plains warriors also worked for wages providing manual labor in local industries. In addition, the Fort Marion inmates earned money in various capacities in the local tourist trade. The confined warriors polished sea beans, made paper toys, and fashioned canes, bows, and arrows. Among the most popular collectibles were the warriors' colorful drawings available for approximately two dollars per book.[3]

The generous supplies of drawing materials and the audience eager to purchase the books filled with vivid drawings, coupled with the captive situation of the artists themselves, created an atmosphere for the production of art never equaled on the Plains, either in pre-reservation or reservation years. With an examination of Fort

Marion drawings, much of the anonymity of Plains art vanishes, and many of the Florida artists emerge as named individuals. This emphasis on individual identities is the direct result of the circumstances under which Fort Marion art was produced. Unlike that of the Plains, the patronage system in Florida encouraged captioned and signed works of art. The concepts that artists should be identified and works of art titled to make them more valuable were the accepted standards of a public oriented to European-based art. Pratt, as well as others, including the fort's interpreter George Fox and the teachers, provided captions for drawings, and the artists themselves occasionally explained the subjects to patrons. Captions were generally concise, simple comments on the activities represented such as Meeting a Friend, War Costume, and Arrival at Saint Augustine. Such explanations were necessary for non-Indian patrons who had no understanding of Plains life and the established system of visual communication from which the Fort Marion inmates drew. The images themselves could not provide the entire story for a foreign audience easily confused by Plains representational conventions.

Fort Marion drawings were created for multiple, complex reasons. They were in many ways a continuation of the Plains practice of artists making drawings as part of a war-honors system in which men earned the right to draw images of their battle exploits through individual bravery; certainly the imprisonment of the men in Florida gave them the right to create images of their experiences both before and during their exile. Florida drawings were also important as explorations of personal creativity and as ways of understanding the new environment in which the prisoners found themselves, while simultaneously allowing the men to record nostalgic memories of the lives and families from which they were separated. Some drawings were sent home to families in Indian Territory and were thus also a means of maintaining contact through visual communication that relayed at least some sense of the lives the prisoners now experienced. While serving all these and undoubtedly additional important functions for the artists themselves, the drawings also fulfilled other roles for Richard Pratt and visitors to the fort. The drawings were given as gifts and sold as souvenirs.[4]

Fort Marion Drawing Books as Gifts

Blank drawing books, pencils, inks, crayons, and watercolors were requisitioned by Pratt as well as provided by interested outside parties, so the exiled artists' supplies were readily available. Pratt encouraged the men to draw not only to create items to be sold to visitors but also to allow the men to record their surroundings. He noted that both the trip to Saint Augustine and the men's new experiences there "made vivid

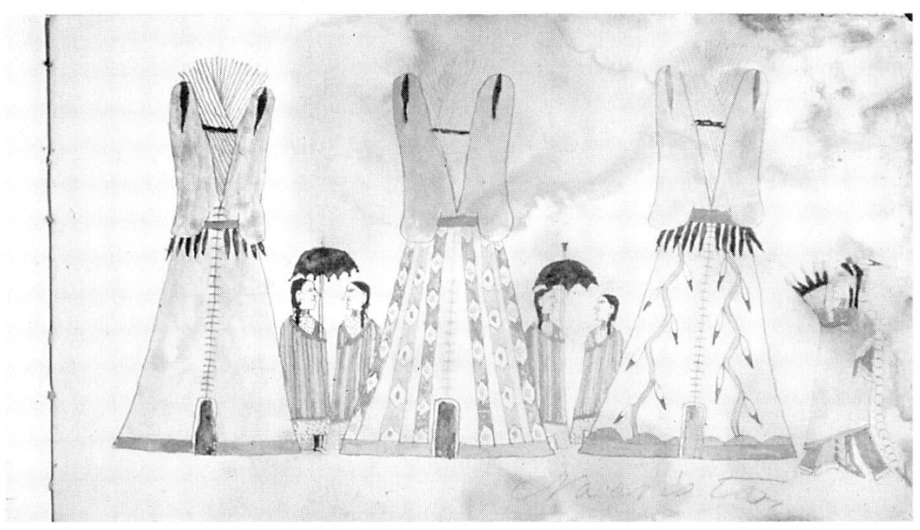

FIGURE 3.1
Bear's Heart, Southern Cheyenne. *Courting Scene,*
ink and watercolor on paper, 4¾ in. x 7½ in.
Oklahoma Historical Society, gift of Marta Lesta
Bertoia.

pictures in the minds of the Indians. . . . Soon the Indians with their pencils and paper began . . . to make pictures of the incidents of their prison life beginning at Fort Sill," where the prisoners had been assembled for transfer to Florida.[5] Pratt even ordered what he termed "picture cards" of locomotives, such as those upon which the men had ridden during part of their journey, and other machinery to be placed in the classrooms at the fort for the men to view.[6] Despite Pratt's proclamation, far more extant Fort Marion drawings present nostalgic views of the life from which the men were exiled than record the long trip to Florida or explore the strange environment in which the men found themselves (fig. 3.1).

While the men themselves had many reasons to make visual records of their new experiences, Pratt soon found he had other uses of his own for the prisoners' drawings. In various instances he presented the Fort Marion drawing books as gifts to important visitors or sent them to influential men and women who might be of future benefit to the Indians. Military and civilian personnel ranging from generals and bishops to wealthy eastern humanitarians received drawing books.

Pratt waged a campaign during his years at Fort Marion for education of the Indians in his charge and for the abolishment of reservations. He saw the future of the

Indian solely through full assimilation into non-Native culture. From mid-1875 to their release in mid-1878, Pratt used the Fort Marion prisoners as examples of what could be achieved through encouragement, discipline, employment, and education, both secular and religious. In correspondence directed to his superiors, Pratt continually emphasized that the men in his charge were as active as possible in seeking employment and earning money. Just a year after their arrival, Pratt reported to Gen. Philip Sheridan that the prisoners had made between three and four thousand dollars through the sale of souvenir items. He also recounted their successes in the classroom. As early as September 1875 he wrote to the adjutant general that "the alphabet, numerals & many english words have already been more or less acquired."[7]

Pratt faced special problems in the care of the prisoners because of government bureaucracy. Technically, the men had been taken prisoner by the army and were, therefore, under the control of the War Department, but the Bureau of Indian Affairs had actual responsibility for the cost of their care in Florida. Pratt, arguing that the advancements the men were making in Florida would be lost when they finally returned to their families, asked that if the men could not be released soon then their families should be sent to Florida to share in the education and assimilation their husbands and sons were experiencing; Pratt's pleas were rejected. In 1877 Pratt tried again, sending a letter of his own to Washington together with one from Making Medicine and one from Eagle Head; these two Cheyenne men represented the younger prisoners in Florida and the older chiefs and leaders, respectively. The letters asked that the exiles either be released or be allowed to work in some way that would ultimately be useful to them when they did return to the reservation. As a result of Pratt's persistence, Commissioner of Indian Affairs John Quincy Smith asked for additional information about the prisoners, and Pratt journeyed to Washington to meet with the commissioner in April 1877. As Herman Viola has suggested, it was probably at this meeting in Washington that a book of Fort Marion drawings by both Making Medicine, a Cheyenne, and Zotom, a Kiowa, was presented to Commissioner Smith. In all likelihood Pratt used the drawing book as part of his campaign to alter the views of government bureaucrats concerning the prisoners.[8]

The joint drawing book presented to Smith is intriguing for various reasons. The first portion of the book includes Making Medicine's drawings and bears a handwritten date of August 1876, while the latter series of drawings, dated March 1877, contains Zotom's drawings. Making Medicine devoted his creative energies to depicting peaceful scenes of life on the Plains, the very life from which the prisoners were exiled, whereas Zotom mainly drew images of the trip to and activities at Fort Marion itself. The combination of these two divergent sets of images, apparently created at different times by artists from the two main groups represented in the prison population, suggests Pratt's involvement and his keen ability as a politician. In keeping with the purpose to which Pratt put the drawings, none of the images contained within Commissioner Smith's book depict battles. While it would be another year before the Fort Marion prisoners were freed, their ultimate release owed a great deal to the efforts of Pratt and the other supporters of Indian rights of the 1870s who assisted him. The book of drawings presented to Commissioner Smith can be seen as part of Pratt's political campaign and his presentation of drawings of nonthreatening subjects, created by two very skilled artists who represented the two largest populations present at the Saint Augustine prison, an ingenious tactic.[9]

Pratt gave books to various other people including Gen. William Tecumseh Sherman.[10] Additional books were presented to people who were well known to the Fort Marion men. Bishop Henry Whipple, an Episcopal bishop from Minnesota very involved in the Indian rights movement, visited the fort and purchased various books but was also given at least one by either Pratt or the artists themselves, perhaps at Pratt's urging.[11]

Fort Marion Drawings as Souvenirs

The timing of the Plains prisoners' incarceration was one that coincided with the beginning growth of Saint Augustine as a vacation destination. As American tourism increased in many locations during the late nineteenth century, souvenirs became far more important as reminders of places to which travelers journeyed and of experiences they had there. Such souvenirs are, by their very nature, incomplete in themselves; narrative needs to provide the supplemental connection for others who may view the objects in the homes of returned travelers or simply for nostalgic memories to be shared at some later time by travelers who took the same excursions.[12] The drawings created by the Fort Marion prisoners fulfilled this specific aspect of narrative through their very existence not only as reminders of a trip to Florida but also through their pictorial nature. Fort Marion drawings, with limited exceptions, present detailed scenes in which action takes place or, in illustrations like those representing Saint Augustine, exacting views not unlike those provided by postcards. If these visual narratives were not sufficient, the traveler also had at his or her disposal the captions and signatures that were frequently placed on the drawings.

Undoubtedly visitors to Fort Marion during the 1875 to 1878 era also purchased drawings that allowed them to meet another kind of desire often associated with tourism—the opportunity to experience the exotic. In Saint Augustine visitors could come into close contact with Plains warriors and chiefs perceived as "dangerous." Although the prisoners were placed in military-style uniforms, they nonetheless represented the "wild" Native inhabitants of the Plains to many Saint Augustine visitors. Indeed, the very timing of the Fort Marion experience coincided with some of the most notorious of Plains battles; Rosebud and Little Big Horn both occurred during the Fort Marion period. The element of danger and the ability to collect drawings created by Plains warriors surely added to the increased interest in the men's drawings. By their very nature, souvenirs are "messengers of the extraordinary," as Beverly Gordon has called them; they are reminders of times, places, and events that were not ordinary in the owner's life. An encounter with Plains warriors in Saint Augustine, Florida, in the 1870s certainly qualified as out of the ordinary.[13]

Pratt added to the lure of his charges as attractions in whom tourists would be interested. As well as sending the Indians out into the Saint Augustine community, he invited visitors to come to the fort. People were encouraged to visit on any day but Sunday, except for those who came then to give religious instruction. A time that was particularly popular with visitors was the period of the day when the men performed their daily exercises or drills. While Pratt wrote of these kinds of contact as attempts to dispel the prejudice and preconceived notions that existed between the Native and non-Native peoples, in some ways he intensified the nature of the prisoners as spectacle, encouraging the touristic gaze. There were archery lessons and archery contests. Various performances took place at the fort, including one in which the Kiowa prisoner Etahdleuh Doanmoe sang a love song and another in which the men engaged in a "bull fight." The bullfight, staged as a contest to prove to the townspeople of Saint Augustine that the prisoners were expert horsemen, was an unabashed center-stage promotion for Pratt. It most certainly demonstrated the skill of the Plains contestants, and by placing the men in a role, if only briefly, that emphasized the realities of their previous existence, Pratt emphasized the "advancements" the men had made under his care.[14] Other glaring examples of staged presentations were the two warrior-style dances that were held for visitors to the fort. As Pratt recorded:

> Many of the early visitors wanted to see an Indian dance and urged their desires on the post commander, and it was concluded to let the Indians give one. Night was selected as the best time. Wood was brought for a bonfire in the court and the terreplein was crowded by the audience. Necessary paint was procured and the best dancers selected. They carried out their home methods of dress and adornment, stripping to the skin, wearing only the gee string and the breech clout which it supported, and painting their bodies most impressively. They made tom-toms, provided a chorus of singers, and gave a varied exhibition of different tribal dances. This was as picturesque and thrilling a performance as any of its kind ever produced on the continent. . . . There

was soon great urgency for another, which was granted, but that ended such performances. They were not calculated to promote any advantage to the interracial respect. I had the consciousness, however, forever after that, that had I been so minded I could have handled the Indians more wisely and out "Buffalo Billed" Mr. Cody in his line.[15]

A third, seemingly contradictory, aspect of the Fort Marion drawings for their purchasers may be found in the statement that they made concerning the effects of "civilization." Dressed in military uniforms and their hair shorn, the men were, by their very exile, being forced into the assimilationist profile the federal government supported (fig. 3.2). Pratt's role was "to kill the Indian but save the man," a role he attempted to achieve through the programs he established at the Florida prison and would subsequently take to Pennsylvania with him when he founded Carlisle Indian School there in 1879. Here, again, Pratt's continued attempts to promote interaction between the prisoners and visitors to the fort were part of a constructed scenario that underscored not only the achievements the men had made but also Pratt's own success in his role as their guardian. The staged performances of bullfights and war dances emphasized what Pratt viewed as advancements through comparison to the daily regimented existence the men followed at the prison. By extension, the opportunity to view the program at Fort Marion might well inspire educational efforts similar to those Pratt had developed or donations from visitors who wished to be of assistance in the Indian cause of the day. Drawing books purchased by Bishop Whipple of Minnesota, for example, were subsequently given to other humanitarians the bishop solicited to provide assistance in the Indian cause.[16]

These various factors provided the major impetus for the purchase of drawings created by Cheyenne, Kiowa, and Arapaho men in Saint Augustine, Florida, between 1875 and 1878. Individual drawing books could simultaneously meet each of these touristic desires by the inclusion of a variety of drawings, some illustrating life on the Plains, others the men's trip to and new existence in Florida.[17] By owning such drawings, visitors to Saint Augustine could well feel that they had experienced something special, that they had been granted a kind of inside information provided by Plains warriors and chiefs. Such drawings underscored the fact that something extremely out of the ordinary was happening in Saint Augustine, where Plains warriors and chiefs, transported from their homes and previous lifestyles, were living in a sixteenth-century Spanish-built fort. There, under the care of an army officer who was also a leading humanitarian of his day, the prisoners wore military uniforms and performed precision drills while also learning to read and write English and moving throughout the community of Saint Augustine working in various capacities and

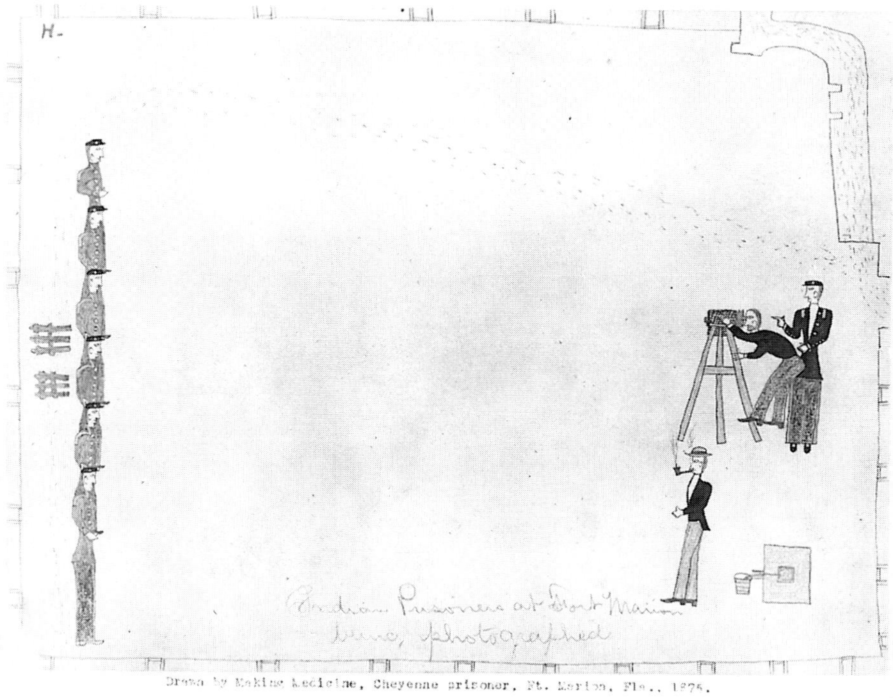

FIGURE 3.2
Making Medicine, Southern Cheyenne. *Indian Prisoners at Fort Marion Being Photographed*, pencil and colored pencil on paper, 8½ in. x 11 in. National Anthropological Archives, National Museum of Natural History, Smithsonian Institution, 39B.

interacting with visitors to the city. It is, indeed, hard to imagine an 1870s tourist experiencing much that surpassed this in being extraordinary.

That the drawings were sold as books not only reflects the ready supply of materials available but also suggests the significance of these images as parts of albums that provide a private view of the lives and experiences the artists recorded, such experiences to be shared, in part, with those who purchased the drawing books. By owning such a book, the purchaser or recipient not only gained a possession filled with mnemonic potential as an object capable of encouraging recollections but also achieved a type of ownership that extended beyond the object itself to include the metonymic capacity of the drawings to stand as substitutes for their creators. While in today's world the monetary value attached to Fort Marion drawings might come immediately to mind, for the purchaser or recipient of the 1870s, the value probably lay more in the capability of the drawings to prove an authentic experience. The importance of the book format itself, most often the kind of commercial drawing book prominent in the era that enclosed unlined pages within board covers bearing marbleized patterns, accentuates the value of the contents, but not a value determined by dollars and cents. There is something automatically select about things bound within protective covers. As Susan Stewart notes, the "interior significance" suggested by the very nature of a book that serves as the repository for memories makes such types of souvenirs even more precious to many.[18]

Autograph Books as Personalized Mementos or Going-Away Gifts

With the exception of occasional books in which two artists drew images, the vast majority of known Fort Marion drawing books were filled with images by one artist. Individual artists approached the pages available to them in their books in different manners, most using the drawing pages exclusively on the horizontal axis. Drawings created on the Plains both before and after Fort Marion also employ the horizontal axis most frequently; thus the Fort Marion artists can be seen working well within Plains formal traditions. Some artists incorporated two facing pages into single compositions thereby achieving a broader pictorial space in which to relay the actions they portrayed. Many books known from Florida contained sixteen or eighteen pages of drawings, while others were larger volumes, having far more blank pages available, and still others contained fewer pages.

Occasionally two different artists shared a single drawing book, each man placing his drawings in a portion of the book. When this occurred, the men working together were most often from the same culture. For example, Howling Wolf and Soaring Eagle, two Cheyenne men, placed eight drawings in a book now in the collection of the Field Museum of Natural History. The first five drawings appear to be by Soaring Eagle while the last three exhibit the stylistic characteristics of Howling Wolf's work.[19]

At least one drawing book with works by two artists crosses tribal distinctions. This is the book that Pratt presented to Commissioner of Indian Affairs John Quincy Smith that includes the work of both the Cheyenne artist Making Medicine and the Kiowa artist Zotom.[20] Both Making Medicine and Zotom created many drawings during their Florida confinement. Each was a very skilled artist in his own way, the two stylistically different. Pratt held both men in high esteem; Making Medicine was the first sergeant of the company of guards, a position of responsibility among his coprisoners, and Zotom became a bugler. In addition, both men remained in the East for further education following the release of the prisoners from Fort Marion.[21] Pratt's gift to Commissioner Quincy of a book filled with twenty drawings by Making Medicine and thirty-seven by Zotom is undoubtedly connected to the specific role the book played as part of Pratt's efforts to have the prisoners released. By including drawings made by two of his star inmates that readily illustrated the peaceful activities of the men, both on the Plains and in Saint Augustine, Pratt added visual weight to his arguments concerning the prisoners' industry.

While the Smith book is an intriguing one and, to date, the only book I know of that includes the work of two artists from two different tribes, yet another type of book exists from the Fort Marion era that further breaks the boundaries held by the majority of drawing books from the prison. I know of three such books. One, in extremely poor condition due to excessive water damage, is now housed in the collection of the Oklahoma Historical Society; the second is contained in Pratt's personal papers at Yale University. The third is part of the Francis Parkman Papers at the Massachusetts Historical Society.

Each of these books differs from others extant from Fort Marion in including the work of various artists of both Cheyenne and Kiowa heritage. Seven or eight artists have work within the Massachusetts Historical Society volume, and the same number included works in the Oklahoma Historical Society book. The Yale volume has the work of twenty or twenty-one different artists.[22] The history of these three volumes is unclear. While the Massachusetts book appears in Francis Parkman's Papers, there is nothing to indicate that Parkman, a noted historian, traveled to Saint Augustine between 1875 and 1878. He was, however, avidly interested in Plains life and might well have obtained the book at some point after the Fort Marion prisoners were released. The Oklahoma Historical Society book was given to the society in 1990 by Marta Lesta Bertoia; the Pratt book came to Yale University with the rest of Pratt's papers.[23]

Although the book from the Francis Parkman Papers is an interesting one deserving of greater study than it has thus far received, it differs markedly from the other two volumes that contain work by many Fort Marion artists. The Parkman book has drawings that are, in many ways, similar to the vast majority of works produced in Saint Augustine. Hunting scenes coexist with battle scenes and nostalgic images of life on the Plains. It is not only a larger format book than the Yale and Oklahoma Historical Society volumes, measuring 8 in. by 12⅞ in., but also has fewer drawings than the much smaller books do. Thirty-seven faces of pages in the Parkman book contain drawings, many having been rendered on both the recto and verso of individual pages. The Oklahoma book is 4¾ in. by 7½ in. and has fifty-one separate drawings; the Yale book, measuring approximately 4 in. by 6¾ in., has forty-nine. The more frequently encountered drawing books from Fort Marion are approximately 8 in. by 11 or 12 in. Each of the two smaller volumes is a commercially produced, leather-bound autograph book filled with unlined pages. It is their nature as autograph books that raises questions not suggested by other Fort Marion drawing books thus far known.

Neither of the autograph books is dated and thus no concrete conclusions can be drawn concerning the timing of their creation or when their owners obtained them. There is an inscription on the inside front cover of the Yale book that reads: "Drawings made by the Indian Prisoners confined in Fort Marion, St. Augustine Fla. 1875 to 1878, representing themselves and incidents in their lives." However, the drawings within the book are consistent in media employed and in no way suggest creation over such an extended three-year time span. The inscription probably refers to the period of the men's confinement, not the amount of time involved in the creation of the drawings included in the volume. The history of the Oklahoma Historical Society book is likewise unclear, more so due to a confusing inscription found within it. Only partially legible and appearing at the beginning of a group of drawings by the Cheyenne artist Bear's Heart, the inscription on the drawing indicates that it was signed by Bear's Heart when he was in Boston on his way to school; this is apparently inaccurate as Bear's Heart, who did stay in the East for school at Hampton Institute in Virginia, did not travel to Boston. The questionable inscription, however, hints at the possibility that the drawing was at least signed at the end of the Fort Marion imprisonment.

The subject matter is varied in each small drawing book and includes a wide range of buffalo and other animal hunts, several battle scenes rendered in miniature, and many genre scenes of village life at home on the Plains (fig. 3.1, plate 3). Neither, however, has any instantly recognizable views of the trip to Florida or the artists' lives there; the Oklahoma Historical Society volume has two drawings that *might* represent scenes from prison life, one of a social dance between men in military clothing and women, and the other a war or Osage dance not unlike the two described by Pratt that occurred in Florida. Even more intriguing than the lack of clear images of Saint Augustine or prison life are several individual self-portraits of a type not frequently found in Fort Marion drawings and certainly not found in drawings known to have been created by Plains artists before the Fort Marion confinement (fig. 3.3). These self-portraits, three of which appear in the Oklahoma Historical Society book and eight in the Yale book, seem to have an entirely different focus and may suggest why these tiny books were filled with images in the first place and by so many different artists.

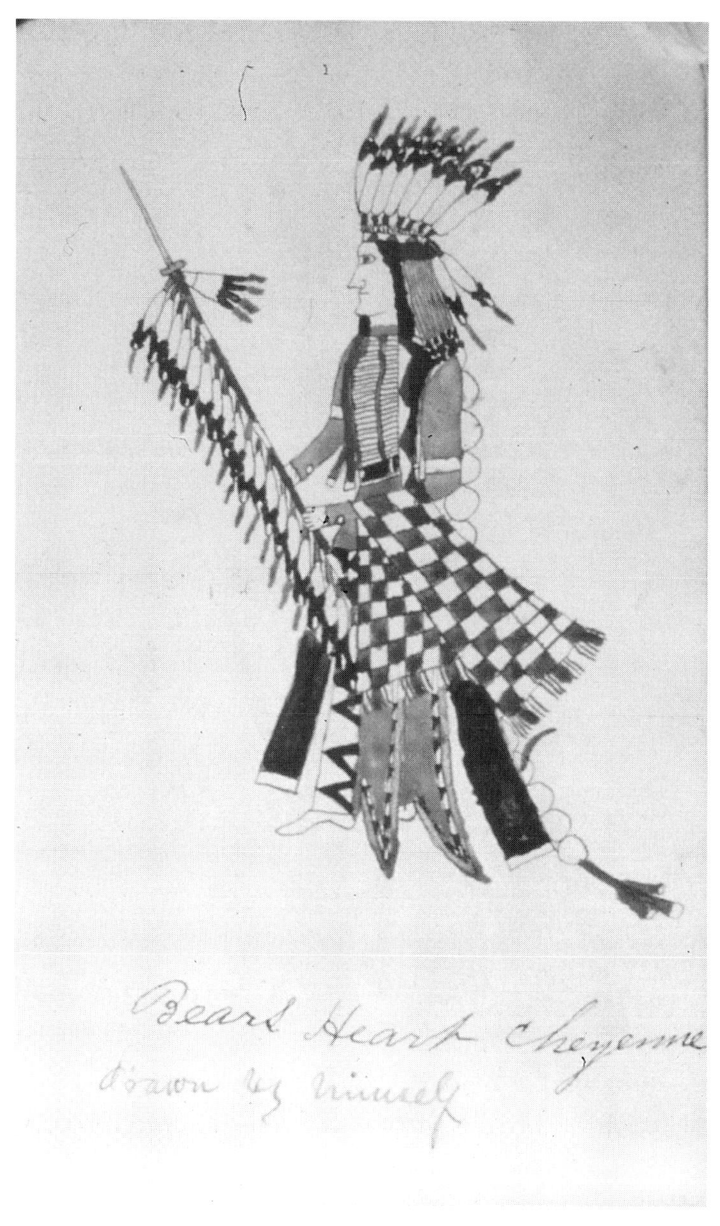

FIGURE 3.3.
Bear's Heart, Southern Cheyenne. *Drawn by Himself*, ink and watercolor on paper, 6¾ in. x 4 in. Richard H. Pratt Papers, Western Americana Collections, Beinecke Rare Book and Manuscript Library, Yale University.

The book found within the Pratt Papers contains work by at least twenty of the twenty-three known artists from Fort Marion. While supplies were available to all the exiles, restrictions that apparently applied to representational painting on the Plains were also at work in the Florida prison. The one woman who was sent to Florida as a prisoner did not draw, as generally women on the Plains did not, nor did the older men; drawing was apparently a younger man's activity on the Plains and so it continued to be in Saint Augustine. Also, the Caddo and Comanche prisoners evidently did not create drawings, their cultures not known for a strong representational art tradition during the nineteenth century. Therefore, most of the artists who made drawings in Florida placed images in the Pratt book.

A smaller number of artists drew in the Oklahoma Historical Society book. In fact, the vast majority of the pages, some twenty-five of them, were filled with images by the Cheyenne artist Bear's Heart. The book contains a smaller number of works by various other Cheyenne and Kiowa men. One of Bears Heart's drawings, however, is of particular significance in suggesting a reason for the book's creation. The drawing is a self-portrait and includes the following partially legible inscription, likely written by the artist himself: "A long time ago I soldier of Indian Soldier & the Cheyennes of Howling Wolf and Miss Alice This Book not forget." Howling Wolf was a fellow Southern Cheyenne inmate and was also an honored member, high in rank, of the Cheyenne Bowstring warrior society, a society to which Bear's Heart apparently also belonged; one of Bear's Heart's self-portraits includes what appears to be a Bowstring Society rattle. While the identity of "Miss Alice" remains open to question, Bear's Heart's affection for her is clear. [24]

If Bear's Heart inscribed his drawing to Miss Alice, was the entire book, then, made as a present for her? The curious inscription indicating that Bear's Heart signed his drawing on the way to school might, then, support a view of the small volume as a gift created for a particular person. The possibility also exists that the Pratt book may have been created specifically for someone, in this case for one or both of the Pratts. Mrs. Pratt was an active teacher in the prison school, a woman with whom the Fort Marion prisoners had repeated contact. In the most detailed account within Pratt's papers that discusses the Florida drawings, Pratt recorded that Mrs. Pratt had "a number of them."[25] The prisoners, of course, also had close contact with Pratt himself. Each autograph book might then be seen as a present intended for a specific person or persons, people the prisoners knew on a more personal basis than they did the other visitors who came to the fort.

As such presents, the small autograph books could have served as specific mementos, as reminders of the men for the people who were given these albums. The format of the small autograph book itself suggests this association and emphasizes the capability of the miniature drawings contained therein to serve simultaneously as mnemonic objects and as metonymic ones much as photograph albums filled with cartes de visite or the slightly larger cabinet cards did for their owners during the same era in which these drawings were made; in fact, the size of the individual pages of these autograph books approximates that of the 4½ by 6½ in. cabinet card. The connection to such photographic albums is additionally strengthened by one of Bear's Heart drawings. In the upper two corners of the vertically oriented drawing appear two triangular forms outlined and filled with black ink (plate 4). These black corners duplicate the effect that would have been achieved in many photographic albums of the 1870s that had precut angled slots for the insertion of the standard-size cartes de visite or cabinet cards, effectively cutting the portion of the photograph to be viewed at oblique angles at each corner. Given the damaged state of the drawing, whether such corners previously existed at the lower edge of Bear's Heart's drawing is unknown.[26]

If these two small drawing books from Fort Marion were created as mementos for specific people, they would probably have functioned as gifts rather than as purchased souvenirs, but they would have been gifts of a very different type from those given by Pratt to humanitarians and bureaucrats. While Pratt's use of drawing books can be seen as political, this second type of gift might better be termed souvenir gifts or personalized mementos. Souvenir gift giving, as Gordon details, often occurs at times of transition. The books might then have been given at the end of the Fort Marion imprisonment, when many of the men were preparing to return home to Indian Territory and thus leave the Pratts and other people with whom they had had close contact in Florida or, in the case of the Oklahoma Historical Society book, when someone of whom the men had grown fond was leaving them.[27]

Further support for the possibility that these two autograph books were mementos given to specific people can be found in the very nature of the drawings themselves. The Fort Marion prisoners kept the money they earned working in various capacities in Saint Augustine and through the sale of items they manufactured, including the drawings they made; many of the men sent money home to their families in Indian Territory. The sale of a book with works by twenty or even seven artists would certainly not have brought much in the way of money to each man; books the men sold for two or three dollars were undoubtedly the ones they created individually or, perhaps, with another artist such as that which Soaring Eagle and Howling Wolf shared. That these two small books are thus far unique in their scale, combined with the rarity of their shared authorship, additionally supports their likely creation for atypical reasons. The anomalous nature of these miniature books is further confirmed by drawings within them.

Miniature Self-Portraits as Individualized Mementos

While the subject matter of the drawings found in the two autograph books is varied, numerous self-portraits stand out from the vast majority of Fort Marion works. These are individualized self-portraits, usually done using the vertical axis of the drawing page as the greatest dimension on which to orient the artist's image of himself. Invariably the men presented themselves in their finest clothing, most certainly not clothing they had with them in Florida, for in the drawings the men have shields and other warrior society paraphernalia in addition to feathered war bonnets and elaborate shirts, leggings and moccasins. Many of the men included their individualized face paint and long hair as well.

These standing portraits are far removed from other Fort Marion art. Here the men are not engaged in action nor are the drawings really part of a view of the life from which the prisoners were exiled. Instead, these vertical self-portraits have their closest affinity to photographs of the day that present people, dressed in their finest, as if for a portrait photographer. The prisoners *were* photographed repeatedly, beginning the day after they arrived in Florida; Making Medicine created at least one drawing recording this practice, the photographer's camera focusing on a line of the men in their uniforms (fig. 3.2).[28] This is how the men were generally portrayed by others who rendered their portraits. The artists also drew images of the Fort Marion confinement that included representations of themselves and their fellow inmates in their prison attire, the military uniforms in which they were required to dress on all but the limited occasions when the public performances orchestrated by Pratt allowed more traditional Plains clothing. It has been argued that at Fort Marion, the Plains prisoners "submerged their identities within the protective personas of accommodation and survived."[29] Within the pages of the two autograph books, however, the men chose how they wished to be remembered, and here they did not "submerge their identities." Their self-portraits are those of men who wished to be seen as individuals within their own societies, as individuals with accomplishments and inherited rights that separated them from other people. Thus the self-portraits include clothing that defines the men as members of their own communities, each man carrying and wearing items of adornment that indicate his position within his culture.

Although traditional Plains painting had developed the custom of differentiating warriors in the action of battle through the detailed rendition of shields, facial paint, and elements of clothing, the concept of an individualized portrait of a figure as a kind of signature and memoir was new. The full-standing profile figures created by eight artists within the Yale book and three within the Oklahoma book are, indeed, the kind of portraits the men would most certainly have wanted to leave rather than portraying themselves in the uniform clothing they wore in Saint Augustine, clothing that did not individualize but, rather, eliminated the differences of achievements and of culture. Kiowa artist Oheltoint even provided a three-quarter-length image of himself positioned next to a detailed representation of his tipi with its painted design, further differentiating him from other men at Fort Marion while simultaneously linking him to his family and the inherited rights that included the design of the lodge. Other images included not only standing self-portraits but also detailed renditions of the warrior's horse, again adding to the individual identity of the artist, his cultural affiliation, and his social standing.[30]

A few other known Fort Marion drawings amplify the connection to photographic images. Both the Cheyenne artist Making Medicine and the Kiowa artist Wohaw (fig. 3.4) created several drawings that either entirely enclose the drawing or set some figures apart from the remainder of the drawing by framing lines or even more elaborate borders.[31] This kind of frame also suggests comparison to the type of embossed borders found in some nineteenth-century photographic albums with die-cut openings into which standard-size photographic images could be slid, the embossed border then serving as a frame for the image it surrounded. Other subjects rendered within both the autograph books reveal no awe at the new surroundings in which the men found themselves when they first arrived in Florida. The Pratt book and very likely the Oklahoma book, despite its current condition, also show many artists very confident of their ability with pen and ink, pencil, and watercolor. Figures are set securely within the tiny pictorial spaces available to them. Such characteristics of style and subject matter support a date of creation for the drawings later rather than earlier within the three-year Fort Marion period.

The order of placement of drawings within the two books may also offer additional information. While the Oklahoma Historical Society book does appear to have drawings that were created by the two Kiowa artists in the first portion of the volume and Cheyenne drawings in the latter, the Pratt book does not neatly segregate the book into Kiowa and Cheyenne halves; rather, the men shared the book across tribal lines. In the Pratt volume, the works of three Cheyenne artists appear first, followed by three Kiowa, followed by three Cheyenne, three Kiowa, three Cheyenne, one Kiowa, two Cheyenne, one Kiowa, one Cheyenne, two Kiowa, four Cheyenne, one Kiowa, and finally one Cheyenne. With one exception, each of the twenty or twenty-one artists drew on two or three pages consecutively. That is, three pages by Making Medicine are followed by four pages by Bear's Heart, then two pages by Nick, then two by Etahdleuh. Only the Cheyenne artist Soaring Eagle seems to have provided two drawings placed in separate locations within the Pratt book; his drawings are found on pages 35 and 49 and each bears the name of Soaring Eagle. This manner of what must have been a constant exchange of the drawing book, passing it back and

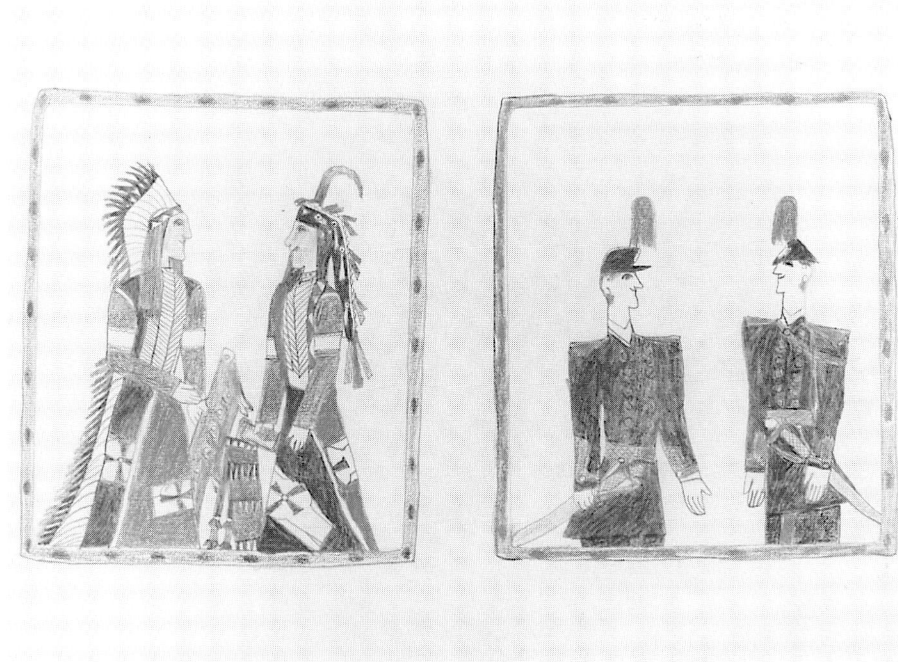

FIGURE 3.4.
Wohaw, Kiowa. Untitled, pencil and crayon on
paper, 8½ in. x 11 in. Missouri Historical Society,
1882. 18.34.

forth from artist to artist, suggests a type of camaraderie and artistic sharing that, indeed, did develop over the years of the Fort Marion confinement as drawings of a very similar nature created by different artists attest.[32]

Many of the Fort Marion men developed a deep bond with Pratt, a bond that continued for the younger men who stayed in the East for further education at Hampton Institute and then at Carlisle with Pratt when the new boarding school opened its doors in 1879. Others continued to correspond with Pratt for years after their release from Fort Marion, informing him of their reservation life, their experiences and frustrations, and, sadly, of their feelings of abandonment by Washington as the years progressed. So, too, some of the men at least developed feelings of affection for various teachers who volunteered their time at the fort. The teachers and others eager to help were numerous, but "Miss Alice" most certainly had an impact on at least Bear's Heart.

The two small autograph books with works by multiple Fort Marion prisoners suggest vastly different reasons for creation than the multitude of Fort Marion drawings. They can be seen as a continuation of the wider nineteenth-century practice of creating friendship albums, a practice that would have been well known to the women who volunteered their time teaching at Fort Marion. Earlier friendship albums had been costly, their expensive leather bindings and rarity making them the property of only the wealthy. Following the Civil War, however, what were actually termed autograph books developed. Such books, generally smaller than their predecessors and fitted with embossed leather covers, contained various types of remembrances offered generally from one woman to another. The sentiments of the later books were, however, vastly different from those of earlier nineteenth-century examples that were romanticized and sentimental. Post–Civil War autograph books were, like literature and art in America in general, more realistic, tempered no doubt by the reality of the war itself.[33]

The two autograph books thus far known from Fort Marion fit well within this concept of personalized remembrances. The men created drawings within the covers of these books that also suggest the tempering of their views by reality and by their desires to be remembered not as they were in Florida—regimented, uniformed, and shorn of their hair—but as they were in their real lives on the Plains. The drawings might even have been made when the men knew their time of exile was soon to be over and they could either return home or continue their education in the East. Either way, the artists who drew in these books left strong visual reminders of their presence, of their individuality, and most certainly of their creativity within the small leather covers of two miniature volumes.[34]

Drawings made between 1875 and 1878 by Plains artists in the strange world of a Saint Augustine prison fulfill many roles, both for their creators and their viewers, past and present. The use of drawings as souvenirs by some, as specific gifts given to others, and as personalized mementos provided, in all likelihood, by the artists themselves emphasizes the complexity of these images. They provide varied narratives of encounter and offer unlimited possibilities for memories to be recalled and shared. Fort Marion drawings are not only evidence of experience, in the larger sense of souvenirs, they are also albums filled simultaneously with miniature drawings and gigantic messages bound protectively within the covers of books. To open such books allows access to private worlds made visual.

Notes

For assistance and research suggestions, especially concerning the sticky problem of photo corners, I thank my colleagues Elizabeth Hutchinson and Geoffrey Batchen of the Department of Art and Art

History; Kathleen Howe, curator of prints and photographs at the University Art Museum at the University of New Mexico; and various reference librarians, especially David Herzel of the University of New Mexico's Fine Arts Library.

1. For detailed accounts of the military wars on the Southern Plains during the 1860s and 1870s, see George B. Grinnell, *The Fighting Cheyennes* (New York: Charles Scribner's Sons, 1915; reprint, Norman: University of Oklahoma Press, 1956); George Hyde, *Life of George Bent Written from His Letters,* ed. Savoie Lottinville (Norman: University of Oklahoma Press, 1967); Donald Berthrong, *The Southern Cheyennes* (Norman: University of Oklahoma Press, 1963); W. S. Nye, *Carbine and Lance: The Story of Old Fort Sill,* 3d ed., rev. and enl. (Norman: University of Oklahoma Press, 1974); James Mooney, "Calendar History of the Kiowa Indians" *Seventeenth Annual Report of the Bureau of American Ethnology 1895–96* (Washington, D.C.: Government Printing Office, 1898), 129–460; and William H. Leckie, *The Military Conquest of the Southern Plains* (Norman: University of Oklahoma Press, 1963).

2. Richard H. Pratt, *Battlefield and Classroom: Four Decades with the American Indian, 1867–1904,* ed. Robert M. Utley (New Haven: Yale University Press, 1964), 105.

3. Karen Daniels Petersen, *Plains Indian Art from Fort Marion* (Norman: University of Oklahoma Press, 1971), 65.

4. That the Fort Marion drawings also played a role as souvenirs does not in any way denigrate them. The term "souvenir" and the phrase "tourist arts" have long held negative connotations as mass-produced objects of low, if any, aesthetic value. Such could not be further from the truth for Fort Marion drawings. Their value and the creative outpouring provided by their creators is not lessened by their role as reminders of trips to Florida for their purchasers.

5. An order Pratt placed in 1876 requested lead pencils; various drawing pencils including seven crimson, nine light blue, ten yellow, and ten green in addition to samples of all available colors; two dozen assorted colored inks; and two dozen drawing books. In requesting the drawing pencils, Pratt wrote that "sharp bright colors suit best." Richard H. Pratt to A. S. Barnes and Co., New York, September 6, 1876, box 14, folder 341, Richard H. Pratt Papers, Western Americana Collections, Beinecke Rare Book and Manuscript Library, Yale University.

Richard H. Pratt, "The Florida Indian Prisoners of 1875–1878," undated manuscript, box 25, folder 676, Richard H. Pratt Papers, Western Americana Collections, Beinecke Rare Book and Manuscript Library, Yale University.

6. Richard H. Pratt to A. S. Barnes and Co., New York, September 6, 1876, box 14, folder 341, Richard H. Pratt Papers, Western Americana Collections, Beinecke Rare Book and Manuscript Library, Yale University.

7. Pratt, *Battlefield and Classroom,* 151–53; Richard H. Pratt to Adjutant General, September 6, 1875, box 19, folder 493, Richard H. Pratt Papers, Western Americana Collections Beinecke Rare Book and Manuscript Library, Yale University.

8. Herman J. Viola, *Warrior Artists: Historic Cheyenne and Kiowa Indian Ledger Art Drawn by Making Medicine and Zotom* (Washington, D.C.: National Geographic Society, 1998), 9.

9. It has been cautioned elsewhere but bears repeating here that the dates placed within Fort Marion drawing books cannot be taken as an indication of when the drawings were actually made, but such dates probably do indicate the date of collection or sale of the books. That the first portion of Commissioner Smith's book bears a date some seven months earlier than that recorded in the second half of the book is of particular interest. I know of no other book from Fort Marion that bears two such divergent dates.

While testimonials exist that the men received no instruction or direction in their drawing activities, this has been questioned. See, for example, Joyce M. Szabo, *Howling Wolf and the History of Ledger Art* (Albuquerque: University of New Mexico Press, 1994), 70–72.

10. Burton Supree with Ann Ross, *Bear's Heart: Scenes from the Life of a Cheyenne Artist of One Hundred Years Ago with Pictures by Himself* (Philadelphia: J. B. Lippincott, 1977), 5. General Sherman's book was later given to what is now the National Museum of the American Indian.

11. Viola, *Warrior Artists,* 13.

12. Susan Stewart, *On Longing: Narratives of the Miniature, the Gigantic, the Souvenir, the Collection* (Durham: Duke University Press, 1993), 136. See, also, Dean MacCannell, *The Tourist: A New Theory of the Leisure Class* (New York: Schocken Books, 1976; reprint, 1989).

13. Beverly Gordon, "The Souvenir: Messenger of the Extraordinary," *Journal of Popular Culture* 20, no. 3 (1986): 135–46.

14. Pratt, *Battlefield and Classroom,* 120. John Urry, *The Tourist Gaze* (London: Sage Publications, 1990) remains the most important study of this aspect of tourism.

A bull was shipped to Saint Augustine from an out-of-state ranch for the bullfight, and two prisoners, one a Cheyenne man, the other a Kiowa, were selected by their fellow prisoners to enter the contest. White Horse, the Kiowa representative, won in a dramatic display that may well have shocked some of the audience not only by what was described as his "practically naked" appearance but also by his actions after killing the bull. Pratt, indeed, got more than he bargained for when White Horse cut the animal's kidney from its warm body and "bit into the tender warm meat, devouring it raw. . . . Ladies fainted, children screamed." See the reprised account in T. L. Craig and Anne Powell, "Florida Bullfight with Redskin Matadors," *Times Journal Magazine,* October 1, 1967, 1, 12–13, Saint Augustine Historical Archives.

15. Pratt, *Battlefield and Classroom,* 120–21.

16. Janet Catherine Berlo, ed., *Plains Indian Drawings, 1865–1935: Pages from a Visual History* (New York: Harry N. Abrams in association with the American Federation of Arts and the Drawing Center, 1996), 116.

17. In fact, most of the Fort Marion drawing books that have been published in full readily demonstrate this variety of types of images within single books. See, for example, Supree, *Bear's Heart;* Moira Harris, *Between Two Cultures: Kiowa Art from Fort Marion* (Saint Paul: Pogo Press, 1989); and E. Adamson Hoebel and Karen Daniels Petersen, *A Cheyenne Sketchbook by Cohoe* (Norman: University of Oklahoma Press, 1964). In *1877 Plains Indian Sketch Books of Zo-Tom and Howling Wolf,* intro. Dorothy Dunn (Flagstaff: Northland Press, 1969), the Kiowa artist ZoTom included drawings of life in Florida and life on the Plains, while Howling Wolf only recorded images of the Plains. Elsewhere, however, Howling Wolf did provide drawings of Florida in drawing books that also contained views of the life from which he was exiled. See Szabo, *Howling Wolf and the History of Ledger Art,* 95–118.

18. Stewart, *On Longing,* 3–36.

See Claude Levi-Strauss, *The Savage Mind* (Chicago: University of Chicago Press, 1966), 22–24, for an important discussion of the connection between art, particularly miniatures, and ownership, and the ability of visual representations to transform people into subjects capable of both understanding and, in part, ownership.

Walter Benjamin explores the collector's passion in general and that for books in particular. Several of his observations concerning the different sense of "value" that a collector attaches to an object compared to the value a noncollector might are particularly pertinent here; Benjamin, "Unpacking My Library: A Talk about Book Collecting," in *Illuminations,* trans. Harry Zohn, ed. Hannah Arendt (New York: Harcourt, Brace and World, 1968).

19. The Field Museum book is 83999. See the discussion of these drawings in Szabo, *Howling Wolf and the History of Ledger Art,* 112–18.

20. See Viola, *Warrior Artists.*

21. Petersen, *Plains Indian Art from Fort Marion,* 171–92, 225–26.

22. The difficulty in determining precisely how many artists have work in the Oklahoma

Historical Society book is caused by the extreme water damage the book has suffered. Watercolor and ink have run throughout the book, leaving ghostly images of the original drawings, while ink inscriptions have blurred, in many cases beyond recognition.

The problem of how many artists have work in the Yale volume comes with the location of two drawings fairly late in the book. Two drawings without identification by artist appear directly following work by the Kiowa artist Zonekeuh. Previous work by Karen Petersen attributed the additional works to Zonekeuh (*Plains Indian Art from Fort Marion,* 258–59); a close examination of details of the two works in question and their comparison to other works by Zonekeuh suggests they are not by the same artist.

23. Parkman did have extensive contact with one Fort Marion prisoner, the Cheyenne warrior-artist Howling Wolf. Both men were treated for vision problems at the Massachusetts Eye and Ear Infirmary at the same time, Pratt having obtained permission and the funding necessary to send Howling Wolf in mid-1877 to what was then the most renowned center for eye disorders in the nation. See the discussion in Szabo, *Howling Wolf and the History of Ledger Art,* 90–91.

The suggestion has been made that Pratt might have sent the drawing book to Boston with Howling Wolf in 1877 as a gift for Parkman (Berlo, *Plains Indian Drawings,* 115), but no correspondence is known to support what is, nonetheless, an intriguing suggestion. However, the same passage states that the book was "completed by mid-1877," using the assumption that it was sent north with Howling Wolf as apparently the sole justification for assigning that date. The volume could just as easily have been completed after Howling Wolf returned to Fort Marion in December 1877.

Lesta Bertoia inherited the book from her grandfather, W. R. Valentiner, who had purchased it in 1946 from Mrs. Irene W. Buckler of Providence, Massachusetts. No further information concerning its history has come to light. Lesta Bertoia to Joyce M. Szabo, August 24, 1999.

24. The probable Bowstring Society rattle, a ring-shaped rawhide form, appears in the twenty-ninth drawing in the book.

25. Pratt, "The Florida Indian Prisoners of 1875 to 1878," 4.

26. For a general discussion of such photographs, see William C. Darrah, *Cartes de Visite in Nineteenth-Century Photography* (Gettysburg, Pa.: William C. Darrah, 1981), especially 8–10. Many separate cases for nineteenth-century daguerreotypes also enclosed photographs in such a manner that the images themselves were framed obliquely at the corners. See, for example, Richard Rudisill, *Mirror Image: The Influence of the Daguerreotype on American Society* (Albuquerque: University of New Mexico Press, 1971), figures 17 and 121.

27. Gordon, "The Souvenir: Messenger of the Extraordinary," 137.

28. The self-portraits can be most closely compared to similar self-portraits that the Mandan chief Mato Tope, or Four Bears, made after contact with both the Swiss artist Karl Bodmer in 1833–34 and with the American George Catlin during the previous year. Both Bodmer and Catlin created many vivid portraits of people they encountered on the Plains, and Mato Tope was among those who were most intrigued by each man's skill in portraiture. Subsequently, the Mandan chief drew his self-portrait as a standing figure, dressed in clothing and carrying objects indicative of his rank and achievements.

The Making Medicine drawing is contained within the collections of the National Anthropological Archives of the Smithsonian Institution, 39B, and is reproduced in Berlo, *Plains Indian Drawings,* 138. Other Fort Marion drawings suggest their inspiration from actual photographs. The Kiowa artist Wohaw set several images within detailed frames; see Harris, *Between Two Cultures,* 91, 97.

29. Edwin L. Wade and Jacki Thompson Rand, "The Subtle Art of Resistance: Encounter and Accommodation in the Art of Fort Marion," 48, in Berlo, *Plains Indian Drawings.*

30. Oheltoint's name has been spelled variously. Ohettoint is closer to the actual Kiowa Aut-

thaui, but on the advice of Kiowa tribal historian Parker McKenzie, the predominant spelling, Oheltoint, has been employed here. Parker McKenzie to Joyce M. Szabo, June 5, 1983.

31. Harris, *Between Two Cultures,* 90–91, 96–97; Berlo, *Plains Indian Drawings,* 140–41.

32. The Oklahoma Historical Society book also, with one exception, has drawings by each artist grouped together. Three drawings by Bear's Heart appear in the midst of drawings by Cheyenne artist Making Medicine. There is one drawing in the Oklahoma Historical Society book suggested to have been made by the Cheyenne artist Howling Wolf. For stylistic reasons, I believe it was made not by him but rather by Bear's Heart. This is the forty-seventh drawing in the volume.

33. Starr Ockenga, *On Women and Friendship: A Collection of Victorian Keepsakes and Traditions* (New York: Stewart, Tabori, and Chang, 1993), 31, 44.

34. Another small autograph book contained in the Pratt Papers (box 34, folder 768) also supports this view of the late date of such small-scale, personalized remembrances. While it may contain drawings by more than one artist, the volume is inscribed: "Chas. Ohetpoint, U.S. Barracks, Carlisle-Pa. Jan. 1880." Oheltoint, a Kiowa inmate at Fort Marion, attended Carlisle Indian School following his release from prison and returned to Indian Territory in late June 1880. An intriguing volume prompting many questions, the autograph book includes miniaturized self-portraits as well as a wide range of other images. If the 1880 date is an indication of either when the drawings were made or when the book came into the Pratts' possession, then this autograph book, too, was one filled by the artist shortly before he left the East and can be viewed as a personalized memento.

CHAPTER 4

Social Power and the Men's Northern Traditional Powwow Clothing Style

AARON FRY

The idea that powwows serve to celebrate "Indianness" has dominated scholarly literature on such events.[1] Authors who rely heavily on this concept have not adequately explored its ramifications and have generally assumed that "Indianness" is a given subsequently displayed through dance; powwow dancing and clothing are often described as the natural extensions of an indisputable identity. Such academic discussions of powwows often lack rigorous theoretical analysis, possibly due to a reliance on obsolete methods. Writers who fear that their works will be challenged by contemporary Native people may be unwilling to make anything but bland, formalistic descriptions of powwow clothing. Critiques by Native people and the obsolescence of certain approaches to Indian art should not be viewed as a limit, but rather a challenge, inspiring more critical and theoretically innovative researches.

This essay shows that powwows and their attendant clothing styles are used by many Native people to actively create, not simply celebrate or affirm, their own identities in response to a diverse range of external pressures and internal issues. Simple, superficial descriptions of contemporary powwow clothes cannot fully prove this point; instead, this chapter examines the historical development and aesthetic character of the men's clothing style that has come to be known as "Northern Traditional" in terms of its context and contemporary function. In the process we may begin to gain an understanding of more plausible indigenous rationales for the current importance and prominence of powwows than those proposed by writers working from implicitly evolutionary frameworks.[2]

For powwow people, the Northern Traditional style is a tool for cultural maintenance and growth that also creates an effective form of resistance to the imposition of power from external sources.[3] However, the word "tradition" itself is so ambiguous and ubiquitous in Native art scholarship that it has become almost meaningless. Nonetheless, this word will be used here, so a definition is needed that is flexible and inclusive, but precisely applicable. "Tradition" is often given wholly unwarranted temporal connotations; it is possible to be both traditional and contemporary at once, challenging ideas that "real" traditional Indians are long gone or peculiar fossils. This chapter proceeds from the position that "tradition" is any ideologically (often religiously) based set of values or practices or both that is produced by and creates social relationships.[4]

In dealing with powwow clothing, a theoretical approach must be utilized that is relatively broad but can be tailored to the specific requirements of a unique, personal assemblage of dance clothes embodying a certain interplay between cultural and individual demands. In 1969 C. R. Hallpike developed a hypothesis concerning the social and ritual meanings of hair. Hallpike's hypothesis is simply that dressing or cutting one's hair signals acquiescence to "a particular disciplinary regime within society." Long hair can indicate that the wearer is in some way liminal to his or her society, while many Native people see hair dressed in braids as an indicator of cultural investments.[5]

Hallpike implies that hair and clothing are parallel sites for the inscription of power on the body.[6] Clearly, more extreme "disciplinary regimes" allow less room for individuality and variation; military organizations, for example, demand submission to rigid codes of behavior, including uniforms and closely shorn hair. In the late 1800s and early 1900s, boarding schools cut the hair of Native students while the federal government enacted "Indian offense policies" outlawing Indian clothes. The government was imposing a certain disciplinary regime, while Native resistance (namely, the continuing use of traditional clothes) was bound within an oppositional and independent system. Discipline, therefore, is not only a type of power but also a mechanism through which it is exercised. As a visual art form, powwow clothing both reflects and creates an indigenous disciplinary regime of social power relations that is, in turn, embodied by networks of relationships.[7]

Resistance is a crucial idea insofar as Native communities must deal with external pressures while maintaining and creating internal social structures. Foucault stated that resistance is engendered by power and is only a localized response to specific manifestations of a vast network of power. Trouillot has noted that such a view ignores the methodological repetition of acts of resistance, especially when such actions are perpetrated by increasingly large groups of people.[8] Successful resistance strategies cannot, therefore, be viewed as singular responses to instances of domination produced by a network of power but instead as an equally dense web of relationships. The Northern Traditional powwow clothing style is bound within Native systems of power and networks of resistance against external impositions. Hence, the "Indianness" that many authors take for granted must be analyzed as a multifaceted structure of power and resistance comprised of the networks of people, visual arts, and songs implicit to powwows. Men's powwow clothing styles tend to be more "pan-Indian," while women's styles can be overtly particular in tribal affiliation.[9] This characteristic of women's clothes can be understood by syntagmatic (internally referential) and associative (externally referential) relationships.[10] For example, modern Kiowa women's Buckskin dresses are often identified by the stylized, beaded oak leaves on the bodice of many dresses, which are internally referential in that the oak leaves only gain a meaning of "Kiowaness" through their relation to, and placement on, the dress itself. A similar oak leaf shape in a ribbonwork design on the bottom hem of a trade cloth skirt might denote "Osageness" rather than "Kiowaness." Hence, to recognize an oak leaf as Kiowa presupposes an associative relationship in that a viewer knows the design in a given context is not Osage, or Ponca, or Muskogee; singular, localized occurrences of an artistic expression are the key to seeing a larger network of tribal and intertribal relations.

Implicit in the relationships that define tribal specificity in dance clothes is an intertribal network; tribalism presupposes intertribalism and vice versa. Men's powwow clothes tend to follow an intertribal structure in that a Lakota man's Northern Traditional outfit would consist of the same basic elements as a Blackfoot man's clothes (such as bustle, apron or breechcloth, breastplate, and so on), with individuality expressed through colors and designs subordinated to a prescribed structure.[11] However, Lakota women's and Blackfoot women's Buckskin dresses could be different in the cut of the yoke, the cut of the skirt, the placement of fringes, and the placement and design of beadwork, so that each dress would have an identifiable tribal character. Because intertribalism and tribalism are interdependently conceptualized, neither gains a position of privilege in the powwow world and both are equally important in creating and maintaining Native identities and mechanisms of power.

This interrelationship challenges ideas of pan-Indianism that underwrite "Indianness."[12] Authors who formulated this concept in the 1950s ignored a contemporary growth of tribalism, led in many regions by women. Sanford silences relevant information in her article on pan-Indianism, and in reference to the 1960 revival of the Kiowa-Apache Manatidie, their Grass or War Dance society, says "that no living person knew how to dance the appropriate dance." She goes on to say that this revival, and by extension others, "bear only the faintest resemblance to any ancient practice of theirs in fact." Her certainty about the supposed "facts" informs her impression that

Indians are ignoring the last vestiges of "their true Indian pedigree" in favor of some recent, unauthentic reconstruction. Her view is that real tradition is bound in the past, an idea repeated more recently by Hobsbawm and Ranger: "where the old ways are alive, traditions need be neither revived nor invented."[13]

What is at stake here is nothing less than control of the definition of authenticity. Clearly, new social meanings are given to old practices, but to assume that this does not happen with traditions that have needed no revival reveals a certain romantic bias insofar as Native people are seen as unchanging anachronisms. More disturbing is Sanford's explication that Native people have achieved full equality with non-Indians when they act like Euro-Americans think they should; in other words, equality and submission are synonymous. Pan-Indianism as envisioned by Sanford and others is not an internal, indigenous strategy, and for powwow people means little in day-to-day social interactions.[14]

The concurrent rise of "pan-Indian" powwows and uniquely tribal practices recalls the interdependence of tribalism and intertribalism: men's clothing articulates tribalism by association, whereas women's culturally specific clothing gains meaning in intertribal networks. Northern Traditional clothes, though comprised of several elements with personal and regional variations, are often identified by the feather bustles worn by dancers at the small of their backs. By examining the history of bustles in general, we can analyze the mechanisms of power and resistance that are intertwined with powwows and the Northern Traditional style in a dynamic creation of meaning.

When living as one tribe long ago, the Omaha, Ponca, Osage, Quapaw, and Kansa peoples created an ornament that elaborated the mythic relationship between warriors and their patrons, wolf and crow.[15] This bustle, the Crow Belt, represented a battlefield after a battle. Two trailers of hide (or later, cloth) hung from the belt and were covered with eagle feathers representing those dropped by scavenging birds fighting over fallen warriors. Two eagle wing pointer feathers protruded upward from the base of the bustle and represented both the rigid bodies of the dead and fatal arrows. The main body of the bustle was made of an eagle skin with head and tail still attached; the eagle was associated with the destructive powers of the Thunder Being and the destructive nature of war. A wolf tail was tied to the right side of the skin; a stuffed crow skin was tied to the left. Wolves and crows were commonly seen scavenging battlefields and were therefore regarded as intermediaries between living and dead warriors.[16]

Among the Omaha, Crow Belt wearers formed an elite class of warriors recognized for their bravery. To earn the privilege of wearing a Crow Belt, a man had to strike an unwounded enemy in battle, be the first to touch a fallen (wounded, but not dead) enemy, be the second to touch a fallen enemy, and then repeat all three feats.[17] Subsequently, a Crow Belt wearer had to maintain this standard of bravery to retain the right to wear the bustle. The Omaha selected their hunting police from the pool of Crow Belt wearers, who wore their bustles on horseback in the hunt; all eligible warriors could wear their bustles into battle. Hence, construction of these bustles was suited to this end. The trailers were split so that one would fall on each side of the horse, and the main body of the bustle was not rigid so that it could be swept out of the way when the wearer was seated. As other tribes acquired the Crow Belt, the eagle skin, wolf tail, and stuffed crow skin (which had specifically Omaha meanings) were often replaced by stripped feathers hanging loose from the bustle base, again allowing the bustle to be worn on horseback.

The Crow Belt is symbolic of how power operated in many historic Plains tribes as well as in the contemporary powwow world.[18] The whole of Omaha society could observe the actions of one bustle wearer, ensuring that his behavior was in line with social expectations; simultaneously, one man, especially when acting as a policeman of a community hunt or as a war leader, could observe everyone else's behavior. The Crow Belt was the conceptual point at which all surveillance was directed and from which all surveillance emanated, thereby ensuring a consensual operation of power insofar as those in leadership positions were under the direct scrutiny of the people they were policing. The late Haddon Nauni, one of Morris Foster's Comanche informants, stated in 1985 that "your life was an open book to your people. You grew up in their sight. Your life is still an open book. It keeps you in line, if you care." Arguably, such concepts of visibility and democratic social control were and are not unique to the Comanche people. Through very similar mechanisms, everyone in pre-reservation Omaha society had a direct investment in the power relations embodied in the Crow Belt.[19]

Crow Belt wearers also wore their bustles when serving as dance leaders in the Omaha Hethushka ceremony. The spread of this dance across the northern Plains in the latter half of the 1800s helped pass along the Crow Belt as well. The Hethushka (commonly called the Grass Dance because of the braids of grass symbolizing scalps worn in the belts of non-bustle wearers) came to the Sioux tribes in the mid-1860s. Shortly thereafter, the northern Cheyenne and Arapaho received the dance and called it the Omaha Dance in reference to its tribe of origin.[20] The Hidatsa bought the dance from the Santee Sioux around 1870; the Crow in turn bought the dance from the Hidatsa.[21] The Kootenai bought two versions of the Grass Dance, one from the Shoshone and one from the Crow, in the late 1800s.[22] On the northern Plains, the Grass Dance moved west, following the encroachment of non-Indians.

On the southern Plains the Grass Dance was a reservation-era (post-1875) phenomenon. In 1877 the Ponca and the northern Cheyenne and Arapaho peoples were removed to Oklahoma, bringing their respective versions of the Grass Dance with them. The Kiowa received the dance from the northern Cheyenne during the latter tribe's brief stay on the Darlington Reservation. The Kiowa called the ceremony Ohoma, a transliteration of the name used by the northern Cheyenne.[23] The southern Cheyenne and Arapaho can be considered geographically distinct from their northern relatives by 1851, the year of the first Fort Laramie treaty, so they did not acquire the dance when the others did in the 1860s. Like the Kiowa, the southern Cheyenne and Arapaho bought the dance from the northern Cheyenne and Arapaho in 1877 but called it the Crow Dance in reference to the Crow Belt bustles worn by the dance leaders.[24] The Osage revived their three I'n-Lon-Schka societies with help from the Ponca, who were influential in spreading the Grass Dance to other tribes living in north-central Oklahoma.[25] As recently as 1969 the Comanche people turned to the Ponca Hethushka society as a model for the Comanche War Dance Society.[26]

Because of the early and widespread popularity of the Grass Dance complex, many authors have posited it as the origin of contemporary powwows.[27] However, this idea presents many problems and is ultimately not as important as the realization that the spread of the Grass Dance makes a distinct statement about Native power structures.[28] Acceptance of the Grass Dance was often a response to an increase in Euro-American disciplinary regimes, whether by military threat or the reservation system; hence, the Grass Dance complex served to emphasize a certain consensual Native power structure embodied in the Crow Belt. By strengthening or slightly reformulating extant systems of power, the Grass Dance created resistance against Euro-American intrusions.

Women's roles were equivalent to men's, and at times even more important. Among the Lakota, a warrior was judged on his bravery in battle and his generosity in giving away beautiful clothes made by his female relatives. The accomplishments of men were inseparable from and intertwined with the artistic abilities of women. During the reservation period, men were no longer able to demonstrate their bravery in battle, so the whole economy of accomplishment and generosity was in danger of collapse. Women, therefore, were left with the responsibility of maintaining Lakota cultural values. Bol has noted that "at first glance it appears incongruous that, precisely when the traditional order was under its greatest stress in Lakota history, the women produced their most elaborate artwork, indeed lavishly covering everything in sight with beadwork."[29] Whether by bullets, short haircuts, or legislative prohibitions against the wearing of Lakota clothes, the U.S. government was imposing an extreme disciplinary regime on Lakota people; increasing quantities of elaborate beadwork became an explication of Lakota values, at once affirming and strengthening them while providing resistance against external impositions.

During the reservation era, Lakota (and other Native) children were often targeted by U.S. assimilation policies. Lakota mothers, in turn, produced for their daughters dresses beaded from the bottom hem all the way to the neck line; for their sons, they fully beaded American-style vests and trousers. Lakota children were literally covered in their own "Lakotaness," as indicated by beadwork. External items, when fully beaded, were stripped of their Americanness, integrated into Lakota culture, and turned into tools of resistance against their own origins by the artistic abilities of Lakota women.[30]

The reservation system, which created the conditions in which art became the primary tool for Lakota cultural maintenance, meant that the rules for wearing the Crow Belt became meaningless, since no one could go to war and gain the necessary war honors. However, instead of disappearing altogether, bustles exploded in number. In fact, the loss of the horse allowed certain changes in the formal character of the Crow Belt. Two trailers were no longer necessary; one large piece of cloth was often used. Likewise, the main body of the bustle no longer needed to be flexible, for men were not wearing their bustles on horseback anymore. Feathers were instead strung in a rigid circular formation, and several layers of feather circles were often sandwiched together. These reservation-era Crow Belts could be worn by any male dancer, indicating that bustles did not help regulate the social order in the same manner as they once had. Instead, bustles followed the same artistic precedent set by Lakota women with beadwork. Anyone who wore a bustle was placing himself within networks of power and resistance, thereby providing a site for the syntagmatic and associative relationships that defined the changing meanings of bustles and beadwork in relation to each other and in opposition to external impositions.

Some contemporary dancers wear Crow Belt bustles with their Northern Traditional clothes. Reservation-era Crow Belts are sometimes seen (plate 5), but are rare in comparison to contemporary bustle styles. These bustles are specific allusions to the period when art became the primary expression of cultural values for many Native people. Indeed, such bustles show how interdependent tribalism and intertribalism are. A Lakota man wearing an old-style bustle would be referencing a certain array of cultural values and historical precedents not necessarily shared by other tribes. An Omaha bustle might include a wolf tail and crow skin that mean nothing to a Lakota man; nonetheless, both bustles gain shared intertribal meanings when worn at contemporary powwows.

When a culture is under such severe external stress that its own institutions and values cannot easily resist externally imposed stresses while maintaining an internal integrity, the whole of the culture may be reformulated via a revitalization movement. The Grass Dance may have served this purpose for some tribes, allowing a realignment of internal power structures to aid in resistance of external impositions. However, the most famous revitalization movement in Native history is undoubtedly the Ghost Dance.[31]

In spite of artistic contributions of Lakota and many other Native women, cultural maintenance was increasingly difficult. The Ghost Dance, popular in the late 1880s and early 1890s, promised the disappearance of intruders and the restoration of old ways of life if Native people denounced alcohol and other external "evils," behaved civilly, wore specific clothing, and danced continually.[32] Because of the massacre at Wounded Knee in 1890, the Ghost Dance has often been described as a failure. Yet it persisted into this century in some regions and its successes were so powerful that they were routinized to define the very nature of contemporary powwows. Powwows embody the idea of dancing for its own sake, ensuring the survival of Native cultures; many contemporary powwow songs specifically elaborate this idea.[33] Dancers continue to use various art forms as tools for cultural maintenance. However, while powwows may symbolize the successes of the Ghost Dance, the clothes of that movement were critically flawed.[34]

The aforementioned doctrines, proposed by the Paiute prophet Wovoka, included clothing thought to carry certain sacred powers; the Lakota, in particular, understood this sacredness to mean "bulletproof." The massacre at Wounded Knee speaks to the failure of this supernatural power, though the real failing of Ghost Dance clothes is more culturally fundamental. Given Bol's documentation of the importance of beadwork as a means for elaborating Lakota values, Wovoka's prescribed clothing, utilizing painted rather than beaded decoration, eliminated the means of visually communicating cultural values.[35]

The process of stripping away materials and ideas of foreign origin from dance clothing, as was the case with Ghost Dance clothes, can be labeled indigenization. Such actions are dependent on a perception that clothing is too heavily influenced by external power, expectations, materials, or all three. Therefore, attempts are made to eliminate those materials altogether. Often, this process goes too far, creating something totally new that is nonetheless justified as being the "old way" or "traditional." By eliminating "foreign" beads as a decorative possibility, Ghost Dance doctrine eliminated the very visual language of beadwork, which was based on the visual language of quillwork. Hence, most Ghost Dance clothes eliminated beadwork and quillwork, which were both culturally integrated artistic expressions, along the way creating new decorative style and logic with limited range of painted designs with limited color schemes.[36]

The decorative style of Ghost Dance clothing was fundamentally disintegrative because beadwork already served multiple functions. Beads were utilized by many

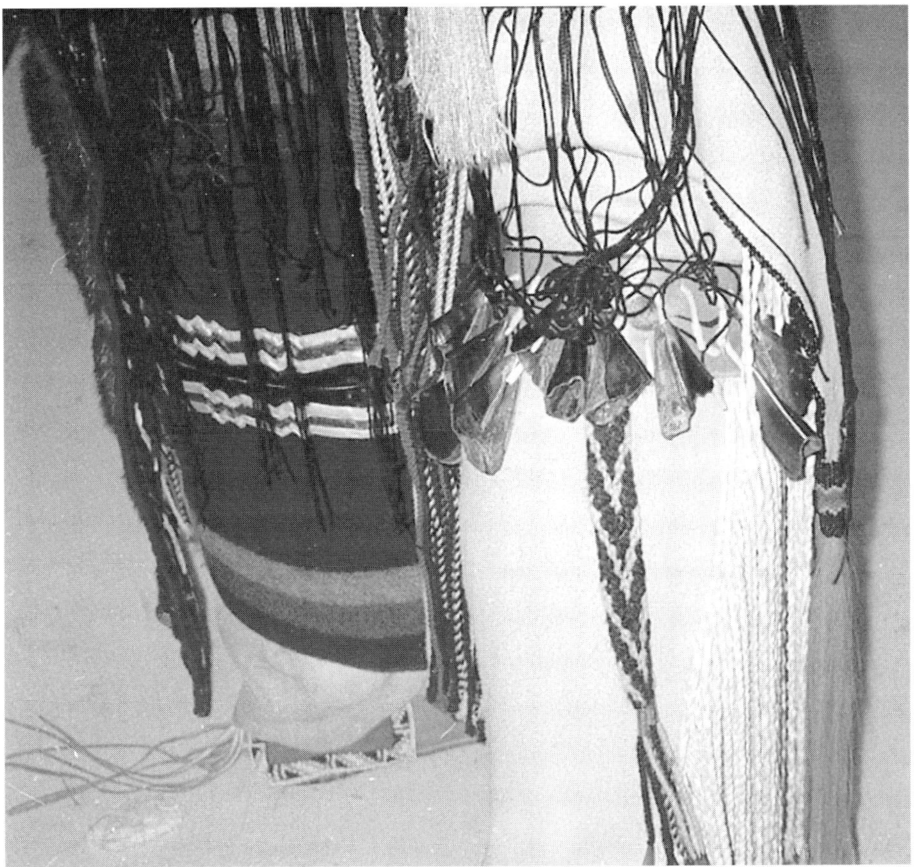

Native peoples as a medium of expression that integrated people and objects into their cultures. Moreover, beadwork styles integrated communicative channels between cultures: Lakotas could recognize Crow or Cheyenne beadwork designs as such and vice versa. As important as the Ghost Dance was to the revitalization of many cultures, it threatened to strip away the extravagant beadwork that had become a crucial means of cultural maintenance for many tribes.

Currently, indigenization tends to occur on a more localized level. Most male dancers at powwows, in every style of dress, wear bells, although some men wear straps of deer toes just below their knees (fig. 4.1). Deer toe "bells" are the indigenized version of bells but have not replaced bells altogether. Neither bells nor deer toes are disintegrative, for both allow a dancer to add to the music to which he is dancing. Nonetheless, deer toes are often referred to as being more "traditional," or the original version of metal bells, regardless of whether such a claim can be substantiated. Hence, the success or failure of indigenization is a matter of degree: the integrative value of innovations must outweigh their disintegrative effects.

The longest-lasting example of indigenization has been the contemporary Northern Traditional bustle. Circular, reservation-era Crow Belts remained popular roughly until the 1920s. In this decade of flappers and the Charleston, the Kiowa and Ponca peoples in Oklahoma began changing the structure of bustles. Young men wanted fancier, flashier featherwork to showcase their increasingly active dancing; they created bustles that were more regular in structure, which became popular throughout Oklahoma. Carefully organized arrangements of feathers with plumes tied on to emphasize motion replaced the thick layers of stripped feathers. For several decades after the invention of the "Fancy Dance" style, Oklahoma men wore either Fancy or Straight Dance clothes. The new Fancy Dance quickly became popular in the northern Plains states as well, where men were either Fancy dancers or danced "old style," wearing reservation-era Crow Belts and attendant clothes. By the early 1960s a new clothing style from North Dakota, the precursor to the contemporary powwow Grass Dance style, was gaining popularity in the northern states but was relatively unknown in Oklahoma.[37] However, until the mid-1960s there was no such thing as the "Northern Traditional" style, which was created as a means of emphasizing internal power structures in the face of external pressures that were threatening Native people.[38]

The 1950s saw the advent of the federal government's assimilationist relocation policies, which forced many families to move to urban centers such as San Francisco, Chicago, and Denver. Those who remained in their home communities could not always rely on tested cultural means for dealing with external pressures such as the blatant anti-Indian racism that was becoming increasingly apparent in the northern Plains states. The American Indian Movement (AIM) was started by urban Indians, victims of relocation, in Minnesota in 1968, but it quickly became involved in combating racism in reservation border towns.[39]

AIM advocated a return to traditional practices such as the Sun Dance as a tool with which Native people could reconstitute their own cultural means for dealing with external pressures. Indian centers sprang up in cities and hosted powwows; dancing itself gained a particularly political meaning as an expression of traditionalism, and in 1971 the Lac Courte Oreilles Anishnabe tribe in Wisconsin hosted the Honor the Earth powwow to protest the relicensing of a dam that had flooded tribal lands fifty years earlier.[40] In 1974 Anishnabe women in Minnesota revived the Jingle

Dress as a tool for stating traditionalist identities, and the dress subsequently spread throughout the northern Plains.[41]

In the Dakotas, the Fancy Dance style became suspect because of its reliance on aniline-dyed hackles of external manufacture for the characteristic bustles. These bustles were essentially indigenized, and the new bustle style was called "Traditional" (plate 6, fig. 4.2). Such bustles were worn with clothes that combined elements from the "old style" and Fancy Dance clothes, with a clear preference for the former. These new Northern Traditional bustles were made of natural feathers, most often eagle because of various religious meanings that such feathers hold for Native people, but were built in a manner similar to Fancy Dance bustles. The feathers are strung together at the base with an additional bridle cord a few inches up the shaft so that when tied to a plywood base a U-shape is achieved. Though the Fancy Dance became exceedingly popular in the late 1960s and never disappeared, by the mid 1970s the new Traditional style dominated on the northern Plains.[42]

As this style spread throughout the nation, a certain aesthetic dichotomy between north and south was created. The northern aesthetic in bustles is characterized by uniformity. Bustles tend to be rather circular, made of one kind of feather such as immature golden eagle tail feathers (plate 6). Whereas Fancy Dance bustles were large and rigidly constructed, with the hackles shaking in time with the dancer's motion, the single bustles of Northern Traditional dancers were relatively small and were designed to open and close like wings as each dancer moved. The indigenization of Fancy Dance bustles succeeded because the new Northern Traditional style did not attempt to disintegrate other ongoing systems of communication. In fact, the new style created a union between the social meanings of bustles and beadwork unlike that any previous clothing styles had. Fully beaded Fancy Dance outfits, although highly valued, place beadwork alongside "nonindigenous" dyed feathers and are an innovation that postdates the creation of the Northern Traditional style. When combined with religiously valued eagle feathers, beadwork gains a deeper level of integrative significance. Beaded vests and cuffs, items of external origin which had long since been culturally integrated, become even more "traditional" when worn by dancers in this new style. The combination of beadwork and eagle feathers in Northern Traditional clothes intensifies the syntagmatic and associative networks that give meaning to beadwork in every dance style on the northern Plains, regardless of whether these other styles use eagle feather bustles.[43]

As the aesthetic character of this new style was being negotiated during the early 1970s by northern powwow people, beadwork was still the primary artistic culture carrier. This trend was followed by southern powwow people who were attracted to this clothing style, but the style itself really did not become popular in the Oklahoma

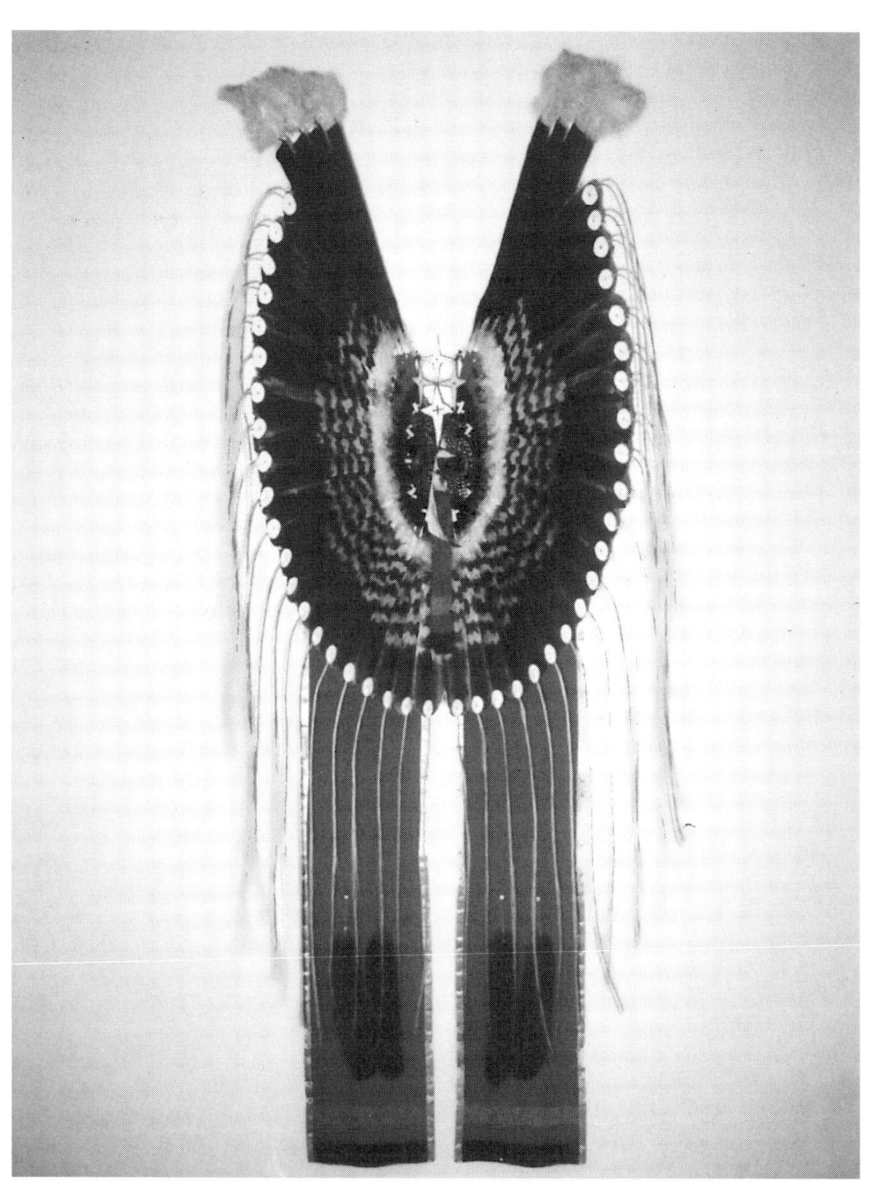

Northern Traditional bustle, 1996. Collection of
author, photo by author.

region until about 1980. The reason for this delay may be the "Great Oklahoma Feather Bust" of 1974. Just as the new Northern Traditional style was becoming a cultural norm for northern powwow people, the U.S. Fish and Wildlife Service arrested fourteen Native people in Oklahoma on charges related to possession of "illegal" feathers. The government's stated rationale for this action was to stop trade in feathers of protected birds, such as eagles and hawks, which was said to be causing the near extinction of these birds.[44]

The sentiment in Oklahoma was that the government's actions had nothing to do with protecting endangered species, which were in greater danger from use of the pesticide DDT. Likewise, sheep ranchers had been killing eagles by the hundreds, stating that the birds represented a threat to their flocks, but had summarily avoided prosecution on similar charges.[45] The government seemed to be making "an attempt to vindicate their feelings against all Indians for political reasons, with overtones resulting from the BIA takeover or the Wounded Knee actions by the American Indian Movement."[46]

An additional government motivation may be found in the fact that the arrests were carried out ten days before Easter, a major Native American Church ceremonial day.[47] Whether motivated by revenge or by fear of the use of peyote by Native American Church members, the government simply ignored its own legislation. The Migratory Bird Treaty Act of 1916, the Bald Eagle Protection Act of 1940, a Joint Resolution of Congress in 1962 (which amended the 1940 law and extended protection to the golden eagle and other predatory birds crossing international lines), and the Endangered Species Act of 1973 each had provisions that allowed the religious use of protected feathers by Native people. Even with such legal exemptions, an ethnic group that constituted at the time less than 1 percent of the U.S. population—and only two-thirds of whom, at most, had a need for such feathers—could not possibly have created an environmental disaster of the scope imagined by the federal government.[48]

Clearly, the environment created in mid-1970s Oklahoma by the government was not conducive to widespread acceptance of a powwow clothing style that placed such heavy emphasis on the use of eagle feathers. Hence, the Northern Traditional style did not become popular in the south until the late 1970s and early 1980s. When the style did gain a widespread southern following, extravagant featherwork, rather than beadwork, was given importance. Just as the government's attempts to legislate against Native clothes in the late 1800s resulted in an explosion of bustles and beadwork, by defining eagle feathers as unacceptable possessions for "proper Americans," the government created a certain disciplinary regime that was resisted by an increased importance placed on feathers by southern powwow people. At the very point where the government exercised its power on the bodies of Native people in Oklahoma, resistance was enacted. However, this resistance was already bound up in a complex network of Native power structures. For some southerners beadwork was still important, but featherwork became even more significant. Large bustles with dowel rod extensions inserted into the feather shafts became popular, as did double-layered bustles. Such bustles necessitated the use of two or even three eagles; the southern bustle aesthetic often used both wing and tail feathers, creating an elliptical shape (fig. 4.2).[49]

In Lynn Huenemann's article on northern Plains dance, figure 143 shows two dancers who are from Oklahoma; this photo was taken at a Comanche powwow, indicating Huenemann's failure to articulate a difference between a northern and southern aesthetic in Northern Traditional clothes. Likewise, Thomas Kavanaugh, in an article on southern Plains dance published in the same book, makes a very confused statement about the creation of extended, double-layer bustles. He says that Fancy Dance bustles became "so large that both the back and shoulder bustles are combined into a single bustle worn at the waist"; he illustrates this statement with an image of a Northern Traditional dancer. Kavanaugh is working from a unilinear evolutionary bias; similarly, Huenemann attempts to homogenize a complex array of regional issues and personal variations. The implicit evolutionism in both examinations of contemporary Plains dance allows the authors to silence relevant social and historical information, subsequently making statements that are simply inaccurate.[50]

Using feathers as a means of resisting government power while strengthening Native power structures did not stop with bustles. Old warrior society emblems revived and elaborated by Northern Traditional dancers in the Oklahoma region quickly spread to other parts of the country. Contemporary shoulder fans (fig. 4.3) may be based on bundles of feathers worn on the left shoulder by historic Kiowa and Comanche warriors as emblems of society membership. Feather visors extending out over the face from under some dancers' porcupine hair roaches may have been an elaboration of pairs of feathers worn in the hair of Ponca Hethushka Society members; both these examples, rather than being directly related to their specific tribal origins, show that southern traditional dancers are covering themselves in feathers just as dancers from the Dakotas cover themselves in beadwork.[51]

The most impressive feather ornaments revived by Oklahoma traditional dancers have undoubtedly been soldier hats. Among many Plains tribes, warrior society members wore particular headdresses that set them apart from other men in the tribe. The most famous image of a man wearing such a headdress was painted circa 1832–34 by Karl Bodmer and is of Pehriska-Ruhpa, a member of the Hidatsa Dog Society. This globelike ornament of magpie feathers with a crest of wild turkey tail feathers had similar counterparts among other northern Plains people, while tribes as far south as the Comanche had their own unique styles of headdresses in the pre-reservation era

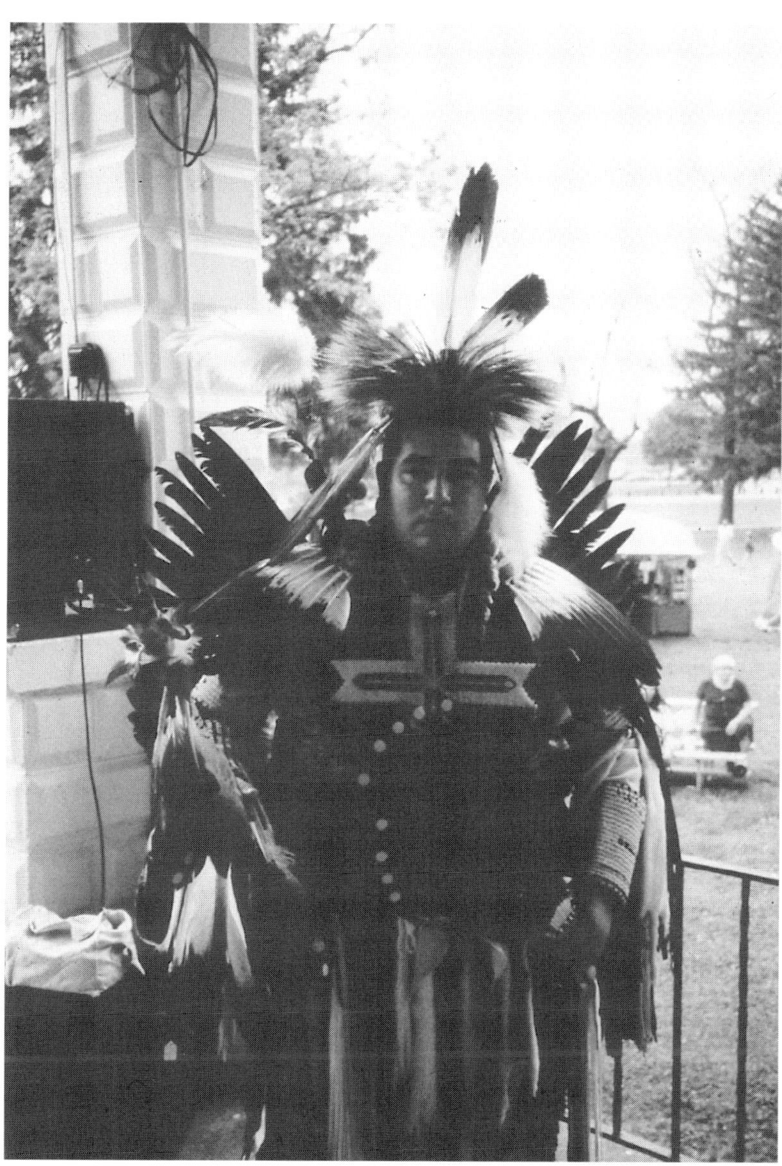

FIGURE 4.3
Wayne Cleland (Anishnabe), 1997. Photo by
author, courtesy Wayne Cleland.

that contributed to social maintenance just as the Crow Belt did among the Omaha and other central Plains tribes. The first soldier hats worn by contemporary Northern Traditional dancers in the late 1980s were of the globe type and, like shoulder fans and visors, quickly became popular outside of Oklahoma.

Such ornaments allowed dancers to cover themselves in feathers, the one component of powwow dance clothing that the government had only recently attempted to control. Furthermore, these hats may cover Euro-American haircuts, so if cutting the hair equals acquiescence to an American disciplinary regime, covering the head with such a headdress draws on a wide range of Native power structures to resist that particular exercise of disciplinary power. However, everywhere in the powwow world the predominant headdress for all male dancers is still the porcupine hair roach (fig. 4.3), which in the past was an emblem reserved for warriors who were members of Grass Dance societies. Currently, roaches implicate male dancers in Native power and resistance relationships in the same manner as these other, more dramatic innovations; indeed, many dancers with short haircuts grow a long scalp lock at the crown of their heads which, when braided, allows their roaches to be worn without being tied on with shoestrings.[52]

Recently, some Northern Traditional dancers from the Oklahoma region have begun experimenting with new, more sculptural forms of soldier hats. Undoubtedly the most innovative artist of these headdresses is George "Cricket" Shields Jr., who is continually experimenting with the shape and mobile character of such ornaments. Shields is able to effectively expand those networks of power and resistance in which all powwow people are engaged by pushing the aesthetic limits of what constitutes a soldier hat, showing that globe-shaped headdresses are but one of a myriad of possibilities for making oneself and others complicit in Native networks of power and resistance. Due in large part to Shields's efforts and innovations, other dancers have been willing to create more mobile and sculptural soldier hats (fig. 4.4). Such continual changes within the bounds of one powwow clothing style draw on a vast network of relationships in order to contribute to cultural maintenance and create the varying identities of Native people.[53]

Clearly the Northern Traditional powwow clothing style articulates very complicated systems of power and resistance while being but one facet of those same networks. The relationships in which traditional dancers are bound, particularly with female dancers in all their respective styles, fully disrupt the logic upon which are based ideas of some essential "Indianness" or pan-Indianism that derives from obsolete evolutionary assertions that powwows are descended exclusively and directly from Hethushka societies. Certainly, the old Grass Dance set historic precedents for powwows and influenced the aesthetic character of the Northern Traditional clothing

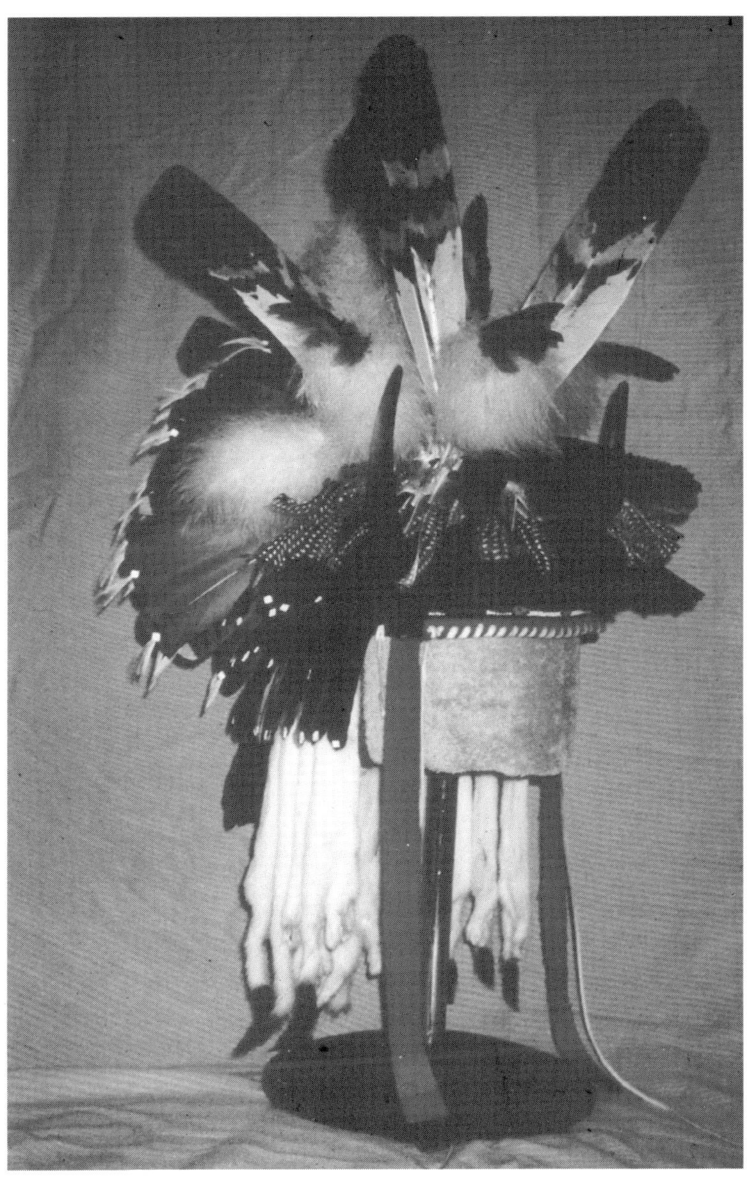

FIGURE 4.4
Contemporary soldier hat, 1996. Collection of
author, photo by author.

style, but such precedents need not presuppose an exclusion of other possible influences. A historic precedent is not necessarily a tradition nor an evolutionary predecessor. Tradition, rather than being a simple concept that is rapidly comprehensible and easily identifiable, is a highly complex and multifaceted dialogue that expands on cultural precursors, ensuring that Native people can create and claim identities that evade simple description.

Notes

This essay is an adaptation of chapter two in Aaron Fry, "The Northern Traditional Powwow Clothing Style and the United States Postal Service: A Study in Conflicting Meanings," master's thesis, University of New Mexico, 1999, 46–96, wherein a lengthier critique is mounted of the discursive construction of "Indianness" as opposed to the creation of multiple identities by powwow people within Native systems of power and resistance. That work would not have been possible without the gracious input and assistance of committee members David Craven, M. Jane Young, and the editor of this volume, Joyce M. Szabo.

1. Some of the more recent authors using this idea include Charlotte Heth, "American Indian Dance: A Celebration of Survival and Adaptation," 1; Lynn F. Huenemann, "Northern Plains Dance," 125; and Thomas W. Kavanaugh, "Southern Plains Dance: Tradition and Dynamics," 105, all in *Native American Dance: Ceremonies and Social Traditions,* ed. Charlotte Heth (Washington, D.C.: National Museum of the American Indian with Starwood Publishing, 1992); William K. Powers, *War Dance: Plains Indian Musical Performance* (Tucson: University of Arizona Press, 1990) 51; and Gloria Young, "Dance as Communication," *Native Americas Special Edition: Native American Expressive Culture* 11, nos. 3 and 4 (1994): 9–15.

2. For a more complete discussion of the construction of and continuing utilization of evolutionary biases, see Fry, "The Northern Traditional Powwow Clothing Style," 7, 21–46.

3. The somewhat awkward and lengthy phrase "Northern Traditional" is used when referring to this powwow clothing style. Generally, this is the name used in Oklahoma; in the Dakotas, it is sometimes called simply the Traditional style or, occasionally, Straight Dance. Northern powwow people refer to the Straight Dance style of Oklahoma as Southern Traditional. The use of "Northern Traditional" is meant to avoid any confusion. Here, Northern Traditional refers to the men's Single-Bustle Dance style, while Straight Dance is used to refer to the Oklahoma Traditional style that uses no bustle.

4. A Marxist distinction between an ideological superstructure created to hide or justify an economic infrastructure should not be read into this definition. Too often ideology is discussed and constructed as the antithesis of a preexisting economic or scientific "truth." It is almost always impossible to determine if infrastructures precede superstructures, and both are discursively interdependent; see Michel Foucault, *Power/Knowledge: Selected Interviews and Other Writings, 1972–1977* (New York: Vintage Books, 1980), 118. Hence, "tradition" should be viewed as the point at which ideology influences economics and vice versa, creating the "truth" of social interactions that are labeled traditional.

5. C. R. Hallpike, "Social Hair," in *Reader in Comparative Religion,* ed. William A. Lessa and Evon Z. Vogt (New York: Harper Collins, 1979), 103.

6. Ibid., 102–4.

7. Michel Foucault, *Discipline and Punish: The Birth of the Prison* (New York: Vintage Books,

1977), 215, 202. For a more extensive discussion of the usefulness and problems of Foucault's writings when applied to Native art, see Fry, "The Northern Traditional Powwow Clothing Style," 15–17, 57, 116n. 9, 118n. 10. Foucault's important contribution here is not so much in a radically new definition of what power is but, rather, the idea that power is not necessarily a possession wielded exclusively by a state or sovereign. The problem with Foucault's view is that he gives the impression of power as such an overwhelmingly pervasive and normalizing force that resistance is implausible.

8. Michel Foucault, *History of Sexuality* (New York: Vintage Books, 1985), 95; Michel-Rolph Trouillot, *Silencing the Past: Power and the Production of History* (Boston: Beacon Press, 1995), 84.

9. Generally, there are four men's and four women's powwow clothing and dance styles:

Men	Women
Northern Traditional	Buckskin
Southern Straight	Cloth Traditional
Grass Dance	Jingle Dress
Fancy Dance	Fancy Shawl

Buckskin and Cloth Traditional dresses are currently the most tribally specific styles. However, the Fancy Shawl style, which was created in the 1950s among the Sioux tribes of South Dakota as a female response to the popularity of the men's Fancy Dance style, has subsequently spread throughout the nation and is currently the most intertribal of the four predominant women's styles. The aesthetic character of this style may have been a response to a certain cultural distortion produced by the relocation policies of the 1950s.

The Jingle Dress originated among the Anishnabe people at Whitefish Bay, Ontario, in the 1920s; by the late 1940s it had all but disappeared, only to be revived in the 1970s. This revival was grounded in a certain politicized concept of traditionalism, so as this dress style spread throughout the nation, specifically Anishnabe cultural proscriptions regarding its use have remained largely unchanged. Even when worn by Comanche or Lakota women, powwow people recognize this dress as an Anishnabe creation, confirming, if not slightly reformulating, the role of tribal specificity in women's powwow clothing.

10. See Terence Hawkes, *Structuralism and Semiotics* (London: Methuen Press, 1977), 26–27.

11. This prescribed structure is, ultimately, created by the very individuals who recognize its restrictions. People can and do reevaluate and change the particular structure of what constitutes a style with some regularity. These may not be drastic changes, but they are changes nonetheless.

12. Charles S. Brant, "Peyotism among the Kiowa-Apache and Neighboring Tribes," *Southwestern Journal of Anthropology* 6, no. 2 (1950): 212–22; James H. Howard, "The Pan-Indian Culture of Oklahoma," *Scientific Monthly* 18, no. 5 (1955): 215–20; Margaret Sanford, "Pan-Indianism, Acculturation, and the American Ideal," *Plains Anthropologist* 16, no. 53 (1971): 222–27; Robert K. Thomas, "Pan-Indianism," *Midcontinent American Studies Journal* 6, no. 2 (1965): 75–83. An early critique of this idea can be found in William K. Powers, "Contemporary Oglala Music and Dance: Pan-Indianism versus Pan-Tetonism," *Ethnomusicology* 12, no. 3 (1968): 352–72; Powers, *War Dance;* and Vine Deloria Jr., *Custer Died for Your Sins: An Indian Manifesto* (New York: Macmillan, 1969), 246.

13. Sanford, "Pan-Indianism, Acculturation, and the American Ideal," 222–23. Sanford simply ignores that the Kiowas, Poncas, and Osages all had functioning Grass Dance societies at the time; certainly they knew how to dance the appropriate dance. Eric Hobsbawm and Terence Ranger, eds., *The Invention of Tradition* (Cambridge: Cambridge University Press, 1986), 8.

14. Sanford, "Pan-Indianism, Acculturation, and the American Ideal," 225–26.

15. Alice C. Fletcher and Francis La Flesche, "The Omaha Tribe," in *Bureau of American Ethnology Twenty-seventh Annual Report, 1905–1906* (Washington, D.C.: Government Printing Of-

fice, 1911), 445–46. This example provides a rebuttal of Hobsbawm and Ranger's fundamental premise that there are invented, unauthentic traditions versus "the old ways." A tradition of bustles was quite consciously invented and has persisted to the present with continually changing meanings. Moreover, this is an example of the interrelation between ideology and tangible, economic reality. Bustles exist at the point where infra- and superstructures intersect.

16. Fletcher and La Flesche, "The Omaha Tribe," 441–42. The name "Crow Belt" should be understood as a product of these Omaha cultural forces; often, the name is misinterpreted as a reference to the Crow tribe. This confusion may be due to the striking similarity between the contemporary bustle style of Crow men and the original Crow Belt bustles; the former is indeed based on the latter and represents an elaboration along a different aesthetic trajectory than that described later for other areas of the Plains. However, many Crow men wear these bustles only at Crow dances, opting for more popular bustle styles at powwows outside southeastern Montana.

17. Fletcher and La Flesche, "The Omaha Tribe," 440–41.

18. This discussion of the Crow Belt, an exclusively male example, as a model of how Native power structures operate is intended to maintain focus on the issue at hand. Many other examples of the same structures could be used: Dog Soldier sashes or women's society emblems, for example. Women's artistic efforts among the Lakota are addressed briefly later and represent different means to the same ends of power and resistance.

19. Quoted in Morris W. Foster, *Being Comanche: A Social History of an American Indian Community* (Tucson: University of Arizona Press, 1991), 141.

20. Kavanaugh, "Southern Plains Dance," 109.

21. C. Scott Evans, *The "Northern Traditional Dancer"* (Denison, Tex.: Crazy Crow Trading Post, 1990), 3; Carolyn Gilman and Mary Jane Schneider, *The Way to Independence: Memories of a Hidatsa Indian Family* (Saint Paul: Minneapolis Historical Society Press, 1987), 159.

22. Louie Ninepipe, "The Grass Dance," in *Gathering of Nations Powwow Program* 9 (1992): 20.

23. Maurice Boyd, *Kiowa Voices,* vol. 1 (Fort Worth: Texas Christian University Press, 1981), 65. The word *Ohoma* is a product of uniquely Kiowa linguistic phenomenon. In the Kiowa language, a nasalized consonant rarely serves as the initial consonant in a word, so the *m* and *h* in "Omaha" were transposed to create a word that is intelligible and compatible with other Kiowa words.

24. James Mooney, "The Ghost Dance Religion and the Sioux Outbreak of 1890," in *Bureau of American Ethnology Fourteenth Annual Report, 1892–1893,* part 2 (Washington, D.C.: Government Printing Office, 1896), 901. Mooney also indicates that since the southern Cheyennes used the Crow Dance as a prelude to the Ghost Dance, their name for the dance may be a reference to one of the sacred birds of Ghost Dance doctrine.

25. Alice Ann Callahan, *The Osage Ceremonial Dance I'n-Lon-Schka* (Norman: University of Oklahoma Press, 1990), 9.

26. This Fort Laramie treaty was the first government document to treat northern bands of the Cheyenne and Arapaho tribes as distinct from the southern bands, who were subsequently recognized as separate political entities by the Medicine Lodge Treaty of 1867. Though the northern and southern groups represent political divisions, each with its own interests and alliances, some cultural interactions continued well after the political distinctions became apparent; see, for example, Kate Bighead, "She Watched Custer's Last Battle," in *The Custer Reader,* ed. Paul A. Hutton (Lincoln: University of Nebraska Press, 1992), 363–77.

By the early twentieth century, bustles had lost their importance in the Ponca and Osage Grass Dance variants. Today, the preferred clothes in the Ponca, Osage, Comanche, and Kiowa dances are Straight Dance clothes. The formation of the Comanche War Dance Society is mentioned only to emphasize the importance of the Ponca Hethushka, which shares its origin with the Omaha Hethushka.

27. Abe Conklin, "Origin of the Powwow: The Ponca He-Thus-Ka Society Dance," in *Native*

Americas Special Edition: Native American Expressive Culture 11, nos. 3 and 4 (1994): 17–21; Evans, *The "Northern Traditional Dancer"*; Huenemann, "Northern Plains Dance"; Kavanaugh, "Southern Plains Dance"; Powers, *War Dance;* Young, "Dance as Communication."

28. The view that the Grass Dance complex is the precursor to modern powwows draws heavily on unilinear evolutionism and Boasian diffusion. Therefore this idea cannot explain any of the supposed changes from Grass Dance to powwow etiquette. For example, women were not allowed in the Grass Dance but are essential to powwows; in the Grass Dance, only certain individuals could wear a feather bustle, whereas any man can wear one in modern powwows. Finally, the idea that Grass Dance societies somehow magically transformed into powwows does not explain the current coexistence of Grass Dance/Hethushka societies and powwows on both the northern and southern Plains.

29. Marsha C. Bol, "Lakota Women's Artistic Strategies in Support of the Social System," in *American Indian Culture and Research Journal* 9, no. 1 (1985):33.

30. Bol, "Lakota Women's Artistic Strategies," 34–37, 49–50. On Lakota children's clothing, see, for example, Barbara A. Hail, *Hau, Kola! The Plains Indian Collection of the Haffenrefer Museum of Anthropology* (Providence: Haffenrefer Museum of Anthropology, Brown University, 1980), 84 fig. 83.

31. For a complete description of the component phases of revitalization movements, see Anthony F. C. Wallace, "Revitalization Movements," in *Reader in Comparative Religion,* 424–27. The most important stage for the purposes of this essay is the phase of routinization, during which new doctrines become the cultural norm and the overt organization of the movement fades from prominence. These stages, especially when applied to the Grass Dance and the Ghost Dance, allow us to see that both these movements have contributed to contemporary powwows.

32. See Mooney, "The Ghost Dance Religion."

33. George P. Horse Capture, *Powwow* (Cody, Wyo.: Buffalo Bill Historical Center, 1989), 10.

34. Among many Plains tribes, men and women had segregated ceremonial societies. The Ghost Dance often represented the first time men and women were sacralized as leaders and participants in the same ceremony. The Grass Dance is no exception, being predominantly male. Therefore, the Ghost Dance's unity of men and women into one ritual structure set a direct and important precedent for contemporary powwows. Ghost Dance participants often wore one eagle tail feather upright at the backs of their heads; this is currently the predominant head decoration among female powwow dancers, showing an even more direct link between the Ghost Dance and powwows. The movement also articulated the idea that dancing for the sake of dancing would ensure the survival of adherents. Looking at contemporary powwows, and following Wallace's model, we can see that this conceptual framework was so successful that the overt organizational structure of the Ghost Dance has been all but forgotten. These ideas served to transform many Native cultures so that they could more easily withstand external pressures and thereby maintain a certain internal integrity.

35. Several good examples of the elaborate Lakota beaded clothes can be found in Hail, *Hau, Kola!,* 97 fig. 100. Though most of the fully beaded clothes (such as dresses, pants, and vests) in Hail's catalog fall within a wide range of dates, from the late 1880s to the 1920s, some dresses with fully beaded yokes were being made by the early 1870s. Lakota Ghost Dance clothes, on the other hand, are curiously rare in publications and museum collections despite their rather well-known association with the events at Wounded Knee in 1890 and the Ghost Dance movement in general.

36. Some examples of Ghost Dance clothes have small amounts of beadwork. The point is that the sheer abundance of beadwork that literally covered people in their own identity was restructured and deemphasized. Currently, indigenized clothes are always inextricably bound to other, non-indigenized clothing, indicating that totally eliminating foreign influences is all but impossible. This concept of integration follows Powers's semiotic analysis of the American flag in Lakota

art; see William K. Powers, "The American Flag in Lakota Art: An Ecology of Signs," *Whispering Wind* 28, no. 2 (1996): 2–15. For an idea, expression, or object to be culturally integrated, it must have a "readable" meaning derived from syntagmatic and associative relationships to the cultural milieu in which it appears. This idea can be problematic insofar as some early acculturationists and relativists used it as justification for the concept of discrete cultures; any change due to cultural interactions was viewed as disintegrative. See Thomas Biolsi, "The Anthropological Construction of 'Indians': Haviland Scudder Mekeel and the Search for the Primitive in Lakota Country," in *Indians and Anthropologists: Vine Deloria Jr. and the Critique of Anthropology,* ed. Thomas Biolsi and Larry J. Zimmerman (Tucson: University of Arizona Press, 1997), 153n. 13; and Edward Sapir, "Culture, Genuine and Spurious," *American Journal of Sociology* 29 (1924): 401–29. Powers's article (as well as his 1968 critique of pan-Indianism) utilizes the idea of a bounded Lakota culture and does not address intertribal interactions and meanings that may be produced by the same integrative processes. Precisely because the issue at hand involves tribal (syntagmatic) and intertribal (associative) relationships, integration must be viewed as a process that organizes cultures internally and their interactions with each other, thereby breaking down the problematic concept of discrete cultural entities.

37. Powers, *War Dance,* 58–59, 71–73. The current Grass Dance powwow clothing style, though probably derived from the clothes of non–bustle wearers in the old Grass Dance, should not be confused with the overt organizational structure of that dance movement. I believe such confusion has legitimated the view that powwows are the descendants of the old Grass Dance complex, which I hope has been shown to be a problematic concept for those reasons cited in n. 27 above, as well as a general view among tribes (especially in Oklahoma) who have Hethushka societies, side by side with powwows, that this ceremony is entirely distinct from the more public dance forms.

38. Both the Kiowa and Ponca tribes claim to be the originators of the Fancy Dance style because of the use of fast war dance songs in their respective Grass Dance societies. This is the subject of some heated debate in Oklahoma, and this chapter is not meant to resolve the conflict; instead, I simply point out that the efforts of many people have contributed to this style and to powwows in general.

39. An accessible account of the early days of the American Indian Movement can be found in Russell Means with Marvin J. Wolf, *Where White Men Fear to Tread* (New York: St. Martin's Press, 1995).

40. Dave Hurley, "Honor the Earth," *Native Peoples* 8 (summer 1995):68.

41. Joe Liles, "Powwow Tales: The Jingle Dress," *News from Indian Country* 10, no. 2 (late January 1996).

42. See Kavanaugh, "Southern Plains Dance," figs. 117, 118, and 124, for good images of contemporary Fancy dancers and their characteristic bustles. However, Kavanaugh states that the man in fig. 117 is a Southern Cheyenne dancer named Dwight White Buffalo. White Buffalo is actually shown in fig. 118 and on the far left in fig. 124.

43. The north-south distinction that is apparent in the powwow world follows certain tenuous geographic boundaries. In this chapter, "north" is used to refer to all Plains areas from Nebraska up to the southern Canadian Plains provinces of Saskatchewan and Alberta, including the Dakotas, Montana, and western Minnesota. "South" refers to Kansas, Oklahoma, north and west Texas, and to a degree, New Mexico and Arizona. Clothing styles, singing styles, and the overt organizational structures of powwows tend to follow this north-south distinction.

44. Tyrone H. Stewart, ed., "Wotantin: Eagle Feather Bust—Oklahoma City," *American Indian Crafts and Culture* 8, no. 6 (1974): 18.

45. Tyrone H. Stewart, "The Great Oklahoma Feather Bust: Some Concerned Opinions," *Indian America* 8, no. 7 (1974): 11, 14.

46. Ibid., 44. Widespread use of DDT by farmers caused the shells of eagle eggs to become very

thin and brittle, costing the lives of countless eaglets. Farm and ranch lobbyists held much more political clout in Washington than did groups advocating Native religious freedom in the 1970s.

47. Ibid.

48. Because of events such as the "Great Oklahoma Feather Bust" and the failure of the government to observe exemptions in wildlife laws for Native religious use, the American Indian Religious Freedom Act was passed in 1978. However, that law was called a "policy [that] has no teeth and has meant nothing to federal agencies"; see Walter Echo-Hawk, "Loopholes in Religious Liberty: The Need for a Federal Law to Protect Freedom of Worship for Native People," *American Indian Religions: An Interdisciplinary Journal* 1 (winter 1994): 8.

49. See Huenemann, "Northern Plains Dance," 129 fig. 143. Currently in Oklahoma there is a growing negative view of these extended bustles. They are often referred to as "satellite dishes," and the dancers are said to have "rear ends shot full of arrows." For the most part this reaction is coming, surprisingly, from younger people.

50. Ibid; Kavanaugh, "Southern Plains Dance," 112.

51. The Comanche Tuuwii (meaning both "black knife" and "crow") Society wore bundles of crow feathers on their left shoulders. Kiowa Tiah Piah society members also used similar shoulder fans attached to their bandoliers. Both these tribes used shoulder bundles of parrot, eagle, hawk, grouse, or other feathers to indicate participation in the peyote religion.

52. See fig. 4.3; the braided scalp lock is threaded up through a small hole in the base of the roach, then through a corresponding hole in the roach spreader (a metal, bone, or rigid leather device that slightly spreads out the porcupine hair; one or two sockets for eagle feathers are attached to the spreader). Next, a thin stick is inserted through the braid as close to the spreader as possible. The weight of the roach and spreader keeps the stick from sliding out, thereby holding the roach on a dancer's head. The use of shoestrings to tie on roaches began in the late 1800s and early 1900s with dancers who had been given short haircuts at boarding schools. The shoestring is looped around the roach stick, passed down through the holes in the spreader and roach, and then tied under the chin.

53. Not all Shields's innovations have been successful. As popular as many of his hats are, Shields is still subject to the very social restrictions he is helping to stretch and reshape, showing the formative role of individuals in creating larger social structures.

CHAPTER 5

JUAN PINO, PUEBLO PRINTMAKER

RUTH LANORE

From late 1925 through 1927 Juan Pino (1896–1950), a Tesuque Pueblo native, created some of the most direct and telling artwork in the Southwest. In a bold and graphic style, Pino broke from the colorful, flattened, and groundless style common to his Native American counterparts. Moving away from a strict adherence to images of ceremonial scenes and dances, Pino depicted Pueblo people actively working and traveling among the village buildings, fields, and mountains. As Pino's work developed technically and stylistically, he turned from "traditional" Indian subject matter and stylistic techniques. He began to explore the subject matter and stylistic elements that were in use by members of the Santa Fe colony of artists. Pino was no mere copyist, however, for although his artwork shows evidence of his investigations, it does not imitate the Euro-American artists' fascination with the New Mexico light or pander to their view of Native peoples as colorful and exotic "props" for images of their ceramic wares or other artistic productions. Instead, Pino's works became complex Pueblo genre scenes with a deep sense of space.

Originally promoted by Charles M. Kassler, the Denver artist who showed Pino how to work in the medium, Pino's prints were soon shown not only at the Museum of Fine Arts but also at the Denver Art Museum's Chappell House. In addition, Pino's friend and patron Jessie G. Hall promoted his work in the Midwest, New York, and abroad. Unfortunately for Pino, Kassler's departure for Europe in 1925 and Jessie Hall's for Paris in 1927, as well as economic and social factors, soon combined to slow his sales and ultimately shortened the period in which he created his strikingly original prints. Without their patronage, and having developed his style far beyond the simple representation of Pueblo dance and ceremonial scenes, Pino's sales slowed dramatically. Ultimately, his portrayal of a broader and more accurate image of Pueblo life than was popular with the Anglo audience almost certainly undid his artistic career. The more his work evolved, the less attention the Anglos who promoted Pueblo artists paid to it. Pino had inadvertently broken an unstated taboo. He had begun to create an art that showed Indians as a part of American culture, often unrecognizable from their Spanish and Anglo neighbors. In addition, he did so in a way in which his own heritage could not be discerned.

By the mid-1920s Santa Fe was actively engaged in creating an image of itself as a land that time forgot. This romantic image, undertaken to lure tourists and wealthy easterners to the region, emphasized the unchanging ceremonials and lifeways of Pueblo cultures. By removing Native American symbols and images of traditional life, as well as stylistic devices such as flattened space, Pino not only ceased creating a marketable "Indian curio" but also unknowingly mocked Santa Fe's attempts to portray the surrounding Native cultures as uncontaminated by contemporary life. As a result, in 1927, after he reached his mature artistic style, the images that were reproduced for the public were of his beginning style: flattened, naive, and undeniably typical of what the Anglo public wanted to see. Compared to the effusive response these early flat and decorative prints received, his more-developed prints drew only a lukewarm reception. This lack of response very likely reflects his rejection of the identifiably Indian look that had initially made his prints so popular. With the exception of a few wood engravings and any undiscovered works, Pino's body of prints was very likely completed by 1927. Despite his lack of economic success, Pino is still one of the most original Native artists of the 1920s.

Juan Pino's Early Artistic Development

In the 1920s Juan Pino was the only Native artist known to work solely in the print medium and the only Native artist in the Southwest to begin creating images in a flat, two-dimensional style, moving toward a convincing illusion of three-dimensionality. He not only developed his technical and artistic skills with rapidity but his work also soon began to evolve in a completely different direction from that of the Pueblo artists who had found a safe and productive market producing images of dances and the occasional genre scene. Although portrayed as a completely untrained artist in early articles, Pino was, instead, a practiced painter of his wife, Lorencita's, pottery, and therefore quite familiar with Tesuque Pueblo's turn-of-the-century style, which included many large, widely spaced geometric floral forms on a white background. His grade-school education included traditional Euro-American artistic training, and his work in Santa Fe further exposed him to this representational style and allowed him easy access to the Fine Art Museum as an artistic resource. In addition, he met many artists through his work, at least three of whom, Gerald Cassidy, Heinz Warneke, and Laura Gilpin, used him as a model.

Pino became well acquainted with Warneke's friend Jessie Hall in 1924. After Kassler's departure, Hall, herself a recognized painter, was to become Pino's primary artistic supporter in Santa Fe, New York, and the Midwest from 1925 to early 1927. Pino met Charles M. Kassler Jr. in the fall of 1924. Pino's first patron, Kassler, a Denver painter staying at John Sloan's residence just off Canyon Road, was himself experimenting with the new medium of linoleum block printmaking.[1] On meeting Pino, Kassler asked him into his studio, briefly instructed him in how to work the material, and gave Pino a square of linoleum and some ink to take home. Several months later, Pino returned with a print and was given more supplies. From that time on Pino completed the blocks with regularity. According to Kassler, each print was better than the last.[2]

From Kassler's glowing report, it is likely that nearly all Pino's early prints were of such quality that they were included in his first exhibition at the Museum of Fine Arts in March 1925. A short review in *El Palacio* lauded the "delightful" work not only for its subject matter of figures and objects from life in the Pueblos but also for its "admirable mastery of line and mass." Kassler was almost certainly responsible for getting Pino's work noticed and hung at the museum, as he was one of only a few people in Santa Fe who would have known about Pino's blossoming talent.[3] Pino's second exhibition followed in May at the Denver Art Museum's Chappell House. The works in this exhibit received high praise in Denver's *Rocky Mountain News* and *El Palacio*. Pino's facility in depicting animals was of special note, but what the author most admired were the ceremonial designs. Here, Kassler was clearly responsible for backing Pino's exhibit. In a review of the exhibit, the author wrote, "Mr. Kassler is, perhaps, more delighted with his Indian protégé than with the progress of his own art while in the Southwest. He believes that he has discovered a genius, and the artists of Santa Fe who have seen his [Pino's] work are inclined to side with him in this view."[4]

It is not surprising that Pino's early prints, all of which are untitled, were so popular. They primarily depict Pueblo ceremonial life, an area with which the Euro-American artists in New Mexico were completely fascinated and upon which Kassler almost exclusively focused his artwork of this period.[5] Judging by their flattened style and lack of anatomical accuracy, five images of Pueblo dances—the Snake Dance, Buffalo Dance, Deer Dance, Basket Dance, and an image of three dancers with rattles—are among Pino's earliest prints. Other early images are of an Indian man on horseback and another hunting deer. While only Pino's print of a man on horseback

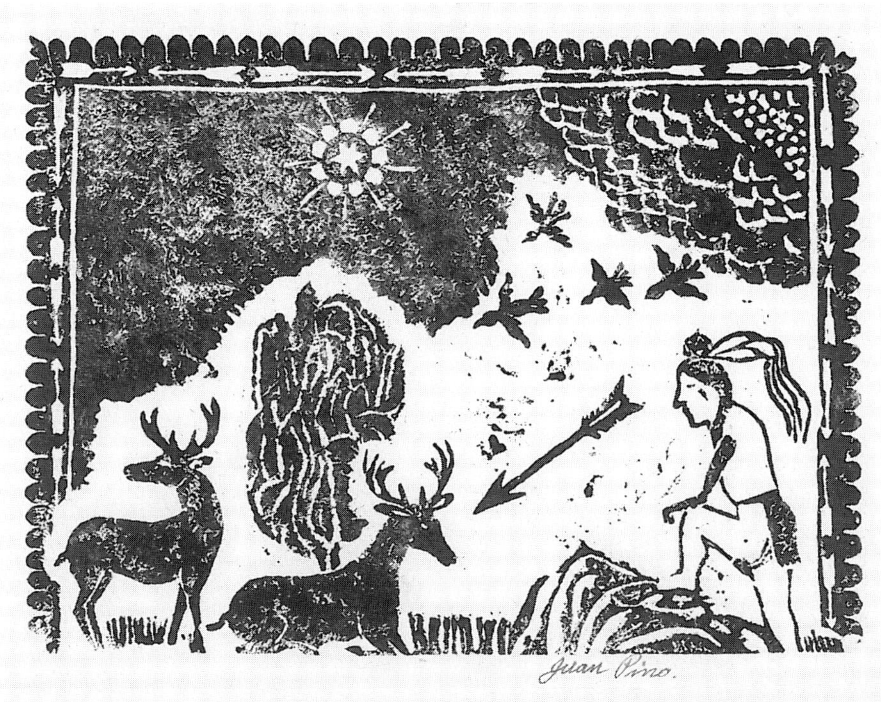

FIGURE 5.1
Juan Pino, Tesuque Pueblo. Untitled *[Man and Two Deer]*, n.d., linoleum block print, 7 in. x 9½ in. Courtesy Museum of Indian Art and Culture– Laboratory of Anthropology, Santa Fe, N.M., cat. no. 55238/13.

can reliably be dated before May 1925, all the prints had been likely completed by that time. Pino's Chappell House exhibit was reviewed on May 3 of that year in Denver's *Rocky Mountain News.* The reviewer included the man on horseback image in his story and mentioned that Pino had completed several prints of ceremonial scenes.[6]

In addition to a strong emphasis on ceremonial subject matter, Pino's early prints share several identifying stylistic traits. As seen in *Man and Two Deer* (fig. 5.1), he rendered animals with a sure and accurate hand yet had a great deal of difficulty with the proportions of human figures; this difficulty gives his early prints a naive quality. Although he could outline figures or portions thereof, in most cases he limited linear elements to the description of details and decorative elements such as borders. These borders bear a strong resemblance to those regularly seen in the prints of the well-known Santa Fe woodblock printmaker Gustave Baumann, which Charles Kassler may have used as well.

Pino's beginning prints share several additional identifying features. Human subjects are depicted with thin, muscle-less arms, extremely small hands, almost equally shapeless legs, and tiny feet that are always seen in profile. Also apparent in these early prints is the flat, unrelieved ground, broken only for the insertion of the image or decorative elements. Rather than outlining the figures against the flat background or carving them into it, Pino carved the linoleum away from the parts of the image he wished to remain dark when inked, such as hair, creating a white "background" around them. For light-colored areas, such as faces, he left the black "background" intact, making his early work appear as though the figures, or parts of them, exist within white "bubbles," while the background prints black. These bubbles, or balloons, in combination with the unmodulated linoleum block surface, further flatten the image and focus greater attention on the print surface. Being relatively unfamiliar with Western expectations of the finished image, Pino likely found it unnecessary to remove more of the linoleum than was absolutely essential for accurate depiction. In these prints, Pino created a narrow space within which the figures move by using the bottom of the image as the horizon line or occasionally carving in landscape details. Indeed, although the bubbles or white areas flatten the images, his figures still retain a strong sense of motion, leaning forward from the waist, with arms and legs bent in dance, and toes pointed. At times, the anatomical inaccuracies create a more convincing sense of motion.

Several of Pino's earliest prints contain decorative linear framing elements. Pino's image of a man and two deer includes geometric motifs linked to the Euro-American conception of Native Americans (fig. 5.1). This print is surrounded by a border of arrows and a geometric sun symbol, whereas in others Pino used stylized feathers and interlocking half-circles that alternately represent cloud forms or are used as decoration. It is likely that Kassler, incorporating Pueblo motifs and subject matter in his own art, encouraged Pino to use the symbolic decorative devices to make the prints appear more Indian.[7]

Varied Influences: Tesuque, Kassler, Rush, and Pueblo Painting

There are striking similarities between the decorative geometric devices Pino used in his prints and the old-style Tesuque black-on-white ceramics that were common in the 1800s. Pino's wife, Lorencita, was primarily known as the last Tesuque artist to make the old-style pottery, and during his lifetime, Juan painted her wares.[8]

In 1930 Kenneth Chapman collected a black-on-cream pot from Lorencito *[sic]*

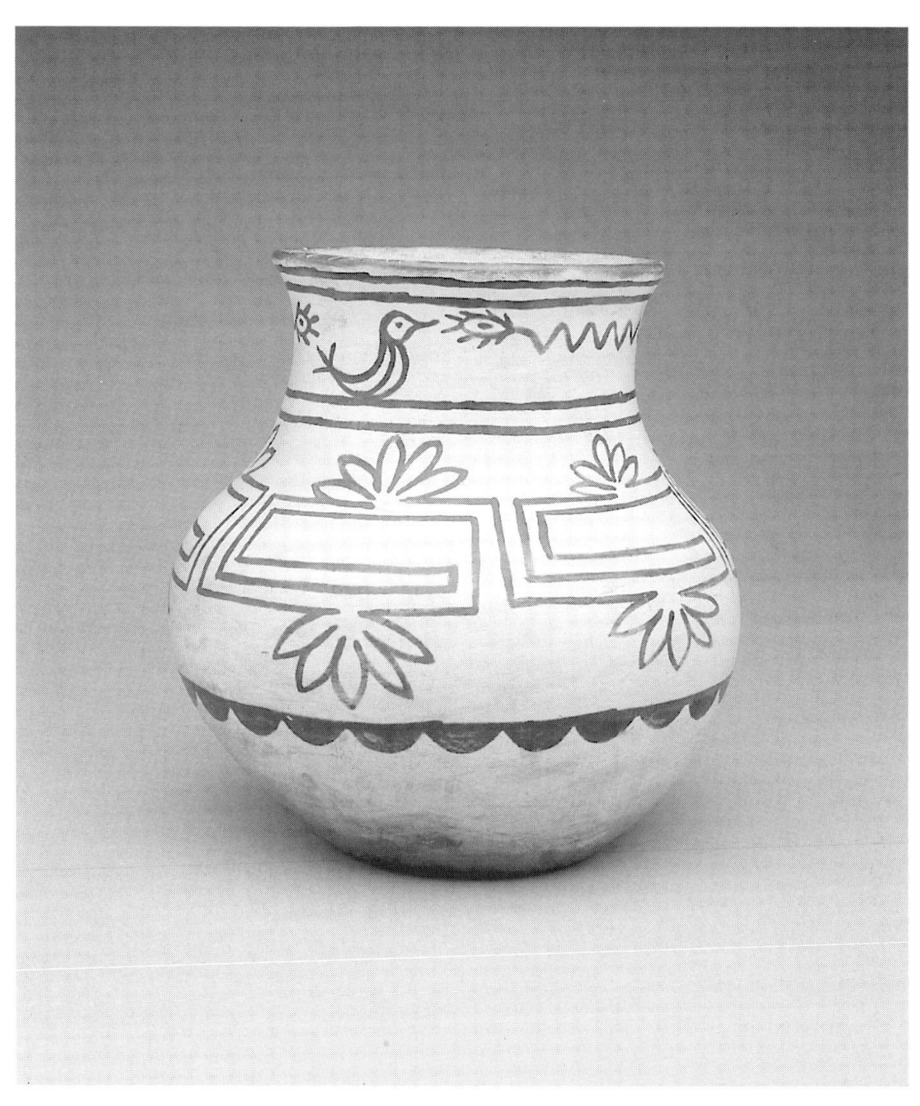

FIGURE 5.2
Lorencito *[sic]* Pino, Tesuque Pueblo. Jar, ca. 1930, height, 8 in. Courtesy School of American Research Collections in the Museum of New Mexico, cat. no. 7836/12.

Pino. The pot, almost certainly completed by Juan, shows a number of distinctive Tesuque design elements, such as flowered meanders, wavy lines, scallops, and a little bird painted within the neck band (fig. 5.2).[9] Such motifs, drawn from revival-style pottery and other examples of Tesuque Polychrome, are obvious in Pino's early prints, as are more generalized stylizations such as gently curving, outlined, and densely filled dark-on-light forms. Tesuque pottery designs maintain a clear figure/ground distinction through the use of outlining and also allow a large white space around the different motifs. This space physically isolates the designs from one another even while the forms visually interrelate. Likewise, Pino's early prints maintain separation between the figures, never letting them overlap one another and, in many cases, not even letting them overlap the ground on which they stand. However, rather than presenting the figures as complete forms that must remain separate from the background as in pottery painting, Pino's prints create a figure/ground division based on the black-and-white values of the figures, whereby light areas of the forms are surrounded by dark areas and vice versa. Pino also provided rhythmic passages by repeating figures in similar poses or surrounding them with decorative designs that make use of the surrounding negative space. Overall, however, Pino's prints emphasize the motions of the figures more than their formal interactions.

Although an outgrowth of Tesuque pottery painting traditions, Pino's early style was likely encouraged and influenced by his first printmaking instructor, Charles Moffat Kassler, Jr., who was already exploring linoleum block printing. Kassler's experiments soon prompted two shows at the Museum of Fine Arts. The first, in March 1925, coincided with Pino's exhibit and included a number of symbolic works, completed in a rhythmic, modernistic style. His second exhibit, in late May or early June, included forty linoleum block prints and a series of paintings, almost all of which depicted phases of Pueblo Indian life.[10] Of Kassler's remaining artworks, the one most closely connected with Pino's work is a handmade linoleum block Christmas card Kassler sent to Olive Rush in 1929 (fig. 5.3). This simple image shares several commonalties with Pino's early work. The central image of a bull is flattened yet active. The bull is viewed directly, from eye level, and stands on a single ground line with no hint of depth. The overall image is bold and graphic, emphasizing large areas of black and white, and it is finished with a decorative top border of zigzags that are highly suggestive of Native American designs. Finally, Kassler's quick strokes of the carving gouge enliven and relieve the black area around the bull and have the same quality as Pino's white bubbles. While one image does not provide much evidence, the correlations between this and Pino's early works strongly suggest that Kassler may have exerted more influence on Pino than his statements attest. By itself, Kassler's Christmas card cannot be considered a fair indicator of his Santa Fe work, being four

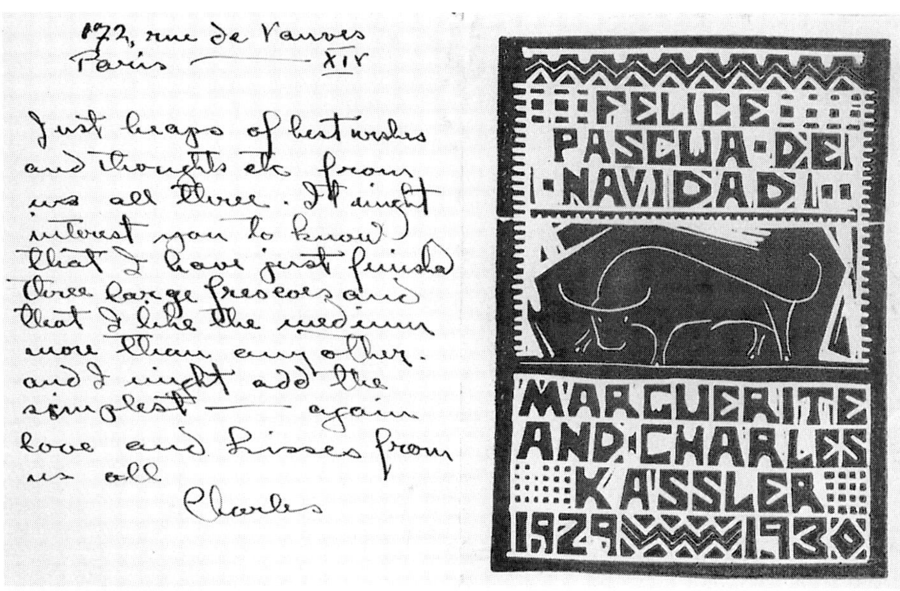

FIGURE 5.3

"Happy New Year" Card, 1929–1930, to Olive Rush from Marguerite and Charles Kassler. Olive Rush Papers 1886–1966, Archives of American Art, Smithsonian Institution.

or five years removed from the work that he and Pino knew. However, this image bears many similarities to the one (or more) that Kassler quickly carved to demonstrate the medium to Pino.[11]

Kassler, who had no known bias about what constituted proper style or subject matter for an Indian artist, likely encouraged Pino's later genre work and its illusionistic development. Certainly he did not appear to censor Pino's early work, which must have been developing in an illusionistic manner before Kassler's departure from Santa Fe in June 1925. After this date, there is no evidence of any contact between Kassler and Pino.[12] While Kassler appears not to have stifled Pino's move toward realistic and illusionistic artwork, Olive Rush, a close friend of the Kasslers, stood strongly against Native American artists "ruining" their art through European mannerisms. Pino's early work was in a suitably traditional idiom, of which she would have approved. Rush's efforts to promote Indian artists were well known in the region. Since her visit in 1914, she had traveled around the Pueblos, decrying illusionistic tendencies and encouraging Indian artists to retain an unspoiled, Native style.[13] Her feelings on the subject were so strong that in 1932 or 1933, while supervising Velino Shije Herrera's preliminary work for the Santa Fe Indian School murals, she wrote in her diary: "When any of the paintings begin to take on a Pale-face look something around my heart seems to collapse and often I turn and walk out of the chapel without a sound. But today, when I saw, or possibly imagined that Velino's buffalo hunt was getting the look, I cautioned—paint Indian, Velino. Don't paint our way."[14]

Rush's somewhat generalized subject matter focused on formal concerns, using the high contrast of the wood block medium to impart a sense of light and atmosphere or to focus on dramatic contrasts between broad masses of dark and light. She used these formal means to create motionless images that elicit an emotional response, producing impressions of solitude or a sense of the spiritual. Pino's early works, on the other hand, demonstrate the importance of accurately portraying the ceremonial life and apparel of Native people. In making these images, he clearly recognized and focused on the kinetic aspects of Pueblo activities.[15]

Pino's early emphasis on ceremonial dance subjects, sharing stylistic similarities with Rush's work, may have been in response to her or Kassler's interests and suggestions, or the expectations of his Anglo buyers. Ironically, Rush's artwork, which depicted women as full participants in daily life, may have provided an unintended stimulus for Pino's further exploration of his artistic options. However, it is highly unlikely that she knowingly encouraged his development from that point. She felt no compunction about borrowing from indigenous styles but would never have induced a Native artist to choose non-Indian subject matter or work in more representational Western idioms. The direction in which Pino was shortly to take his own art makes it clear that Rush's opinions had little power over him. They did not dissuade him from using her work as a source of inspiration any more than they stopped him from drawing on the other Santa Fe artistic styles. Pino's early work certainly conforms to the Anglo expectations of Native American art that Rush shared. It is flat, decorative, and descriptive of Pueblo life and ceremonial subjects. These expectations were undoubtedly shared by Pino's enthusiastic Denver audience, as Kassler was busy taking orders for Pino's prints before the first Denver exhibition.[16]

The works of the four most prominent Pueblo painters of the time—Awa Tsireh, Fred Kabotie, Otis Polelonema, and Velino Shije Herrera—almost exclusively focused on ceremonial dances and occasional Pueblo genre scenes. By 1925 these four artists were well known in Santa Fe. By 1925 Awa Tsireh, who rarely included shadowing in his paintings, was developing an increasingly decorative and flattened style. Kabotie's and Polelonema's works were the most illusionistic of the group, but even they generally removed background elements. Instead, in order to portray depth, these artists paid careful attention to vanishing point perspective, the placement of figures within the composition and their relationship to one another, as well as shadowing and atmospheric perspective. Starting in 1920 the School of American Research provided the four favored artists with jobs, studio space, materials, and time to refine and explore their images. On the other hand, Pino almost certainly created at home, with few materials, and limited time between his wood delivery and construction jobs and his Pueblo duties. While he had been attempting to create and sell art at least since 1919, time constraints and lack of formal training put him at a disadvantage when compared to the sponsored artists.[17]

Initially Pino's prints bore a strong resemblance to those of the other Pueblo artists, but whether Pino was influenced by them directly, was asked to imitate them by his patrons, or developed his style independent of them is unknown. What is clear is that in late 1924 and early 1925, his art fit the expectations and preconceptions of the Santa Fe Anglos who were purchasing and promoting Native art.

Pino's Later Style

Pino's work developed and was produced with such rapidity that in August 1925 eighteen of his prints were shown at the Santa Fe Fiesta's Southwest Indian Fair. This exhibition revealed the incredible development the artist had made in his work. In the few months since his initial exhibits, Pino had made great strides in developing the human figure, overlapping objects in space, and, most obviously, resolving the figure/ground problem that had previously forced him to surround his figures with bubbles.[18] Although an exact account of the development of his works is not possible, a vague chronology can be suggested by looking at the progress Pino was making in correcting anatomical inaccuracies. Apparently, in some of these transitional images, while he experimented with the use of light and shadow, perspective, and the figure's position within the composition, he temporarily returned to the use of familiar but less illusionistically convincing devices. It also appears that Pino nearly abandoned the use of ceremonial subject matter during this period.

When a review of the fiesta appeared in July 1926, Pino, the only Native artist working on paper to be mentioned, was praised for deviating from the typical images of ceremonial dancers so many others had depicted. "It was gratifying to see some other subjects attempted," the reviewer wrote, noting, "in black and white, Juan Pino has done some excellent things, such as horsemen mounting a steep hill." Pino's prints were also mentioned as being among the best-selling items at the fair, commanding good prices from collectors and dealers alike.[19]

Some of Pino's early transitional images make changes while retaining the simple, flattened style of the earlier period. These works, however, put far less emphasis on details of costuming or the manner in which fabric drapes, allowing the contrast of

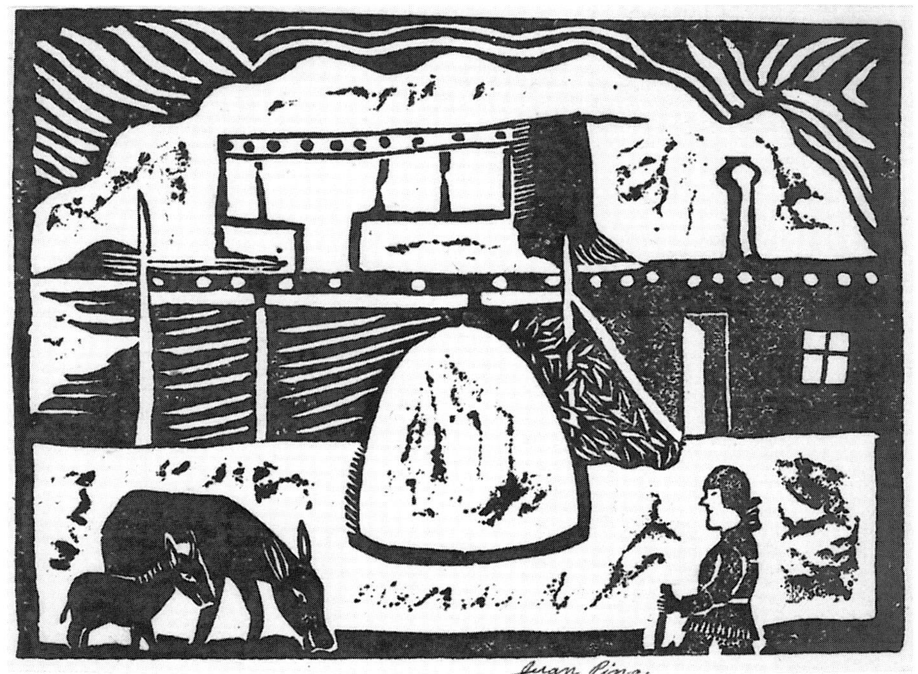

FIGURE 5.4
Juan Pino, Tesuque Pueblo. Untitled *[Pueblo Scene with Two Burros and Walking Man]*, n.d., linoleum block print, 6¾ in. x 9 in. School of American Research, cat. no. IAF.P156.

uninterrupted dark and light areas to create a more dramatic image. From this point, all Pino's figures have well-formed bodies, overlap the tools with which they work, and move in a space unhampered by the dark backgrounds that characterized earlier prints. During his transitional period Pino focused primarily on nonceremonial genre scenes in which women participate on an equally important and active level as their male counterparts. Pino also explored a variety of viewpoints, from below eye level to high above, as though he were floating almost directly overhead. In contrast, his Pueblo contemporaries painted their images as if they were seen from a rooftop some distance away. This eye-level viewpoint makes Pino's compositions immediately and strikingly different from those of the Pueblo painters. An example of this difference is Pino's *Pueblo Scene with Two Burros and Walking Man* (fig. 5.4). One of the images included in the 1925 Indian Fair, it shows just how far Pino's work had progressed technically and stylistically. It is also an example of the somewhat larger format and much more active and narrative images Pino began to create around this time.

In later works he focused on scenes of everyday Pueblo life, as seen in *Harvesting Grain* (frontispiece), preferring to depict individuals working or traveling in an outdoor setting. Rather than close-up views of undifferentiated individuals, Pino pulled back and began to show a much wider panorama in these images. He maintained his central position and, like many Anglo painters in Santa Fe, pictured each of his scenes from eye level, generally looking across an open space and then up to the mountains or buildings. From this point, Pino's figures always carry out their activities within a landscape that rises behind them or within a village where buildings are depicted with an intuitive understanding of perspective. Pino's figures were now included within a specific environment, with recognizable houses and landscape elements.

Pino also began to experiment with the representation of reflected light, although, like his intuitive understanding of perspective, it was never clear from which direction the light originated. Pino's mature images, however, use line and shape to represent light and shadow and more clearly define the folds, weight, and volume of clothing, as well as create a sense of light and energy within the environment. Repeated lines more convincingly express the patterns of clouds, rays, and warmth of the sun and the textures of trees, grass, and walls. While he did not produce images of complete three-dimensional illusionism, he was able to create a convincing sense of space and atmosphere.

Pino's most-developed images are wood engravings that make further narrative, technical, and stylistic advancements. These complex prints completely avoid the previous problems in depicting anatomy and perspective. One of the engravings depicts a man in overalls walking toward the left side of a fenced yard (fig. 5.5). Behind him are two adobe houses, a *horno,* or beehive oven, and several tall trees. By eliminating the typical Pueblo attire of baggy, belted white shirt and loose pants from the figure, Pino removed the final signifiers of "Indian-ness" from the image. While clearly a continuation of his mature style, this print could have been done by anyone, of any culture, who had experience with wood engraving and good observational skills. Through this documentary image, Pino notes the changes taking place in the Pueblo, and makes evident his interest in depicting the actuality of the Pueblo and its people rather than stereotypes. While Pino's *Pueblo Scene with Man in Overalls* may well fit into the output of the Anglo artists in the region, it was an unusual and unexpected image from a Native artist, exploding the image of the Indian locked within an unchanging, if mythic, world. In addition to recording the changes occurring within the Pueblo, Pino also used this print to freely explore a more striking use of pattern, texture, and the effects of reflected light and cast shadow. Ranging from

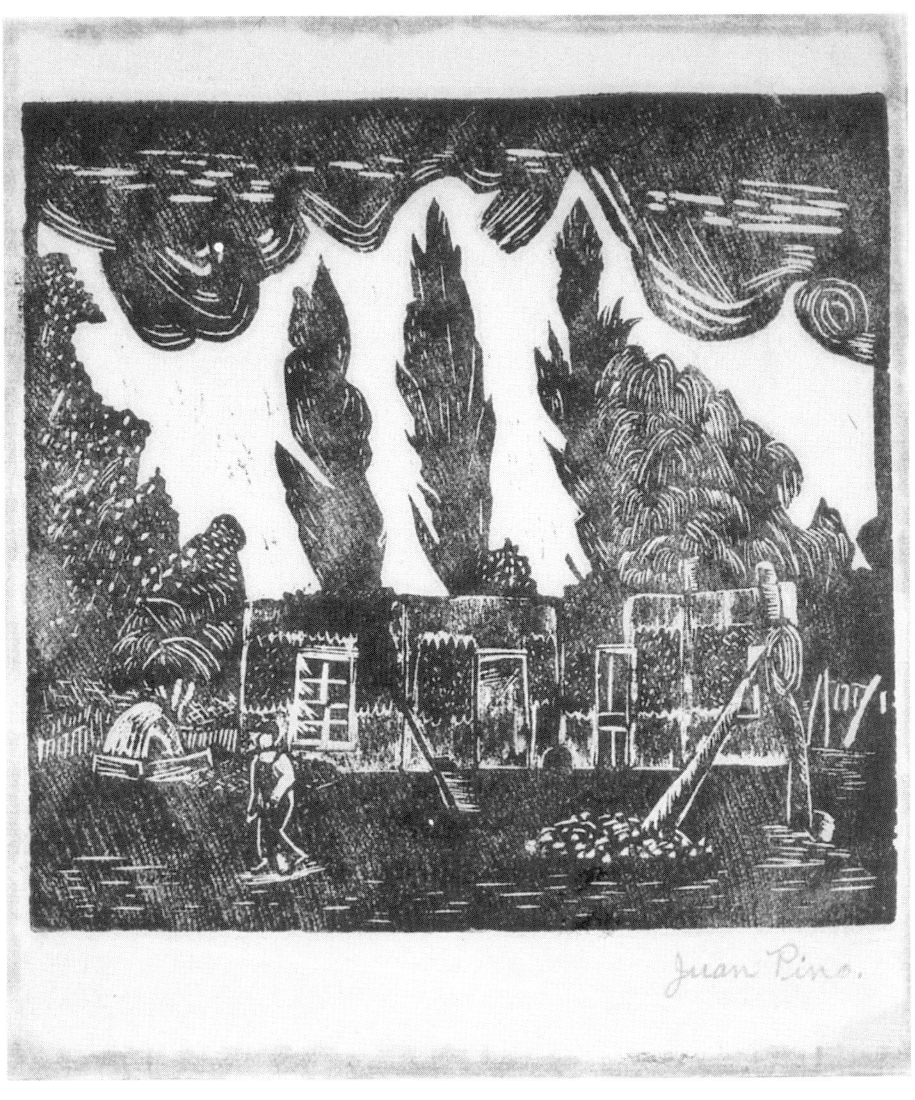

Figure 5.5
Juan Pino, Tesuque Pueblo. Untitled *[Pueblo Scene
with Man in Overalls],* n.d., wood engraving, 5½ in.
x 5¾ in. Denver Art Museum collection, gift of
Mrs. Ben Charrington, cat. no. 1953.439.

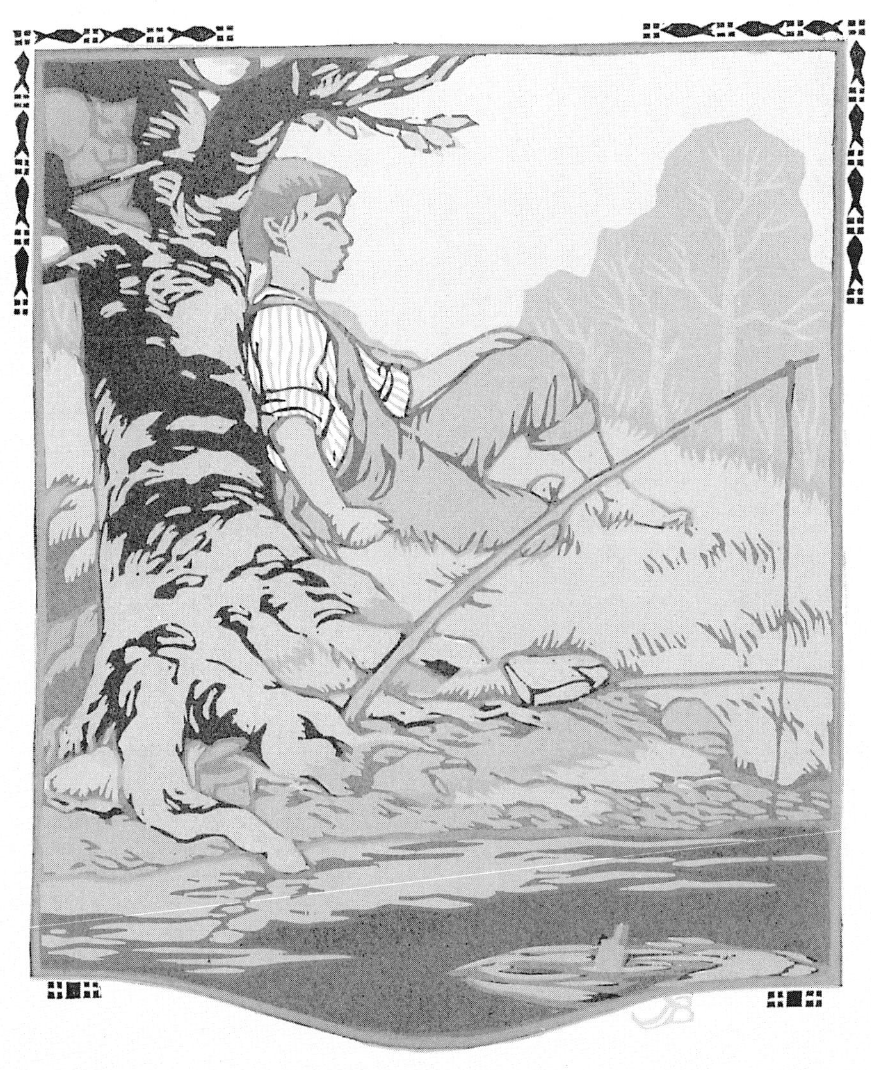

FIGURE 5.6
Gustave Baumann. *July,* 1912, color woodcut, 8 in. x
6½ in. Collection of Robert Bell, M.D. Illustration
for *All the Year Round,* n.p.

wide to narrow, Pino's lines now create tone as well as shadow. Moreover, the negative space created by the contrast of stark white space between dark trees and rolling clouds further enlivens the image. Pino had become not merely an excellent Indian artist but a fine artist in his own right, producing works that ultimately show a sophistication and growth rarely matched in such a short period of time. His final works demonstrate a technical and artistic refinement that was a genuine, unstudied product of his own imagination.

The relative speed with which Pino experimented with new graphic depictions may, in part, be explained by the number of printmakers and painters active in Santa Fe from the 1910s through the 1930s. Birger Sandzen was one of the first artists in New Mexico to use a variety of print media unapologetically, including lithography, woodcuts, and linoleum cuts. He had his first exhibition at the Museum of Fine Arts in 1919, within months of his arrival in Santa Fe. His prints use the busy, choppy strokes of van Gogh and the swirling lines of Munch to create a buzzing, glowing life in his depictions of trees, landscapes, and portraits. While Pino's village scenes were not as highly organized or patterned as Sandzen's, there are clear connections between his work and Pino's active, swirling, and repetitive use of line in fabric, trees, clouds, and fields of grain, as seen in *Harvesting Grain* (frontispiece).[20]

It is the work of the well-recognized Santa Fe artist Gustave Baumann, however, that Pino's compositions, and his use of line and point, most resemble. This is not surprising, as Baumann's work was regularly shown at the museum and was enthusiastically purchased by the public. Like many of the borders used by Baumann in his woodcuts of the 1910s, three of Pino's early prints include decorative top and side borders. In particular, the border of repeated arrows in *Man and Two Deer* (fig. 5.1) bears a strong resemblance to the small repeated symbolic, geometric, and natural elements with which Baumann framed the original prints used in 1912 to illustrate James Whitcomb Riley's poetry in *All the Year Round* (fig. 5.6). These prints, like Pino's transitional and mature works, are carved in a simple, graphic manner with wide unmodulated surfaces, thick linear elements, and strong outlines.

Several of Pino's transitional and mature pieces include decorative swirling clouds and landscape elements that clearly resemble the use of line in Baumann's 1917 *Excavated Area of the Aztec Ruin* (fig. 5.7).[21] This monochromatic print contrasts striking black mountains against boldly patterned clouds within a choppy, impressionistic landscape. Both artists left large areas of flat white or light-colored backgrounds against which buildings and trees are silhouetted, and the textural trees and grasses depicted in Pino's mid to late works bear strong similarities to Baumann's busily carved foliage of masses of repeated dots and lines as well.

By the mid-1920s Baumann's prints were full of color and were less linear. These

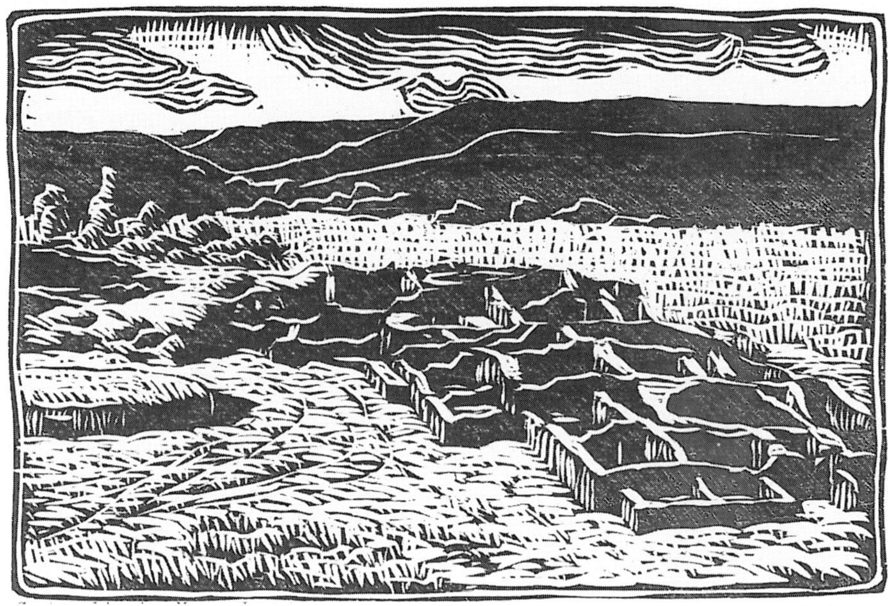

images most strongly suggest the connection between Pino and Baumann. In terms of subject matter, Baumann's prints regularly include picturesque southwestern images of grazing burros, Pueblo ceremonials, and people visiting before their adobe homes. In early 1925, just as Pino was learning his medium, several of Baumann's picturesque images were shown at the Museum of Fine Arts.[22] In his landscapes, Baumann used a typical compositional device. The horizon line is high in the image and the viewer appears to be observing the scene from a centered, eye-level foreground, across a lower midground, and up toward the background mountains or buildings. Pino adopted this compositional form during his transitional period and applied it to nearly all his subsequent images.

Pino's prints also share a simple and naive quality with Baumann's, largely due to a simplification of figures, buildings, and other objects. Baumann, an accomplished draftsman, was deliberately making his images plain and removing any traces of individuality from his figures. In Pino's case, this naïveté is more likely a natural outcome of self-training and the lack of practice necessary to accurately render human anatomy and perspective. In addition, the many examples of stylized and modern art seen in Santa Fe would not have convinced him that anatomical accuracy or linear perspective was essential to the creation of good artwork. Pino was adapting his techniques to fit what he was seeing in the work of Euro-American artists. However, his techniques were not tailored to the expectations of those accustomed to traditional academic standards nor were they deliberately modernist. They did not depict the most sensuous aspects of Pueblo life nor did they abstract mountains and other landscape elements into sharp, geometric forms. Instead Pino was simply picturing what he found of interest, images of daily life he knew intimately and that other Santa Fe artists valued and depicted.

Printmakers were not the only individuals to influence Pino's work. The easel paintings of the frequently exhibited Santa Fe artist John Sloan may also have affected Pino's mature work. Sloan depicted chunky, moderately simplified figures within choppy and slightly stylized landscapes or cityscapes with thickly applied paint. Like Pino's mature work, Sloan's figures and landscape elements are harshly lit with highly contrasting areas of light and shadow. Overall, however, Sloan, who later became president of the Exposition of Indian Tribal Arts, may have left his strongest impression on Pino through his philosophy rather than his artwork.[23] Sloan was among many artists who were strongly affected by the modernism of the 1913 Armory Show. Many, such as Alfred Steiglitz and his circle, championed modern art, often to the exclusion of recognizable subject matter. Sloan, on the other hand, was strongly opposed to this position and felt that art should remain available to, and understandable by, everyday people. A fiercely independent individual, Sloan made several pointed statements deploring majority influence over artistic matters. He said repeatedly: "It may be taken as an axiom that the majority is always wrong in cultural matters. . . . Voting on matters of taste always results in selection of the mediocre or commonplace. . . . Politically I believe in democracy, but culturally not at all. . . . Whenever a cultural matter rolls up a majority I know it is wrong."[24]

Rather than mandate appropriate subject matter for Native artists, Sloan reserved his censure for those works that struck him as, in the words of J. J. Brody, "insincere stereotypes pandering to non-Native aesthetic criteria." For this reason he harshly criticized the Oklahoma painters known as the Kiowa Five for creating "a cheap vaudeville treatment encouraged by tourists."[25] Yet unlike the majority of Santa Fe Indian art patrons, he championed the Native artist's right to individuality. Clearly, Sloan felt that the mold into which Native artists were being pushed was deleterious to their art, just as it would have been to any other artist. While Sloan's values were often inconsistent with his pigeonholing of Native American art, it is likely that he would have supported Pino's exploration while it retained its somewhat naive appearance. Pino's much more polished and aesthetically developed wood engravings, however, very likely went beyond what Sloan considered acceptable Indian output.

The swift development of Pino's work from his transitional phase forward makes it clear that his desire was to search out new stylistic, technical, and artistic challenges—refusing the limitations of stereotypical images and styles. Instead, among his most obvious sources were the artwork of several Santa Fe artists whose images were commonly used to decorate Santa Fe homes, public facilities, and the Fine Arts Museum walls. Pino's ability to draw ideas from these very popular sources without plagiarizing them makes his work stand out from that of Native and non-Native artists alike.

After his fiesta exhibit, Pino's works were shown at the Saint Louis Public Library's Art Room in October 1925. A brief article in the *American Magazine of Art* stated that his exhibit had attracted considerable attention and was "of real merit." This exhibit was almost certainly arranged by Pino's patron Jessie Hall, as her permanent residence was not far from Saint Louis. Jessie's personal and professional assistance to Pino is made clear through correspondence from Pino. In a letter dated March 31, 1926, Pino asked Jessie what had happened to a group of prints her husband had taken to New York. He also asked Jessie to sell the prints she had taken to Saint Louis and take any that remained with her to Europe. He certainly trusted her, since he asked her to keep the money from these sales until her return. Additionally, he inquired whether she had received two prints he had recently completed and mailed. The two new prints Pino referred to were probably included in an exhibition of newer and more finished works that was shown at the Santa Fe Museum of Fine Arts in April 1926.[26]

While it appears that Pino believed Mr. Hall was the person taking his prints to New York, Jessie's son Edward T. Hall believed that, in late 1925 or early 1926, it was Jessie who took a group of prints to the Weyhe Gallery in New York. The Weyhe Gallery specialized in prints and carried the wood blocks of Howard Cook, Barbara Latham, Arnold Rönnebeck, and Gustave Baumann, all of whom either lived, or spent time, in Santa Fe during the 1924–27 period.[27] Jessie was a close friend of Carl Zigrosser, the Weyhe Gallery's director, and it was she who interested him in carrying Pino's work. Zigrosser's interest was so strong that the gallery gave Pino a one-person show in 1925 or 1926.[28]

Pino wrote again to Jessie Hall in September 1926 indicating that he had not done any printing during his intervening trip to Colorado. He and Lorencita had taken their artwork to sell, but while all Lorencita's pottery sold, he only sold some of his prints. Two more letters followed in early and mid-December 1926. However Pino made no mention of his prints or printmaking in either letter; the death of the Pino's first child and other worries took precedence.[29] The lack of artistic comment in these letters suggests that Pino may have ceased making new works. *El Palacio,* which had closely followed his career, made no mention of any new prints in his two subsequent exhibitions. Perhaps Jessie Hall had set in motion an interest in Pino's work that might have continued had she not left for Paris in early 1927, not to return for four or five years.[30]

The selection of one of Pino's early prints, *Four Bow Dancers,* for the cover of the March 1927 periodical *Arts* was almost certainly a result of Jessie's earlier efforts in New York on his behalf, as was Pino's second exhibit at the Denver Art Museum in June 1927.[31] This show did not receive the same media attention as had the 1925 exhibit, yet reviews of the exhibit were generally positive, stating that Pino's work was "typically Indian in feeling" and "worth study." Apparently this show was arranged through Arnold Rönnebeck, the new director at the Denver Art Museum, who likely saw Pino's work at the Weyhe Gallery where he also showed. While there are no references in *El Palacio* to further exhibitions by Pino, there are suggestions that he may have continued to print after June 1927. In 1929 *El Palacio* included an article entitled "Picturesque Games and Ceremonial[s] of Indians," which noted that a ceremonial concluded "disclosing such artists as the Natives Awa-Tsireh, Fred Kabotie and Juan Pino." At least for that author, Pino was still an artist worth mentioning and one whose work he considered on a par with that of Awa Tsireh and Kabotie.[32]

Pino's final exhibit most likely took place in December 1931. The first exhibition of *The Exposition of Indian Tribal Arts,* held at the Grand Central Art Galleries in New York, included two of Pino's linoleum block prints. However, as no photographic record of the prints survives, there is no way of knowing what they were. Unfortunately, Pino's prints were cut from the well-publicized two-year traveling exhibit that followed. The catalog for the traveling exhibit makes no mention of Pino nor is any explanation available to clarify why Pino's works were excluded. Since only a few of the more than six hundred works in the initial exhibit were cut, the exclusion of Pino's works makes a larger statement.[33]

The image of Indian art as a *traditional* art form was quite important to the organizers of the exposition. They had defined the purpose of the exposition as being "to gain recognition and a wide discriminating market for the Indian artists, and thus encourage them to continue their own Native arts *within the best of their traditions*" (emphasis added).[34] If this "tradition," approximately fourteen years old in 1931, had been allowed to develop on its own, it seems likely that the choice of media, subject matter, and style used by Native artists would have broadened as individuals expressed their personal preferences. Yet the groundless style and symbolic, ceremonial subject matter with decorative motifs popularized by Awa Tsireh, Kabotie, Polelonema, and Herrera had become encoded and crystallized. Maintained through selective Anglo patronage and assistance, this style was followed by all but a few of the Pueblo artists.[35] Admittedly a function of the marketplace, this Indian art style had turned into a set of unstated rules about what constituted the proper form for Indian artists to create. At times, this assistance was subtle, the style encouraged through suggestions or purchase, but at other times it was enforced. As early as 1921 Edgar Lee Hewett, director of the Museum of New Mexico, had created a policy (that could be enacted at will) of denying museum access to Native artists working in oils or "the white man's manner." Curiously, this censorship was broadly supported by the same art and museum communities that also supported the Fine Art Museum's open-door policy for Anglo artists.[36]

The decision to cut Pino's prints from *The Exposition of Indian Tribal Arts* was probably made because the style and subject matter did not fit the Anglo image of Native American art. Certainly the realistic, workaday aspects of Pino's prints were dramatically different from the ceremonial, dancing, and hunting scenes produced by the majority of Southwest Indian painters. These "traditional" images were what the public had come to know as Indian art and what major collectors, such as William and Leslie Van Ness Denman, had begun collecting as early as 1919. The Denmans, like the organizers of the exposition, preferred ceremonial images and those that spoke of Indian spirituality.[37] As such, Pino's later prints would likely have been of little interest if not of immediately identifiable Indian subjects. His early prints, on the other hand, while of the correct subject matter, were much less anatomically and stylistically refined, and might not have fared well when judged against the work of the other exhibitors. Ultimately, the Anglo fascination with Native American spirituality, combined with the desire of Santa Fe Indian art patrons to keep the work an uncontaminated, original American art form, almost certainly played a major part in Pino's inability to find new patronage.

After the departure of Kassler and then Hall, Pino discovered that his work did not sell as well as his wife's pottery. And although the Weyhe Gallery was an excellent and prestigious outlet, the art of Native Americans was just beginning to be appreciated in New York. Even if Pino's prints sold well, it is doubtful these sales could have provided his whole income. As a result, no matter how much he enjoyed the process, Pino probably could not afford the time and energy to create an item that would not sell well.

To all appearances, Pino dramatically slowed his production of linoleum block prints somewhere in early 1927, although the wood engravings are likely of a later date. After this period, it seems doubtful that he continued to receive much financial

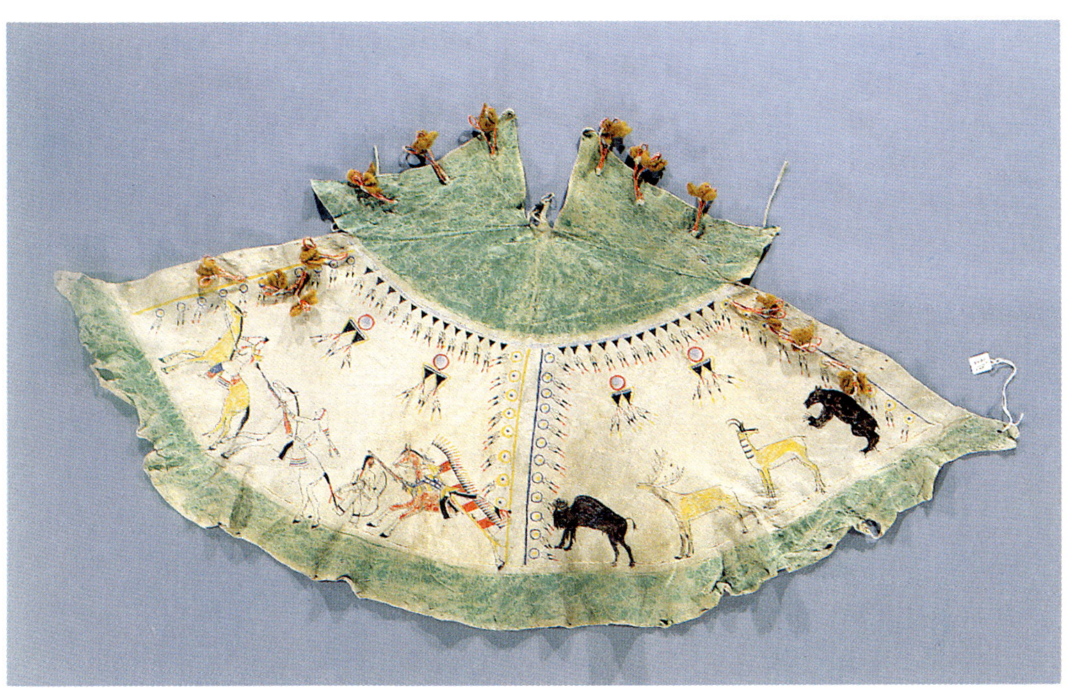

P L A T E   1
Plains, Miniature Tipi, n.d. Hide, pigment, quills,
cloth, thread, 112 cm x 60 cm. Color transparency
6396, American Museum of Natural History Photo
Studio, courtesy Dept. of Library Services,
American Museum of Natural History.

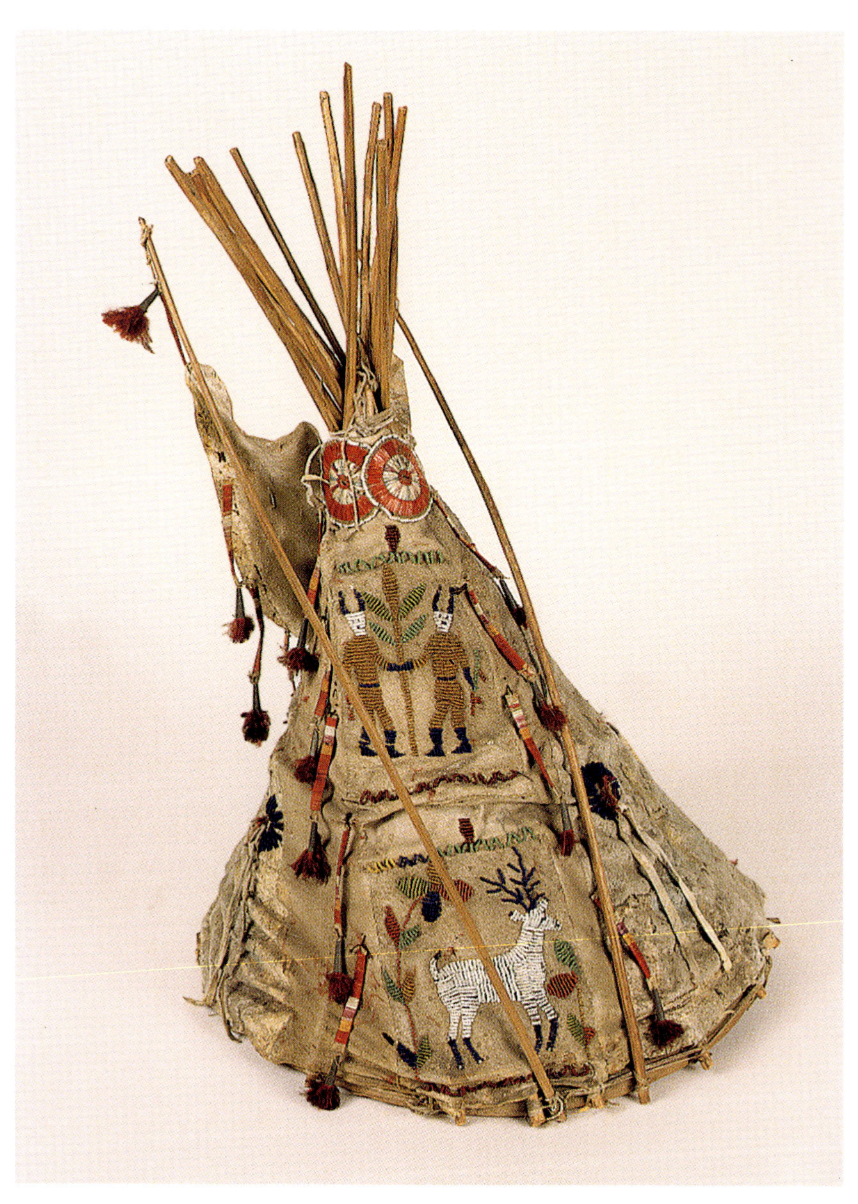

PLATE 2
Sioux, Miniature Tipi, 1880–1900. Buckskin,
beads, quills, pigment, feathers, tin cones, 100 cm.
high. State Historical Society of North Dakota,
11996.

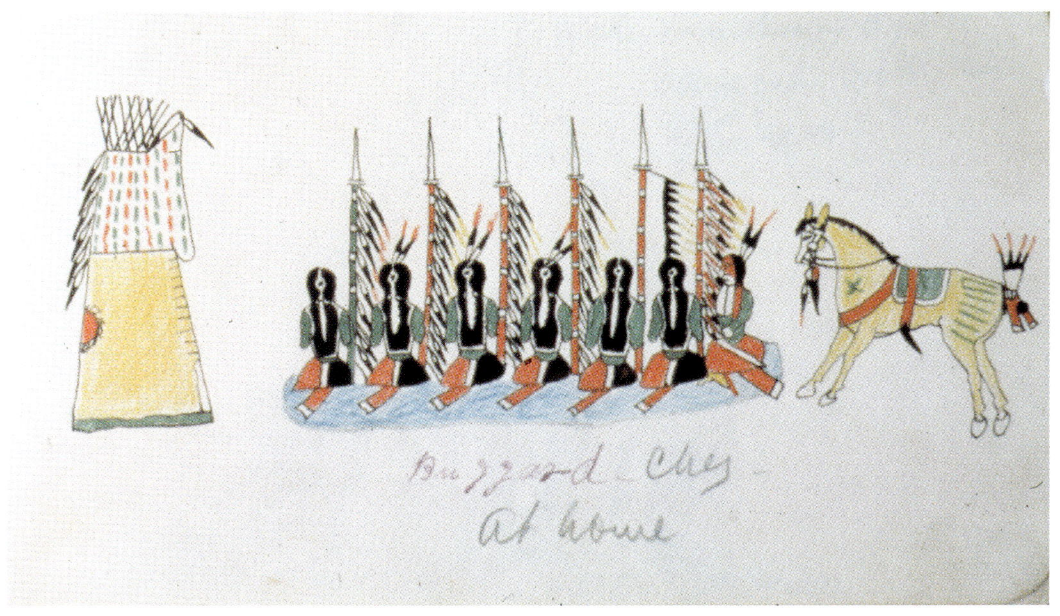

PLATE 3.
Buzzard, Southern Cheyenne. *At Home*, ink and watercolor on paper, 4 in. x 6¾ in. Richard H. Pratt Papers, Western Americana Collections, Beinecke Rare Book and Manuscript Library, Yale University.

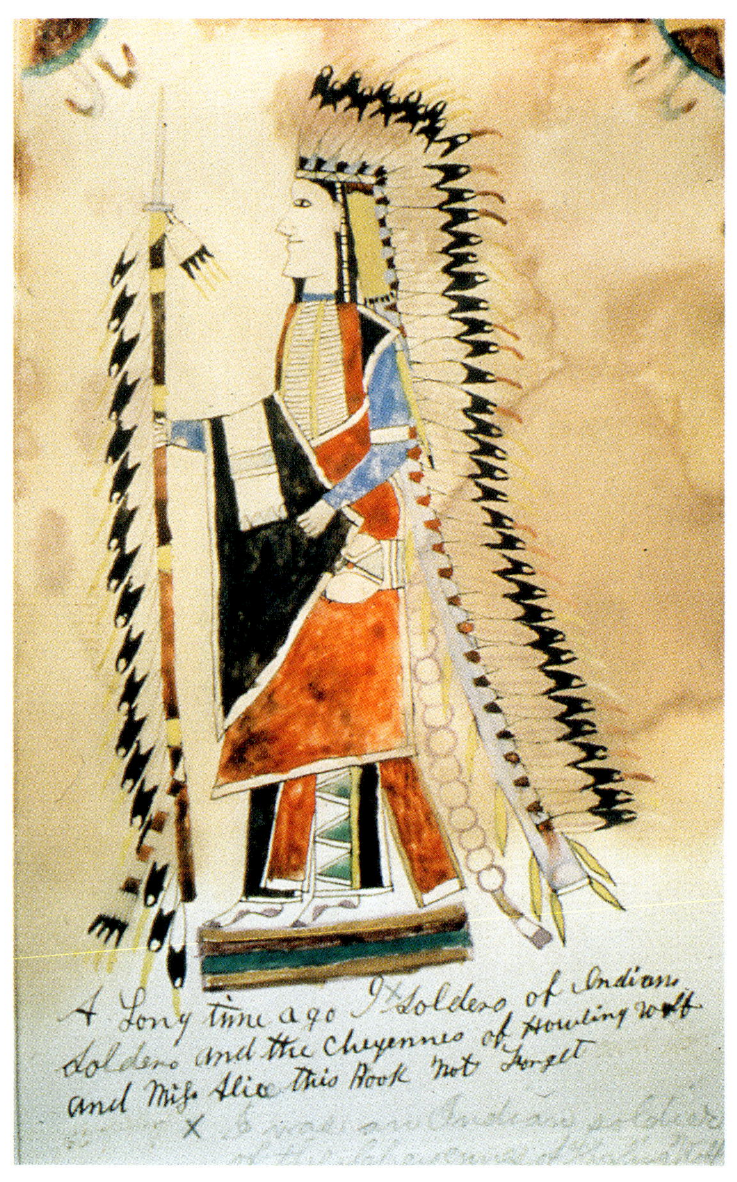

Plate 4.
Bear's Heart, Southern Cheyenne. *Self-Portrait*,
ink and watercolor on paper, 7½ in. x 4¾ in.
Oklahoma Historical Society, gift of Marta Lesta
Bertoia.

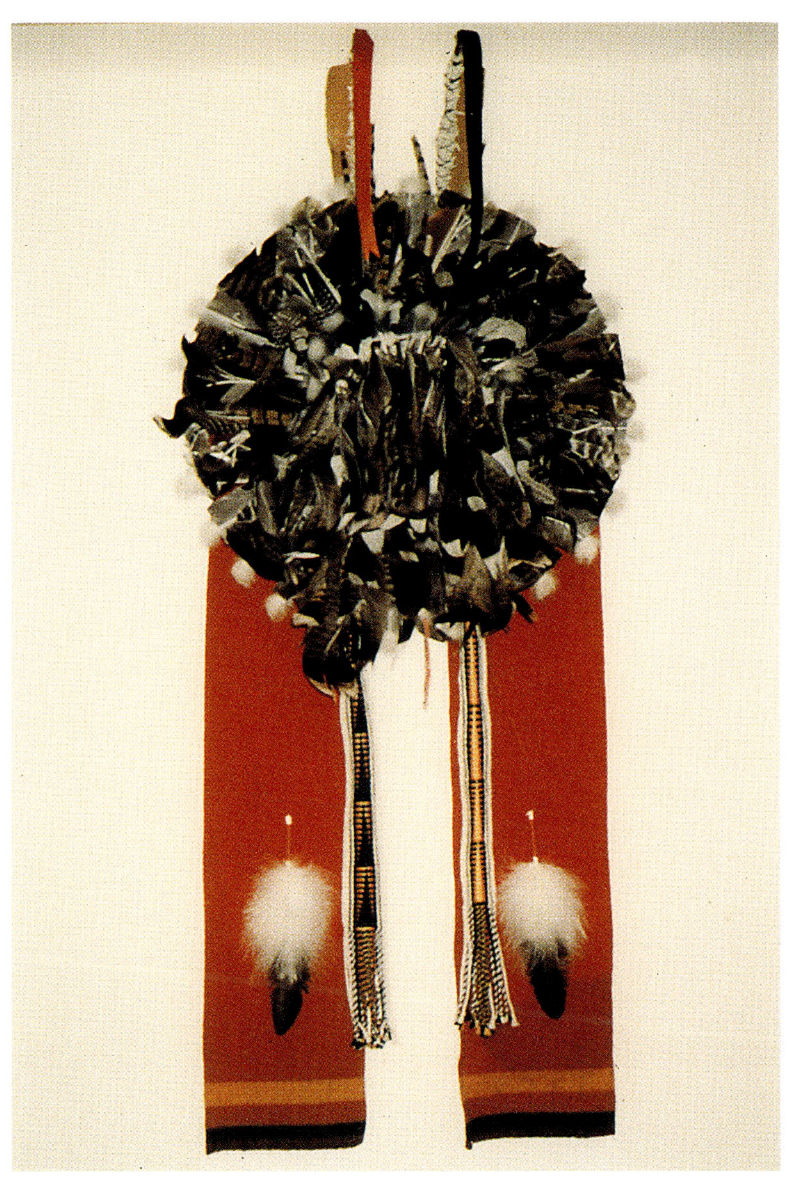

PLATE 5
Old style bustle, ca. 1993. Collection of author,
photo by author.

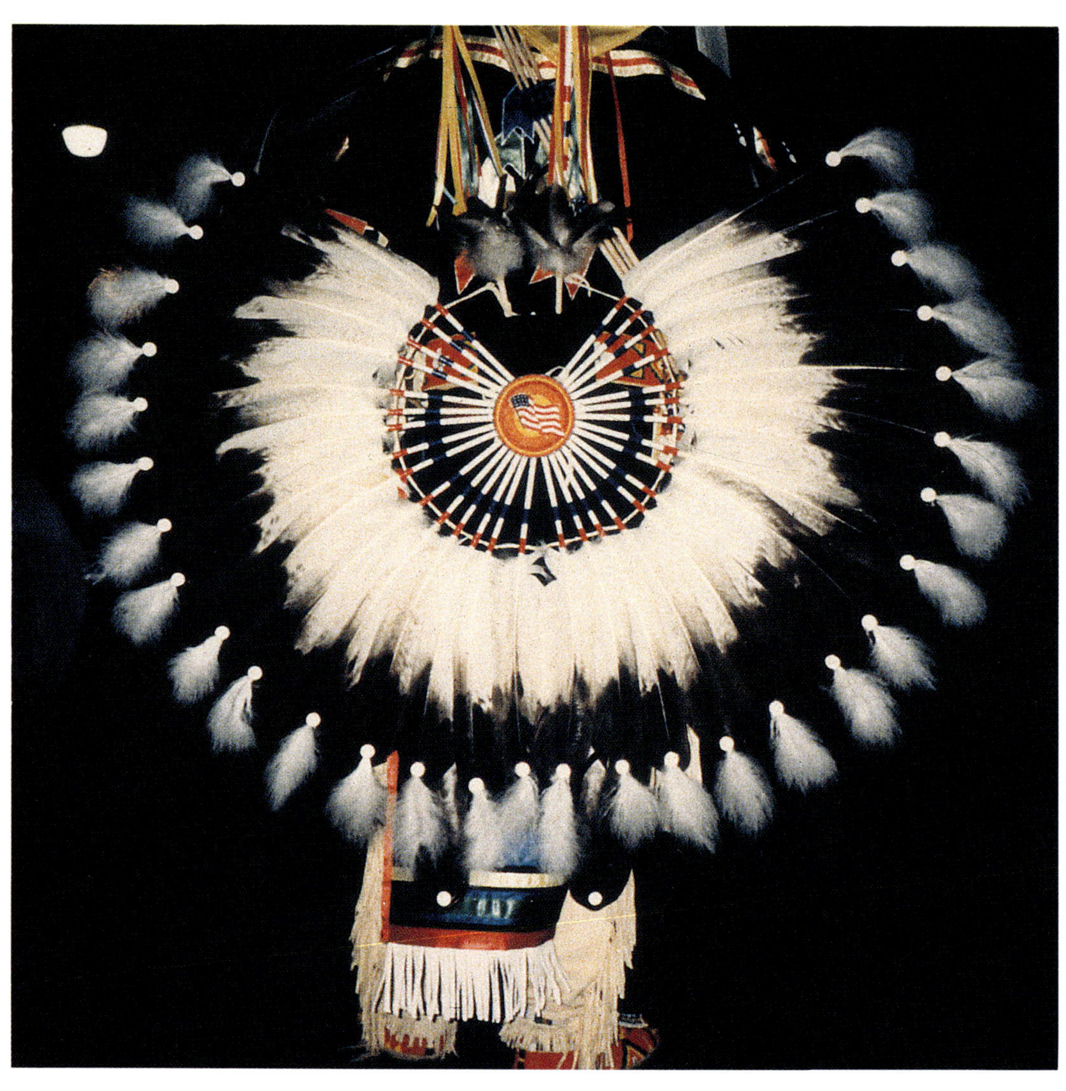

PLATE 6
Northern Traditional bustle, 1995. Photo by author,
courtesy Joe Little.

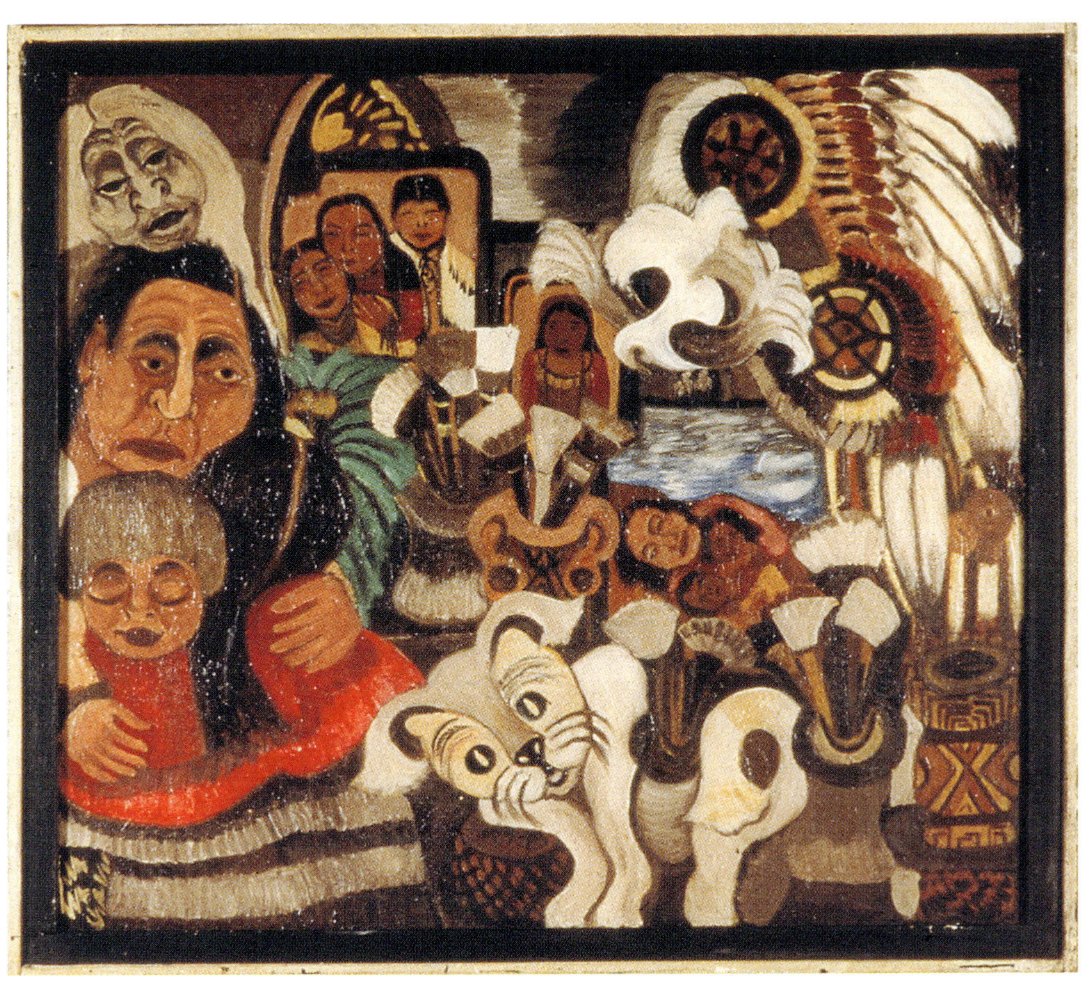

PLATE 7
Bonita Wa Wa Calachaw Nuñez. Untitled, n.d., oil
on canvas, painted wood frame, 111 cm. x 124.4 cm.
Photo by Gina Fuentes. Courtesy, National
Museum of the American Indian, Smithsonian
Institution, 25.1156.

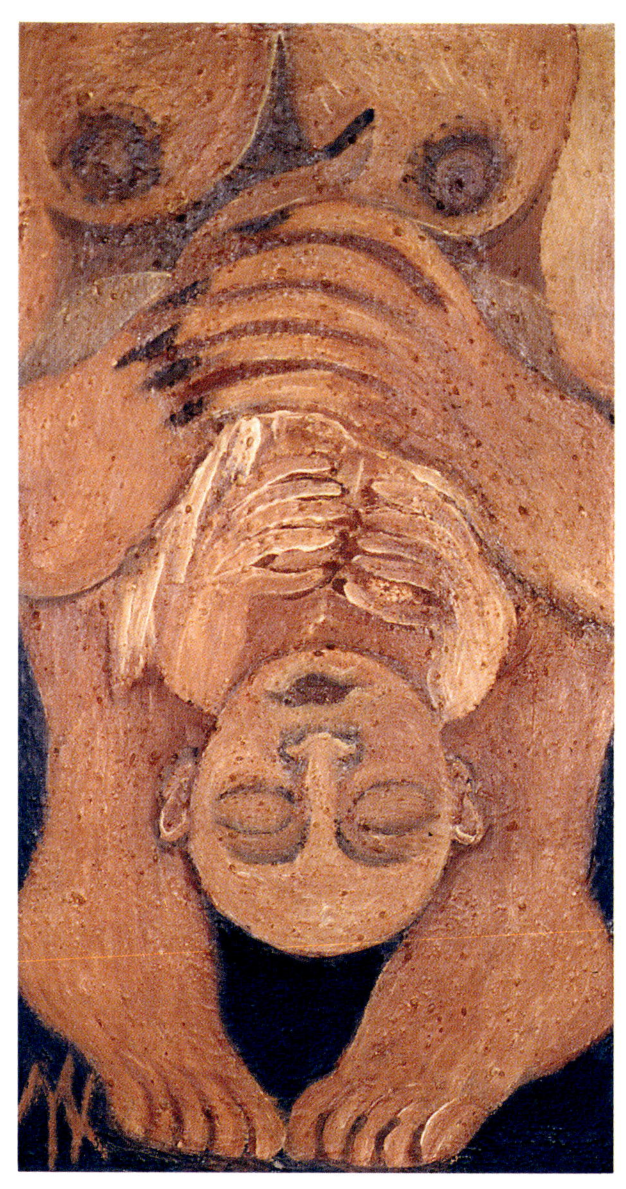

Plate 8
Bonita Wa Wa Calachaw Nuñez. *Birth of a Baby,*
before 1959, oil on board, painted wood frame,
27 in. x 17 in. x 2 in. Gift of Esther N. Finkelstein.
Photo by Cynthia Frankenburg. Courtesy, National
Museum of the American Indian, Smithsonian
Institution, 25.5031.

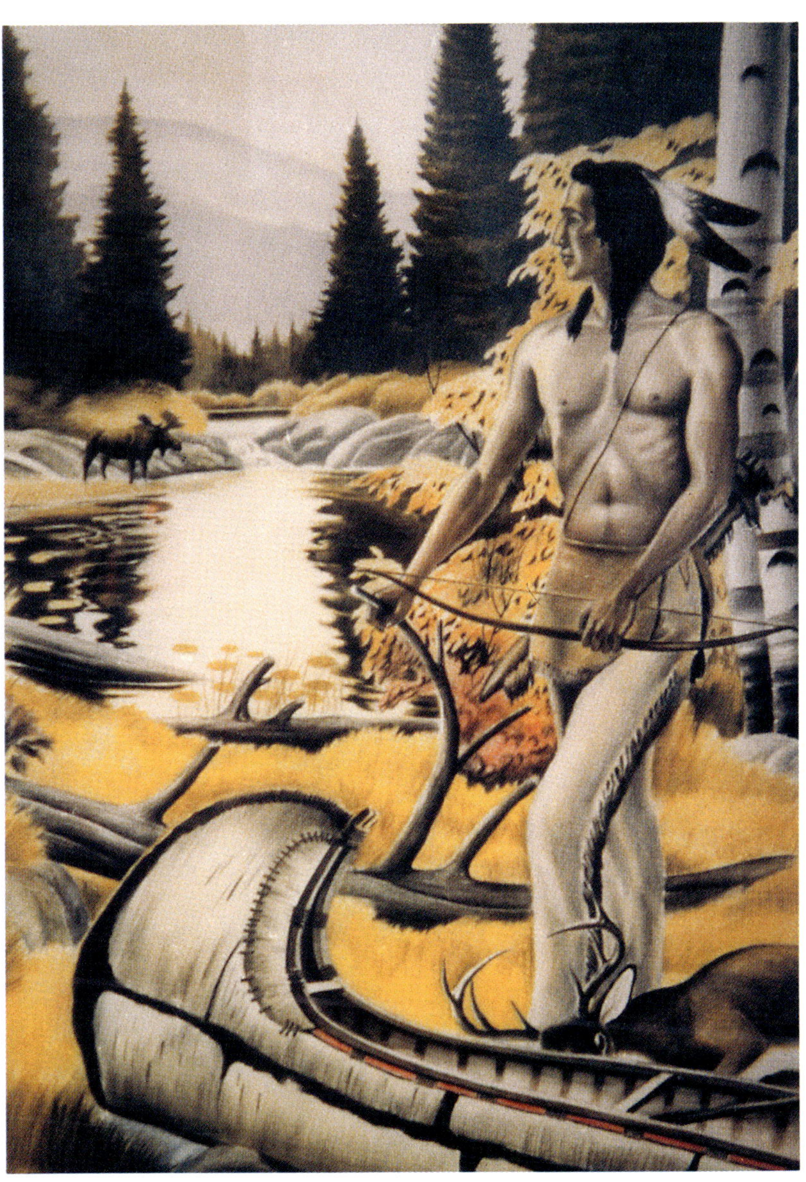

P L A T E 9
Clarence Monegar. Untitled, n.d., pencil, crayon,
watercolor on paper. Location unknown. Photo
courtesy of Joann Dougherty.

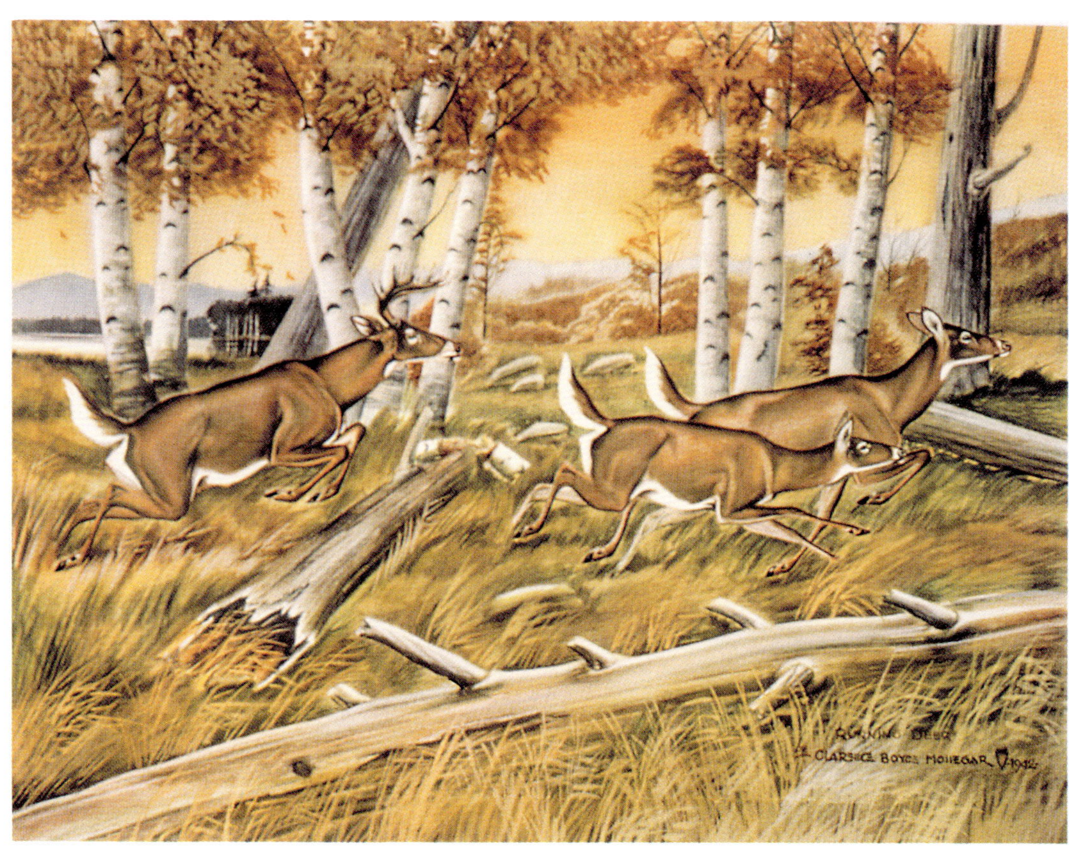

PLATE 10
Clarence Monegar. *Running Deer,* 1942, watercolor on paper. Location unknown. Photograph courtesy of Elvehjem Museum of Art, University of Wisconsin-Madison.

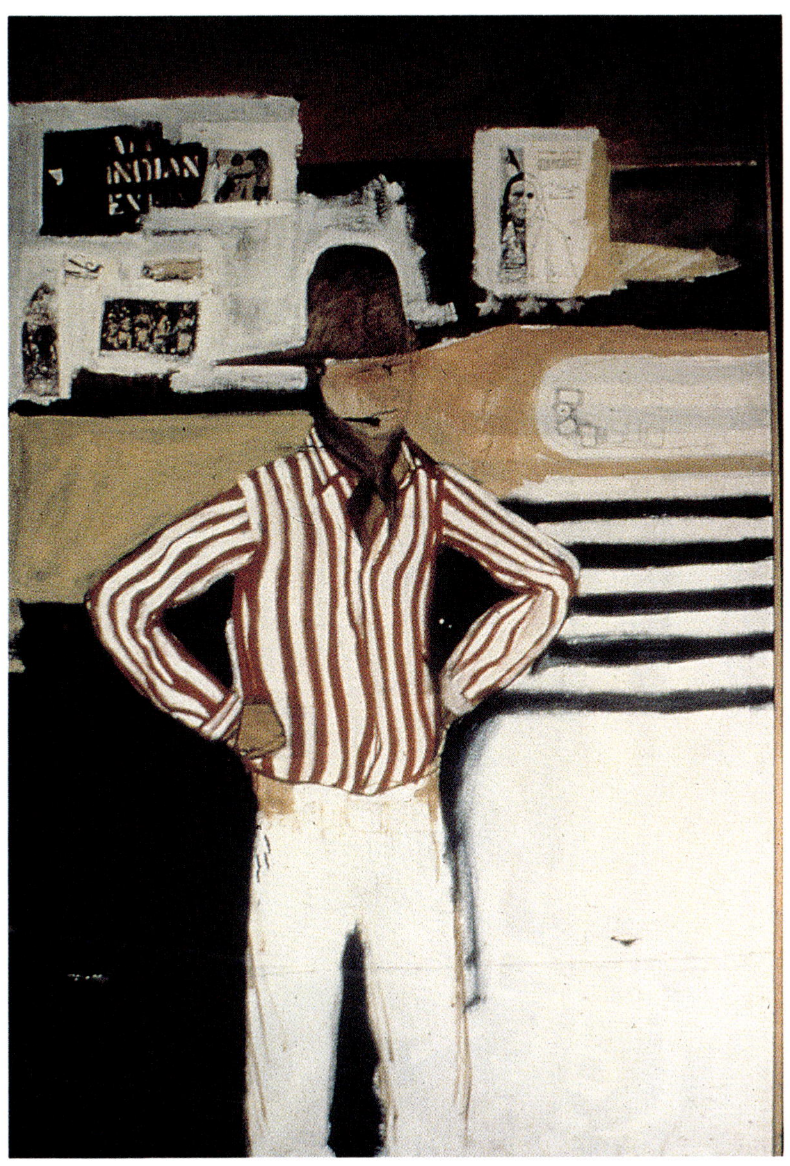

PLATE 11
T. C. Cannon. *Made in Japan with Exception of
One,* 1966, mixed media 71½ in. x 46 in. Institute
of American Indian Arts Museum.

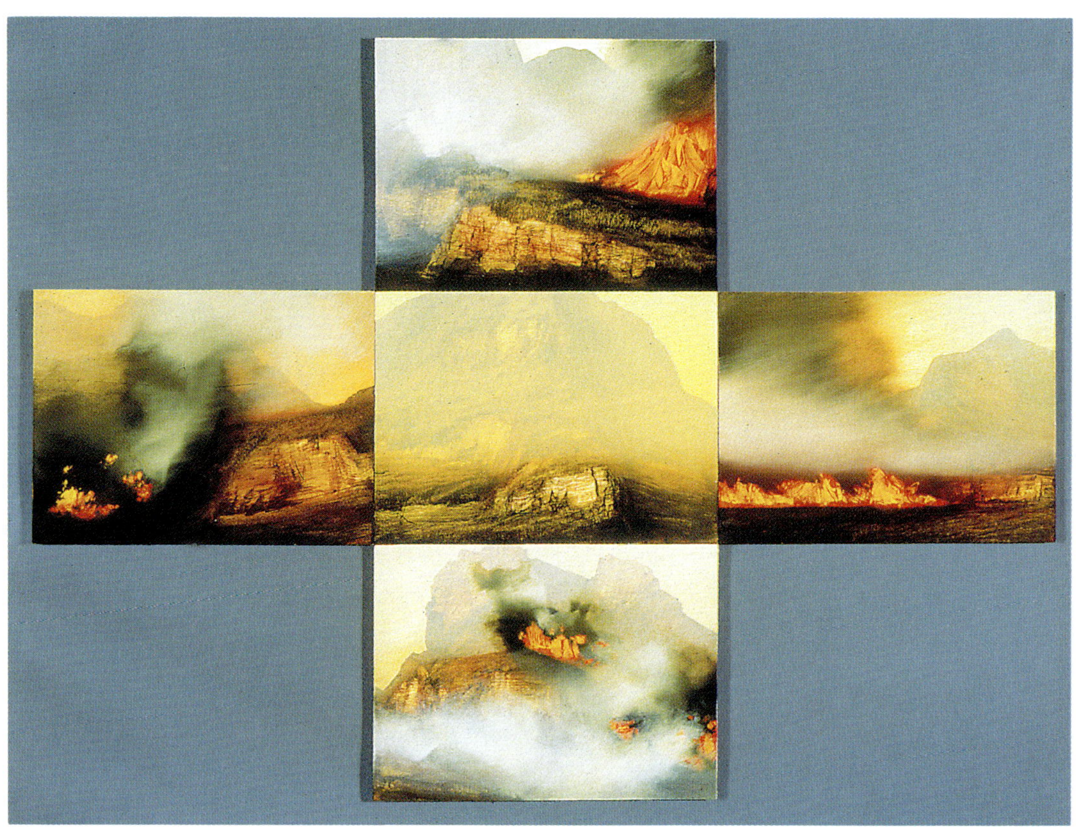

PLATE 12
James Lavadour. *Nest of Suns,* 1998, oil on board,
72 in x 96 in. Courtesy of the artist.

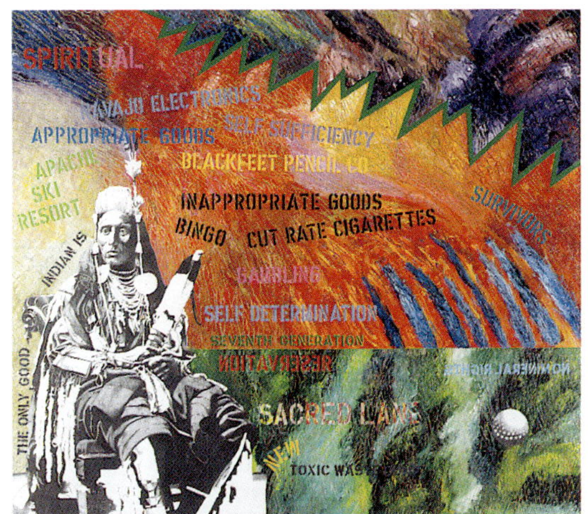

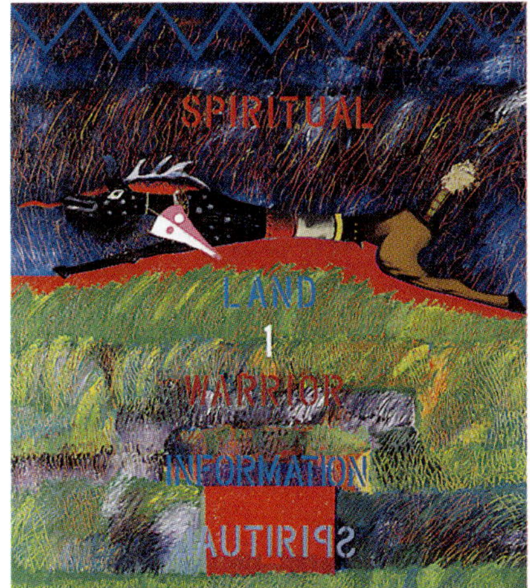

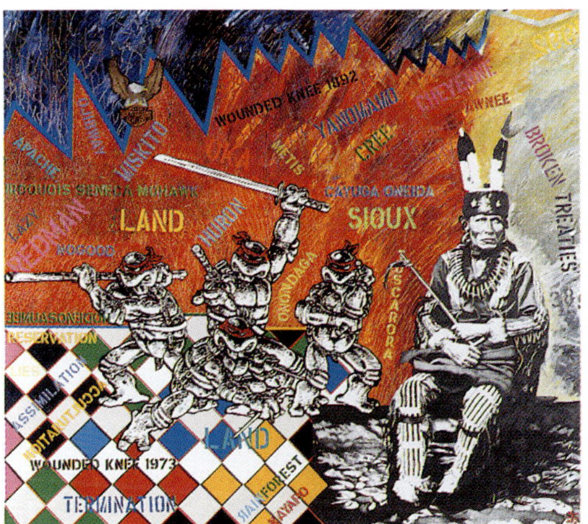

George Longfish. *The End of the Innocence,* 1991–92 installation, mixed media, three panels, top: 96 in. x 102 in.; center: 96 in. x 84 in.; bottom: 96 in. x 102 in.

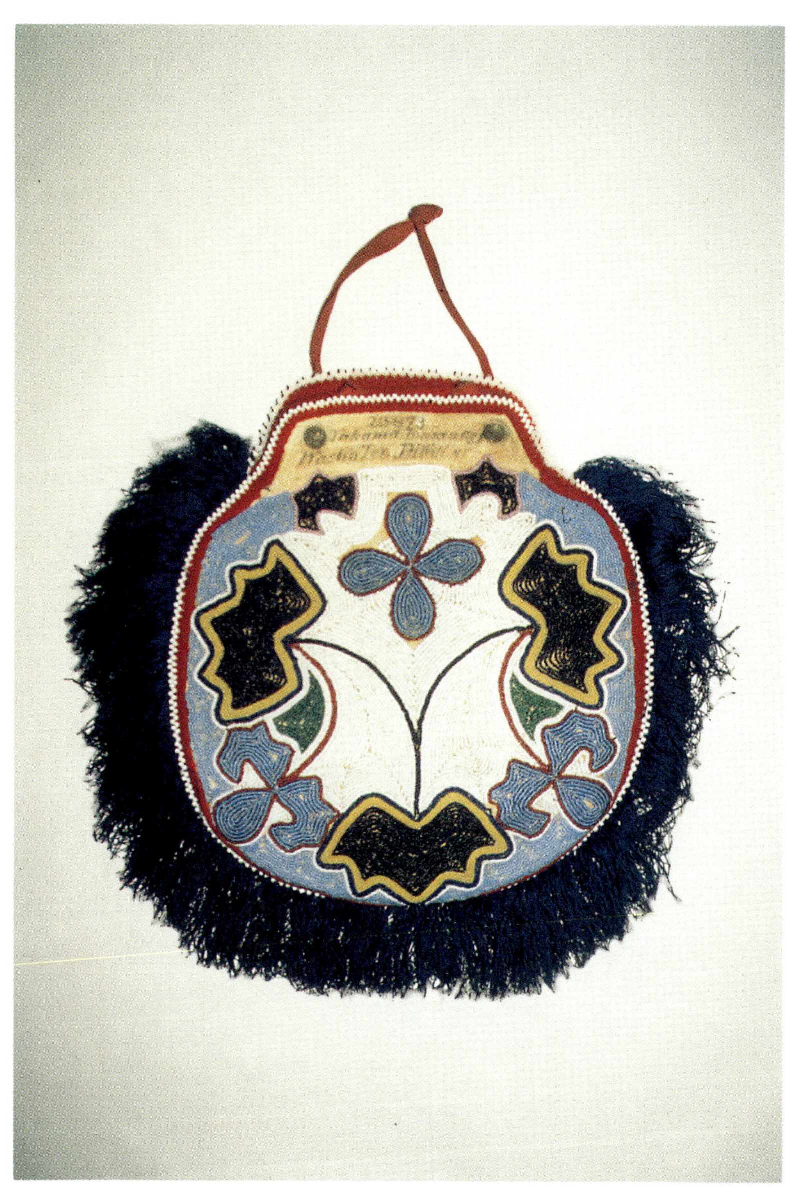

P L A T E   14
Yakama Double Saddle Pouch, collected 1876.
Department of Anthropology, Smithsonian
Institution, cat. no. E23873. Photo by author.

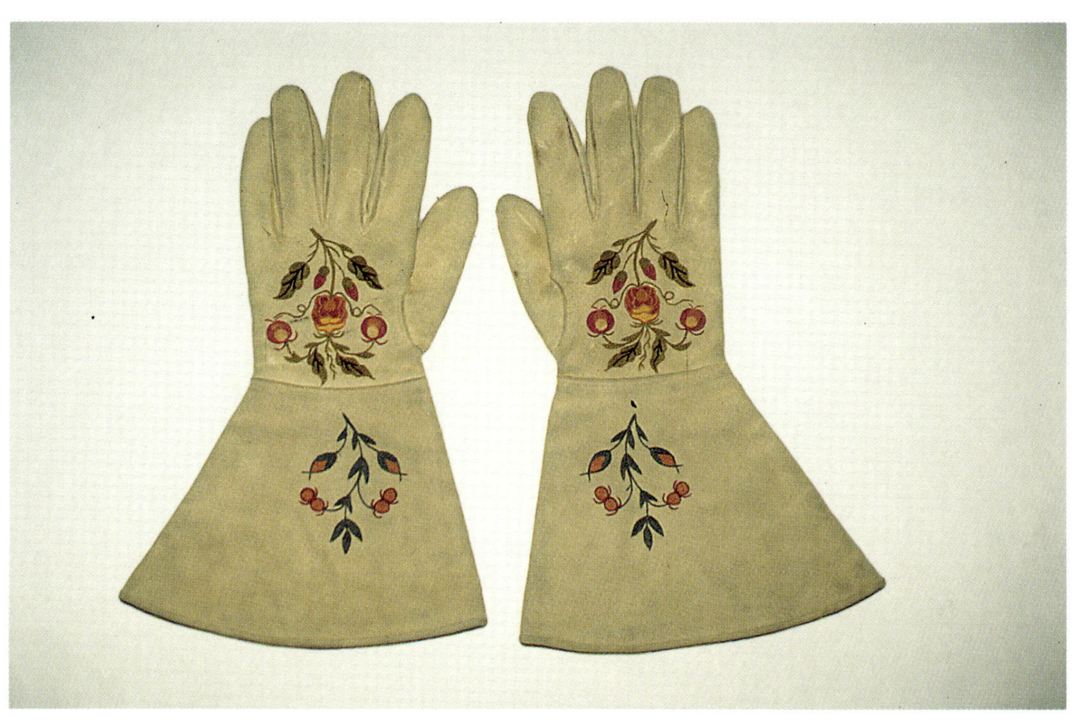

PLATE 15
Colville Gloves, collected 1878–79. Department of
Anthropology, Smithsonian Institution, cat. no.
E131245. Photo by author.

reward. His oldest son, Joseph, born in 1927, only vaguely remembers seeing one completed work when he was very young.[38]

Pino's early work, initially drawn from his experience in painting pottery, conformed closely enough to the expectations of his mentor Charles Kassler and the Santa Fe and Denver audiences for it to be heavily promoted and praised. After Kassler's departure, Jessie Hall assisted Pino by taking examples of his work to Saint Louis and to Erhard Weyhe's gallery in New York. Weyhe obviously thought enough of Pino's work to give the artist a solo exhibition and to submit a print to *Arts* magazine for publication. Clearly, the magazine's editorial staff concurred with his judgment. Indeed, Pino's art was considered sufficiently noteworthy to be included in the 1931 *Exposition of Indian Tribal Arts*. Unfortunately, it was not stereotypical enough to prevent it from being cut from the two-year traveling exhibition.

With Jessie Hall's move to Europe in 1927, Pino's art almost completely disappears from the record. By that time, his work had already strayed significantly from the expected subject matter and style of Indian art, and it is doubtful he had the power to arrange his own exhibitions. In the 1920s, as in the 1930s, it was very important to Anglo purchasers and promoters of Indian art that it conform to a style that was identifiably Indian. As a congressman of the 1930s remarked, "Who wants to go West to buy a picture painted by an Indian of three apples on a plate?"[39] Native people knew this and had tailored their wares to meet the tastes of Anglo tourists since the coming of the railroad. Pino, however, ignored this fact in his rapidly developing art, until neither the images nor their creator could be readily identified as Indian.

In addition, his works continued to show Native peoples in a contemporary environment, working and traveling in an existing world. Compounding this faux pas was the fact that the Santa Fe art and cultural community was attempting to create an indelible image of Santa Fe as an unchanging, harmonious world, separated from the realities and ills of actual life. Pino's artwork contradicted these tourist fantasies, acting as reminders that even Pueblo life was changing. Under these circumstances, it is not surprising that Pino was unable to find another patron. Pino's works were created at a time when the U.S. art and museum communities had a variety of agendas. In many cases a legitimate concern for the economic welfare of Native peoples overlapped with their desire to reinvent the history of the Southwest. Native artists such as Pino were caught in the middle, not content to have their work censored or channeled into more "acceptable" forms.

For Pino, coming from an artistic heritage that emphasized flat, stylized patterns and their formal relationships to one another and the pottery surface, the similarities and differences between Pueblo art forms and Euro-American styles must have created an exciting artistic challenge. When looking at Pino's art and observing its genuine technical and stylistic development and artistic sophistication, it is clear that Pino did not limit his creations in order to fulfill others' expectations of what was right for him as a Native American; instead, he created within the context of the entire artistic environment, an environment of which he himself was a part.

Notes

1. Edward T. Hall, *An Anthropology of Everyday Life* (New York: Doubleday, 1992), 245; "Kassler in Santa Fe," *El Palacio* 18 (April 1, 1925): 150–51.

2. M.A.C., "Art Work of Tesukue Indians to Be Shown in Linoleum Print Blocks at Chappell House: Dealer in Pinon Wood Displays His Ability When Given Opportunity," *Denver Rocky Mountain News,* May 3, 1925.

3. "March Exhibits," *El Palacio* 18 (March 16, 1925): 124.

4. M.A.C., "Art Work of Tesukue," 10; "Block Prints by Juan Pino," *El Palacio* 18 (June 1, 1925): 237–40.

5. "Exhibit by Charles M. Kassler Jr.," *El Palacio* 18 (June 1, 1925): 235–36.

6. M.A.C., "Art Work of Tesukue," 10.

7. "Exhibit by Charles Kassler," *El Palacio* 18 (March 16, 1925): 125.

8. Marcella Leaf and Joseph Pino, daughter and son of Juan I. Pino, personal communication, April 18, 1993; School of American Research, Indian Arts Research Center, anonymous, undated note attached to catalog card number 2937a and b.

9. It had long been the practice among Pueblo artists to note only the potter and not the painter of the pottery pieces. Anglo collectors maintained this practice.

10. "Exhibit by Charles Kassler," 125; "Exhibit by Charles M. Kassler Jr.," 235–36.

11. Olive Rush, block printed Christmas card sent by Charles Kassler from Paris, 1929, OR-AAA, reel 1628, no f. no. Archives of American Art, Washington, D.C.

12. "Exhibit by Charles M. Kassler Jr.," 235–36.

13. Dorothy Dunn, *American Indian Painting of the Southwest and Plains Areas* (Albuquerque: University of New Mexico Press, 1968), 227.

14. Olive Rush, diary entry, Thursday, August 17, 1932, OR-AAA, reel 1629, f. 1195, Archives of American Art, Washington, D.C.

15. A good resource for images of Olive Rush's work is Stanley L. Cuba, *Olive Rush: A Hoosier Artist in New Mexico* (Muncie, Ind.: Minnetrista Cultural Foundation, 1992).

16. M.A.C., "Art Work of Tesukue," 10.

17. An excellent overview of these four artists' works can be found in J. J. Brody, *Pueblo Indian Painting: Tradition and Modernism in New Mexico, 1900–1930* (Santa Fe: School of American Research Press, 1997).

18. Museum of New Mexico, negative no. 22951; "Premium List: Fourth Annual Southwest Indian Fair," *El Palacio* 18 (May 1, 1925): 202.

19. "The Fiesta of 1925 as Viewed by One Observer," *El Palacio* 21 (July 1, 1926): 2–20.

20. Birger Sandzen, *The Graphic Work of Birger Sandzen* (Lindsborg, Kans.: Birger Sandzen Memorial Foundation, 1957); Clinton Adams, *Printmaking in New Mexico, 1880–1990* (Albuquerque: University of New Mexico Press, 1991), 8.

21. "At Work on Taos and Rito Pictures," *El Palacio* 6 (January 1919): 18.

22. "Wood Block Prints by Gustave Baumann," *El Palacio* 15 (January 18, 1925): 35–36.

23. Dunn, *American Indian Painting*, 234.

24. Van Wyck Brooks, *John Sloan: A Painter's Life* (New York: E. P. Dutton, 1955), 100.

25. Brody, *Pueblo Indian Painting,* 180; Brooks, *John Sloan,* 166.

26. *American Magazine of Art* (November 1925); Juan I. Pino to Jessie Hall, March 31, 1926, collection of Edward T. Hall, Santa Fe; "April Exhibits," *El Palacio* 20 (May 1, 1926): 185–86.

27. Adams, *Printmaking in New Mexico.*

28. Edward T. Hall, personal communication, April 2, 1994.

29. Juan I. Pino to Jessie Hall, September 9, 1926; Juan I. Pino to Jessie Hall, December 5, 1926; Juan I. Pino to Jessie Hall, December 19, 1926; collection of Edward T. Hall, Santa Fe, N.M.

30. Hall, *An Anthropology of Everyday Life,* 21–22, 64–71.

31. The cover illustration was provided courtesy of E. Weyhe, the Weyhe Gallery owner, *Arts,* table of contents; Adams, *Printmaking in New Mexico,* 35.

32. M.A.C., "Wood Block Exhibition Is Worth Study," *Denver Rocky Mountain News,* June 12, 1927; Alexandre Hogue, "Picturesque Games and Ceremonial[s] of Indians," *El Palacio* 26 (March 2–23, 1929): 182.

33. Exposition of Indian Tribal Arts, *Catalogue: The Exposition of Indian Tribal Arts, Inc., Grand Central Art Galleries,* December 1–24 (New York: Exposition of Indian Tribal Arts, 1931).

34. Dunn, *American Indian Painting,* 234.

35. Brody, *Pueblo Indian Painting,* 114–17.

36. Ibid., 111; Alexandre Hogue, "Pueblo Tribes Aesthetic Giants, Indian Art Reveals," *El Palacio* 24 (March 24, 1928): 215–16.

37. Tryntje Van Ness Seymour, *When the Rainbow Touches Down* (Seattle: University of Washington Press, 1988), 320, 326–27.

38. Sometime in the 1970s, after Lorencita had passed away and twenty years or more after Pino had died, his family cleaned out the couple's old house. There, they found Pino's blocks and press. Having no idea of their importance, however, the family did not preserve the items; all were lost or destroyed. Joseph Pino and his sister, Marcella Leaf, do not believe any of the blocks remain in existence.

39. Margretta S. Deitrich, "Their Culture Survives," *New Mexico Magazine* 4 (February 1936): 45.

CHAPTER 6

INDIAN IDENTITY AND EVALUATING THE PAST

Bonita Wa Wa Calachaw Nuñez,

an Indian Princess Painter

KATHLEEN E. ASH-MILBY

"I am sure that it is to our mutual distress that I must report that the paintings of 'Princess' Wa Wa Chaw may be the property of the Museum!"[1] With these impassioned words by the head curator of the Museum of the American Indian–Heye Foundation a collection of more than thirty paintings by Bonita Wa Wa Calachaw Nuñez (1888–1972) were officially, though reluctantly, deemed a part of the museum's collection in 1979. In the weeks before her death in 1972, the artist made her donation to the museum through the director, Frederick Dockstader.[2] Over the next seven years the paintings were neither accessioned nor exhibited. When a dispute arose over their ownership in 1979, museum staff did not eagerly defend their title. Despite the artist's parting gesture to posterity, the question of her authenticity as a Native American artist and the subsequent obscurity of her name and work have remained.

Nuñez, or "Wa Wa Chaw," as she signed her paintings and was popularly known, was to many a Native American painter of little consequence, active primarily in the 1940s to 1960s.[3] Although she appears in several biographical guides to Indian painters, women, and leaders, her name generates little recognition by most scholars in Native American art history. With the exception of a little-known publication of her diaries and some of her paintings and drawings in 1980, and her brief mention in a few other publications and unpublished studies, her work has not received note-worthy attention.[4] This history begs the question why her work has been neglected, underrepresented, and essentially rejected as legitimate Native American art. Several reasons can explain these phenomena. First, Wa Wa Chaw was removed from her

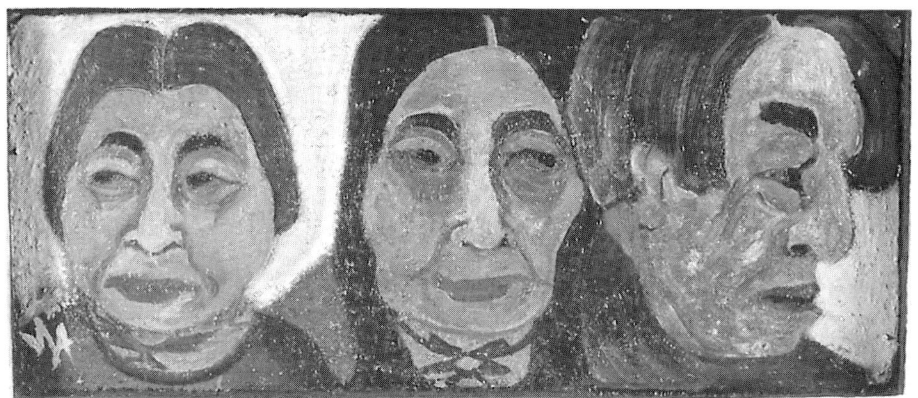

FIGURE 6.1
Bonita Wa Wa Calachaw Nuñez. Untitled, n.d., oil
on canvas, painted wood frame, 30.5 cm. x 68 cm.
Photo by Gina Fuentes. Courtesy, National
Museum of the American Indian, Smithsonian
Institution, 25.1151.

Native community as an infant and spent the majority of her life in the urban environment of New York City. In addition, her painting itself, largely self-taught and in its very execution wildly expressive and decidedly emotional, was a challenge to established mid-century Indian painting conventions. Further removal from serious consideration was the use of the title "princess" in her name. Even by the 1970s the title was a source of derision.

Wa Wa Chaw left behind an impressive oeuvre, including more than forty-five paintings now in several museum and private collections. Her subjects ranged from complex autobiographical compositions to intimate portraits of individuals and small groups (plate 7, fig. 6.1). A notable collection of her diaries and more than fifty pen-and-ink drawings also survive, now residing in the National Cowboy Hall of Fame archive. Despite the exclusion of her work from previous consideration, a close examination of her paintings reveals early work of a new type of Native artist, reflecting an urban, feminist perspective, open to modern art influences and not afraid to explore her mixed and complex identity.[5]

Birth of a Baby

> I was born on Christmas . . . I was told later in my life By Mother Mary
> Duggan who was passing though Calif. on her way East and having to make

connections for her return home She had to waite *[sic]* for two or three days . . . Wondering *[sic]* along the Roads . . . Mother stopped at a wooden *shack.* And in that *shack* was my real Mother Indian having *Labor Pains. Mother* Mary Dugg*an* Took things into *her hands* and in a few minutes I was *born* Mother Gave me to her. . . . The Poverty of The Shack was alway a memory in Mary Duggan['s] Mind. Three or four days it took Mary Duggan before she was on her way Eastward bound.[6]

Wa Wa Chaw was both blessed and cursed by the circumstances of her birth. According to her diaries, she was born to a Luiseño mother of the Rincon band in 1888, near Valley Center, California. She was immediately adopted and brought east by a Euro-American suffragist and Indian sympathizer, Mary Duggan, and her physician brother, Cornelius. Wa Wa Chaw spent the majority of her youth and adult life in Manhattan. Wa Wa Chaw was raised in the Duggans' wealthy home on Manhattan's Upper West Side. From a young age she was surrounded by an elite group of humanists, intellectuals, and prestigious individuals who visited the Duggans, including Sir Arthur Conan Doyle and Carrie Chapman Catt. Many of these visitors were concerned and involved with the welfare of Indians.[7] Dark-skinned and Indian, Wa Wa Chaw was surely a curiosity to most New Yorkers whose lives were distant from Native communities and concerns.[8] Public opinion at the time, sometimes referred to as the "age of the vanishing Indian," considered Indians to be heathens, and the Duggans were challenged on more than one occasion for adopting a creature barely considered human.[9]

At the time of Wa Wa Chaw's adoption, Native people were perceived as savages that should either be eliminated or "saved" through religion and education. Mary Duggan was clearly a proponent of the latter solution to "the Indian problem." Gen. Richard Pratt, an acquaintance of the Duggans, began his campaign "to save the man by killing the Indian" through education and literal separation of Native people from tribal influence.[10] During the 1870s Pratt first practiced this approach with a group of southern Plains Indian prisoners held at Fort Marion, Florida, and later continued his campaign with the founding of the Indian School at Carlisle, Pennsylvania. His influence on federal Indian policy would be felt for decades to come. By removing Wa Wa Chaw from her Native family and giving her a formal Euro-American education, the Duggans probably felt they were rescuing her from a life doomed to poverty and perceived as backward.[11]

From her diaries it appears that Wa Wa Chaw's childhood was privileged, though isolated. She claimed to have had no childhood friends and spent her time with the Duggans and their social circle. Her formal education consisted primarily of tutors,

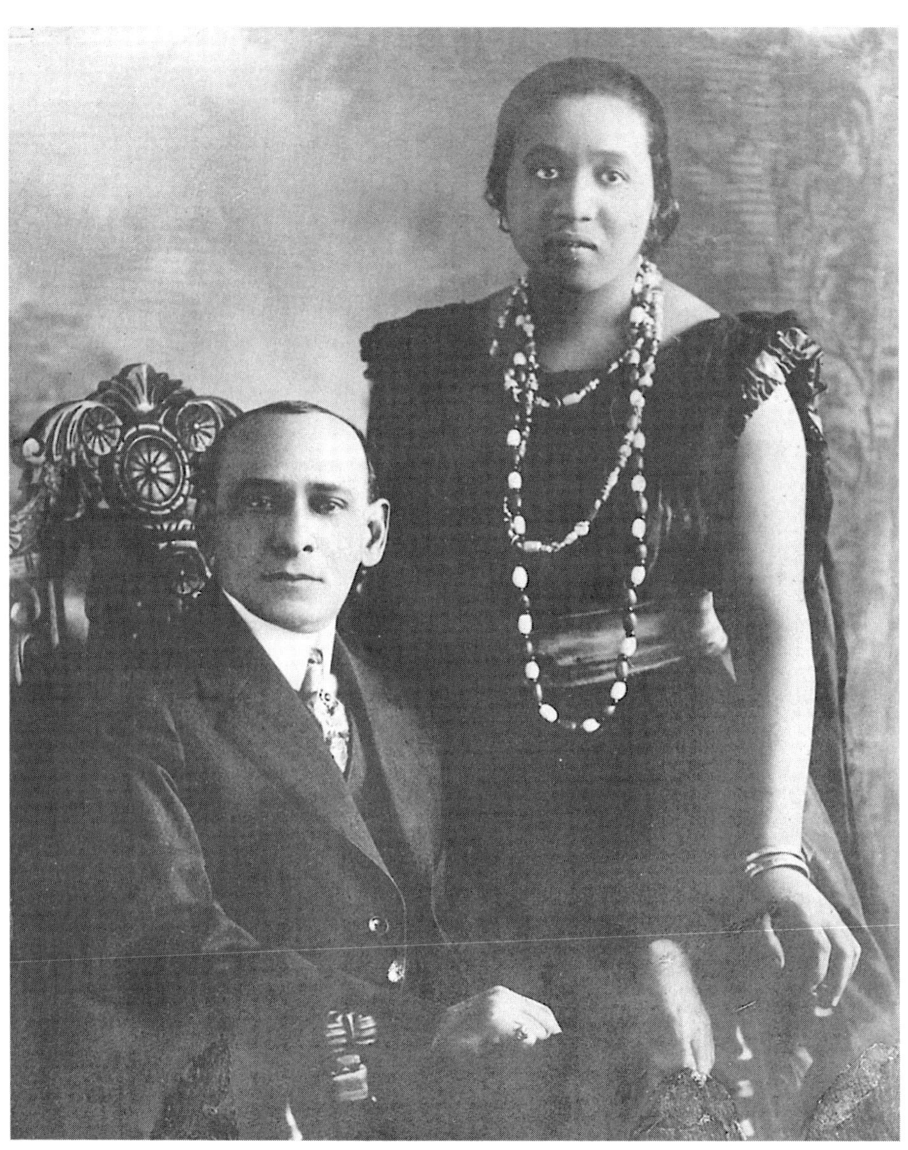

FIGURE 6.2
Wa Wa Chaw and her husband, Manuel Nuñez, from about 1910, 4⅜ in. x 3⅛ in. Photographer unknown. Arthur and Shifra Silberman Collection, National Cowboy Hall of Fame, Oklahoma City, Oklahoma.

although she does mention a brief (one- or two-year) residence at the Sherman Indian School in Riverside, California.[12] Even after her marriage to Puerto Rican cigar manufacturer Manuel Carmonia-Nuñez about 1910, she spent most of her time with the somewhat overprotective Duggans (fig. 6.2). Dr. Duggan, who felt that Wa Wa Chaw's body was "a little late in maturation" with delicate bone structure, was very concerned that she be kept from having children for at least two years after her marriage. The couple did eventually have at least one child who died in infancy.[13]

Although Wa Wa Chaw could not remember her biological mother, the involuntary removal that physically separated her from her Native community and family of origin never lost its emotional resonance. Growing up she was forced to rely completely upon her adopted parents for the details of her Indian identity. Her conflicted relationships to both her birth and adoptive mothers, in addition to her own difficult experiences with motherhood, were often explored as subjects in her paintings.

Birth of a Baby is a powerful and profound painting that explores the artist's mixed feelings about her own origins (plate 8). Collected in 1959 this maternal nude is an arresting, unconventional, and graphic treatment of the rare subject of birth.[14] Crowded within the frame in a twist of squarely defined limbs, a baby emerges from the body of a woman. The dark-lipped infant's eyes are closed and the expression serene, if not melancholy. In this unusual depiction, the artist has paid particular attention to anatomical details, such as the inclusion of the afterbirth and the prominence of the mother's breasts. Wa Wa Chaw has reduced her portrayal of this woman to the very essence of biological motherhood: the moment and experience of birth. The focus, however, is upon the infant, not the mother; the face of the woman is absent, having been obscured by the top boundary of the frame. Viewed in the context of Wa Wa Chaw's own birth, it can be argued that this painting is indeed a self-portrait. Despite the extreme intimacy of this moment—the child still physically connected to its mother—the mother in this composition remains anonymous to the viewer, just as the artist's biological mother remained a stranger to her.

In Western non-Indian art, historically the nude was presented as an idealized form absent disturbing "wrinkles, pouches, and other small imperfections." The traditional depiction of mother and child is that of the Madonna, defined by the immaculate (asexual) conception. Maternal nudes, or nude women depicted during pregnancy and childbirth, continue to be rare, if not taboo, subjects. Within twentieth-century Native American painting, complete nudity is unusual with few exceptions such as *Pollination of the Corn* (1948) by Waldo Mootzka (Hopi, 1903–38), a semi-abstract image with a fertility theme, and a number of paintings by Frank Day (Maidu, 1902–76) relating to death and origin stories. *Birth of a Baby* stands in marked contrast to traditional, idealized Western depictions of the sexless Madonna as well as the use of the nude within Native American painting. Wa Wa Chaw's mother is a sexual being, who, though not named or identified is depicted as a real person, not an abstract concept or separated from contemporary mothers through time or death.[15]

At the approximate time *Birth of a Baby* was created, maternal nudes were found in the work of German artist Paula Modersohn-Becker (1876–1907). Becker's portrayal of maternity emphasized the close intimate relationship. According to Linda Nochlin "animal physicality" fills works such as the sleeping mother and infant in *Mother and Child* (1906). Although Becker's experiences as a mother herself were limited to a brief relationship with a stepdaughter and Becker later lost her life due to complications after the birth of her natural daughter, her depictions of pregnancy and motherhood, like that of Wa Wa Chaw, were frank, unapologetic explorations of maternity. Unlike Becker and other women artists from the late nineteenth and early twentieth centuries who explored the theme of maternity, such as Käthe Kollwitz (1867–1945) and Mary Cassatt (1844–1926), however, Wa Wa Chaw did not receive formal, academic training.[16]

A Self-Taught Artist

Wa Wa Chaw's artistic career was strongly influenced by her treatment within the Duggans' home. From a very young age she was viewed in a romantic light and treated as a mystic with powerful perception and natural, intuitive, artistic abilities. Out of concern for the quality of Indian boarding schools, and possibly from over-protectiveness, the Duggans educated their adopted daughter through at-home tutors; her education may have included some limited art studies.

Largely self-taught, Wa Wa Chaw began her artistic career as a child creating medical illustrations for Dr. Duggan, an early cancer researcher. He was particularly fascinated by the visual perception she exhibited in her medical drawings. The doctor remarked that observing the same specimens with a "microscope revealed nothing new."[17] These skills helped her later in life as she continued producing and selling medical drawings on a freelance basis. Wa Wa Chaw also made line drawings of the various people she met throughout her life, as well as historic figures who shaped her opinions about the Indian situation. Individual portraits often included the names, descriptions, and significance of the subjects. She sometimes even added comments they had made. For instance, on a portrait of Carlos Montezuma, a prominent American Indian-rights activist she greatly admired, her notation reads: "Keep talking Freedom Wa-Wa[.] Let no one stope *[sic]* you. Right thinking can never be wrong. Protect Ever[y] other American, Dr. Carlos Montezuma By Wa-Wa Chaw."[18]

Wa Wa Chaw may have begun experimenting with oil painting and ink as early as her teens.[19] Unfortunately she did not date her paintings. The earliest documented painting is from 1946 when she began entering the Philbrook Art Center Indian Annual painting competitions.[20] Regardless, in a biographical form she submitted for the competition, she claimed to have painted as a hobby all her life.[21]

Wa Wa Chaw's paintings include a wider range and greater sophistication in composition and subject matter than her drawings of medical subjects and portraits. The majority are large in format, ranging from approximately 25 by 19 inches to more than 5 by 3½ feet. Of forty-six identified paintings, only four are unframed: two paintings on board panels and two others on round or oval canvases. Almost all her paintings were constructed with deep frames, thickly painted, sealing them to the canvas or board foundation. The frames appear to have been an integral part of each painting; some frame elements were even applied to the face of the painting support.[22] A series of six smaller paintings, all measuring less than 18 by 18 inches may have been created to sell on the street, as she exhibited and sold her work in Greenwich Village street fairs and outdoor exhibitions, probably during the 1940s and 1950s. The smaller format would have made the paintings easier to transport and sell in this context.[23] In contrast, her largest extant paintings were part of the collection donated to the Museum of the American Indian (MAI) in 1972; these paintings, which remained in her apartment until the year of her death, may have been difficult, if not impossible, for her to informally exhibit and sell in her later years.

Although detailed analysis has not been conducted, it appears that Wa Wa Chaw used an undetermined oil-based paint combination, possibly including industrial paints.[24] This may indicate that these paintings were made later in her life when she struggled financially without the support of her adoptive parents. The surfaces of her paintings are deeply textural, often showing evidence of being reworked several times during the long drying process. Many of her paintings are similar in subject to her drawings, focusing primarily upon portraiture. For example, an untitled painting of three unidentified men exhibits very distinctive hairstyles and facial characteristics (fig. 6.1), which may be clues to their identity. A portrait purchased by the Philbrook Art Center from their 1947 painting competition is titled *Chief Runs Them All*. Rather than working from models, Wa Wa Chaw probably worked from memory. She stated, "My painting[s] are Creative[.] I never need one to pose[,] for me My Friends Live for ever in my Thoughts."[25]

In a smaller number of her paintings, but particularly in her two-tone panels and ink drawings, Wa Wa Chaw draws the focus from the human figure to pattern and design. These images, though still containing figures, concentrate on abstracted reproductions of totem poles and designs that appear to be taken from Native American objects and artifacts. Wa Wa Chaw was a frequent visitor to the Museum of the American Indian in her later years; the museum was located not far from her home in Spanish Harlem.[26] She would have had many opportunities to visit the permanent exhibitions, which consisted primarily of overcrowded, geographically arranged cases brimming with cultural artifacts, rich with the chaotic combinations of design found throughout Wa Wa Chaw's work.

Modernist Influences

The work of Bonita Calachaw Nuñez is all but unknown in the field of contemporary and twentieth-century Native American art studies. This may be attributed to her lack of exposure through the burgeoning Southwest Indian art market in the 1930s to 1950s or even to her low profile as an eastern, urban-based, self-taught artist with little or no institutional support and recognition. However, she was an active participant in the Philbrook Indian Annual, exhibiting in six competitions between 1946 and 1965.[27] In addition, the Museum of the American Indian and the Philbrook Museum of Art, together, acquired more than thirty of her paintings between 1947 and 1972. Instead of a lack of visibility or opportunity, or even the casual disparaging descriptions of her work as "ugly" or "oatmeal paintings," Wa Wa Chaw's work may have remained in relative obscurity because its authenticity as Native American painting has continued to be questioned.[28]

Wa Wa Chaw's painting stands in marked contrast to the established "traditional" Native American painting that developed in Santa Fe and Oklahoma from the 1930s to 1950s. Despite the groundbreaking work of many contemporary Native American artists in the last thirty years, the image of Indian painting that still comes to mind for most is the Southwest, or Studio, style characterized by the use of flat colors with little or no modeling, minimal or absent background detail, and the frequent use of outline.[29] Although there have been some notable exceptions to this rule, such as the work of Ernest Spybuck (Absentee Shawnee, 1883–1949), the Studio style of painting became regarded as a traditional and pure form of pan-Indian painting, which controlled the market and shaped expectations for decades.[30]

While the established aesthetic canon became the marker of authenticity for the judgment of many early Native American artists, the content was also judged. Among the most popular subjects were scenes of Native people participating in traditional dances or activities, the paintings often incorporating design elements from traditional arts such as pottery design. Contemporary references or outwardly emotional scenes, such as the returning soldier in *First Furlough* (1943) by Quincy Tahoma (Navajo, 1921–56), were unusual. Painting in a narrative style that did not fit stylistic conventions was often accepted not for its artistic merit but for the ethnographic information it contained. Interestingly, many of these artists freely used European conventions such as depth of field, modeled figures, and fully fleshed-out backgrounds.[31] Wa Wa Chaw's painting did not fit into the conventions of "traditional Native American painting" in style or content. As an independent, self-taught artist, she developed her work as a personal form of self-expression and exploration of her identity as an urban Indian. Wa Wa Chaw was probably influenced by modern European and Euro-American artists and movements rather than the expectations and confinements of the growing Indian art market.

As a young woman in the Duggans' home, Wa Wa Chaw surely had many opportunities to meet and discuss ideas with artists. She once mentioned receiving instruction from Albert Pinkham Ryder, who taught her to "tone down" her color.[32] Following the pattern set by the Duggans, Wa Wa Chaw, as an adult, opened her home to other artists and Native American visitors to New York City. In a 1947 letter to Bernard Frazier of the Philbrook Art Center, Wa Wa Chaw explained the influence of the New York modern art scene on her work:

> My home is almost a center.
> I read Art News sometimes and Art Digest[,] there are many more.
> They have a[n] outdoor Art Exhibitions.
> It is to *[sic]* much work for me you know I cannot keep up with them the New York *Artist*. You *don't know it* But [the] *Philbrook* has made a *discovery*[.] I have had so many *people* talking [to] me On the painting *idea* that I really don't know how I ever made up my *mind* to *send* out any of my painting.[33]

It is likely that Wa Wa Chaw had many opportunities to view the work of modern American and European artists throughout her career. The Metropolitan Museum of Art, the Museum of Modern Art, various art galleries, and local exhibitions were all accessible to her. In addition, reproductions in *Art News* and *Art Digest* would have exposed her to a variety of styles and modern art movements, as well as kept her informed about national and local art news and exhibition opportunities.[34] In contrast, Wa Wa Chaw's exposure to Native American painting was quite limited. As a New York resident, she had two major opportunities to view contemporary painting: the *Exposition of Indian Tribal Arts* held in the Grand Central Galleries in 1931 and the Museum of Modern Art exhibition *Indian Art of the United States* in 1941. While these were both major exhibitions of Native art, contemporary painting was only a small component. Label copy in the exhibitions was sure to promote and describe Native American art in limiting terms. In the catalog for *Indian Art of the United States,* for instance, a Haida slate carving of *The Bear Mother,* a mother grimacing as she nurses her half-bear child, is "celebrated . . . largely because it displays a personal emotion foreign to traditional Indian work."[35]

While the work of artists inspired by the Studio style was the essence of control, Wa Wa Chaw's work was the extreme opposite. Instead of painting delicate, steady, even lines and figures with watercolor or acrylic paint, she stood before a large canvas with an odd mixture of oil-based paints and attacked the surface in broad, expressive strokes, reworking the canvas to her satisfaction. The people she portrayed are not delicate and beautiful; her subjects have thick, earthy limbs, their lips are dark with sly smiles; they laugh, cry, and embrace each other. The sheer emotion of her work stands in marked contrast to tranquil scenes rendered by other Native American painters of her time. Far from the subdued work of "traditional" Indian painting, the painterly, emotional, and expressive quality of Wa Wa Chaw's work suggests a strong influence from Expressionism. Her preference for intense color and contrast, as well as expressionistic brushwork, suggests the influence of several European artists, including Edvard Munch and Emil Nolde. Even in her graphic work she combines forceful, dramatic images with self-reflective subjects, frequently addressing Indian social concerns.[36]

German graphic artist Käthe Kollwitz used a similar approach, combining bold, expressive imagery with a compassionate approach toward her subjects. Like Wa Wa Chaw, Kollwitz also exposed the suffering of the underclass, intending "her art to be one of urgency and social purpose." In her series *War* (1922–23), an image titled *The Sacrifice* poignantly illustrates the strife of mothers whose children were sacrificed for the war effort (fig. 6.3). Kollwitz's graphic antiwar efforts reflect her own grief after losing one of her two sons in World War I. She effectively uses the maternal nude in this context to expose the vulnerability of the mother and child as well as to create a symbolic representation of all mothers.[37]

Wa Wa Chaw's subjects reflect personal experiences and concerns as an urban Indian and an advocate for Indian rights. Rather than depicting idyllic scenes of untroubled traditional Indian life, Wa Wa Chaw used her art as an opportunity to expose the poverty and desolation she witnessed as a visitor to Indian reservations with Mary Duggan. Influenced early in her life by non-Indian sympathizers for the Indian cause, as an adult Wa Wa Chaw joined other Native people who were products and advocates of the Euro-American education system in protesting the deplorable conditions most Native people suffered. Through organizations such as the Society of American Indians, founded in 1911, these Indian advocates demanded the abolishment of the reservation system and fought for the rights of Indian people as individuals. Wa Wa Chaw's frank, unromantic portrayals, particularly strong in her ink drawings, were in themselves a protest against the suffering and neglect of her people.

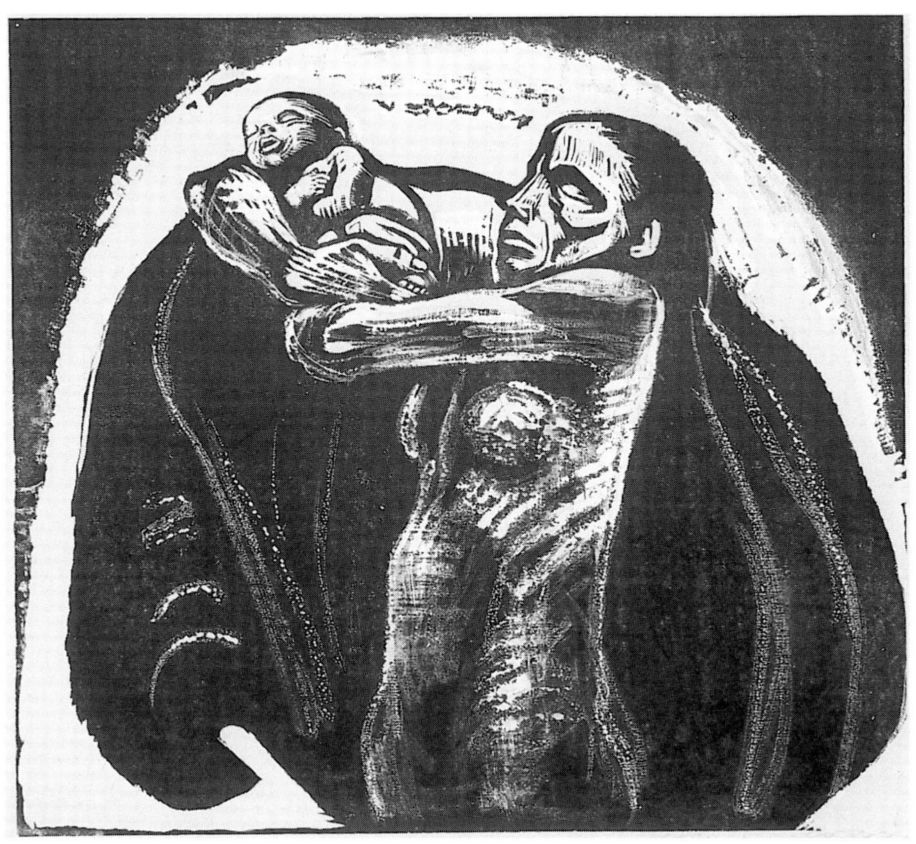

Other paintings and drawings focus on explorations of her own history. In . . . *Her Memory* Wa Wa Chaw's biographical approach is apparent (fig. 6.4).[38] The focus of the painting is a grief-stricken young woman holding what appears to be a very small baby or fetus. This figure is likely a self-portrait of Wa Wa Chaw with her deceased child. She is flanked on either side by her two mothers. Mary Duggan appears as a well-dressed society woman, with her grey hair swept under a black hat. Wa Wa

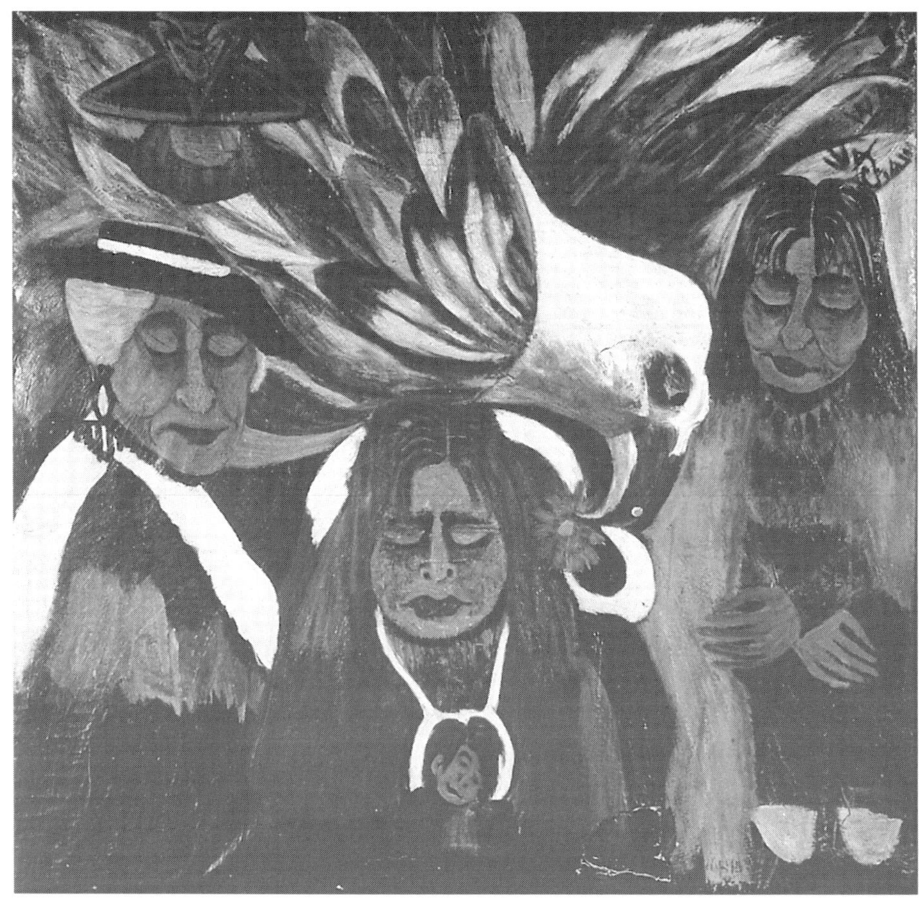

FIGURE 6.4
Bonita Wa Wa Calachaw Nuñez. . . . *Her Memory,*
n.d., oil on canvas, painted wood frame, 124 cm. x
125 cm. Photo by Katherine Fogden. Courtesy,
National Museum of the American Indian,
Smithsonian Institution, 25.1161.

Chaw's Native mother, in a simple dress and orange cape, her dark hair loose, also joins this mourning scene. Images of embracing Indian women and children, common throughout Wa Wa Chaw's work, seem to suggest the relationship she deeply missed with her biological mother. A deep emotional edge emerges in an untitled painting of a gray-haired elderly woman holding a young sleeping woman (fig. 6.5). The dramatic position of the young woman's head, her slightly disheveled hair hang-

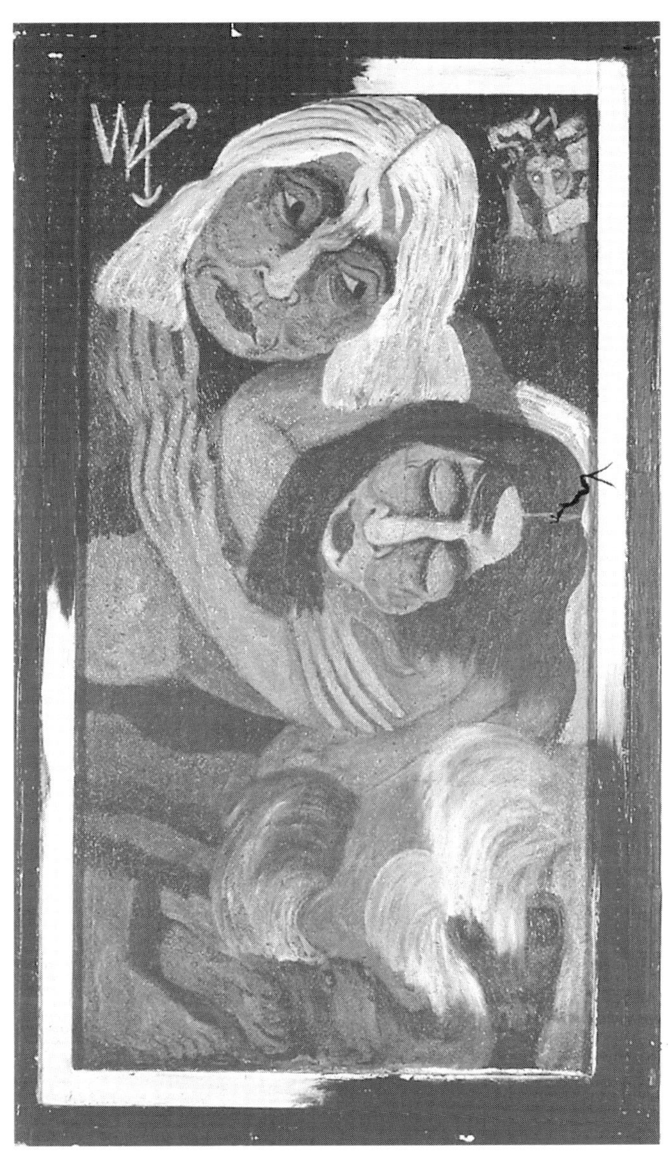

FIGURE 6.5
Bonita Wa Wa Calachaw Nuñez. Untitled, n.d., oil
on canvas, painted wood frame, 137.2 cm. x 72.4
cm. Photo by Katherine Fogden. Courtesy,
National Museum of the American Indian,
Smithsonian Institution, 25.1159.

ing in her face, and her nudity communicate a complete submission and vulnerability to the elderly woman's protective and affectionate embrace. The elderly woman, who is barefoot and wears a simple red-and-black dress, appears to be Native, possibly representing a wise Indian grandmother or mother. This elderly figure appears as a caring protector to the sleeping figure, who may be only unconsciously aware of her presence.

Depictions of the unconscious in Wa Wa Chaw's work are not uncommon. Like other New York artists in the 1930s and 1940s, she was probably exposed to the popular belief in the inherent spirituality of Native American art, as well as Jungian theories that linked the collective unconscious to the primordial consciousness.[39] Wa Wa Chaw may also have believed that through her unconscious experience she could connect with her Native ancestors, just as theorist John D. Graham explained in *Systems and Dialectics of Art*: "The purpose of art in particular is to re-establish a lost contact with the unconscious, . . . with the primordial racial past."[40]

From her childhood, Wa Wa Chaw was touted as a visionary with sensitive, extrasensory perception. Her parents appear to have been members of the Society for Psychic Research, which she believed was grounded in "scientific research." Wa Wa Chaw mentioned in her diaries that Mary Duggan was the host to one of the recognized pioneers in the spiritualist movement from Great Britain, Sir Oliver Lodge, and participated in seances held with Lodge at the home of May Pepper Vanderbilt. During this visit, Lodge even claimed to have known her already, perhaps through some psychic connection.[41] These supernatural relationships and influences can be seen throughout Wa Wa Chaw's paintings. She likely depicted mystical relationships with animals, spirits, and her racial past through the unconscious mind as part of her own experiences as a Native American woman. In a particularly moving detail of a largely autobiographical painting, a sleeping or dreaming woman (perhaps the artist?) is pictured clutching two small children to her chest while appearing to lie underwater (fig. 6.6). If this is a self-portrait, the depiction may represent a link between her unconscious mind and children lost in infancy.

Many of Wa Wa Chaw's paintings include prominent animals. In . . . *Her Memory* (fig. 6.4), a large bird hovers over the three central figures, its wings outstretched and a flower in its beak. In another, (fig. 6.5) a long-haired dog, possibly an Afghan hound, in the lower-right corner of the picture plane, is tucked protectively beneath the arm of the sleeping figure. Various animals, especially dogs and birds, appear throughout Wa Wa Chaw's work, suggesting a transformative or mystical relationship with the human subjects. Spirits also appear frequently, often rendered as grisaille figures sometimes interacting with the living. In one example three generations of women appear in the left of the frame, the oldest, a gray spirit figure (plate 7). In an unusual

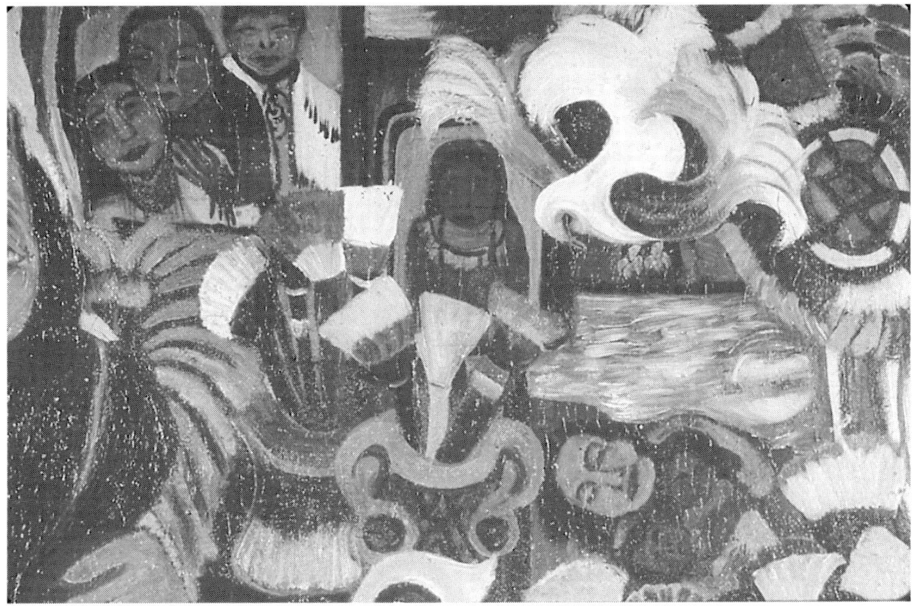

FIGURE 6.6
Bonita Wa Wa Calachaw Nuñez. Detail of
Untitled, n.d., oil on canvas, painted wood frame,
detail of plate 7. Photo by Gina Fuentes. Courtesy,
National Museum of the American Indian,
Smithsonian Institution, 25.1156.

grisaille painting the artist included what appears to be an entire village of spirits, most with melancholy expressions and closed eyes. The figures are twisted together, their hands long-fingered and clawlike. One female spirit, tucked beneath a large white bird, looks out from the picture frame smiling at the viewer.[42]

An Indian "Princess" Painter: Authenticity and Identity

The authenticity of Wa Wa Chaw's work as Native American art continues to be in question years after her death. The artist's own struggles with her identity as a Native woman and artist are boldly explored in her art and diaries. Today federal guidelines strictly define who can be "officially" recognized as an authentic Indian artist, but how do we define and authenticate Indian identity for a Native artist born in the nineteenth century to a tribe of displaced peoples?[43] At the time of Wa Wa Chaw's birth many southern California tribes were poverty-stricken and homeless. For the

Luiseño the 1880s were a tumultuous time. By 1889 their population totaled only 901. Land rights for Native people in southern California, previously referred to as "Mission Indians," were not firmly established. Although reservations had been established for some bands as early as 1870, others were evicted from their homes and displaced. The encroachment of Euro-American squatters on Indian settlements was a constant problem, forcing Native communities onto largely barren land with little or no supportable water supply. The first tribal enrollment for the Rincon Band of Luiseño did not occur until 1923.[44]

Although Wa Wa Chaw deeply missed the relationship with her culture of origin and biological family, as a young woman she was unable to locate her mother or family during a trip to reservations in southern California.[45] Horrified by the poverty, abuse, and neglect she witnessed, her traumatic experience may have exacerbated her conflicted feelings about betraying her adoptive parents. Despite rumors of people who knew her family, named "Calac," Wa Wa Chaw returned to New York. She was grateful for her privileged life and believed she had been rescued from a grim life of suffering. Removed from her biological family as an infant, she was raised entirely by non-Indians who had biased, late nineteenth-century stereotypical ideas about Indians and race. She learned about her culture from her adoptive parents and through a variety of Indian individuals with whom she came into contact because of their interest in the Indian cause. From her diaries it is apparent that Wa Wa Chaw was made aware of her status at an early stage in her life. The Duggans took pleasure in proudly showing off their "little Indian." Though surely considering themselves good Samaritans, they objectified and used her as an example of how the Indian could be saved from the heathen ways of Native culture.

Wa Wa Chaw was a child when she became an active representative and spokesperson for American Indians. Her first lecture on behalf of Indian women and the Indian cause occurred when she was about ten years old as she spoke to a women's group concerned with Indian welfare. A photograph taken about this time shows her in Native dress reading a dictionary. The significance of her identity as an educated Native woman is reflected in her attachment of newsprint copies of the photograph as a marker (or perhaps proof) of her identity on the back of many of her paintings. In addition to her signature, "Wa Wa Chaw," she also included the following biographical information in part or whole: "Born December 25 1888, Luiseño, Rincon Band (Mission Indian), Valley Center, California."[46]

A further influence on her identity was her reported participation in a traveling actors' troupe. As a young woman, she apparently lectured and performed throughout the country, especially on the Chautauqua circuit in the northeastern United States.[47] Her Indian identity was further reinforced, and like many other Indian performers (genuine and not), she probably adopted the designation "Princess" during this time. As a female Indian artist, her continued use of the title "Princess" was not unusual. Other contemporaneous "Indian princess" painters included Pop Chalee (Taos) and Jimalee Burton (Cherokee).

Wa Wa Chaw's concern for the Indians' welfare and her strong identification as an Indian woman led to her continued advocacy for American Indians. Carlos Montezuma was a particularly strong influence. A Yavapai from Arizona, he was adopted as a boy by a Euro-American man and raised in Chicago. Although trained as a medical doctor, he became an influential Indian activist and strong advocate for the abolishment of the reservation system and the Bureau of Indian Affairs. Like Wa Wa Chaw, he also worked throughout his life defending Indian people while struggling with his own identity as an adoptee, removed and raised outside his community of origin. His premature death from tuberculosis in 1923 was a profound loss for Wa Wa Chaw. They had become correspondents, possibly meeting through his involvement in the Eastern Association on American Indian Affairs in the early 1920s.[48]

Wa Wa Chaw's identity as an artist was also significant. In one of her autobiographical paintings, she included what appears to be a small self-portrait, a painting within a painting, depicting herself in Indian dress (fig. 6.6). The portrait is placed next to a second miniature portrait of a Native family; a man stands behind a woman embracing a child. Both pictures are directly behind two containers holding numerous paintbrushes. Using a similar convention in another painting, the artist appears to have depicted herself painting her own portrait. Her acceptance as both an Indian and an artist was extremely important as demonstrated in her experiences with the Philbrook Art Center.

Two of Wa Wa Chaw's paintings were purchased by the Philbrook Art Center in 1947 after their entry in the first two Annual American Indian Painting Exhibitions.[49] However, her later entries in the 1950s were rejected as were the works of other artists such as Oscar Howe (Yankton Sioux, 1915–83), who did not paint in the established "traditional" Indian style, defined by the Philbrook as "flat 2 dimensional." Wa Wa Chaw sent a bitter response to her repeated rejections. "To my Friends of Philbrook Art Center=I am a Portrait Painter=I feel you *are* not *interest*[ed] in that type of *Art.* Altho *[sic]* I was one of the first to enter the competitions. My paintings has *[sic]* always *been* return[ed] without results. I just cannot continue to Put Myself in *debt.*"[50]

In the reply to her protest, the curator implicitly expressed the Philbrook's institutional desire to preserve a style that was doomed to disappear, much like the vanishing Indian. "We at Philbrook realize that the traditional style of Indian painting will someday be no more, and while it still exists we would like to show it."[51] Ironically, Wa Wa Chaw's existence as an urban Indian was the result of the non-Indian's desire to save the Indian. The Philbrook's effort to preserve what they saw as the traditional style of Indian painting through the exclusion of other styles was an artificial attempt to freeze Indian art and expression in a timeless and unchanging past. Several years later, in 1965, her last entry to the competition was accepted.

Wa Wa Chaw's experiences with the Museum of the American Indian were similarly frustrating. Although she periodically stopped by the museum in the 1960s for a friendly chat with the assistant director, and later director, Frederick Dockstader, she was unable to convince the museum to purchase any of her paintings. At first unwilling to donate her paintings, she shared her frustrations in a 1963 letter to Jeanne Snodgrass, Indian art curator at the Philbrook. Wa Wa Chaw did not understand how museums could expect artists to donate, rather than sell, their work: "Come down to Earth!"[52] In her last effort to be recognized by the MAI, she made her large donation of paintings only two weeks before her death. Although the collection was eagerly accepted by the museum through Dockstader, the paintings were later misidentified as Modoc and "Culture Unknown" and were never exhibited.[53] At least one painting was sold at auction in 1975.[54]

In the late 1970s the publisher of *Spirit Woman* arranged for the paintings to be removed from the museum and photographed for the publication. After a dispute over the ownership was quickly and amicably settled in 1979, the majority of the paintings were accessioned. The remaining six were accessioned in 1997. Due to the artist's anonymity and the radically different character of her work, the paintings remained unappreciated and largely forgotten until recently.

Wa Wa Chaw was a powerful, complex woman, not shy about expressing her feelings and opinions verbally, on paper, or on canvas. Although she was raised in a non-Indian, urban environment, her Indian identity informed and influenced her work as an advocate for the Indian cause and her art. She did not fit expected definitions or expectations of Native people in the early twentieth century; neither did her art. Like all practicing artists, Wa Wa Chaw was strongly influenced by the art produced in her community. For this Indian artist, her world included the art of avant-garde New York and European artists. Her exposure to Indian culture and her understanding of Indian art were subject to the same biases and theories of other artists working in New York in the mid-twentieth century. In contrast to the work of her Indian artist contemporaries, her work reflects her Indian identity as an outsider rather than as a cultural insider.

The rejection of her art as authentically "Indian" based on her physical separation from her Native community only perpetuated restrictive, romantic preconceptions of Indian identity as existing in a pure and isolated state. Thousands of contemporary

Native people who live in urban communities today would surely protest this limiting definition of the Indian experience. While earlier scholars dismissed her by applying the same restrictive standards and expectations used for other Native American artists working in a different style under different circumstances, Wa Wa Chaw's work should be evaluated and appreciated within its context. The fact that her painting style and content is radically different from other Native American artists of her time should not negate her contribution to Native American art history.

If the worth we attribute to Indian art is there, as Richard Shiff has stated, "simply because the work has been done by people considered authentically 'native,'" we will compartmentalize Native art and miss the great depth and breadth that has remained undiscovered. Unless we look at the work of Wa Wa Chaw as reflecting the life and identity of an urban Indian, a woman displaced from but unwilling to give up her culture, then we discount and ignore a very real portion of the twentieth-century Native experience. The experience of removal and rediscovery of Indian identity continues today for many Native people, as it will continue in the future. Involuntarily separated from her culture of origin, as an artist Wa Wa Chaw expressed the pain and joy of this now-familiar Indian experience. Despite her struggle for recognition as an American artist, Wa Wa Chaw's identity as a Native American woman and as an individual was hers to claim and acknowledge in her art, whether it is accepted today or not.[55]

Notes

1. Roland Force, James Smith, Stan Steiner, William Stiles, and Douglas Latimer, miscellaneous correspondence, 1979, National Museum of the American Indian (NMAI), Registration Files, Cultural Resources Center, Suitland, Md. The collection of the Museum of the American Indian–Heye Foundation was transferred to the National Museum of the American Indian, Smithsonian Institution in 1989.

2. Frederick J. Dockstader, personal communication and interview, New York, 1997.

3. Wa Wa Chaw did not date her paintings. These dates are gleaned from documented entries in museum exhibitions.

4. See references to Wa Wa Chaw in the following sources: Gretchen M. Bataille, ed., *Native American Women: A Biographical Directory* (New York: Garland Publishing, 1993); Frederick J. Dockstader, *Great North American Indians: Profiles in Life and Leadership* (New York: Van Nostrand Reinhold, 1977); David M. Fawcett and Lee A. Callander, *Native American Painting: Selections from the Museum of the American Indian* (New York: Museum of the American Indian, 1982); Robert Henkes, *Native American Painters of the Twentieth Century: The Works of Sixty-one Artists* (Jefferson, N.C.: McFarland, 1995); Patrick Lester, *The Biographical Directory of Native American Painters* (Tulsa: Servant Education and Research Foundation, 1995); Jeanne Snodgrass, *American Indian Painters: A Biographical Directory* (New York: Museum of the American Indian, 1968); Lydia L. Wyckoff, ed., *Visions and Voices: Native American Painting from the Philbrook Museum of Art* (Tulsa: Philbrook Museum of Art, 1996).

Stan Steiner, ed., *Spirit Woman: The Diaries and Paintings of Bonita Wa Wa Calachaw Nuñez, an American Indian* (San Francisco: Harper and Row, 1980). See plates 207–9 and caption written by Edwin Wade (with Arthur Silberman) in "Controversy in Native American Art" in Wade, ed., *The Arts of the North American Indian: Native Traditions in Evolution* (New York: Hudson Hills Press, 1986), 235. Her work was included in two recent exhibitions and catalogs: Wyckoff, ed., *Visions and Voices,* and Sarah E. Boehme et al., *Powerful Images: Portrayals of Native America* (Seattle: Museums West in association with the University of Washington Press, 1998). See also Jennifer Jean Flint, " 'A Woman's Experience: From the Collection of Bonita Wa Wa Calachaw Nuñez.' An Exhibit Design," master's thesis, Oklahoma State University, 1998.

5. Wa Wa Chaw's diaries, drawings, and two paintings were collected from her apartment by Steiner in 1972 and later sold to collector Arthur Silberman. The Arthur and Shifra Silberman collection, containing Wa Wa Chaw's diaries and drawings, was acquired by the National Cowboy Hall of Fame, Oklahoma City, in 1997.

6. Steiner, *Spirit Woman,* 242–43.

7. Ibid., 100.

8. Robert G. Hays, *A Race at Bay: New York Times Editorials on "the Indian Problem," 1860–1900* (Carbondale and Edwards: Southern Illinois University Press, 1997), 16–17.

9. Steiner, *Spirit Woman,* 13–14.

10. Richard H. Pratt, *Battlefield and Classroom: Four Decades with the American Indian, 1867–1904,* ed. Robert M. Utley (New Haven: Yale University Press, 1964).

11. Dockstader, personal communication.

12. The Sherman Indian School archive does not confirm this claim.

13. Steiner, *Spirit Woman,* 76–77. Although I have found only one reference in her diaries to a child who died (Steiner, *Spirit Woman,* 83–84), Steiner suggests there may have been more (xiv).

14. Esther Finkelstein, personal communication and interview, Vestal, New York, 1998.

15. The quotation is from Kenneth Clark, *The Nude: A Study in Ideal Form* (Princeton: Princeton University Press, 1956), 7. According to Rosemary Betterton, in rare Christian depictions of the Virgin pregnancy "the Madonna's body becomes [a] symbol of the 'virginal maternal,' the impossible duality of inviolable and fertile body which is at the heart of the Christian ideal of womanhood"; "Mother Figures: The Maternal Nude in the Work of Käthe Kollwitz and Paula Modersohn-Becker," in *An Intimate Distance: Women, Artists, and the Body* (New York: Routledge, 1996), 33.

16. Ann Sutherland Harris and Linda Nochlin, *Women Artists, 1550–1950* (New York: Knopf and Los Angeles County Museum of Art, 1976), 66.

17. Steiner, *Spirit Woman,* 15.

18. Many of her medical and other drawings are intact and currently stored with her diaries at the National Cowboy Hall of Fame in Oklahoma City. Copies of her diaries, as well as some original correspondence, are in the collection of the Huntington Free Library, Bronx, New York.

19. Flint, " 'A Woman's Experience,' " 17.

20. The Philbrook Museum of Art was formerly known as the Philbrook Art Center.

21. Bernard Frazier to Wa Wa Chaw, with handwritten response from Wa Wa Chaw, June 23, 1947, Archives, Philbrook Museum of Art, Tulsa, Okla; Bonita Wa Wa Calachaw Nuñez, response, written on letter from Bernard Frazier, 1947, Archives, Philbrook Museum of Art, Tulsa, Okla.

22. Leslie Williamson, NMAI conservator, personal communication, 1997.

23. These six paintings are currently in a private collection in Manhattan, originally sold at auction in 1995. See *Fine American Indian Art,* Sotheby's Auction Catalog, Sale 6783, 1995.

24. Williamson, NMAI conservator, personal communication, 1997.

25. Nuñez, response to Bernard Frazier.

26. Dockstader, personal communication.

27. Lydia Wyckoff to Charles Putney, October 24, 1994, Archives, Philbrook Museum of Art, Tulsa, Okla.

28. The comments were made to me by an NMAI staff member, 1996.

29. Rather than give complete credit for the development of this style to Dorothy Dunn and her students as the term "Studio style" implies, Margaret Archuleta and Rennard Strickland use the term "Southwest style" in *Shared Visions: Native American Painters and Sculptors in the Twentieth Century* (Phoenix: Heard Museum, 1991), 72.

30. J. J. Brody, *Indian Painters and White Patrons* (Albuquerque: University of New Mexico Press, 1971), 128.

31. See Ernest Spybuck, *Procession before the Shawnee War Dance,* National Museum of the American Indian, Smithsonian Institution (02.5735).

32. Nuñez, biographical information form, n.d. [after 1946] Archives, Philbrook Museum of Art, Tulsa, Okla.

33. Nuñez, response to Bernard Frazier.

34. *Art Digest* regularly posted regional, state, and national exhibition opportunities in the column "Where to Show."

35. Frederick H. Douglas and Rene d'Harnoncourt, *Indian Art of the United States* (New York: Museum of Modern Art, 1941), 151.

36. Arthur Silberman compares her work with these artists in Rennard Strickland, "The Silberman Collection," *Persimmon Hill* (winter 1996): 29–36; Henkes, *Native American Painters,* 195, refers to these artists as her "painting heroes," although his source is not clear.

37. Harris and Nochlin, *Women Artists,* 263.

38. The entire title of this painting, written in pencil on a backing of brown paper, has been obscured. The fragmented title reads " . . . tingale, Her Memory."

39. W. Jackson Rushing, *Native American Art and the New York Avant-Garde: A History of Cultural Primitivism* (Austin: University of Texas Press, 1995), 97.

40. John D. Graham, ed., *Systems and Dialectics of Art* (London and New York: Delphic Studios, 1937), 15. For a full discussion of the relationship between Jungian theory and Native American art, see Rushing, *Native American Art,* 121–68.

41. Steiner, *Spirit Woman,* 27–29.

42. Not illustrated: Bonita Wa Wa Calachaw Nuñez. Untitled, n.d., oil on canvas, painted wood frame. National Museum of the American Indian, Smithsonian Institution, 25.1154.

43. The American Indian Arts and Crafts Act of 1990 stipulates that it is unlawful to falsely suggest an item for sale or display is Indian produced. The definition of "Indian" is stated as a "member of a federally-recognized tribe or a state-recognized tribe, or a person who is certified as an Indian artisan by an Indian tribe"; PL 101–644, Sect. 104.

44. Lowell John Bean and Florence Shipek, "Luiseño," in *California, Handbook of North American Indians,* ed. William Sturtevant, vol. 8 (Washington: Smithsonian Institution Press, 1978), 558.

45. Steiner, *Spirit Woman,* 110–12.

46. The original photograph has not been located. Newsprint copies referenced here are also found pasted in her diaries and pasted to a copy of her poem "The Indian Game," *The Indian: The Magazine of the Mission Indian Federation,* 1922, located in the Arthur and Shifra Silberman Collection, National Cowboy Hall of Fame, Research Center. A reproduction of the poem and image can also be found in Steiner, *Spirit Woman,* 109.

47. Dockstader, personal communication.

48. Ultimately Montezuma applied for enrollment in his tribe but was rejected for political reasons after making too many enemies in the federal government; Peter Iverson, *Carlos Montezuma*

and the Changing World of American Indians (Albuquerque: University of New Mexico Press, 1982), 153–60. For information on the Eastern Association on American Indian Affairs, see Arlene B. Hirschfelder, "Association on American Indian Affairs," in *Native America in the Twentieth Century: An Encyclopedia,* ed. Mary Davis (New York: Garland Publishing, 1994), 64–66.

49. Frazier to Wa Wa Chaw; Nuñez, response to Bernard Frazier.

50. Jeanne Snodgrass to Wa Wa Chaw, October 25, 1957; Nuñez to Jeanne Snodgrass, October 9, 1957, both in Archives, Philbrook Museum of Art, Tulsa, Okla.

51. Snodgrass to Wa Wa Chaw.

52. Nuñez to Jeanne Snodgrass, April 15, 1963, Native American Artists Resource Collection, Heard Museum, Phoenix, Arizona.

53. *Indian Notes and Monographs* (New York: Museum of the American Indian, 1973), 91; Fawcett and Callander, *Native American Painting,* 71.

54. This painting was item number 57 on the Museum of the American Indian Benefit Auction list, dated January 29, 1975. The painting was purchased by Charles M. Putney, a private collector who now lives in New Mexico; personal communication, 1998.

55. Richard Shiff, "The Necessity of Jimmie Durham's Jokes," *Art Journal* 51:3 (1992): 74.

The Hunt for Identity in Clarence Monegar's Wildlife Paintings

SAMUEL E. WATSON III

*I*n February 1942 the noted regionalist painter John Steuart Curry wrote to his dealer in New York City from his home in Madison, Wisconsin, urging him to consider the work of a successful local painter of "animals and birds," Clarence Monegar. In his enthusiasm for the artist, Curry praised the anatomical accuracy of Monegar's renderings as well as his unerring color sense.[1] While such actions typified Curry's generosity as artist-in-residence at the University of Wisconsin, this particular episode deserves closer attention, for subsequent praise heaped upon Monegar went beyond his technical proficiency as an artist. Indeed, while Curry's excitement at his "discovery" was focused primarily upon Monegar's artistic talent, the enthusiasm of others would be marked by a variety of social, artistic, and cultural discourses that centered upon Monegar's identity as a "full-blood Winnebago." As a Native American painter, Monegar's tale is both familiar and singular, for like many others, Monegar's initial success can be traced to a relationship with a famous Euro-American painter. However, Monegar's brand of mimetic illustration distinguishes his work and places it firmly outside the parameters of accepted Indian painting of the time. By foregrounding Monegar's Native American identity, as most writers of his day did, I examine how the Wisconsin artist's paintings were understood by patrons to possess something characteristically "Indian." To some degree, this corresponded with attitudes toward paintings being produced by other Native painters affiliated with the easel-painting movement centered in the Southwest. What is dramatically different, however, is the extent to which such attitudes would shape the imagery that was produced in each region.

In the past twenty-five years many facets of Native American easel painting have been explored in a wide variety of scholarly books and essays, as well as museum exhibitions. This attention has helped to make this once-neglected area of research one of the more significant in the field of Native American art history. Still, within the broader context of American painting, works by Native Americans continue to be largely ignored. This exclusion is particularly baffling considering how easily Native painting fits into the established canon of American art. Two factors seem primarily responsible for this artistic segregation. The first, and most obvious, is that Indian painting has historically been understood and promoted as a racial product. From its inception, Indian painting existed on a separate plane from current American artistic practices, and Native artists were encouraged to create only those works that communicated authentic tribal traditions. Thus salable paintings were to depict decorous Indian lifestyles and be stylistically indebted to supposedly traditional forms of Indian painting. Iconographic and stylistic evidence of Euro-American influence interfered with the romantic primitivism of this construct and was to be erased from all works. The painter John Sloan was a great advocate of this viewpoint, "[Indian painters] could never 'learn' anything from Modern American art. They should be kept away from extraneous influences and given sufficient encouragement to grow by expressing themselves in their own way. . . . So far there have been no American art exhibits in the pueblos—and may the Lord forbid it for many years to come!"[2]

The other related factor that contributes to the marginalization of the genre is that historic Indian painting continues to be defined largely by those same "authentic" stylistic and iconographic markers that were first articulated in the Southwest. The pervasiveness of this trope, which immediately calls to mind images of Pueblo or Navajo dancers painted in a flat, decorative manner, is actually quite similar to a problem inherent in American art generally. This problem is one of regional hegemony, in which work from one geographic region has dominated or even defined the artistic discourse of the entire nation. Just as the Northeast has historically defined Euro-American painting in this country, so has the Southwest governed our understanding of Native American painting in the twentieth century. Indeed, at midcentury, the aesthetic markers of Southwest Indian painting would come to define a pan-Indian style that was propagated by such institutions as the Santa Fe Indian School and the Philbrook Art Center in Tulsa. This would have unsettling consequences for Native American painting as the identification with one particular painting style would either pigeonhole artists into a singular mode of artistic expression or entirely exclude those whose work differed from its culturally defined stylistic parameters. Such an essentialist and reductive view has precluded serious scholarly inquiry into the careers of those artists not historically associated with the Indian painting movement. With a few exceptions, these painters have been doubly excluded: their cultural identity as Native American marks them as marginalized "other" within the larger context of American art, while their idiosyncratic artistic identity has divorced them from the context of Native American art.[3]

This essay represents an effort to deconstruct this paradigm by focusing on the career of Clarence Monegar, a Hochunk (Winnebago) painter of wildlife who worked far from the centers of Indian painting and whose works were neither stylistically nor iconographically "Indian"—at least insofar as this term was understood by promoters of Indian painting. Yet in Wisconsin, as in Santa Fe and Tulsa, Monegar's works were primarily understood to be products of his cultural identity. While this association did not manifest itself in any imposed stylistic guidelines, it clearly shaped Monegar's production and marketing of his works. This essay considers the implications of this primitivist reception of Monegar's work in order to understand the representational strategies Monegar would implement over the course of his career. In viewing Monegar's paintings it is important to remember that until recently, few marginalized artists were able to articulate overtly the psychic and physical conditions that marked their tenuous social positions while continuing to work within the dominant culture's representational systems. Because of this, the pictorial results of such artists have been perceived as conservative, if not altogether conformist. Recent studies have suggested, though, that a bit of atextual coaxing may disclose that such images can be read as "operating somewhere between resistant affirmation of cultural specificity and total accommodation to the host culture." Monegar's wildlife paintings seem to occupy such an ill-defined, liminal space. Although his works are fully immersed within the established traditions of wildlife painting, itself a field marginalized within art history, Monegar's identity as a Native American would become an important aspect of their meaning both to the artist and to his patrons.[4]

Life and Early Career

Clarence Boyce Monegar was born in Shawano County, Wisconsin, in 1910. While he was still a child attending the Indian Parochial School in Wittenberg his artistic talent was recognized and encouraged by the Reverend T. M. Rykken. Later, Monegar would receive his first regular art instruction at the Tomah Indian School where an instructor apparently took a special interest in Monegar and may have provided him with wildlife prints by John James Audubon after the boy had expressed an interest in nature drawing. After leaving the Indian School, Monegar attended Wittenberg High School for one year before he was forced to drop out in order to help support his mother and family after the death of his father. Years passed during which Monegar held a variety of jobs—usually as a seasonal laborer, occasionally as a sign painter. One notable exception occurred in 1927 when Monegar embarked upon a stint with a circus, which allowed him to travel the country for six months.[5]

In 1932 he married and settled near Black River Falls until 1940. It is from this period that the earliest extant works (1936) by Monegar were completed. Although what prompted Monegar to begin producing and peddling his paintings remains unclear—it was most likely out of sheer economic necessity—he soon found a regular patron in J. Bruce Van Gorden who owned a flour mill in the town. In addition to the modest sales of his paintings, Monegar continued to find employment as a laborer during this period; however this environment of relative stability came to an end in 1940 when Monegar's wife and the mother of his four children contracted tuberculosis and subsequently died. Soon afterward Monegar was charged with failure to adequately support his children and was imprisoned in the county jail at Neillsville. In jail, Monegar spent part of his time drawing pencil sketches of wildlife that so impressed his captors they provided the artist with additional art supplies. With these, Monegar painted and drew images of wild animals in realistic settings, which he then sold to his jailers and other law enforcement personnel. Eventually, Monegar was paroled to the care of the district attorney who personally drove Monegar and his paintings to the campus studio of John Steuart Curry in Madison with the hope that Curry would recognize Monegar's talent and possibly help the artist develop his artistic skills into a lucrative occupation. Although the extent of the training Monegar received at the hands of Curry is unclear—at the time Curry was not teaching regular art classes and did not accept students—Monegar stayed for several months in Madison, where he received some form of instruction from Curry. Later, Monegar would recall the experience as the turning point of his life.

By all accounts, Curry was immediately struck by the quality of Monegar's work and was eager to help him succeed. From his initial letter to his dealer, Reeves Lowenthal of Associated American Artists, in February 1942 until the last of his Monegar correspondence in June of the same year, Curry's writing bristles with enthusiasm over his artistic discovery. Curry was not only impressed by the self-taught craftsmanship evident in Monegar's paintings but also excited by the ready market he imagined Monegar would find for his work. Curry repeatedly emphasized Monegar's sales success in Wisconsin and urged his dealer to find other patrons for the artist in New York. Curry's letters represent the only writings about Monegar that do not focus primarily upon his identity as a Native American painter. Instead, Curry was moved by Monegar's artistic talents.

> I think you can sell these [Monegar's paintings] almost as fast as he can make
> them. . . . He has had no formal art training whatsoever, and has learned all his

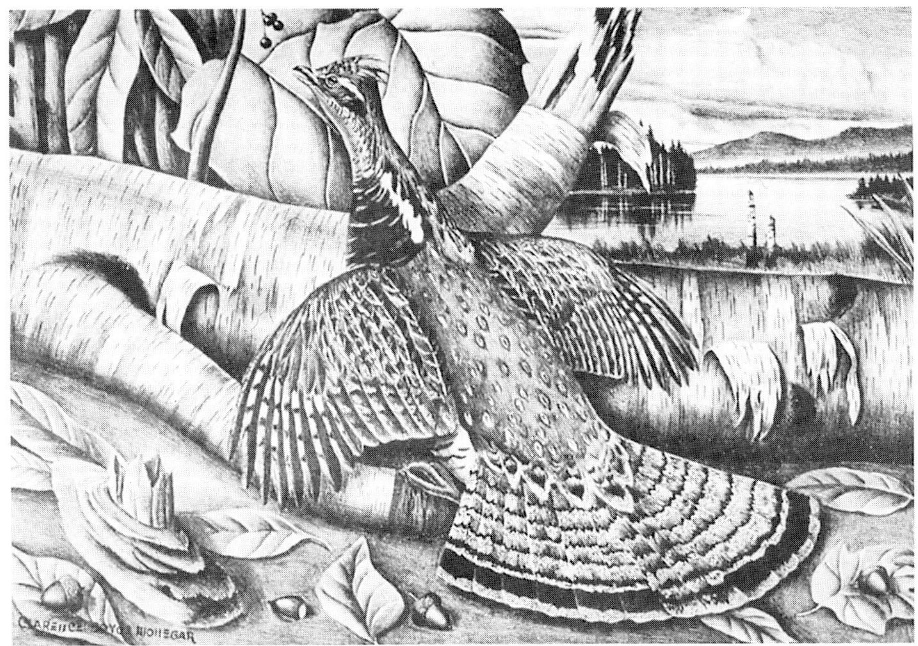

FIGURE 7.1
Clarence Monegar. *Feeding Grouse*, 1943,
lithograph. Private collection.

form from magazines, lithographs, etc., and natural history books. I am certain he does not lift his work as I have been up to his studio watching him work. In my opinion he is vastly superior to those other animal and bird artists, particularly in his rendering of color and textures. He has a beautiful color sense. People who know say his deer and birds are absolutely correct, which means a great deal to sportsmen, etc. I think a possibility is that you could sell his work commercially to sporting magazines. Also I am certain, as I said before, that sportsmen will like them at once. They certainly have out here.[6]

Soon after their first meeting, Curry gave Monegar a lithograph stone that had been in Curry's studio and encouraged him to try his hand at lithography. Curry reported good progress on Monegar's first effort (a "dandy") although it was turned down by the dealer. A later lithograph, *Feeding Grouse* (fig. 7.1), was more successful and an edition of sixty was printed and quickly sold. Monegar had additional success at the annual Rural Arts Show at the University of Wisconsin where he regularly submitted paintings and routinely sold all that he displayed. In 1945 this period came to an end for Monegar when he was drafted into the army and served as an ambulance driver. Upon his return to Wisconsin in 1946, Monegar went to Chicago and attended classes at the Art Institute. Monegar eventually settled in Milwaukee where he continued to paint wildlife scenes and to exhibit them until his death in 1968.

The Van Gorden Collection

While Monegar gained regional fame with his wildlife paintings, an examination of Bruce Van Gorden's collection of early works by Monegar reveals that the artist's oeuvre was initially more diverse. Based upon the work in this collection, later exhibition lists of his works that are currently unlocated, and oral histories, a loose framework can be established in which it appears that early in the painter's career he most frequently painted romantic images of Indians that fully embraced Native American stereotypes. Indeed, at least some of these early works appear to have been directly copied from paintings and illustrations by non-Native artists. Over time, however, Monegar would virtually abandon such iconography to focus instead upon painting the detailed, carefully nuanced images of wild animals that would garner strong sales and for which the artist would receive regional acclaim. Before this success, however, the work that Monegar produced and that Van Gorden purchased during the late 1930s was an eclectic mix, suggesting a great deal of experimentation by the young and inexperienced artist. While all are rendered in a finely detailed graphic style that emphasizes illusionistic, three-dimensional space, the subject matter varies considerably. Of the ten paintings and drawings still in the Van Gorden family's possession, two are portraits of family members, three depict Plains Indians on horseback, three portray Woodlands hunters with their prey in a forest setting, and two are highly detailed paintings of wildlife set in the Wisconsin landscape.

The two portraits from this period testify to Monegar's willingness to experiment with form and subject matter and to his commitment to naturalistic draftsmanship. The first of these is a portrait that depicts S. H. Van Gorden, Bruce Van Gorden's father (fig. 7.2). To realize this portrait, Monegar was given a photograph by the younger Van Gorden, which he faithfully reproduced in pencil and pastel. The resulting image is a very competent translation of a photographic subject into a graphic one with wide areas of flatness, a subdued palette, and a stiff frontality attesting to the work's photographic source. While Van Gorden's body is somewhat blocky and angular, Monegar's rendering of the face is nevertheless quite sensitive. Another work that was also based upon a photograph presents Mr. and Mrs. Bruce

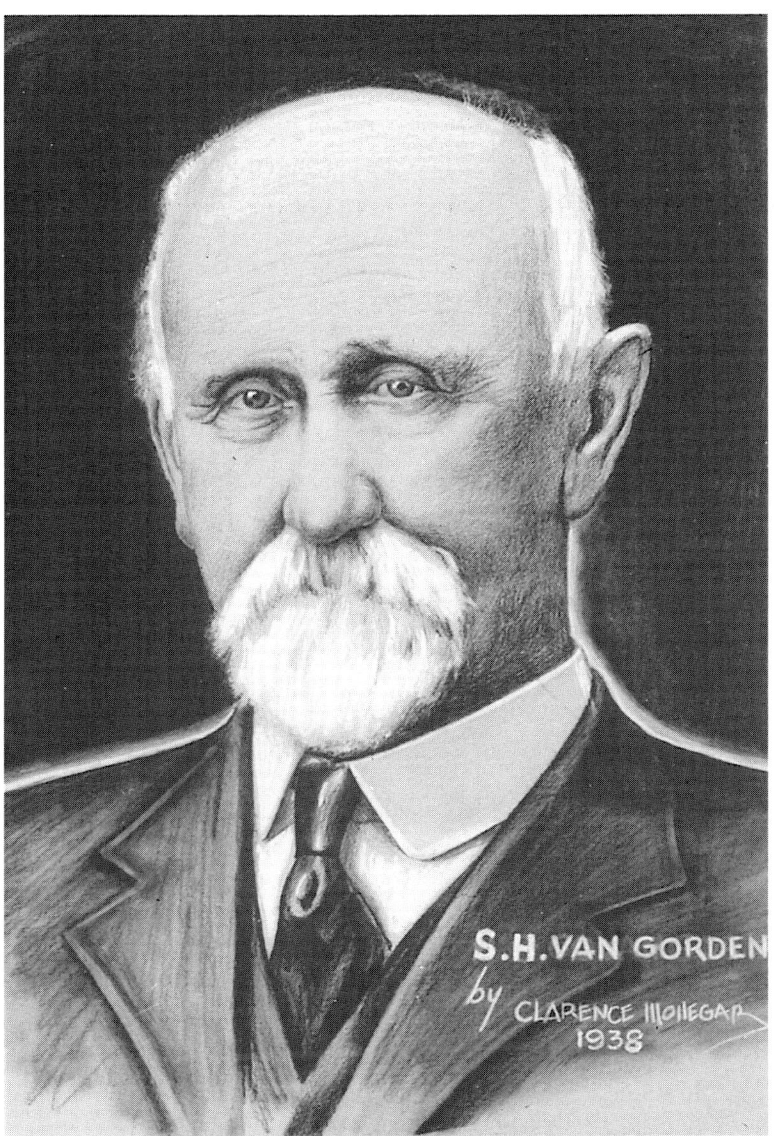

F I G . 7 . 2
Clarence Monegar. *S. H. Van Gorden,* 1938, pencil
and pastel on paper. Private collection.

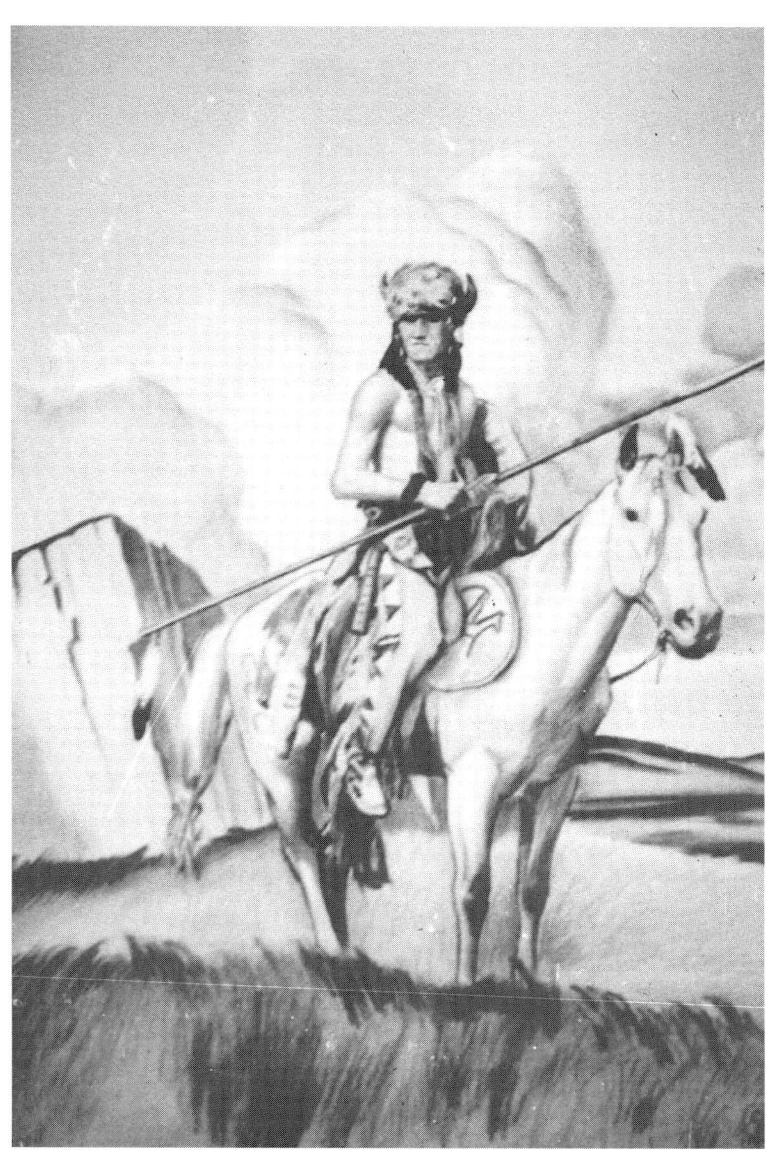

FIGURE 7.3
Clarence Monegar. Untitled, 1940, pencil, crayon,
watercolor on paper. Location unknown. Photo
courtesy of Joann Dougherty.

Van Gorden as they appeared before leaving for a costume party. The two were dressed as a Hochunk couple in clothing they had borrowed from a local Hochunk family. In neither painting is there any background setting; instead the figures exist against a neutral void.

Two pendant works from 1940 each illustrate a generic Plains male astride his horse. In one (fig. 7.3), the figure appears to be a warrior, as he wears a buffalo headdress, carries a feathered lance and a painted rawhide shield, and sits atop a horse that is adorned with eagle feathers. Set in a grassy landscape accented by sheer rock bluffs in the middle ground and rolling hills in the background, the warrior and horse pause and stare out of the painting as if scanning the horizon for signs of life, while behind the figure ominous thunderclouds gather. In the other work, the male figure lacks any heraldic regalia, wearing only moccasins and a breech cloth, with one eagle feather in his hair (fig. 7.4). Unlike the warrior, this figure, which Monegar titled *Scout,* stares out of the picture frame directly at the viewer. The landscape is quite similar to that of the former work, with identical grassy plains and stone outcroppings; however, in the distant background low-lying, blue mountains can be seen. In these paired images, Monegar was clearly learning about visual design and spatial relationships as these figures are the compositional inverse of each other. While the warrior sits astride a horse that frontally faces the left side of the composition, the scout's mount faces the rear and right half of the composition. Similarly, the warrior is presented frontally with an emphasis on the right half of his body, while the scout is seen from the rear as he pivots in his seat and presents the viewer with the left side of his body. These compositions are not the original work of Monegar but are copies of works by W. H. D. Koerner, a popular painter and illustrator whose works appeared as numerous magazine covers and story illustrations during the 1920s and 1930s. A comparison of Koerner's 1931 *Warrior's Hand of Battle* with Monegar's identical *Scout* of 1940 reveals that Monegar "lifted" the subject and composition from Koerner.[7]

A related group of works depicts solitary Native American hunters in forest settings. These works demonstrate a greater emphasis on three-dimensional illusionism, an increased compositional complexity, and a richer use of color, which stands in marked contrast to the starkness of the Plains illustrations. Typical of these works is an untitled painting (plate 9) in which a large, shirtless male hunter holds a bow and stands behind the lifeless body of a deer he has just killed. In the immediate foreground, the prow of a birch-bark canoe rises at the hunter's feet and directs the viewer's eye toward the back of the composition, as does the backward glance of the hunter. Here, a moose, dwarfed by giant fir trees and a mountain range in the distance, tentatively steps into a river or lake. The change in Monegar's palette is striking as he chose a rich, saturated yellow for the long grass that covers the foreground

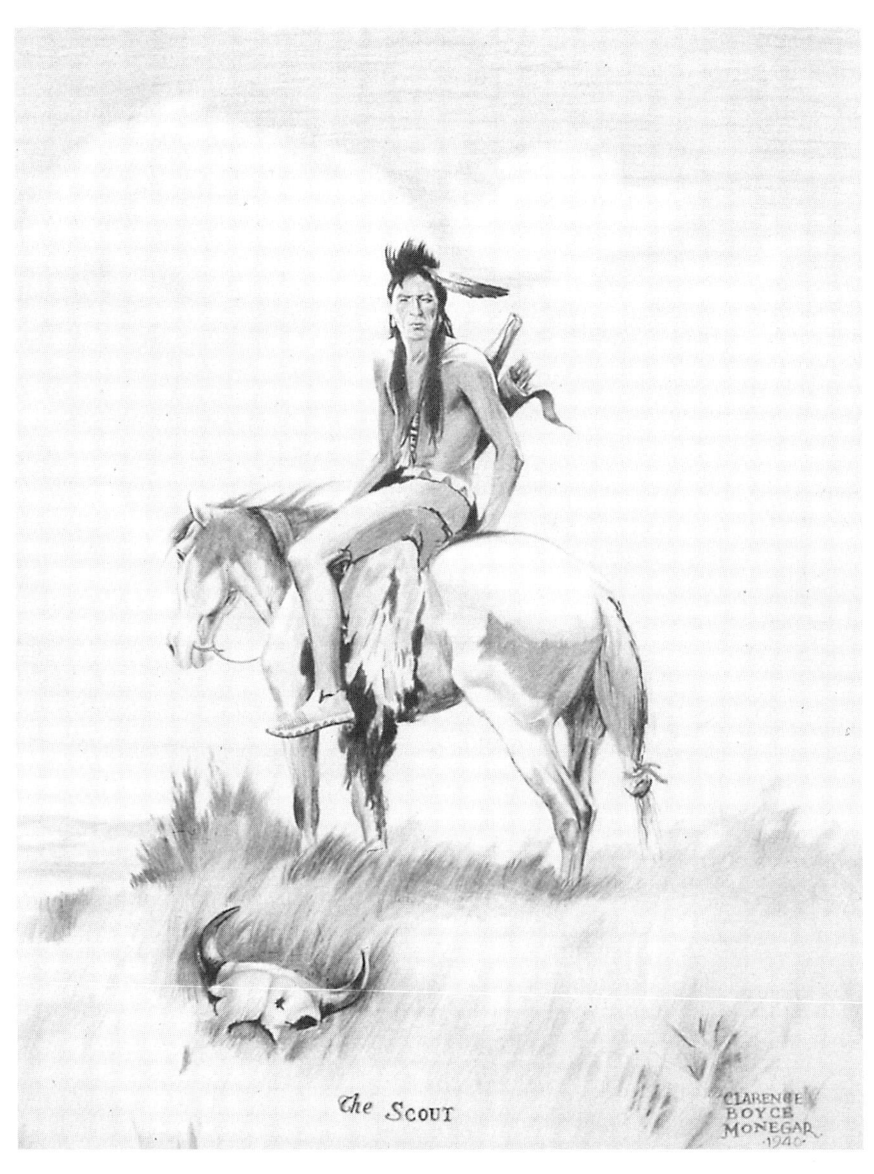

FIGURE 7.4
Clarence Monegar. *Scout,* 1940, pencil, crayon,
watercolor on paper. Private collection.

as well as the distant background. The darkness of the evergreens in the distance anchors and balances this liberal use of yellow, as does the bright reddish orange of a small bush in the middle ground that further isolates the figure of the hunter. Two other paintings are similar in subject matter and pictorial intricacy: one depicts a hunter paddling a birch-bark canoe with a slain deer in the bow; the other presents a hunter retrieving ducks he has just shot with his bow and arrow.

Yet even as certain of Monegar's hunting scenes seem to exhibit both a greater formal sophistication and a compositional elaboration, his choice of subject matter, like that of his Plains subjects, continued to be highly dependent on a romanticized type of Indian image constructed by Euro-American artists and illustrators. The Indian hunter with his prey who stands silhouetted against a forested, watery backdrop is a nostalgic trope that closely links Native Americans with wild, untamed nature and is a common motif in paintings and illustrations of the time. While it is doubtful that Monegar would have had any direct experience with those paintings that defined this romantic type, by the 1930s the theme had become a familiar enough staple through its dissemination in popular prints, magazine illustrations, and especially in advertisements.[8] The perpetuation of such conventions by a Native artist illustrates the degree to which false or stereotyped representations of a colonized group that are created and distributed by the dominant society can come to shape the very people who are being inaccurately portrayed. Charles Taylor writes: "Our identity is partly shaped by recognition or its absence, often by the misrecognition of others, and so a person or group of people can suffer real damage, real distortion, if the people or society around them mirror back to them a confining or demeaning or contemptible picture of themselves. Nonrecognition or misrecognition can inflict harm, can be a form of oppression, imprisoning someone in a false, distorted, and reduced mode of being."[9]

Gerald Vizenor ironically refers to such stereotypes of Native Americans through the use of the lowercase, italicized *indian*. For Vizenor, this term embodies both the initial and the continual misidentification and misrepresentation of Native peoples by Euro-Americans and signifies the absence of authentic Native expression. In this sense, Monegar's early paintings should more properly be considered as depicting this *indianness*, as signifying absence. Though the markers of *indian* are present in the work, these depictions have little relevance to the life of the Hochunk Clarence Monegar, or to any other twentieth-century Native American. Rather, Monegar illustrates those *indians* who most accurately reflect the romantic nineteenth-century constructs that continued to resonate with the wider Euro-American public of the time.[10]

Absence seems further encoded in these romantic images when viewed alongside the portraits of Van Gorden family members. The disparity between Monegar's

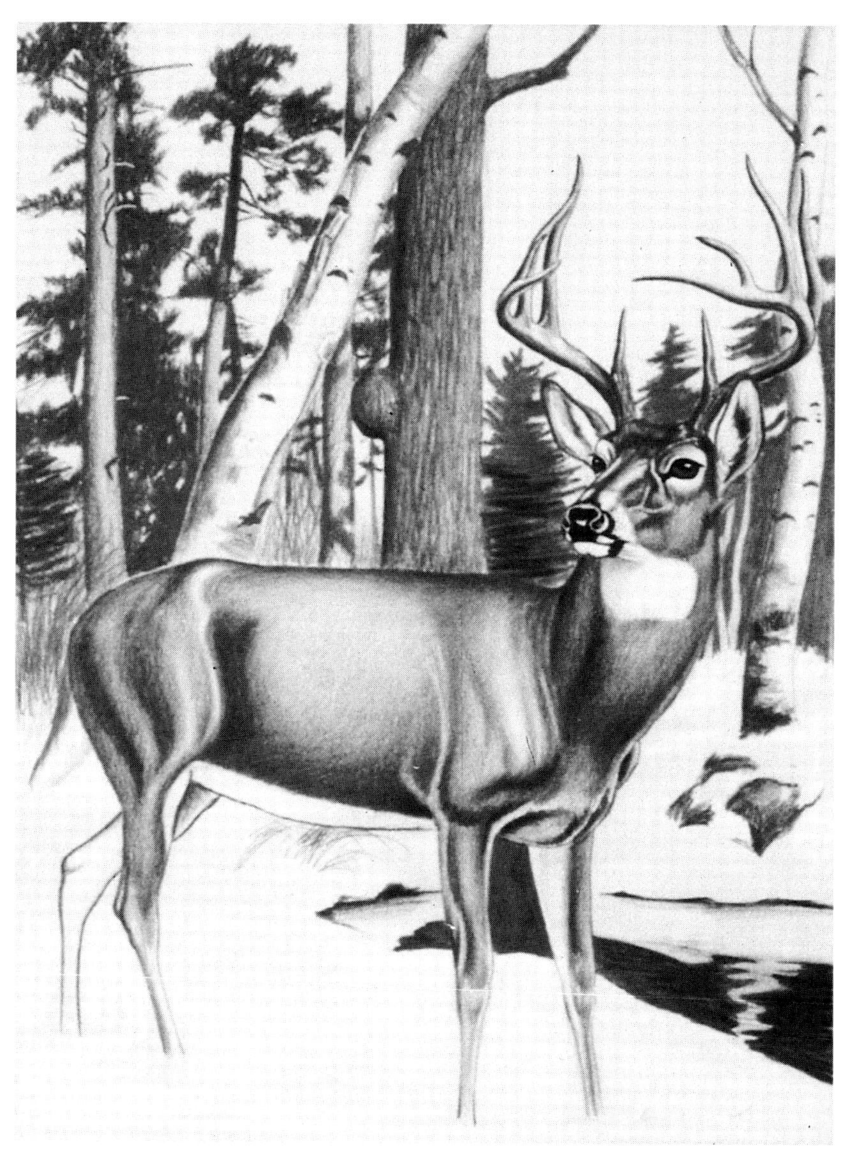

FIGURE 7.5
Clarence Monegar. *Buck in the Snow,* 1942, pencil
on paper. Private collection.

images of imagined *indians* and his depictions of actual Euro-Americans is formally based upon the artist's use of photographic sources for the latter images and conceptually linked to assumptions of photographic veracity. Because Monegar was working from photographs, his images of the Van Gordens are marked by a commitment to a mechanically reproduced naturalism, seen most notably in the closely rendered facial details, which seems to impart an actual historic presence that belies the lack of any contextual background setting. Thus, it is particularly ironic (and tragic) that the image of Mr. and Mrs. Bruce Van Gorden masquerading as Hochunks seems somehow more "authentic" (in a veristic sense) than those paintings that illustrate generic warriors and hunters *(indians)* occupying landscape scenes that seem wholly derivative and constructed.[11]

At this early stage, Monegar was also producing the wildlife scenes for which he was to later receive local acclaim. While these and later wildlife paintings by Clarence Monegar may seem innocuous enough, their production over the course of Monegar's career can be understood as the realization of an artistic exploration in which complicated issues of identity, personal as well as social, are played out. That these works can be interpreted as something more than mere illustration is evident in the undated *Buck in the Snow,* which presents a large male deer pausing as if just sensing danger (fig. 7.5). The buck is shown from the side standing beside the bank of a stream. The surrounding wooded forest has been blanketed in snow, creating an atmosphere of quiet and stillness that pervades the image. While the emphasis on wildlife is a departure from the other paintings in Van Gorden's collection, a comparison between the pose of Monegar's Plains warrior and that of the white-tailed buck suggests that the two are ideologically linked, both embodying themes of nature, freedom, and impending conflict. In the two works, a central horned figure stands cautiously in a wilderness landscape with his head cocked to the right. Dressed for combat, the warrior is poised for action as he strains to locate his enemy in the nearby surroundings, while similarly the alert buck scans his environment for signs of danger. Despite the implied precariousness of their situation, both figures exhibit confidence and strength in their respective environments.

Nevertheless there is a major difference between the two images: one depicts a human on the grassy plains; the other, a deer in the northern woods. Still, it would be a mistake to dismiss the similarities between the two based solely on this disparity in subject and setting; for while it initially appears that human presence has been erased in *Buck in the Snow* it may be that effacement has taken place rather than total erasure. In other words, the *indian* has been removed from the wilderness composition, only to be replaced by a barely concealable symbol of the Native American, the wild animal. Indeed, if we press further, this symbolic Native American can be interpreted as Clarence Monegar himself. If such a claim seems preposterous, consider the context in which Monegar was working.

Monegar painted in an era in which Indians were supposed to paint in a definably Indian style. This form of cultural relativism shaped the Indian painting movement in the Southwest where Pueblo artists were held to a centuries-old style of painting by patrons and promoters who understood artistic innovation to be akin to cultural degradation. In Wisconsin, a state comparatively devoid of the large numbers of anthropologists and cultural do-gooders who clustered around Santa Fe, there is little to suggest that ideas of cultural relativism impacted the arts of Native Americans. If such ideas had been prevalent its advocates would have been hard-pressed to single out any indigenous artistic practice among the Hochunks to which Clarence Monegar could lay claim in his painterly pursuits. Indeed, the internal disorganization and seeming rootlessness of the tribe by the 1930s appears almost as the antithesis to the sedentary, traditional life of the Pueblos.[12]

Yet to a degree, Indians were thought to be Indians and if their art could not be understood in terms of any authentic style, people would turn to subject matter in order to find something innately Native. In this regard, Monegar's work could be understood as the unique expression of an Indian sensibility if strong associations were made between his identity as a Hochunk and as a painter of wildlife. In the following biographical sketch of the artist the animalistic qualities ascribed to Monegar clearly link him to the wildlife that he paints. "Brooding, restless, of full-blood Winnebago stock, Clarence Monegar in his temperaments, habits, and art seems to express typical Indian characteristics. He is nomadic, taciturn, childlike; the subjects of his paintings are running deer, feeding grouse, and flying ducks in the woods and by the rivers of his native homeland. He is a keen observer of both man and nature. He can converse on the art and society of his times in excellent English." Similarly, a journalist would write, "Paintings by Monegar focus on the forests and fields of Wisconsin with a perception that is not only accurate but temperated [*sic*] with knowledge and respect inherited from generations of devotion." Clearly these authors understood Monegar's production of wildlife paintings to have been extensions of his Native American identity. As a consequence, Monegar's meticulously rendered wildlife scenes were seen as proof of the romantic belief that Native Americans lived in harmonious interdependence with nature.[13]

While Native Americans had been conceptually linked with their natural environment by Europeans since contact, during the 1930s this romantic construction was being specifically utilized by proponents of environmental conservation and wildlife management. In this decade human destructiveness had resulted in a series of environmental disasters that dramatically raised public awareness of the need for rethinking man's relationship with nature. From his home in Wisconsin, Aldo Leopold became a leading proponent of "biocentrism"; the idea that all living things are connected and that all living things have the right to function in their natural environments.[14] Over time Leopold specifically developed his "land ethic," which sought to "enlarge the boundaries of the community to include soils, waters, plants, and animals, or collectively: the land." Native Americans were often invoked by Leopold, and other early conservationists, for their intuitive understanding of this land ethic. In this way, Leopold perpetuated the construct of the natural, environmental Indian in contrast to the overcivilized, conquering European. While Leopold's aim was to laud the environmental consciousness of Natives, he most frequently relegated them and their contributions to the past. In an explanation of the concept of food chains and how they have been irreparably altered by consumption patterns, Leopold wrote, for example, "thus soil-oak-deer-indian is a chain that has now been largely converted to soil-corn-cow-farmer." If we understand this equation to be one of increasing domestication, and thus by degrees a separation from nature, the Indian/farmer dichotomy reveals Leopold's failure to conceptualize Native Americans as anything other than pure nature. Clearly his system of direct contrasts (oak/corn, deer/cow) also implies that the farmer can only be understood as non-Native or European. The corollary would further suggest that the Indian was incapable of acting as a farmer and could only occupy the role of hunter.[15]

During this period of awakening environmental consciousness, Euro-American hunters and sportsmen would take a leading role among wildlife advocates. Recognizing the need for the preservation of natural habitats, as well as the protection of species once considered expendable, hunters formed powerful alliances that lobbied Congress for legislation to protect the country's interior.[16] Among this group, most recognized the superiority of Native American ecological habits and viewed Native American hunting practices and philosophies as admirable and worthy of emulation. Readers of books and magazines of the era were instructed that Native Americans were the country's first hunters and exemplified high moral standards. One writer bemoaned the difference between Indian hunters of the past and hunters of his era. "How different it has been with the white man of today. His lust for the sporting hunt must be tightly controlled by laws. Even the laws do not always deter for there has been a particular breed known as the game hog. He has no reasoning, no compassion, no foresight. He shoots to fill the pile. He takes all and gives nothing in return. Luckily, the tide is beginning to turn. . . . Perhaps someday we may have the humbleness, the gratefulness, and the reverence of those who came before us, the Indians of the Woodland."[17]

Often, hunters alone in the wilderness stalking their game imagined themselves sharing a primal kinship with Indians of the past. José Ortega y Gasset understood this aspect of hunting to be its ultimate nature. He saw hunting as a transcendence of the present and as a way of invoking an inner "natural man" who exists beneath the surface of man's civilized façade. In the United States this "natural man" was most immediately knowable as an Indian. In the Southwest, Aldo Leopold experienced this elision of identities as he hunted a deer among the architectural ruins of a prehistoric Indian site. "I overshot, my arrow splintering on the rocks the old Indian had laid. As the buck bounded down the mountain with a goodbye wave of his snowy flag, I realized that he and I were actors in an allegory. Dust to dust, stone age to stone age, but always the eternal chase!" While Leopold does not invoke the Native American by name, the setting of the incident as well as his choice of the bow and arrow as his weapon have clearly provided the context for the hunter's identification with the Native.[18]

In targeting hunters and sportsmen as the primary patrons of his wildlife paintings, Clarence Monegar surely understood the romantic appeal of linking hunting with the Native. Indeed, his early images of *indian* hunters effectively embody this trope. Monegar's actions suggest that he further encouraged a conflation of his own personal Native American identity with that of his wildlife iconography, for at some point after 1942, Monegar began painting a small red arrowhead after his signature as a signifier of his Indian identity. People came to believe that this was some type of pictographic representation of his Hochunk name ("Red Arrow"), and, at Monegar's death, obituaries would list it as such. In fact, however, according to the artist's brother, Monegar's Hochunk name actually translates as "Little Rain." The red arrowhead was an invention of Monegar's that he incorporated into his signature as a way of communicating his Native identity to a primarily Euro-American audience. Monegar felt that this detail appealed to those many who wanted to purchase a painting by an authentic Native American.[19] In addition, the inclusion of the red arrowhead was an act that assured the elision of Monegar's identity with the wildlife he painted. The juxtaposition of this arrowhead, a symbol of the ancient hunt, with its animal targets marks the scene as authentically primal like Monegar (the "full-blood" observer of nature) himself. Additionally, this strategy legitimated his observations of nature by using his Native identity (and its implied closeness to nature) as a seal attesting to the veracity of the wildlife images he created. In this way, his works clearly conflated ideas of the Indian and nature in an easily discernible manner that would have been understood by those hunters who purchased Monegar's wildlife images.

An additional strategy utilized by Monegar can be seen in his treatment of the landscape. As Monegar concentrated on the production of wildlife paintings, he moved from the generalized settings found in his *indian* paintings to very specific locales found in central and northern Wisconsin. Patrons applauded this celebration of the local and were eager to own such works. Such an emphasis needs to be understood within the larger context of American art in the 1930s and 1940s, for it corresponds with the trend toward regionalism and localism that marks the years between the two world wars in this country. As Thomas Craven put it, "the only outlet, the sole means of escape for the American painter lies in the discovery of the local essence, after which we may hope for a viable native school." In addition to Monegar's work with Curry, who undoubtedly meted out similar advice, the Hochunk painter would have been further exposed to such ideas through his frequent associations with the annual exhibition of the Rural Arts Program at the University of Wisconsin.[20]

The Rural Arts Program was the logical outcome of this commitment to nativism espoused by Craven, Curry, and others. The program was conceived by Curry and Chris Christensen, dean of the College of Agriculture at the University of Wisconsin, in 1939 as a means of encouraging artistic production among the residents of Wisconsin rural farming communities. It operated quite simply; county agents were alerted to watch for local painters and sculptors, who were then encouraged to submit their work to Curry for possible inclusion in the annual exhibition. Curry judged the works and put together an exhibition that was part of the school's yearly "Farm and Home Week." From its first year the program was a great success and by its second, the show was attracting more than fourteen thousand visitors and the attention of *Life* magazine, which did a photographic feature on the event. For many of the artists involved with the program, like Monegar, this was an inestimable opportunity to exhibit their works and reap the rewards of their efforts, whatever those may have been. In a 1949 letter to John Barton, director of the program, the rural artist Lela Smith undoubtedly expressed the sentiments of many: "My art may not mean a lot to the rest of the world, but it has changed my whole life for the past nine years."[21]

Monegar's affiliation with the Rural Arts Program offered him more than personal satisfaction; it redirected his life toward an art career. The exhibitions of the Rural Arts Program brought his paintings before large numbers of potential patrons who would otherwise never have heard of the artist. While Monegar was never able to survive off the sale of his work alone, he received regional acclaim for his talents and continued to sell his work in great numbers for the duration of his life. Additionally, the show provided a context in which to place Monegar. As a rural artist, Monegar was understood to be part of a larger artistic group that found support from an enthusiastic public. Individually these artists may have been viewed as idiosyncratic, but together they formed an important cross-section of Wisconsin citizens. While Monegar's Native American identity would always mark him as different within this group, it was nevertheless certainly mediated by this artistic identity.[22]

A key to understanding the identity issues with which artists such as Clarence Monegar must have grappled, at least subconsciously, can be found in certain post-colonial texts that have sought to define the dislocated or fragmented position occupied by the oppressed within the colonial system. In his consideration of the writings of Franz Fanon, for example, Homi Bhabha writes of the multifaceted conditions that underlie the process of identification for the disenfranchised. Fundamental to this process for Bhabha is the realization that "to exist is to be called into being in relation to an otherness"; in other words, the "them" always defines the "us." In this dialogic encounter, the Native experiences a psychic split when he desires that position of power held by the colonial oppressor and yet still wishes to retain defining aspects of traditional character. Bhabha further summarizes the dilemma of identity: "The question of identification is never the affirmation of a pregiven identity, never a self-fulfilling prophecy—it is always the production of an image of identity and the transformation of the subject in assuming that image. The demands of identification—that is, *to be* for an Other—entails the representation of the subject in the differentiating order of otherness. Identification . . . is always the return of an image of identity that bears the mark of splitting in the Other place from which it comes." Monegar's early works speak of this struggle for identification and can be understood in light of such a process. From Plains warrior to Woodlands hunter to wildlife scenes, Monegar's oeuvre can be seen as an illustrated quest for the appropriate representational means of communicating his unique identity in 1930s and 1940s midwestern America.[23]

The artist's decision to imprint his Native identity in the form of the red arrowhead on his wildlife compositions clearly indicates the presence of such representational strategies. Yet ultimately the identity best symbolized by this arrowhead was not Monegar's personal, Hochunk one, but his public *indian* one. In a sense, this was Monegar's act of dressing in feathers or of playing Indian; in other words, he was providing the public with a symbol of Indianness they had come to desire. The real Clarence Monegar was not "Red Arrow," but a Hochunk man whose life was one of hardship—marked by tragic deaths and personal and tribal estrangement. In short, his life was not the romantic, close-to-nature existence his nature paintings would imply.[24]

This is not to say, however, that his wildlife paintings were in any way fraudulent or false; rather if we imagine that the animals portrayed by Monegar acted as surrogate selves for the artist, and thus a means of escape, I think we get a closer sense of Monegar as an individual and a truer idea of the importance of the paintings. To understand this identification, consider that while languishing in jail Monegar began to paint, in earnest, his images of birds and animals that roamed freely through the rural Wisconsin landscape, often in flight from some unseen danger (plate 10). These were acts of creation that not only allowed him to temporarily transcend his immediate surroundings but also would eventually lead to his release from jail and provide a lifelong means of financial support.[25] It seems easy to imagine that for the remainder of his culturally determined life, Monegar would want to continue to identify with symbols of freedom and transcendence, if only in his private longings. To be sure, this conflation of Monegar-as-wildlife invokes the same stereotype of Native-American-as-nature mentioned earlier. Yet if Euro-Americans were looking to Monegar's works as some form of mediation between their overcivilized selves and the freedom of nature, who is to say that Monegar himself did not make similar psychological investments.

Finally, Monegar's identification with a fleeing deer or a flying bird seems much less eccentric if we consider that his artistic mentor, John Steuart Curry, similarly associated himself with animals and even plants. In an article from a 1943 *Newsweek,* Curry's friend Reginald Marsh noted that Curry's 1937 painting *Ajax,* which depicts a massive bull grazing in the Kansas countryside, was in fact a self-portrait of the midwestern artist. More recently, Charles Eldredge has convincingly argued that Curry and his fellow regionalist Thomas Hart Benton each found self-expression through portraits of midwestern crops. Eldredge views Curry's 1933 *Kansas Cornfield* as well as Benton's *Wheat* of 1967 as barely concealed symbols of the artists, as self-portraits in "regional, vegetal guise." Just as these regionalist painters reworked images of mundane crops and livestock into meaningful personal metaphors, Monegar's affinity for wildlife can be seen in a similarly solipsistic light.[26] Although the identity represented by these works remains determined, to a degree, by the primitivist assumptions of the dominant culture, Monegar's wildlife paintings can nevertheless be seen as the culmination of a variety of representational strategies through which Monegar sought to construct an identity (both personal and pictorial) for himself as a Hochunk painter in mid-America at midcentury.

Notes

1. John Steuart Curry, Madison, Wisconsin, to Reeves Lowenthal, Associated American Artists, New York, 3 February 1942, Curry Papers, Archives of American Art, Smithsonian Institution, Washington, D.C., microfilm role 165, frame 430.

2. This view was most clearly articulated in J. J. Brody, *Indian Painters and White Patrons* (Albuquerque: University of New Mexico Press, 1971). John Sloan quoted in Ruth Laughlin Barker, "John Sloan Reviews the Indian Tribal Arts," *Creative Arts* 9 (December 1931): 445–47.

3. For a consideration of the problem of regional hegemony in Euro-American painting, see Angela Miller, *The Empire of the Eye* (Ithaca and London: Cornell University Press, 1993). The dismissive term "Bambi style" has been used to categorize the pan-Indian-style trend at its most

formulaic. Rebecca Dobkins has recently addressed the difficulty of classifying such idiosyncratic Native American painters in her article "The Work and Influence of Maidu Painter Frank Day," *American Indian Art Magazine* 23 (autumn 1998): 54–67.

4. The quotation is from Norman L. Kleeblatt, "MASTER NARRATIVES/minority artists," *Art Journal* 57 no. 3, 30. For a recent attempt at "mainstreaming" wildlife painting see Nicholas Hammond, *Modern Wildlife Painting* (New Haven and London: Yale University Press, 1999).

5. In constructing this brief biography, I used the following sources: "Berg Jewelry Displaying Monegar Pictures," *Black River Falls (Wisconsin) Banner-Journal,* January 29, 1964; "Indian Monegar's Art on Display," *Black River Falls (Wisconsin) Banner-Journal,* July 9, 1969; "Indian Artist Receives Honor In His Own Land," unattributed 1943 newspaper article found in the Jackson County History Room in the Black River Falls Public Library; John Rector Barton Papers in the State Historical Society of Wisconsin, Madison; John R. Barton, *Rural Artists of Wisconsin* (Madison: University of Wisconsin Press, 1948); John Steuart Curry Papers in the Archives of American Art; Donald Key, "His Art Overcame Tragic Life and Jail," *Milwaukee Journal* (6 July 1969); Tom Lawin, "Fame Game Comes a Bit Late for Jackson Artist," *Eau Claire (Wisconsin) Leader and Daily Telegram,* November 21, 1969. R. A. Scott, "Clarence Boyce Monegar—Wisconsin Artist," *Wisconsin Tales and Trails* 4 (November 1963): 26. In addition, interviews were conducted with Monegar's brother, Russell Monegar (telephone interview, October 12, 1998), and Joann Dougherty (Black River Falls, Wisc., June 2, 1998), daughter of Bruce Van Gorden. Research in Wisconsin was made possible by a Summer Research Fellowship from the Graduate School at the University of Kansas.

6. Curry to Lowenthal, 16 February 1942, Curry Papers/AAA role 165, frame 434.

7. I have not yet located the original source in which Koerner's illustration appeared. However, the same work appears in popular print as the cover illustration for the August 1973 edition of the magazine *American History Illustrated.*

8. Indeed, Curry identifies such items of popular culture as influences upon Monegar; see Curry to Lowenthal, 16 February 1942, Curry Papers/AAA role 165, frame 434.

9. Charles Taylor, *Multiculturalism and "the Politics of Recognition"* (Princeton: Princeton University Press, 1992), 32.

10. Gerald Vizenor, *Fugitive Poses: Native American Indian Scenes of Absence and Presence* (Lincoln and London: University of Nebraska Press, 1998), 14–15.

11. This sense of historical presence is aided by the simple fact that the identities of these individuals are known.

12. For a useful account of how this same form of cultural relativism shaped anthropological encounters with Native Americans, see Thomas Biolsi, "The Anthropological Construction of 'Indians:' Haviland Scudder Mekeel and the Search for the Primitive in Lakota Country," in *Indians and Anthropologists: Vine Deloria Jr. and the Critique of Anthropology,* ed. Thomas Biolsi and Larry J. Zimmerman (Tucson: University of Arizona Press, 1997).

13. Barton, *Rural Artists of Wisconsin,* 105; Lawin, "Fame Game Comes a Bit Late," 3.

14. See Lisa Mighetto, *Wild Animals and American Environmental Ethics* (Tucson: University of Arizona Press, 1991). See also Gary G. Gray, *Wildlife and People* (Urbana and Chicago: University of Illinois Press, 1993), 101.

15. Aldo Leopold, *Sand County Almanac* (1949; reprint, Oxford: Oxford University Press, 1987), 204, 206–7, 215.

16. The passage of the Duck Stamp Act in 1934 and the Federal Aid in Wildlife Restoration Act of 1937 attest to the success of such groups. In addition, Pres. Franklin Roosevelt launched several programs during the 1930s that focused on environmental preservation. See Gray, *Wildlife and People,* 38–41.

17. Fred Blessing, "The Woodland Indian—Conservationist," in *Outdoor Horizons,* ed. L. Brings (Minneapolis: T. S. Denison, 1957), 154.

18. José Ortega y Gasset, *Meditations on Hunting* (New York: Charles Scribner's and Sons, 1972), 134; Leopold, *Sand County Almanac,* 150–51. For a cogent discussion of how nature and nature skills have been inscribed as "Indian" see Philip J. Deloria, *Playing Indian* (New Haven and London: Yale University Press, 1998). His discussion of the indoctrination of boys and girls into this ideology through organizations such as the Camp Fire Girls, Woodcraft Indians, and the Boy Scouts beginning early in the twentieth century seems particularly relevant here. See his chapter titled "Natural Indians and Identities of Modernity."

19. Telephone interview with Russell Monegar. One source estimated the number of paintings sold by Monegar during the last twenty years of his life as being more than eight thousand.

20. Donald Key, "His Art Overcame Tragic Life and Jail." Also, Joann Dougherty in the June 2, 1998, interview noted that residents of Black River Falls were most interested in those works by Monegar that depicted nearby scenery. Thomas Craven, *Modern Art* (New York: Simon and Schuster, 1934).

21. "Rural Art," *Life,* March 31, 1941, 76–79; Lela Smith to John R. Barton, John R. Barton Papers in the State Historical Society of Wisconsin. Box 5, folder 3.

22. Apparently Monegar's work was even reproduced on greeting cards produced in the area, and several paintings were published as covers of local magazines; R. A. Scott, "Clarence Boyce Monegar . . . 1910–1968, Memorial Exhibition," exhibition brochure, Charles Allis Art Library, July 8–31, 1969.

23. See Homi Bhabha, *Location of Culture* (New York: Routledge, 1994), particularly his chapter "Interrogating Identity"; the quotation is on p. 45.

24. For a general consideration of the phenomenon of providing the public with a symbol of Indianness, see S. Elizabeth Bird, "Introduction: Constructing the Indian, 1830s–1990s," in *Dressing in Feathers,* ed. S. Elizabeth Bird (Boulder, Colo.: Westview Press, 1996). See also Deloria, *Playing Indian.* As a child, Monegar witnessed the death of his father and two siblings, and later in life, his wife. His tribal estrangement is briefly noted in Donald Key's article and was further elaborated upon by Joann Dougherty. Monegar's inability to fit into Euro-American society was considered at length in a letter by John Barton. See Barton to John and Ruth [?], John R. Barton Papers, State Historical Society of Wisconsin, Box 7, folder 14.

25. Initially, it was his lack of financial means that landed him in jail.

26. "Curry of Kansas," *Newsweek,* 15 November 1943, 80; Charles C. Eldredge, "Prairie Prodigal: John Steuart Curry and Kansas," in *John Steuart Curry: Inventing the Middle West,* ed. P. Junker (New York: Hudson Hills Press, 1998), 105. Indeed Curry's cow (bull) and Monegar's deer seem to play out Aldo Leopold's romantic equation.

CHAPTER 8

MADE IN JAPAN WITH THE EXCEPTION OF TWO

Native American and Appalachian Arts Come of Age

JOY L. GRITTON

*I*n 1966 a young Caddo-Kiowa Indian from Oklahoma named T. C. Cannon painted an image of a solitary figure he entitled *Made in Japan with Exception of One* (plate 11). The work was most likely conceived as a commentary on the unique status of Native peoples among Americans, a status that defined Cannon not only as an individual and tribal member but also as an artist. The painter was one of a small group of Native American high school students studying at the Institute of American Indian Arts (IAIA), a magnet Bureau of Indian Affairs boarding school that had set up shop in Santa Fe, New Mexico, in 1962. The school's director, George Boyce, promised a program "unique and important in the world of arts" that would "open doors of opportunity for self-expression" to Indian youth of "high artistic talent." Such talent was an "economic resource" that, when developed, could result in excellent "make-a-living" careers.[1] In addition to their occupational value, the arts were perceived as transcending linguistic and cultural barriers, and so they comprised the heart of the institute's secondary and postsecondary curriculum in an effort to improve cross-discipline academic performance while instilling pride in cultural heritage. Like his classmates, Cannon was attracted by the opportunity to use his Native background while training as an individual creative in his own right.[2]

While Native American students painted at the federally funded school in New Mexico, a young Whitesburg, Kentucky, lawyer penned a book that was to focus the country's attention on another group of unique Americans. "It is the story of how a proud, stubborn, self-reliant people has been reduced to serfdom," wrote Sargent Shriver of Harry Caudill's *Night Comes to the Cumberland: A Biography of a Depressed*

Area. Though the Kennedy administration's poverty initiatives highlighted the plight of the Indian and other minorities, the political seeds of its agenda had been sown in the West Virginia coal mines of the 1960 presidential campaign, seeds that would only fully germinate with the War on Poverty of the Johnson era.[3]

Caudill's exposé of the Appalachian region's timber and coal industries brought the national conscience to bear on a people who seemed as remote and timeless as the Indian. His work received official sanction from the administration in the form of a foreword by Secretary of the Interior Stewart Udall (whose wife, Lee, was an ardent supporter of IAIA). Describing the Cumberland Plateau as an "anachronism, a remnant of an ugly chapter of our history," Udall found tragic irony in the reality of the "fiercely independent frontiersman" of Daniel Boone country living "today in bleak and demoralizing poverty almost without parallel on this continent." The following year, desperate images of hard times in Letcher County, Kentucky, featured in Charles Kuralt's "Christmas in Appalachia," inspired donations of clothing, food, and toys to be delivered by the truckload.[4]

As in Indian country, mountain workers had for the past seven decades looked to the arts for remedies against Appalachia's "ills." It came as no surprise then that a 1962 "comprehensive" survey charged with assembling "current information on social, cultural, and economic conditions as a basis for sound programs" in the region included a chapter entitled "The Revival of Handicrafts." While its author, Bernice Stevens, showed less optimism than Boyce for crafts' potential to provide Appalachian youth with "make-a-living" careers, she nevertheless expressed concern that the public schools were not teaching crafts "either as a practical subject or as a cultural foundation for pride in a mountain heritage." The region's institutions of higher education were adding craft courses to their curricula but few were "stressing crafts as a part of the culture of the area." Stevens feared that unless the mountain craftsman understood his own cultural heritage and developed its possibilities, the area would "cease to make a unique contribution to our national culture." A similar state of affairs in Indian arts had been one impetus for the founding of the Institute of American Indian Arts and its predecessor, the Southwestern Indian Art Project.[5]

Even as Stevens maintained that the primary value of crafts was individual creative satisfaction, she acknowledged that *Appalachian* crafts had always been anchored in "economic necessity," first in the survival of pioneer forms and then in the early promotion of the craft revival.[6] And as with Indian arts, the revivals had not been wholly homegrown:

> By the latter half of the nineteenth century, factories, mills, and growing cities
> gradually released most American homes from the necessity of being self-

sufficient. In most of the country, handweaving died out with the Civil War. Other crafts followed into near-extinction, in the Appalachians as well as in the rest of the country. . . . In the last decade of the nineteenth century, however, interest in crafts began to revive, largely through the efforts of out-siders, who came to the mountains for a vacation or a stint of teaching, fell in love with the highland area, and stayed to devote their lives to its people.[7]

Appalachian and Native American arts had both long been enmeshed in issues of economic development, cultural preservation, social change, and outside interven-tion and patronage. By the 1960s the related cultural institutions, arts and crafts markets, educational programs, exhibition venues, and the arts themselves all re-flected the imprint of these forces. And so it was that in the last years of the decade, at a time of resurgence of interest in folk traditions and things "Indian," J. J. Brody set about to critically explore the relationship between outside patron and indigenous artist in the history of Native American painting.

Brody defined the "relevant questions" as follows: "(1) To what degree is modern American Indian painting an extension of aboriginal pictorial form and content, and to what degree is it a novelty? (2) To what degree is modern American Indian painting an extension of aboriginal pictorial functions and to what degree an accommodation to postconquest realities?" Other issues, Brody explained, would naturally arise from the inquiry. "If there are novel factors, can they be isolated and their sources deter-mined? If postconquest social conditions have affected the art, can they be isolated and their effects enumerated? Is it possible that the forms are aboriginal but the func-tions modern? Can the reverse have happened, with novel forms being applied to an-cient functions?"[8] Ten years later David Whisnant would frame essentially the same problem as it related to Appalachian arts with the phrase "the politics of culture":

Clearly, cultural intervention is a complex process which has taken many forms and whose results are subject to a variety of interpretations. We will begin to understand these episodes and processes in our cultural history only when we look at them in detail *as* intervention, and not as benign incidents which produced a collection of slave songs, or a revival of handweaving, or a colorful festival. In short, we must begin to understand the politics of culture— especially the role of formal institutions and forceful individuals in defining and shaping perspectives, values, tastes, and agendas for cultural change.[9]

While it is true that for all peoples and arts across history there has existed a thick web of patronage, market, audience expectations, and foreign influence that infuses the artist's work, for this particular time and these particular artists there was the added dimension of larger power inequities that were not limited to an individual relationship but were pervasive to the entire group as a whole.

Though Native American and Appalachian artists have shared a parallel legacy in this respect, the outcomes of their relationships with outside teachers, collectors, promoters, and markets have in many ways been decidedly different. Indeed, it is through this divergence as much as through the similarities that the dynamics of tangled motives and agendas become even clearer. An overview of some of the most significant and lasting of the "interventions" illuminate this point.

Accounts of the history of Appalachian crafts generally begin with one art form—hand weaving. The choice is most probably not without significance.[10] It was with weaving that John Ruskin had launched the Arts and Crafts movement, and it was certainly at the earliest core of both the Appalachian and the Native American arts revivals. Perhaps the most recognizable name synonymous with Appalachian arts today is Berea. It was there in 1893 that college president William Goodell Frost launched his "extension tours" into the mountains, bringing back homespun coverlets as evidence of the worthiness of his work with "our contemporary ancestors." Three years later Frost held the first homespun fair during commencement week. Premiums offered for the best coverlets, blankets, and linsey-woolseys spawned competition and a thriving annual market. Soon, stories of industrious Appalachian youths paying their way through college with the products of mountain looms were rife upon the land.[11]

Frost was also able to assure immigrant-leery and industry-weary urban potential donors that the mountaineer belonged to the "category of the 'native born'" and yet was distinctively different from the prospective benefactors themselves. While lacking the "intelligence which is the leading trait of latter-day Americans," Frost noted, the mountaineer had the "unjaded nerves which the typical modern lacks." This opposition between the modern and the Appalachian was, in fact, seminal to the emergent artist-patron relationship at the turn of the century, thanks in large part to local-color writers who for two decades had plied popular magazines with images of backward children of nature subsisting in rustic log cabins perched on picturesque ridge tops. Horace Kephart in his classic study of mountain life likened the folk there to castaways left on some unknown island, "unaided and untroubled by the growth of civilization." Time had stood still for these backwoodsmen of the Blue Ridge and Unakas, and "the progress of mankind from that age to this is no heritage of theirs."[12]

Hettie Wright Graham echoed this tone in her article on Berea College's Fireside Industries for Gustav Stickley's *Craftsman* in 1902: "To visit this region is to lose a century of the inventions which are regarded as the necessities of life in the larger

American cities and towns. Ships, steam-engines and even row-boats are there un-known, and the only means of travel is upon horse-back. Civilization has left these poor mountaineers far behind in all that makes for outward refinement and knowl-edge of the world." Graham had been hired by Frost to teach weaving in the Fireside handicrafts program. She worked out of a log cabin whose furniture had been crafted in the school's woodworking class. Emphasizing that the textiles produced at Berea were "devoid of that unmistakable commercial quality found in all manufactures created for an indefinite 'market,'" Graham seemed to be following at least the spirit of her predecessor, Susan B. Hayes, who had frowned upon the use of aniline dyes and taught the students to spin linen thread from the twelve acres of flax grown on school land.[13]

Stickley's readers would have been sensitive to the distinction between the natural materials and individual craftsmanship of the Berea goods and those mass-produced for their own abundant consumption. The Arts and Crafts movement was both fostered and nourished by an industrial alienation that the nonmodern, both of the human and material sort, seemed to remedy. Thus, as Becker has observed, reformers, folklorists, anthropologists, and artists had since the end of the century "sought out the people who, they imagined, lived in tightly knit societies, close to the soil," where "the community took care of its members, human and spiritual values reigned, and beauty lay in carefully crafting from raw goods the material necessities of everyday domestic life."[14]

Many saw their mission as one in which they would work to preserve the tradi-tions of these "primitives" and rescue them from some as yet undetermined modern fate. Graham, for example, took pains to warn of the imminent changes that threat-ened the mountain folk. "Already," she reported, "saw-mills are supplying boards for frame school-buildings and dwellings, with which to replace the old log-houses," and "agents of sewing-machines are finding their way to the most obscure hamlets." She concluded that "it becomes a question whether the baser elements of modern life shall be passed on to them without protest, and whether honest handicrafts shall be allowed to decline and disappear among them, as they have everywhere failed, when brought into competition with the factory-system of production."[15]

Mountain workers with both religious and private affiliations established a legion of schools in the first decades of the twentieth century that struggled to check the flow of sewing machines and other industrial evils into Appalachia's hills and hollers. Most were a curious mix of acculturative education and primitivist philosophy. Katherine Pettit and May Stone, founders of Hindman Settlement School in Kentucky, de-scribed their intent as being "to live among people in a model home, to show them by example the advantages of cleanness, neatness and order, and to inspire them to use pure language and to lead pure, Christian lives . . . hoping thereby to elevate and uplift them." In addition to basic academic skills, girls were taught to cook and sew, to do laundry and iron clothes, to weave and make baskets. Boys learned carpentry, blacksmithing, and woodworking skills. The schools' promotional literature painted a benevolent picture of ardent local support, with earnest stories of community elders such as "Uncle" William Creech or "Uncle" Solomon Everidge walking miles to plead that mountain children might have the opportunity to learn the ways of the world.[16]

A few programs, such as the John C. Campbell Folk School at Brasstown, North Carolina, came to focus on the arts as a form of culturally appropriate vocational education. Generally, some degree of economic independence and self-sufficiency was seen as a critical element in these educational crusades. Craft cooperatives and training centers began to mushroom across the hills. Francis L. Goodrich, one of the earliest figures in the mountain weaving revival, was a social worker for the Women's Board of Home Missions of the Presbyterian Church living in Brittain's Cove, North Carolina, in 1895, when she was first given a forty-year-old coverlet and the draft from which it was woven. She was immediately interested in the proposition of producing the coverlets at a moderate cost and finding a market for them. The ensuing operation, named Allanstand Cottage Industries, was to combine financial incentives with social altruism and cultural preservation, according to the expressed goals recounted by Eaton: "to bring money into communities far from market and to give paying work to women in homes too isolated to permit them to find it for themselves; to give to these women a new interest, the pleasure of producing beautiful things, the delight of the skilled worker and artist of feeling themselves sharers in the work of the world; to save from extinction the old-time crafts while producing things of value and beauty."[17] Goodrich advertised an expanded line of goods—including portieres, lounge-covers, and tablecloths—in missionary magazines and northern newspapers and opened a permanent salesroom in 1908. Allanstand pieces were included in Stickley's 1903 arts and crafts exhibition and were used in First Lady Ellen Wilson's Blue Mountain Room in the White House.[18]

For some ventures, the cottage business component superseded any pretense of revived "traditional" forms or even contemporary expressions of mountain aesthetics or experiences. Winogene B. Redding, founder of the Pi Beta Phi Settlement School Weavers Guild in Gatlinburg, Tennessee, remembered designing the weavers' pieces because she feared they would not know how to best translate their work into useful items for other people's homes. She saw this as simply a "question of bringing back ideas from the outside world to be interpreted by their skill." Goodrich also provided designs to Allanstand workers. Still, apparently not all products were destined for an outside market. Evelyn Bishop, first head resident at Pi Beta Phi, told Eaton that the school's handwoven curtains, table runners, and towels were showing up in area homes and that several women had come to night classes so as to weave cloth for their children's dresses.[19]

In addition to featuring Appalachian arts, the *Craftsman* also published articles on Native American arts, music, and mythology.[20] Attention was focused primarily on the Southwest, where other revivals and survivals were assuming prominence. Eastern buyers who purchased a Berea weaving for their table, might very well be in the market for a Navajo rug for their floor. The coming of the railroads in the 1880s had made commercially produced clothing and Pendleton blankets widely available to the Navajos and lessened their own demand for the handwoven wearing blankets and mantas favored for nearly two centuries. At the same time, the iron rails brought surges of tourists primed by Fred Harvey promotions to purchase a piece of Indian America. These urbanites were, again, searching for the inversion of their own modern lives. In Harvey's Indian Building in Albuquerque, Navajo weavers demonstrated for train travelers at looms curiously lashed to potted trees to simulate outdoor weaving on the reservation, an ambiance presumably designed to reinforce buyers' own predilections for the natural.[21]

Trading posts established on the reservations after the Navajos' return from their Bosque Redondo exile in 1868 had for twenty years supplied the aniline dyes and commercial yarns that produced dynamic eye-dazzlers and pulsating wedge weaves, but the bright greens, purples, and oranges of the recently emergent style did not fit the expectations of these new patrons. Now traders began to buy only those wares made from the natural dyes and hand-spun wool that seemed appropriate for those who lived "close to the soil." Since Navajo weavers had not actually worked to any great extent with vegetal dyes and were no longer accustomed to dying with indigo, the DuPont Company was commissioned to develop commercial dyes that replicated the soft natural tones. Enterprising weavers soon experimented with locally available plants, however, with some eighty-six different dyes being isolated by Nonabah Bryan, a Navajo teacher at Wingate Vocational High School.[22]

Juan Lorenzo Hubbell, whose family enterprises included some fourteen trading posts, limited weavers solely to the black and blue synthetic dyes that seemed to emulate traditional classic-style textiles. Oil paintings of these older Navajo blankets were hung at his Ganado post as models.[23] Classic blankets also served as inspiration for Mary Cabot Wheelwright of the Eastern Association on Indian Affairs, who in the 1920s facilitated the development of a regional style of weaving at Chinle. The association, like the New Mexico Association on Indian Affairs and the American Indian Defense Association, had been organized to protect Indian rights in response to endangered Pueblo land claims. Much like the mountain workers of Appalachia, these antiassimilationist groups advocated the arts both as stalwarts against cultural erosion as well as sources of desperately needed income for isolated Native communities. Wheelwright and her friend L. H. (Cozy) McSparron of the Chinle Trading Post encouraged weavers to reproduce the patterns and colors of the classic-style textiles whose photographs they displayed in Navajo schools and trading posts.[24]

Those non-Navajos who intervened between artist and buyer seemed to have perceived of themselves as having single-handedly saved a pure dying art from the misguided bastardizations of the artists themselves. Sallie Lippincott, who together with her husband, Bill, sought to replicate the revival at Chinle in the Wide Ruins area, remembers that she had high hopes for what the weavers there could do, if only they were enlightened as to some truer Navajo "beauty":

> When my husband and I bought the post, the Navajos in that area were making very poor rugs, the kind that were sold from knocked together stands along Highway 66. . . . The wool was not well cleaned or well spun. The bordered designs were the kind that originate in Oriental rugs or were crossed arrows and swastikas, and the colors were red, black, and white. Admittedly, these were the designs thought of as "Indian." But we had come to the reservation to work in the National Park Service at Canyon de Chelly. . . . We had seen the really beautiful rugs that the weavers there produced and were sold at Cozy's post. We hoped to guide the Wide Ruins weavers into the production of beautiful rugs too. We knew they were capable of such work.[25]

Lippincott's words echo those of Jennie Lester Hill, who came to manage Berea's Fireside Industries in 1903. "Once both indigo and madder were common plants in many mountain gardens," lamented Hill, "but in none of them are they found now. Too often, alas, has our weaver departed from the traditions of her mother; she has used the cheaper aniline dyes and her work has degenerated with her."[26]

For the most part, the Appalachian and Navajo weaving revivals were limited primarily to a resurgence of certain styles or media rather than a return to original functions or consumption. An art form once worn by and traded among Navajos was now produced for easterners' rugs. Mountain social workers such as Hill expressed little confidence that the products of Appalachian looms would find much use in the homes of those that produced them: " 'What is the future of these fireside industries?' we are sometimes asked. 'Will they die out as the mountain region is opened to trade, and machine-made products take the place of the homespun?' So far as the uses of the mountaineers themselves are concerned, this will probably be the case. But for real well-made homespun products there is an ever growing demand. Nothing is more artistic for furnishing country houses or for country wear. The mountain girl may choose the flashy, shoddy goods at the country store in preference to her mother's homespun, for it is new to her, but the golf girl will not." Hill goes on to urge "friends of the mountain people" to help them adapt their products to "modern methods of living." "The woman who can weave a coverlid, can weave portieres and table draperies when she is shown what they are," she argued. "Instead of linsey and blankets for her own use, she can weave golf skirtings and homespun suitings."[27]

Modern applications of traditional forms would fast become a familiar theme in the promotion of Appalachian arts but one that remained carefully tempered by a distinctively nonmodern, primitive appeal. "Adapting mountain industries to these changing times is the fascinating occupation of the 'Spinning Wheel,'" wrote Clementine Douglas of the craft center she had established at Asheville, North Carolina, in 1924. Yet the center's woolens, linens, hooked rugs, and other products were arranged among pioneer household utensils in a log cabin showroom so that they would "blend with the setting of by-gone days." In a similar fashion, the weaving, basketry, and woodworking of the Blue Ridge Weavers in Tryon, North Carolina, were displayed in a salesroom "where many old objects of early mountain life are exhibited." And while Mrs. F. D. Huckabee of the Pine Burr Studio in Apison, Tennessee, acknowledged that the hooked rugs they crafted were sold in larger cities (to the tune of ten thousand dollars in sales for one community's work in 1930), she was quick to add that "we have nothing that savors of factory work. Each piece is made in the home of the worker with a small hook resembling a crochet hook."[28]

When representatives of these cooperatives and schools met at Penland, North Carolina, in 1928 to begin organizing what would become the Southern Highland Handicraft Guild, the disparity between the expectations of patrons and the realities of the mountains and its artists was evident. Discussion topics ranged from the economic significance of handicrafts in homes and schools to the influence of crafts on the character of the workers, from use of native materials to partial use of machinery in handmade articles. Creation of new objects and designs to meet market requirements was also on the agenda.[29] Barker notes that the guild was to continually run a gauntlet between preservation and change, beginning with a 1931 exhibition that featured both pioneer crafts and modern weaving from the St. Louis Handicraft Guild. Interested parties were divided into what one Tennessee Valley Authority worker characterized as the "Purists" and the "Liberals," with the former maintaining that mountain crafts must be of only traditional types, worked with crude tools, and primitive in aesthetic, and the latter readily adopting modern designs, which sold better.[30]

An article that appeared in *American Magazine of Art* in 1933 betrays a similar ambiguity regarding the balance between old and new in mountain baskets. "In the Southern Highlands of this country, a greater variety and number of handicrafts are produced than in any other large section," the author reported. "The traditional crafts have persisted there because of the more primitive level on which life is lived and because of the lack of communication and interchange with the outside world." Yet the viewer could rest assured that the baskets, like the other craft articles, did not represent "slavish copies of traditional models." The old designs were constantly being adapted and re-created by the individual craftsman. These crafts were not "mere perfunctory repetitions but works of contemporary art."[31]

That same year the Southern Highland Handicraft Guild debuted their first national exhibition at the Country Life Association's convention in Blacksburg, Virginia. The association, founded in 1919, worked to slow the outward migration of youth from farm to city by addressing issues of poverty and isolation critical to rural populations. Work in the *Handicrafts of the Southern Highlands* represented thirty-three craft centers and was juxtaposed with color reproductions of bucolic scenes. With the help of the American Federation of Arts, the show traveled to several other venues, including the Corcoran Art Gallery in Washington, D.C., the Brooklyn Museum in New York, the Milwaukee Art Institute, and the Everhart Museum in Scranton. The Everhart also featured southwest Indian pottery, textiles, and paintings during this same time period.[32]

In a similar vein, southern Appalachian crafts figured prominently in the 1937 *Rural Arts Exhibition* sponsored by the U.S. Department of Agriculture, the Department of the Interior, the Work Projects Administration, the Farm Security Administration, the Russell Sage Foundation, the American Federation of Arts, and the Southern Highland Handicraft Guild and Southern Highlanders. Here contemporary crafts were once again highlighted against a backdrop of farms and fields. Also included among this show's rural craftsmen were Native American artisans.[33]

Native arts had been found in a somewhat more rarefied atmosphere at the *Exposition of Indian Tribal Arts* exhibit in New York in 1931. Organized by John Sloan and Amelia White and sponsored by the commissioner of Indian affairs, the secretary of the interior, and the College Art Association, the show was billed as "the first exhibition of American Indian art selected entirely with consideration of esthetic value." The show's catalog, written by Sloan and Oliver LaFarge, chided museums that exhibited "the choice vase and the homely cooking pot side by side" and declared that they hoped their show of "fine and applied arts, selected from the best material available," would give the Indian a "chance to prove himself to be not a maker of cheap curios and souvenirs, but a serious artist worthy of our appreciation and capable of making a cultural contribution that will enrich our modern life."[34]

The exhibit introduced a new "modern application" for traditional arts. Indian cultures were being discovered by American modernists attempting to forge a uniquely New World heritage for their own conceptual work. They followed on the heels of European surrealists, who had begun to exhibit their own art alongside that of Native peoples, seeing in indigenous arts an expression of a primordial order lost to Western man.[35] In this context Native arts were no longer viewed as a mere quaint relic that offered refuge from modern life but as an affirmation of a universal truth that modern art also sought to reflect, as Sloan's catalog introduction reveals: "The Indian artist deserves to be classed as a Modernist, his art is old, yet alive and dynamic, but his modernism is an expression of a continuing vigour seeking new outlets and not, like ours, a search for release from exhaustion. . . . He is a natural symbolist. He is bold and versatile in the use of a line and colour. His work has a primitive directness and strength, yet at the same time it possesses sophistication and subtlety. Indian painting is at once classic and modern."[36]

The more than six hundred pieces of pottery, jewelry, textiles, sculpture, basketry, beadwork, and paintings exhibited in the exposition were now modern by virtue of their supposed affinity with contemporary American arts, rather than by some contrived adaptation to the needs of middle-class decor. "The art of the Indians, so eloquent of this land, is American art, and of the most important kind," proclaimed Walter Pach in a *New York Times* review of the show. "Indian abstraction is seen to be something radically unlike that of any of the modern European 'isms,'" added Edward Alden Jewell. "The Indian artist would not know what to make of cubism and futurism; yet he knows a great deal about simplification and stylization, methods of working that have sprung directly from the employment of symbolic forms."[37]

The germ of this change in status was to mature in 1939 at the *Indian Art in the United States and Alaska* exhibit organized for the Golden Gate International Exposition of 1939 by the Indian Arts and Crafts Board in cooperation with the Federal Art Project of the Works Progress Administration. Like its predecessor the Southern Highland Handicraft Guild, the Indian Arts and Crafts Board had been formed in 1935 to address issues such as quality of craftsmanship and materials, development and regulation of markets, and arts training and promotion. Unlike the guild, it operated as a government agency under the aegis of the Department of the Interior. The exhibit was marshaled by the board's general manager, Rene d'Harnoncourt.[38]

D'Harnoncourt was careful to draw correlations in his displays between the Native work exhibited and its modern vanguard counterparts. In this way an Inuit shaman's mask was described as revealing a "surprising affinity between certain phases of modern art and primitive art," a coincidence all the more astonishing, marveled d'Harnoncourt, when one considered that the "founders of the corresponding modern schools were entirely unfamiliar with Eskimo carvings and paintings." Another mask revealed the "seemingly illogical grouping of form elements . . . typical of surrealism in modern art," while an eighteenth-century Iroquois club anticipated modern sculpture in its "treatment of balanced masses."[39]

Viewing the exhibition as an opportunity for Indian artists to explore new markets for their products, d'Harnoncourt devised the salesrooms he provided as practical laboratories for merchandising: "In the first of these rooms, Indian handicrafts were shown under conditions resembling those of a modern quality gift shop, stressing artistic merit and the quality of every piece rather than its romantic associations. . . . Another salesroom was arranged to look somewhat like the usual Indian Trading Post so as to determine what type of background would prove more stimulating for the purchase of Indian goods. It is interesting to note here that almost all quality sales were made in the shop decorated in the modern gift shop style." More conventional notions of "modern applications" were also applied in the redirection of certain art forms' functions to meet the needs and tastes of potential buyers. The "gift shop" featured model rooms showing the use of Pueblo, Plains, and eastern Woodlands arts in the context of the modern home, with items such as pottery, kachinas, a drum, and a mask serving as interior decor accents. "No attention was paid in this shop to tribal origins," noted d'Harnoncourt, "and the articles were grouped in a manner to make the individual pieces appear at their best."[40]

The San Francisco show was the forerunner of the expanded *Indian Art of the United States* exhibition at the Museum of Modern Art in 1941. Here the museum's lower floor featured an "Indian Art for Modern Living" display that included Navajo rugs and jewelry, Pueblo pottery, a Cherokee "wastepaper basket," and wearing apparel designed by Swiss clothing designer F. A. Picard that incorporated Pawnee ribbonwork, Osage beading, Seminole patchwork, and Navajo hammered silver buttons.[41]

The main exhibit's promotion and critical response was likewise dominated by the interplay between the Native and the modern. "Good Indian work, done without the interference of whites," explained d'Harnoncourt in the catalog, "includes restrained colors as well as bright ones, and usually leans to economy rather than complexity of design." It was this "subtle control of its elements and the close relationship between function and form," he concluded, that brought "Indian work so near to the aims of most contemporary artists and make it blend with their surroundings that are truly of the twentieth century." Now Indian arts, the "most American of any we have in this country," were both inherently modern, as well as applicable to modern life. "That a museum dedicated to modern art stages this show is no haphazard event," wrote Jean Charlot for the *Nation,* "for Indian crafts are one of the sources of our own modern style." Secretary of the Interior Harold Ickes concluded that the exhibit was "a picture of the ancient Indian moving out into modern American and world life while holding fast to his ancient genius and devotions."[42]

The show's popularity led to other exhibits of Native arts, including one at the Betty Parsons Gallery in New York in 1946 that featured Northwest Coast painting. In the catalog Barnett Newman, one of the rising New York abstractionists who had organized the exhibit, effectively summarized Native arts' appeal to the new American art: "Here, then, among a group of several peoples, the dominant esthetic tradition was abstract. . . . There is an answer in these works to all those who assume that modern abstract art is the esoteric exercise of a snobbish elite, for among these simple people, abstract art was the normal, well-understood, dominant tradition. Shall we say that modern man has lost the ability to think on so high a level?"[43]

America's other "simple people" were being rendered in quite different terms. While Indian arts were displayed in the Museum of Modern Art and reviewed in prestigious and avant-garde publications, Appalachians could find their crafts in rural life shows and home living magazines. Allen Eaton's seminal *Handicrafts of the Southern Highlands,* published in 1937 by the Russell Sage Foundation, was still rooted in an aesthetic dominated by preservation and economic survival. His discussion of artist cooperatives, regional styles, and traditional techniques was punctuated by Doris Ulmann's timeless faces of old-time craftsmen and women working on mountain cabin porches. Eaton not only felt compelled to save a way of life he perceived to be endangered but also to counter negative moonshining, feuding images of Appalachia popularized by Paul Webb's *Esquire* cartoons, Snuffy Smith, and Li'l Abner.[44] A people who had once been revered as the last treasured survivors of premodern life were now ridiculed as ignorant holdouts unable, or unwilling, to join the progressive twentieth century.[45]

There were those working in the Appalachian craft world who were beginning to challenge the status quo, however. Mary Ela, director of Berea's art program in 1940, called on members of the Southern Highland Handicraft Guild to explore new directions for mountain crafts: "Who has the courage to stop whittling trinkets and to focus his energy upon wood sculpture which is stirring in these mountains. . . . Who is as concerned with the handicraft today as with the remembrances of what handicraft was, yesterday? Who dares to experiment with new materials, and who has the strength to find new and significant ways of handling a material as familiar as our native cotton?"[46] When the guild met in Asheville in 1943 the associate director of the Rockefeller's General Education Board was in attendance, and the following year the foundation made available a grant of six thousand dollars to support an arts survey directed by Marian Heard of the University of Tennessee. For the next seven years the

Rockefeller organization helped to both chart and fund the guild's work in the areas of arts education and marketing.[47] Weaver Anni Albers of the Black Mountain College in North Carolina gave one of the first Rockefeller-guild sponsored workshops on color and design in 1945, despite being herself unimpressed with mountain weaving that "simply reproduced set patterns from the past."[48]

Workshops "where all weavers may have their work evaluated and learn from nationally known experts" continued to be a guild staple over a decade later when Emma Weaver published her survey of mountain arts in 1958. Weaver noted that the craft revival had brought many artisans to work in the highlands who were not native to the region. With "training and taste for today's newest forms and designs," these artists had created an eclectic mix in the mountains. Today's southern highland craftsman, she reported, may read the *New Yorker* or *House Beautiful,* be a farmer's wife or a medical technologist, and work in silk screening or braided rugs.[49] Still, *Crafts in the Southern Highland* began by paying homage to the classic story of the region's history:

> These highland settlers brought little book learning with them, and sparse baggage except the skills of their English, Scotch, Irish and German forebears, together with the ballads, folk tales and festival dances of their ancestral homelands across the ocean. A treasured bedstead or clothes press, perhaps; a cumbersome loom; cook pots of iron, a banjo, fiddle, possibly a dulcimer. Remote from each other in their coves, isolated from the tide of industrial progress that soon began to sweep the lowlands, they continued for generations to make what they needed or do without. To the wealth of new materials at hand they adapted traditional methods to create forms and patterns of their own, but the old patterns were preserved, and the names they'd always gone by, no one knew why.[50]

Thereafter, modern tweeds, rugs, upholstery, and draperies were introduced by way of their ancestral "kiverlids," woven on a rough hearthside loom. Tales of chair carvers hauling their wares to market on muleback were juxtaposed with elegantly appointed model dining room furniture (fig. 8.1). The products of loom, potter's wheel, and workbench said to complement modern interiors and executive offices were all firmly rooted in a premodern past.[51]

Rockefeller intervention took a different turn in Indian country, probably due to American modernists' early patronage of Native arts. The year following Weaver's Appalachian survey, art educators, dealers, and traders convened at a Rockefeller-sponsored conference entitled "Directions in Indian Art." Acting as a consultant for

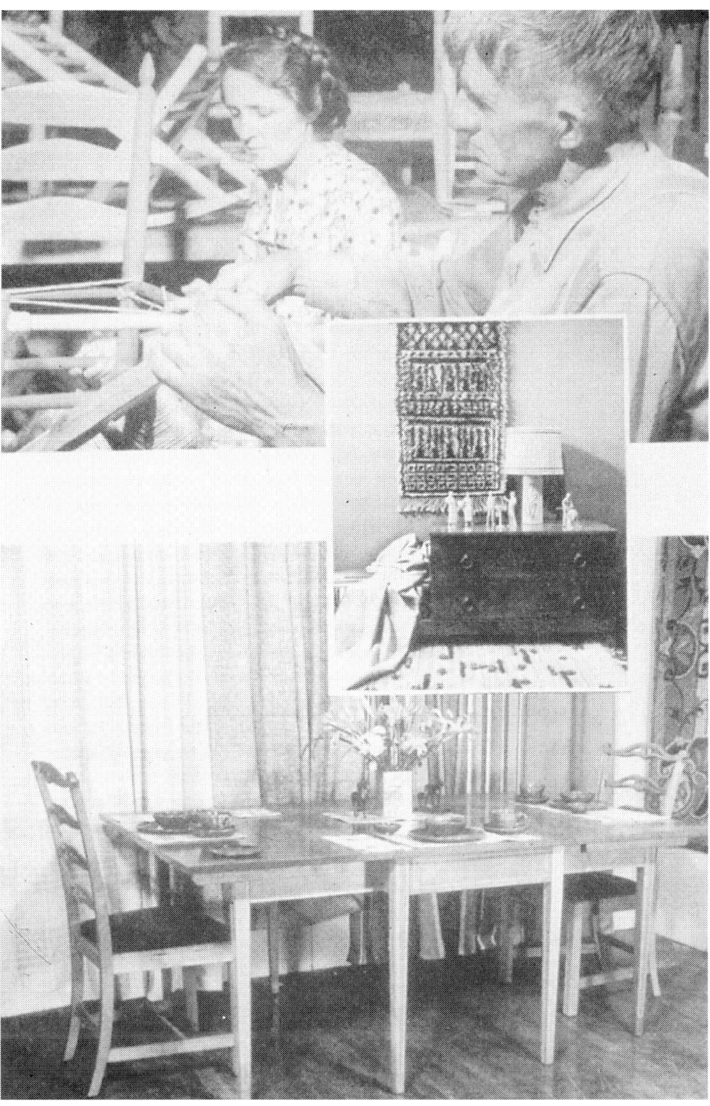

Chair Workers Preparing Seats and a Model Dining
Room Arrangement Showing Modern Applications
of Appalachian Arts. Published in *Crafts in the
Southern Highlands* (Southern Highland Handicraft
Guild: Asheville, 1958), 25.

the conference was Cherokee artist Lloyd New, who urged the foundation's director of humanities, Charles B. Fahs, to consider an approach to arts education that reflected the realities of contemporary Indian life. "We criticized the institutions that existed up until then," New recalls, "because . . . we had a tendency in our radical way to label all the art school movements up till that point as being more or less dedicated to the preservation of art forms, rather than trying to find out what art forms might suit the dynamics of Indian culture."[52]

Conference discussion focused on ways to expand the ethnic art market through modern adaptations. "The craftsman must make a revision of his own work," charged Hopi artist Charles Loloma. "He must find newer ways of doing things. New forms can come out of Indian backgrounds." Some speakers noted the obstacle of an arbitrarily defined traditional ideal that was rooted in initial outside collecting activity. "If these people lived in Basketmaker times," complained art dealer Tom Bahti, "they would object to pottery in the belief that it was not traditional and therefore not Indian." A consensus emerged that circumstances demanded a break with tradition. "The future of Indian art lies in the future, not the past," New declared. "Let's stop looking backward for our standards of Indian art production. We must admit the heyday of Indian life is past, or passing."[53]

The conference led to the funding of a series of workshops for young Indian artists held at the University of Arizona from 1960 to 1963. As with the Southern Highland Handicraft Guild workshops, there was a blend of Native and non-Native instruction. "Few believe that the force needed to produce this impetus could be generated wholly within Indian cultural circles," organizers explained, and there was an "obvious need for closer educational and working relationships between young Indian artists and non-Indian professional groups capable of assisting the development of indigenous talent."[54] Students not only experimented with a variety of media in the studios but also were saturated with lectures on design fundamentals and art history, and viewed a wide range of films. Printed programs for the project's 1961 culminating show proclaimed the undertaking a success: "This exhibition of student work demonstrated clearly that traditional tribal expression and a progressive contemporary approach are compatible."[55]

The project was a springboard for the Institute of American Indian Arts in Santa Fe. While part of the curriculum resembled that of the mountain schools in that students were instructed in such subjects as home management and consumer buying with the intent that they would assimilate to a mainstream American lifestyle, the arts pedagogy and ideology differed markedly from that of the previous Appalachian or Indian arts revivals. Though a traditional techniques course was offered, the school's exhibits and publications favored "new directional" work that expressed the students' tribal heritage in nontraditional media and styles. "Each is expected, in the name of personal freedom," explained Art Director Lloyd New, "to determine the meaning to himself of this unique background. . . . He is charged with the responsibility of evolving from his traditions a way of life that fits him, however far it may vary from the cliché expectations of the purists and the traditionalists."[56]

Despite declarations of radical change, Jim McGrath, who organized and mounted the school's exhibits, cautiously displayed student work in tandem with traditional pieces, making clear the relationship between source and departure. The catalog for a 1964 IAIA show held in conjunction with the *First American Indian Performing Arts Festival* in Washington, D.C., likewise carefully traced the works' lineage:

> This is the first time that the newest experimental directions of contemporary Indian artists and craftsmen from throughout the United States . . . are being exposed along with the traditional forms of past cultural achievements out of which the experimental developments are growing. For example, the ceramic forms of a young Comanche artisan growing out of her tribal buffalo hide, feather bonnet carrying cases; the Snohomish weaving experiments of cedar bark, shell, horse hair coming from traditional Snohomish weaving materials; new paintings from the Sioux and the Crow artists growing out of the three-dimensional shield cultural pattern where actual objects are suspended from the shield; the Eskimo jewelry designer who is building his experiments around the dance rattles that have movable parts; and the hard-edge Colville painter basing his expressions on the plateau parfleche and corn husk bags.[57]

In 1965, two years after he drafted the foreword to Caudill's *Night Comes to the Cumberlands,* Stewart Udall wrote the catalog introduction for an IAIA exhibit at the Riverside Museum in New York. Unlike the despairing portrait he had painted of Appalachia, Udall's sense of Native cultural expression was forward looking and enthusiastic. "Though its roots go deep into the past," he explained, "Indian art today, as exemplified in this collection, is fresh and stimulating. While preserving ancient symbols and traditional designs, it employs new mediums and modes of expression that are in keeping with life in space-age America." The show's critical reviews were reminiscent of the self-congratulatory prose elicited by *The Exposition of Tribal Arts* in 1931 or *Indian Art of the United States* ten years later—modernists had once again found a kindred spirit: "That two artists without knowledge of each other and sharing not even a similar culture or geography could work in the same style, perhaps with the same intention or meaning strikes our wonder. . . . Whereas our artists have consciously explored new expressive modes in the exotic arts of Africa and the Orient, the young American Indian, using elements of his own heritage and found objects from the reservation, creates with but an introduction to oil painting works immediately suggestive of our most modern art."[58]

What can be said of these outside interventions in Native and Appalachian arts from the 1880s until the 1960s—this transforming period of artistic adolescence? T. C. Cannon, reflecting on outside intervention in a painter's work, concluded, "I believe that an artist, regardless of the influence he obtains from others, can not afford to be influenced by that which is told to him by others who wish to form him or it will cause the destruction of his idiom as a painter." The task of sorting the influence that these artists willfully chose to adopt and adapt from that which was imposed by those who "wished to form them" has not yet been fully addressed.[59]

As Becker has suggested, questions of authenticity are largely meaningful only for outsiders, for the process of cultural change allows for the invention of tradition and the rewriting of history. These are choices that Whisnant seems to deem inappropriate when he complains that "one of the paradoxes of intervention-induced cultural change is its very durability and the degree to which imported forms and styles are accepted and defended by local people whose actual cultural traditions they altered or displaced." His categorizations of "strictly traditional," "quasi-traditional," and "frankly imported" have more in common with the interveners he seeks to expose than with the locals he implies are too ignorant to know the difference.[60]

Tremblay, referencing the Pueblo pottery revival that paralleled the interventions discussed above, notes that the artistic standards imposed by etic perspectives seem to differ not only from emic points of view but also from those of the art world at large:

> Certain issues keep reappearing in Native American craft like a refrain. Some nonnatives who claim that work is purer, more authentically indigenous, or more beautiful because it is inspired by precontact art believe innovation and outside influence cost the loss of one's culture. Others, usually outsiders, feel that one must let go of tradition to be modern and important, to be in the vanguard. Looking at craft in the dominant culture since the turn of the century, however, one sees evidence of appropriation from every culture on earth. In a similar spirit, it was Maria Martinez's prerogative to make blackware pottery inspired by pre-Columbian work and plates inspired by European dinnerware, and to let her husband paint them with traditional designs slightly altered by the Art Deco aesthetic of the time, itself often reflective of Native American forms.[61]

Tremblay also points out that potters such as Martinez and Nampeyo helped their families enter the cash economy while at the same time remaining in their home communities. That a good many artists in Indian country and Appalachia viewed their work as primarily an economic venture is a reality the intervener's nonmodern constructions frequently ignored. A Department of Labor's Women's Bureau field study conducted in 1933 revealed that 90 percent of all the craftswomen in southern Appalachia worked for commercial businesses. Hours were long and the pay was poor, and most were probably not concerned with whether the textile they wove or the chair they caned was strictly indigenous to their region or not. Their work's authenticity derived from the sweat of their brows and the ache in their backs.[62]

The monetary compensation customary for Appalachian arts was perhaps one of the hardest legacies of the outside interventions. While IAIA's Director Boyce boasted of turning out "$25,000 a year Indians," Stevens was warning in her survey that craft work was "painstaking and slow, and many craftsmen estimate that their actual hourly wage is very low."[63] The coupling of Indian arts with the American art vanguard insured their access to a fine arts market that was rarely available to the Appalachian artist.

Moreover, following the innovations of the Rockefeller summer projects and the Institute of American Indian Arts, continuity with the nebulous nonmodern "traditional" was not defined for Native art by any particular medium, style, or technique. This was not true for mountain arts. The very image of Appalachia demanded simplicity to the point of coarseness. For Caudill writing in 1963 this quality was both genetic and environmental, if not also irrevocable:

> The influx to the Blue Ridge was composed almost entirely of the unskilled or the little-skilled. They were men and women who, with rare exception, had known little or no experience with artfully wrought things of beauty. They had not owned or lounged upon skillfully carved chairs or beds and, as a generality, they were not people who had ever been called upon to maintain or create graceful or attractive things. . . . His every effort at manufacture was crude and in the extreme, and his descendants through the intervening generations have been unable to add either design or skill to his meager handicrafts.[64]

The "Appalachian" of this construction could not be simultaneously modern and ancestral. Its roots could not mesh with Udall's "life in space age America." Barker notes that even the Southern Highland Handicraft Guild's name employs a term "seldom used by craft professionals except as a derogatory term." The dichotomy has had consequences other than the price artists can command for a pot or a weaving. Young mountain artists studying in university art programs fear their degrees will tarnish their folk artist status, while their Native American counterparts proudly display biographical statements at the annual Santa Fe Indian Market listing advanced degrees from IAIA, the San Francisco Art Institute, or the California College of Arts and Crafts.[65]

Other accommodations to Brody's "postconquest realities" are less clear, for the story has only been partially told. The analysis of interventions usually tells us more about what outsiders do with the culture in question than the reverse. The forms and functions reserved for use within the indigenous community often go undetected or are purposely ignored by those who do not live, work, or worship in those communities. As Tremblay has documented, it is within this context that the mirror image of the intervention comes into focus. The objects associated with healing or ceremony or the marking of rites of passage such as births, weddings, or deaths are not the stuff of revival interventions or ethnic art markets, yet they may reflect their influence.[66] In an ironic twist of circumstance, they may in fact be the art forms that bring the needs of the outsiders and insiders into step, as Blaustein suggests:

> The rhetoric of folk revivalism has given rise to new realities, to the selective reconstruction and reinterpretation of older cultural symbols to suit contemporary social needs, not only of the people who were born and raised in Appalachia but also of newcomers who have come to identify with the region.
>
> To make sense of the complete spectrum of Appalachian artistic expression, we need to stop trying to distinguish the authentic from the synthetic. We should pay more attention to the universal human needs which all forms and genres of art fulfill.[67]

Perhaps the difficulty arises in trying to reconcile "universal human needs" with "postconquest realities." Arts interventions in both Native American and Appalachian communities have largely been based upon ethnocentric assumptions about just what those needs were and how they were most wisely met through arts production. Gross power and economic inequities (i.e., postconquest realities) allowed many outsiders to define poverty for each group as well as to attribute it to perceived inherent inadequacies. Cross-cultural ignorance prevented others from fully understanding the deeper functions the arts served within Native and Appalachian communities. Self-interest, whether of an economic or personal sense, led revivalists to focus on romantic perceptions of nonmodern life and particular media and techniques, rather than dynamic arts of diverse media that facilitated healthy integration of rapid social and technological change. The arts' remunerative potential has only complicated these issues.

Still, outside intervention has been a constant force in Native American and Appalachian arts maturation. Thoughtful reflection upon its many legacies is critical for those who wish to redefine or strengthen the role of the arts in the mountains or Indian country today. As these unique American cultural traditions continue to grow and evolve, how *will* the arts meet their universal human needs?

Notes

1. Promotional press release reprinted in Alvin C. Warren, "Institute of American Indian Arts to Open at Santa Fe," in *Education for Cross-Cultural Enrichment: Selected Articles from Indian Education, 1952–1964,* ed. Hildegard Thompson (Haskell, Kans.: Haskell Institute Press for the Bureau of Indian Affairs, U.S. Department of the Interior, 1964), 139–41.

2. This was the school's charge as outlined by Boyce in a letter sent to Bureau of Indian Affairs area directors in 1962; see George Boyce to Martin N. B. Holm, April 13, 1962, George Boyce Papers.

3. Shriver quote from back dustcover, Harry M. Caudill, *Night Comes to the Cumberlands: A Biography of a Depressed Area* (New York: Little, Brown and Company, 1963); Allen Batteau, *The Invention of Appalachia* (Tucson: University of Arizona Press, 1990), 165.

4. Stewart Udall, foreword, in Caudill, *Night Comes to the Cumberlands,* vii; Batteau, *The Invention of Appalachia,* 7, 162.

5. W. D. Weatherford, foreword, v; Bernice Stevens, "The Revival of Handicrafts," 286–87, both in *The Southern Appalachian Region,* ed. Thomas R. Ford (Lexington: University of Kentucky Press, 1962).

6. Stevens, "The Revival of Handicrafts," 279.

7. Ibid., 280.

8. J. J. Brody, *Indian Painters and White Patrons* (Albuquerque: University of New Mexico Press, 1971), xv.

9. David E. Whisnant, *All That Is Native and Fine: The Politics of Culture in an American Region* (Chapel Hill: University of North Carolina Press, 1983), 15.

10. Jane Kessler, "From Mission to Market: Craft in the Southern Appalachians," in *Revivals! Diverse Traditions, 1920–1945: The History of Twentieth-Century American Craft,* ed. Jane Kardon (New York: Harry N. Abrams in association with the American Craft Museum, 1994), 128.

11. Allen Eaton, *Handicrafts of the Southern Highlands* (New York: Russell Sage Foundation, 1937; reprint, New York: Dover, 1973), 60.

12. William Goodell Frost, "Our Contemporary Ancestors in the Southern Mountains," *Atlantic Monthly* March 1899, 318; see also Batteau, *The Invention of Appalachia,* 63. Horace Kephart, *Our Southern Highlanders: A Narrative of Adventure in the Southern Appalachians and a Study of Life among the Mountaineers* (1913; reprint, Knoxville: University of Tennessee Press, 1976), 17–18. For further discussion of the local-color movement and Appalachia, see Henry D. Shapiro, *Appalachia on Our Mind: The Southern Mountains in the American Consciousness, 1870–1920* (Chapel Hill: University of North Carolina Press, 1978), 3–31. Examination of the opposition between modernity and folk culture appears in Jane S. Becker, *Selling Tradition: Appalachia and the Construction of an American Folk, 1930–1940* (Chapel Hill: University of North Carolina Press, 1998), 16–20.

13. H. W. Graham, "The Fireside Industries of Kentucky," *Craftsman,* January 1902, 45, 47; Eaton, *Handicrafts of the Southern Highlands,* 61.

14. Becker, *Selling Tradition,* 3–4.

15. Graham, "Fireside Industries," 45–46.

16. Katherine Pettit and May Stone, "The Kentucky Mountaineer," *Report of Reception and Musicale* (Boston: Eastern Kindergarten Association, 1902), 7–9, cited in Whisnant, *All That Is Native and Fine,* 29. Eaton, *Handicrafts of the Southern Highlands,* 73–74, 70–71; for further discussion of the settlement, mission, and folk schools see Whisnant, *All That Is Native and Fine.*

17. Eaton, *Handicrafts of the Southern Highlands,* 66; see also Frances Louisa Goodrich, *Mountain Homespun* (1931; reprint, Knoxville: University of Tennessee Press, 1989).

18. Becker, *Selling Tradition,* 65; Eaton, *Handicrafts of the Southern Highlands,* 66.

19. "Winogene B. Redding," n.d., and transcript of interview with Winogene B. Redding, Pigeon Forge, Tennessee, 18 March 1965, Membership Biographical Data Files, Southern Highland Handicraft Guild Papers, Folk Art Center, Asheville, N.C., cited in Becker, *Selling Tradition,* 73; Becker, *Selling Tradition,* 65; Eaton, *Handicrafts of the Southern Highlands,* 72.

20. Harvey Green, "Culture and Crisis: Americans and the Craft Revival," in *Revivals!* 33.

21. Alice Kaufman and Christopher Selser, *The Navajo Weaving Tradition, 1650 to the Present* (New York: E. P. Dutton, 1985), fig. 109. The Harvey "intervention" is discussed in Kathleen L. Howard and Diana F. Pardue, *Inventing the Southwest: The Fred Harvey Company and Native American Art* (Phoenix: Heard Museum, 1996).

22. Charles Avery Amsden, *Navaho Weaving: Its Technique and Its History* (Santa Ana: Fine Arts Press, 1934; reprint, Glorietta, N.M.: Rio Grande Press, 1974), 225–27; Kate Peck Kent, "From Blanket to Rug: The Evolution of Navajo Weaving after 1880," *Plateau* 52, no. 4 (1981): 19; Kaufman and Selser, *The Navajo Weaving Tradition,* 95–96; Nonabah G. Bryan and Stella Young, *Navajo Native Dyes: Their Preparation and Use* (1940; reprint, Palmer Lake, Colo.: Filter Press, 1978).

23. Kent, "From Blanket to Rug," 10–11, 14; Kaufman and Selser, *The Navajo Weaving Tradition,* 67–69.

24. For further discussion of these organizations see Lawrence Kelly, *The Assault on Assimilation: John Collier and the Origins of Indian Policy Reform* (Albuquerque: University of New Mexico Press, 1983), 213–54, and Kenneth Philp, *John Collier's Crusade for Indian Reform, 1920–1954* (Tucson: University of Arizona Press, 1977), 26–54.

25. Quoted from a manuscript by Sallie Lippincott Wagner, in Ralph T. Coe, "Native American Craft," in *Revivals!* 69.

26. Jennie Lester Hill, "Fireside Industries in the Kentucky Mountains," *Southern Workman* 32 (April 1903): 208.

27. Ibid., 212.

28. Eaton, *Handicrafts of the Southern Highlands,* 82–83, 79.

29. Ibid., 237, 241.

30. Garry G. Barker, *The Handcraft Revival in Southern Appalachia, 1930–1990* (Knoxville: University of Tennessee Press, 1991), 19. For further discussion of the guild and its history, see Eaton, *Handicrafts of the Southern Highlands,* 237–54; Becker, *Selling Tradition,* 73–92; and Whisnant, *All That Is Native and Fine,* 161–64. Memorandum, G. A. Schweppe to W. L. Sturdevant, September 25, 1934, 4, cited in Becker, *Selling Tradition,* 84.

31. "Mountain Baskets," *American Magazine of Art* 26 (December 1933): 546.

32. H. Green, "Culture and Crisis," 35; Eaton, 253–54; Becker, *Selling Tradition,* 212.

33. Becker, *Selling Tradition,* 99–100.

34. John Sloan and Oliver LaFarge, *Introduction to American Indian Art* (New York: Exposition of Indian Tribal Arts, 1931), 5–6, 56, 53. Sloan was a long-time patron of Indian arts. As president of the Society of Independent Artists he had organized previous shows of Indian paintings in association with the society's annual exhibitions from 1920 until 1922. Amelia White was secretary of the Eastern Association on Indian Affairs and a founding member of the Rockefeller-funded Indian

Arts Fund. For further discussion of the *Exposition of Indian Tribal Arts,* see W. Jackson Rushing, *Native American Art and the New York Avant-Garde: A History of Cultural Primitivism* (Austin: University of Texas Press, 1995), 125–26.

35. Elizabeth Cowling, "The Eskimos, The American Indians, and the Surrealists," *Art History* 1, no. 4 (1978): 486, 488. For further treatment of the surrealists and their relationship with indigenous cultures, see Barbara Braun, "Art from the Land of the Savages, or Surrealists in the New World," *Boston Review* 13, nos. 5–6 (1988): 5–6, 18–19, and Braun, *Pre-Columbian Art and the Post-Columbian World: Ancient American Sources of Modern Art* (New York: Harry N. Abrams, 1993); Aldona Jonaitis, "Creations of Mystics and Philosophers: The White Man's Perceptions of Northwest Coast Indian Art from the 1930s to the Present," *American Indian Culture and Research Journal* 5, no. 1 (1981): 1–45; and Evan Maurer, "Dada and Surrealism," in *"Primitivism" in Twentieth-Century Art,* ed. William Rubin, vol. 2 (New York: Museum of Modern Art, 1984), 541–84.

36. Sloan and LaFarge, *Introduction to American Indian Art,* 6.

37. Walter Pach, "The Indian Tribal Arts: A Critic's View of the Significance and Value of a Unique American Asset," *New York Times,* November 22, 1931; Edward Alden Jewell, "The American Indian Exhibition: A Tradition Lives On," *New York Times,* December 6, 1931.

38. For an exhaustive discussion of the board's history, see Robert Schrader, *The Indian Arts and Crafts Board: An Aspect of New Deal Indian Policy* (Albuquerque: University of New Mexico Press, 1983).

39. *Indian Art in the United States and Alaska: A Pictorial Record of the Indian Exhibition at the Golden Gate International Exposition,* prepared by the Indian Arts and Crafts Board of the U.S. Department of the Interior at the Federal Building on Treasure Island, San Francisco, 1939 (Ann Arbor, Michigan: University Microfilms).

40. Ibid.

41. Frederick H. Douglas and Rene d'Harnoncourt, *Indian Art of the United States* (New York: Museum of Modern Art, 1941). Further analysis of this landmark show is provided by W. Jackson Rushing, "Marketing the Affinity of the Primitive and the Modern: Rene d'Harnoncourt and 'Indian Art of the United States,'" in *The Early Years of Native American Art History: The Politics of Scholarship and Collecting,* ed. Janet C. Berlo (Seattle: University of Washington Press, 1992), 191–236.

42. Douglas and d'Harnoncourt, *Indian Art of the United States,* 199–200; "All-American Art," *Art Digest,* January 1, 1941, 17; Jean Charlot, "All-American," *Nation* 152, no. 6 (1941): 165; Harold Ickes, "Department of the Interior Press Release, 13 January 1941," Indian Rights Association Papers, Microfilm, reel 120, plate 92, cited in Schrader, *The Indian Arts and Crafts Board,* 231.

43. Barnett Newman, *Northwest Coast Indian Painting* (New York: Betty Parsons Gallery, 1946).

44. Rayna Green, introduction to the Dover Edition, in Eaton, *Handicrafts of the Southern Highlands,* xvi; Batteau, *The Invention of Appalachia,* 127–28, 132.

45. Batteau, *The Invention of Appalachia,* 87, 127.

46. Mary Ela, "Made by Hand," *Mountain Life and Work* 16, no. 3 (fall 1940): 7, cited in Barker, *Handcraft Revival in Southern Appalachia,* 37.

47. Barker, *Handcraft Revival in Southern Appalachia,* 40–41, 43; Stevens, "The Revival of Handicrafts," 282.

48. Whisnant, *All That Is Native and Fine,* 175; Barker, *Handcraft Revival in Southern Appalachia,* 42.

49. *Crafts in the Southern Highlands* (Asheville: Southern Highland Handicraft Guild, 1958), 21, 12–13.

50. Ibid., 7–8.

51. Ibid., 14, 21, 27.

52. *Shared Visions: Native American Painters and Sculptors in the Twentieth Century,* proceedings

of a conference held at the Heard Museum, May 8–11, 1991 (Phoenix: Heard Museum, 1991), 74. For further discussion of the conference and the related Southwestern Indian Art Project, see Joy Gritton, *The Institute of American Indian Arts: Modernism and U.S. Indian Policy* (Albuquerque: University of New Mexico Press, 2000).

53. Frederick J. Dockstader, *Directions in Indian Art,* proceedings of a conference held at the University of Arizona, March 20–21, 1959 (Tucson: University of Arizona Press, 1959), 26, 19, 28.

54. "A Proposal for an Exploratory Workshop in Art for Talented Younger Indians," October 15, 1959, 1, Rockefeller Foundation archives, RF 1.2 Series 200 R, Box 430, Folder 3708.

55. David L. Patrick et al., *Southwest Indian Art: A Report to the Rockefeller Foundation Covering the Activities of the First Exploratory Workshop in Art for Talented Younger Indians Held at the University of Arizona in the Summer of 1960* (Tucson: University of Arizona Press, 1960), 36–37; "Exhibition: Student Work, Second Annual Southwest Indian Art Project—1961," University Art Gallery, July 21—August 4, 1961, Rockefeller Foundation Archives, RF 1.2, 200 R, Box 431, Folder 3709.

56. Lloyd New, *Young Indian Painters from the Institute of American Indian Arts* (Santa Fe: Museum of New Mexico, 1966).

57. *American Indian Performing Arts Exhibition* (Washington, D.C.: U.S. Department of the Interior, 1964), 10.

58. *Young American Indian Artists* (New York: Riverside Museum, 1965), 1; Harvey Stahl, "Recent Exhibitions," *Arts Magazine* 40, no. 4 (1966): 52–54.

59. "An Evening with the Young Indian Painters from the Institute of American Indian Arts," printed program, Museum of New Mexico, Santa Fe, March 11, 1966, p. 3, Institute of American Indian Arts Archives.

60. Becker, *Selling Tradition,* 39, 9; Whisnant, *All That Is Native and Fine,* 100, 63.

61. Gail Tremblay, "Cultural Survival and Innovation: Native American Aesthetics," in *Revivals!* 80–81.

62. Becker, *Selling Tradition,* 127.

63. George Boyce to Martin N. B. Holm, 13 April 1962, George Boyce Papers; Stevens, "The Revival of Handicrafts," 286.

64. Caudill, *Night Comes to the Cumberlands,* 29–30.

65. Barker, *Handcraft Revival in Southern Appalachia,* 20.

66. Tremblay, "Cultural Survival and Innovation," 77.

67. Richard Blaustein, "Beyond Nostalgia," *Now and Then* 6, no. 3 (fall 1989): 3, cited in Barker, *Handcraft Revival in Southern Appalachia,* 218.

CHAPTER 9

P*ICTURING* S*OVEREIGNTY*

Landscape in Contemporary Native American Art

KATE MORRIS

Every part of this soil is sacred in the estimation of my people.
Every hillside, every valley, every plain and grove has been hallowed
by some sad or happy event in days long vanished.

SEEALTH (CHIEF SEATTLE), DECEMBER 1853

*I*f the basic tenet of sovereignty is the exercise of control over access to resources, information, and knowledge, then it stands to reason that to witness sovereignty is oftentimes to encounter silences. This chapter concerns one such silence: the absence of an entire genre of painting in the oeuvre of contemporary indigenous art. That genre, landscape, is conspicuously absent, given the preeminence of land in the matrix of Native culture, economics, and politics. As Seealth's words remind us, the physical land is the fabric from which a people's history is woven. In more academic terms, a people's occupation of, and connection to, the land is the defining aspect of the words indigenous, aboriginal, and native.

Today, Native land claims against the United States and Canadian governments number in the hundreds, while tribal pursuit of avenues of economic development of physical and natural resources is coupled with the resurgence of Native environmentalist movements. In the realm of art, a plethora of contemporary works by indigenous artists have both reflected and championed these causes; however, even in exhibits devoted to the subject of land, there is a dearth of paintings that might reasonably be defined as landscape paintings. As curator Jaune Quick-to-See Smith wrote in her introductory remarks to *Our Land/Ourselves: American Indian Contemporary Artists* (1990): "The artists in this exhibit take multiple approaches to describing land/landscape. It is more rare to find a horizon line than not. It is more rare to find political content than not. It is more rare to find realism than not."[1]

Quick-to-See Smith notes that what is missing from the oeuvre is the quality that defines the European landscape tradition: perspectival illusionism. In *Our Land/Ourselves,* for instance, only a handful of the paintings convey any sense of spatial depth. More often, the artists have compressed the pictorial space and affirmed the physical surface of the work by affixing collage elements, massing the paint, or writing on the canvas. These techniques are common to modernists, who, according to critic Clement Greenberg, eschew perspectival illusionism in favor of the pure, irreducible qualities of painting—the physical surface of the canvas, the flatness of the picture plane, the textural quality of paint. Illusionism, however, is not merely a formalist phenomenon. As James Duncan has written, this type of representation has its origins "in the practice of art in Renaissance Italy and in philosophy as it was revolutionized by Descartes." Parallel developments in art and science were predicated on the notion that the system of linear perspective could be used to reveal or record truth. Duncan summarizes: "Perspectival painting became one of the first Western projects which, in the name of science, reason, and objectivity, denied its artifice and claimed to offer a mimetic reproduction of the world of experience." Two aspects of this statement are precisely relevant to the study of landscape paintings: first, that formal developments in painting are inexorably linked to cultural phenomena such as philosophic and scientific systems, and second, that perspectival painting in particular is associated with a deeply ingrained notion of objectivity. While the former assumption continues to be reinforced in writings on landscape, Duncan and other theorists have thoroughly discredited the latter. The myth of objectivity—which Duncan refers to as the "denial of artifice"—has been exploded, leaving in its wake the absolute certainty that illusionist, European-style landscape paintings have illustrated, and continue to illustrate, something more than an objective view.[2]

The exact nature of a landscape's subjectivity is still a matter of debate. Are landscapes a predominantly personal projection of the imagination onto wood, water, and rock, as Simon Schama suggests in *Landscape and Memory* (1995)? Or are landscapes "social hieroglyphs," to be deciphered as textual systems, as suggested by W. J. T. Mitchell in *Landscape and Power* (1994)? In the former view, the shaping perception of the artist/viewer is acknowledged to be the agent that transforms raw matter into landscape; however, the emphasis is placed on the individual mind, rather than on a larger sociocultural construct. Schama writes: "Although we are accustomed to separate nature and human perception into two realms, they are, in fact, indivisible. Before it can ever be a repose for the senses, landscape is the work of the mind. Its scenery is built up as much from strata of memory as from layers of rock."[3]

Whether landscapes are personal or political constructs, they are nonetheless highly subjective expressions, laden with culturally specific meaning. Thus landscape depictions by artists with dramatically divergent worldviews—especially regarding land—might be expected to be correspondingly dissimilar. The remainder of this chapter enumerates the ways in which depictions of land by indigenous artists differ from those by European painters, in form, in content, and in ideological intention.

From the time of the earliest European voyages to the New World, navigational charts and coastal profiles drawn up by ships' crews were complemented by landscape paintings produced by professionally trained shipboard artists. Though rarely free of romantic conventions, the works produced by these artists were regarded as scientific documents, and the landscapes were reproduced and distributed alongside hundreds of illustrations of the flora and fauna of the New World. For example, upon the return of Captain James Cook's *Endeavor* to England in 1771, the amassed pencil sketches, watercolors, and oils of the ship's three artists were entrusted to John Hawkesworth, who oversaw their conversion to engravings and their publication alongside the journal entries of the *Endeavor*'s crew. Hawkesworth's volumes became best-sellers in their day, and the engravings therein inspired everything from popular entertainment to interior decor.[4]

As the age of exploration gave way to the era of the Grand Tour, more and more members of the European gentry journeyed to places heretofore known only through travel narratives. Perhaps in deliberate imitation of the popular expedition illustrations, many travelers either painted or sketched the lands they visited or bought souvenir paintings abroad. Back home in Europe, these paintings served a dual purpose: on the private level, they provided a personal memento of the trip; on the public level, they could attest to the veracity of the tourist's account of his or her travels. In this sense, landscape paintings were not unlike the spears, shrunken heads, and other trinkets found in the "curiosity cabinets" of the truly wealthy. Mitchell has argued that this practice continues today, making landscape painting the ultimate form of tourist art.[5]

The public consumption of landscape paintings in Britain, however, was not limited to those paintings that described exotic and far-off locales. The English gentry, for instance, had for centuries been commissioning paintings of their estates, either as landscapes per se or as backdrops to family portraits. By the mid-nineteenth century, the middle class had joined in, buying paintings, not of their own land, but of the English countryside.[6] Given the fact that this practice flourished after the passage of the Parliamentary enclosure acts—which bolstered the gentry's monopoly on land-holding—it might be concluded that the middle class regarded the ownership of landscape paintings not only as a status symbol but also as a substitute for the ownership of land itself.[7]

Late eighteenth-, early nineteenth-century landscape paintings served three principal functions: first, as descriptive accounts of unseen places; second, as status objects; and third, as the embodiment of a desire to possess the land depicted therein. Whether the landscapes in question picture "homelands" or foreign soils, whether they be for public or private contemplation, they are all irrevocably bound to a prevailing historical process: colonialism. As Mitchell has testified, the great moments in the development of landscape painting coincide with periods of imperial expansion: "Is it possible that landscape, understood as the historical 'invention' of a new visual/pictorial medium, is integrally connected with imperialism? Certainly the roll call of major 'originating' movements in landscape painting—China, Japan, Rome, seventeenth-century Holland and France, eighteenth- and nineteenth-century Britain—makes the question hard to avoid."[8]

Support for this theory can be found not only in the history of the production and consumption of landscape paintings but also within the pictures themselves. Consider, for instance, the formal, rather than ideological, aspects of perspectival illusionism. By definition, linear perspective—the pictorial system in which all orthogonals in a composition meet in a single vanishing point—creates the illusion of depth, of recession into space. In some perspectival paintings the picture plane is reimagined as a window onto the painted world. In the case of landscape paintings, the surface is regarded not so much as a window but as a door. Where the eye leads, the mind follows, drawing the viewer, at least in his or her imagination, into the landscape. Ann Bermingham has written: "Traditionally, when viewing a landscape painting, we expect the organization of light and color to highlight what is important and to lead the eye in stages into the distance. We also expect objects to be arranged in a way that facilitates this movement." Elizabeth Helsinger concurs; she has demonstrated that nineteenth-century English landscape paintings often incorporate an open space or road in the foreground, providing a point of entry into the picture plane. If European landscape paintings are expected to "direct the eye on its journey to the horizon," then the formal construction of such paintings is perfectly suited to the colonialist process, which is itself characterized by the relentless push into the peripheries of an ever-expanding empire.[9]

When the colonial peripheries are the subject of European landscape paintings, the *manner* in which the landscape is represented is no less suited to the industry of expansion than the formal characteristics are. In texts, for instance, the peripheries were often depicted as if devoid of any civilization. For example, Mary Louise Pratt has characterized John Barrow's *Account of Travels into the Interior of Southern Africa in the Years 1797 and 1798* (1801) as "a strange, attenuated kind of narrative because it does everything possible to minimize all human presence. . . . Barrow's book exemplifies a kind of discursive division of labor common to much travel writing of his time: the main narrative deals with landscape, while indigenous peoples are represented separately in descriptive portraits."[10]

The obfuscation of indigenous life, whether deliberate or unintentional on the part of the author, supports the myth of the inveterate European explorer as a solitary figure, "alone in deepest Africa," according to Duncan. Duncan concludes that "the tropes of solitude used to describe the explorations of Europeans who invariably traveled with and among large numbers of Africans only make sense within a discourse which rhetorically makes Africans absent by representing them as less than human. Such rhetoric of absence could only be believable to a European audience that was deeply racist. The encoded message in such [descriptions] was that Africa was a land of disorder and savagery and that the European stood as the sole representative of order, the only rational, civilized presence there."[11]

For artists, the periphery never seemed quite as "dark" as it did to writers; however, the artist considered himself no less alone than his counterpart. The Australian artist George Angas (1822–86), for instance, is well known for his romantic portrayals of New Zealand and its inhabitants—both Native and settler. Nonetheless, Angas consistently diminished the Maori presence in his writings, dismissing the Natives as "savages":

> The view of Tongariro from this spot was magnificent, as it appeared lit up with all the resplendent tints of evening: the glow of the setting sun fell with a roseate warmth on the steeps of the mountain; and after the orb [sank] below the horizon, leaving the deep valleys veiled in gray and purple twilight, its glory gilded the snow-streaked crater, and tinged with ruby and orange the volumes of vapour that rolled up from that vast cauldron. It was indeed a majestic scene: sublime in its grandeur; and I wished there had been other than savages to have gazed with me upon its glories.[12]

According to Pratt, such descriptions, and by extension painted depictions, "not only partook of the European aesthetic codes favouring panoramic views, but also portrayed a country that was rich in resources, vast, and most important, empty: a place, in other words, that was open to European imperialism."[13]

The same strategy holds true in landscape depictions of North America, where even the explorer's presence was diminished in the vast emptiness of the American West. Albert Bierstadt, the quintessential European painter active in the American West in the post–Civil War period, depicted the landscape in the same manner that Angas described Tongariro—majestic, sublime, and largely empty. Europeans rarely inhabit Bierstadt's landscapes; when Native Americans appear, they are almost incidental, an extension of nature. Schama describes them as such, in his discussion of Bierstadt's *Giant Redwood Trees of California* (1874): "Instead of the sentimental, inanimate elegy for the vanished redwood redskin [Schama is referring here to 'native' trees], Bierstadt includes three Indians, a brave with his son seated by the pool and a squaw *[sic]* returning with a basket on her back, a Native American version of the Georgic idyll. Most crucially, the tepee-like triangular opening in the side of the foremost tree is evidently the Indians' dwelling place. It is the most literal translation of what John Muir . . . meant when he wrote of returning to the American woods as 'going home.'" Schama is correct in identifying the function of the Natives as evocative of "the Georgic idyll"; however, he fails to note the significance of the minute scale of the human figures. Whether evocative of nature or of savagery, the Native presence is elided in representations of the periphery so as not to deny the potential for European entrance into the scene.[14]

Nevertheless, as Charles Harrison has stated, "There is no such thing as a landscape without human figures, whether or not figures exist there." Harrison is technically correct, given the root of the word itself. The Dutch word, *landschap,* derived as it is from the German, *Landschaft,* denotes a unit of human occupation.[15] The perceived contradiction here, that landscape is defined as occupied but depicted as if empty, is only resolved when one considers the tense of the representation. While romantic landscapes are understood to represent a mythic, pastoral, or edenic past, depictions of the colonial periphery unmistakably represent the future, the *potential* for occupation or exploitation. As John Hanning Speke recalled his first glimpse of Lake Victoria, Nyanza, Africa, in the 1860s: "The pleasure of the mere view [vanished in favor of] those more intense emotions which are called up by the consideration of the commercial and geographical importance of the prospect before me." In this passage, the explorer is considering the "prospect" before him. The word *prospect* can describe a view "of things within the reach of the eye," but being from the Latin *prospicere,* "to look forward," the term more commonly denotes an expectation. With reference to landscape paintings of the periphery, a third connotation of the word is equally appropriate: the verb "to prospect" specifically describes the act of seeking mineral wealth to wrest from the earth.[16]

All three connotations are evoked in the mid-nineteenth-century landscape photography of Carleton Watkins. Watkins trained his eye (and his lens) on many of the same subjects as his close contemporary Bierstadt did—the "grizzly giants" and the monuments of Yosemite—however, he did so in the employ of the California State Geological Survey. Under this aegis, Watkins carefully documented the actual and the potential exploitation of California's natural resources. Joel Snyder has described the

philosophy underlying Watkins's works: "His views of the Pacific Coast from California to Oregon often cast it as an unspoiled and unspoilable Garden of Eden—as places
to visit, but also to live in. In other words, Watkins's landscapes address the Pacific
Coast as potential real estate and as a site for eastern investment and development."
Snyder finds these photographs "essentially invitational in character," a description
that might be applied to any European depiction of the New World landscape.[17]

As viewers trained to perceive the landscape through the filter of colonialist
representation, we tend to regard all references to land as "invitational." How then are
we to regard references to the land in paintings by indigenous artists, who have every
reason to avoid issuing further invitation into an already relentlessly appropriated
landscape? Might we expect to encounter only deliberately subversive expressions?
The landscape has been a subject for Native American painters since the inception of
Native American painting. J. J. Brody writes, "The Mimbres people [circa 1000 C.E.]
drew the world around them as they conceived it. . . . They drew animals, mythical
creatures, abstractions of mountains, clouds, and plants as they saw, remembered,
and imagined them." One thousand years later, artists such as Emmi Whitehorse
(Navajo), George Morrison (Chippewa), Truman Lowe (Hochunk), Alex Janvier
(Dene), Joe Feddersen (Colville), and many others continue to draw the world as they
experience it; they have transformed landscape paintings into evocative personal and
political expressions.[18]

Nest of Suns (1998; plate 12) depicts the western landscape, and in certain formal
respects it resembles Watkins's photographs of the same subject. In each of five 24-in.-
x–32-in. panels, majestic landscape features such as mountains, valleys, and escarpments are barely contained within the limits of the canvas. *Nest of Suns* is the work of
Walla Walla painter James Lavadour, a self-taught artist who has been painting
landscapes on the Confederated Tribes of the Umatilla Indian Reservation in northeastern Oregon for more than twenty-five years. Unlike the explorers and tourists
discussed thus far, Lavadour is a true "insider," and that aspect of his identity results in
paintings that are fundamentally different from those of the European landscape
tradition. For instance, while Lavadour affirms that the lands outside his studio
inspire his paintings, he insists that the works represent something more than an
objective view. "Rather than the depiction or representation of a specific landscape
scene my object has been to display the occurrence of landscape inherent in the act of
painting."[19]

"For every application of paint," Lavadour says, "there's a landscape." This sentiment is borne out by the artist's method, which involves the gradual buildup of layers
of paint on the surface of the canvas. Each layer of paint is wiped with a cloth or
worked with a palette knife; as many as one hundred layers may accrue in this

manner. Lavadour does not object when critics compare this process to "the natural course of mountain building—deposition, erosion, accretion," for he believes that the relationship between the artist and the landscape is a reciprocal one, rather than one of exploitation. "Whatever is in the earth is in me and whatever is in me is what I make art out of. I view making art as an expressive event of nature. . . . In paint there is hydrology, erosion, mass, gravity, mineral deposits, etc.; in me there is fire, energy, force, movement, dimension, and reflective awareness."[20]

This sense of intimate connection to the land is shared by many contemporary Native artists. Cherokee artist Jimmie Durham explains: "We do not traditionally see the earth as a mother but as a process that intimately includes us. . . . The land is exactly part of us and vice versa. Our collective and individual spirits are then exactly part of the process." For Truman Lowe, where you live "runs through your body" and evolves into your work. Ultimately, according to Ojibwa artist Carl Beam, "all landscape is internal." In this respect, then, it seems that landscapes painted or sculpted by these artists (if not all Native American artists) must be regarded as highly personal expressions—projections of the imagination onto wood, water, and rock, as Schama suggests—rather than as the textual systems that Mitchell considers them.[21]

Yet Lavadour's paintings are laden with intention beyond personal expression. Critic Ron Glowen regards the multipaneled compositions such as *Nest of Suns* as "metaphors for the division of land into parcels subject to ownership and exchange." After all, Glowen points out, Lavadour was at one time a land-use planner for the Confederated Tribes of the Umatilla Indian Reservation. He concludes that "the fragmentation of each ensemble represents the ruptured unity and harmony of nature." In fact, the artist's incorporation of as many as twelve discrete panels into larger compositions does not fragment the imagery; rather, it compounds it. In Lavadour's work, the composite imagery conveys greater meaning or expression than the components would individually. There is, for instance, a dynamism generated by the juxtaposition of the panels; an almost stormlike energy radiates from the center of *Nest of Suns*. Another effect of the grouping of the panels is that the resultant compositions constitute abstract, even symbolic forms, such as crosses, arches, and open rectangles. Once the viewer perceives the abstract element of the composition, the illusionism of the individual canvases is tempered. Lavadour's compounded imagery, coupled with his mitigation of the perspectival qualities of the paintings, may frustrate the viewer because both serve to block the viewer's access to the landscape.[22]

Other formal aspects of Lavadour's work serve the same purpose. In *Nest of Suns,* for instance, the scale of the landscape changes in each of the panels, as does the degree of recession into the picture plane. Each time the viewer's eye begins to follow the orthogonals into the perspectival space, the relatively shallower plane of an adjoining panel draws the eye back to the surface. Further, the open space or road that Helsinger located in the foreground of English landscape paintings is entirely absent from these paintings; Lavadour provides neither literal space for the viewer to occupy nor means to enter it. In contrast to Watkins's "invitational" works, Lavadour's landscapes prove essentially inviolable.

In addition to Lavadour's manipulation of the formal characteristics of landscape painting, the artist's iconographic mainstay, fire, is also psychologically alienating to some viewers. The recurrence of flames in works such as *Under Fire* (1990–91), *Honey Tongue* (1997), and *Nest of Suns* has led at least one critic to describe the paintings as "apocalyptic visions."[23] In the European landscape tradition, by contrast, the destructive force of fire is acknowledged, yet celebrated. In New Zealand, where the dense native foliage was put to the torch by colonists, ostensibly to accommodate British agricultural practices but also in an effort to naturalize the still-alien landscape, the "frozen flame" and the "slain tree" became powerful iconographic symbols of nation building.[24] In the 1830s the "slain tree" motif entered the vocabulary of landscape painting in the United States through the works of the Hudson River school painters. According to Barbara Novak, the tree stump motif became a symbol of progress, sometimes to be mourned, sometimes celebrated, nonetheless evocative of "the march of civilization." In New Zealand as well as America the felled tree in landscape paintings "defines new values, replacing myth with history, the individual with the community. The stump, then, signifies the community participation that constructs social fabric." In other words, European landscape paintings act in the service not only of colonialism but also of nationalism.[25]

A critical double standard operates here; as flames in European landscape paintings are understood to reference constructive histories, they constitute positive reinforcement of the immigrant status quo. In Lavadour's work, on the other hand, a landscape on fire is considered an "apocalyptic vision." Lavadour vigorously contests this interpretation, in part because of its moralizing tone, but also because he regards the flames as a creative force, rather than a destructive one. "In me there is fire, energy, force, movement, dimension, and reflective awareness," he avers, and the titles of his works, such as *New Blood* (1990), *Blossom* (1990), and even *Nest of Suns,* reinforce this creative aspect. Finally, it must be acknowledged that Lavadour's flames engage the viewer viscerally, even if the viewer remains "outside" the landscape. In *Nest of Suns* four of the five panels are "on fire," yet the central panel is not; this creates a vortex around which the energy of the outer panels rotates. This vortex activates the space between the viewer and the work, simultaneously drawing the viewer into the landscape and fixing him or her outside of it.[26]

If, according to Lavadour, "whatever is in the earth is in the artist, and whatever is

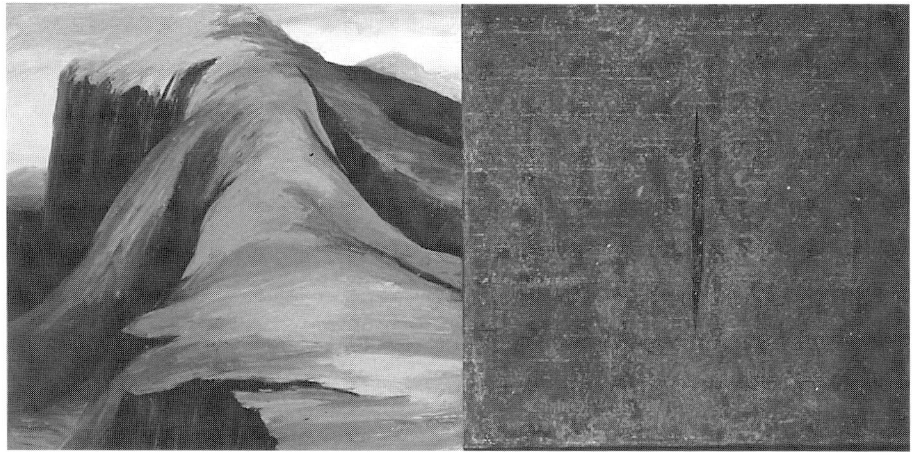

in the artist is what he makes art out of," we might also regard *Nest of Suns* as a metaphoric extension of the artist's body. The link between the canvas, the artist, and the landscape is made explicit in the title of Lavadour's most recent exhibition of landscape paintings at PDX Gallery in Portland, *My Body's Edge.* In *Nest of Suns,* Lavadour claims for himself a place of calm, from which his creative and expressive energy radiates. Moreover, Lavadour asserts that the landscape he depicts is not empty; the artist himself inhabits it.

Lavadour's interest in the liminal spaces where interior and exterior are joined is shared by Cherokee artist Kay WalkingStick. In the 1980s WalkingStick was working with "pure abstraction . . . about the visual world as well as the interior world," an exploration that would ultimately lead the artist to the diptych format that has become the foundation of her work. The diptychs, such as *The Abyss* (1989), *Letting Go from Chaos to Calm* (1990), *Spirit Center* (1991), *Remnant of Cataclysm* (1992), *With Love to Marsden* (1995), and *Venere Alpina* (1997; fig. 9.1), each pair an abstract or symbolic form with a representational landscape image. As WalkingStick recalls, the landscape imagery evolved gradually, out of abstract forms. She had been working with layers of beeswax and acrylic, scratching through each successive layer to reveal the colors in the layers below. After thirty or more layers, WalkingStick says, the paintings just began to look like landscapes, despite her lack of intention to produce such images.[27]

The paintings became more and more about the earth, the landscape, and they looked, many of them, like seeing the earth in the geological diagrams one sees of the different-layered remains of the various eons of the history of the earth. The paintings had this feeling of accruing the way the earth has accrued with layers of rock and sediment. The surface itself looks very much like limestone. . . . And it has, because of the wax, a very organic quality, so that it related to the earth itself, to the ancient earth, to the earth as seen from thousands of miles up.[28]

The "imagistic" quality of the landscapes resulted from an equally unanticipated atmospheric effect. "I had gone from a very flat paint to a very manipulated color. And as soon as you manipulate color you're manipulating atmosphere; you see space. And so they were taking on more and more of not a landscape abstraction but a look of real landscape because they were becoming atmospheric." As the landscape aspect of these paintings became more and more prevalent, WalkingStick recalls that she was reluctant to abandon abstraction. She began to pair the landscape panels with purely abstract counterparts, and she found "a kind of symbiosis there that was quite remarkable, that [she] would not have predicted."[29]

Critics, even Native ones, tend to interpret the two aspects of the diptychs, abstract and realistic, as "two different perceptions of the world, Cherokee and Anglo-American." WalkingStick is half Cherokee, raised in Syracuse, far away from her Cherokee father, whom she barely knew. Many of her early works, including diptychs, address the question of her biracial identity. *Talking Leaves* (1993), for instance, is an eighteen-page book in which WalkingStick juxtaposes gouache self-portraits with insensitive remarks people have made about her mixed heritage.[30]

Especially given the artist's own stated interest in issues of biculturalism, we can reasonably regard the two panels of the diptychs as versions of a common quotation, expressed in different languages. WalkingStick, moreover, regards the two aspects as essentially complementary, engaged in conversation with one another. "One is not the abstraction of the other," she says; "one is the extension of the other. I want the two portions to resonate with one another like the stanzas of a poem."[31] If they diverge at all, WalkingStick explains, it is not in expressive language but in content. "The two portions represent two kinds of knowledge of the earth. One is visual, immediate, and particular, the other is spiritual, long-term, and nonspecific. . . . One side refers to the present while the other side refers to both the past and the future."[32] In this respect WalkingStick's diptychs are almost the physical embodiment of Schama's book title *Landscape and Memory*. As the artist describes them, the representational side is not only immediate and particular but "short-term," a "snap shot" of the landscape, while the abstractions are about a different kind of memory, "that memory that goes back eons but forward eons as well."[33]

The two components of *Venere Alpina* are engaged in a slightly different dialogue than that of WalkingStick's earlier diptychs. In particular, this diptych is unusual in that it is the abstract side, not the imagistic panel, that has a layered effect. The right panel is composed of wood, canvas, steel mesh, and other mixed media, while the left is simply oil on canvas without the addition of wax. On the right, a rent in the steel mesh reveals a subsurface of blue sequins and red and black glitter. The copper-colored patina of the steel mesh and the glistening red that is exposed within the gash are suggestive of the human body. At the same time, the abstraction evokes the landscape; a glimmer of riches beneath the surface both attests to and confronts a legacy of exploitation of the earth's natural resources. As WalkingStick has stated, the incorporation of various metals into the diptychs "represents the economic urges underlying the rape of our land."[34]

Whether the diptychs are about kinds of memory or about the artist's "view of the earth and its sacred quality," WalkingStick is adamant that the paintings are not landscapes.[35] At least, she says, "they are not landscapes in the sense that Thomas Cole or Church painted landscapes." WalkingStick's insistence on this point is due to her clear understanding of the role European landscape painters and their creations played in the colonization of the Americas. As she told Lawrence Abbott: "These artists brought in the notion of Manifest Destiny and that the earth is there to be exploited for mankind's use, which is one of the things that has destroyed our United States. Not just the aboriginal inhabitants, but the earth itself." WalkingStick's comments regarding many of the formal qualities of her work must be reconsidered in light of this statement. For instance, WalkingStick has stated that she adheres to a prescribed mathematical formula when determining the dimensions of her diptychs. This formula is based not on the size of the landscape image but on the size of the geometric form in the abstract panel. Thus, though perfectly balanced, her composi-tions place an imperceptible emphasis on the symbolic element. Further, Walking-Stick frequently builds up the abstract panel to a greater extent than the landscape panel, so that, when hung on the wall, the former literally overshadows the latter. The intent, according to the artist, is to "maintain that sense of it being an object, of it being concrete: it is real."[36] In *Venere Alpina,* the panels are slightly different sizes and deliberately offset. A small gap between the panels acts as a "speedbump. . . . It forces you to slow down, to look at one side, then slowly look at the other, then look back."[37]

By continually asserting the primacy of the abstract panel, by repeatedly endeav-oring to "activate the surface" and otherwise affirm the objecthood of both sides of the diptychs, WalkingStick, like Lavadour, effectively mitigates the illusionistic qualities of the landscapes in her work.[38] Nevertheless, WalkingStick strives to preserve the expressive quality of those landscapes. "There is a primalness . . . a larger-than-life quality to them. They're not tamed, they're not controlled, they're not farmed, they're not pruned. . . . The landscape I like is not untouched but relatively raw; I like that in paintings—raw and edgy."[39]

One of WalkingStick's recent works, *Il Minotauro* (1998), is both raw and edgy; a primal, barren landscape spans both panels of the diptych. A jagged edge speckled with aluminum bisects the composition; it is but a remnant of the "speedbump" that WalkingStick provided her earlier diptychs. In the absence of both that break and an abstract panel, there would be little to bar the viewer's access to the landscape, were it not for the presence of the Minotaur, a naked, horned, featureless male on all-fours, who kneels facing the picture plane in the right panel. Though only an outline, the Minotaur constitutes an effective guardian of the landscape; he does not occupy the landscape, but hovers over it, existing on an intermediate plane, situated between the viewer and the landscape. With a deft touch, WalkingStick has cropped the edges of the canvas in such a way that the horns and fingers of the figure seem to extend out of the top and bottom of the composition. Any predisposition on the part of the viewer to enter, let alone exploit, WalkingStick's landscape is summarily dismissed as the Minotaur comes forth in challenge.

A final aspect of WalkingStick's diptychs is relevant to the discussion of landscape representation in Native American art. WalkingStick has described the diptychs as her "way of unifying the double life" that "all Native people, whether living on a reservation or separated from a tribal experience are living in some way." Walking-Stick's life is doubled by biculturalism, by "two kinds of knowledge of the earth," by the tension of remaining "Indian" while availing herself of the "technology of the late twentieth century." Her experience is also shaped by the fact that she does not live on a reservation; she paints from a vantage point removed from the tribal landscape. Jimmie Durham has described this predicament: "We Cherokees were driven from our homeland, and it seems we cannot go back, so we must then search always for ways to be part of some other, some broader homeland." Through her work, which she describes as the product of memory and invention, WalkingStick preserves her personal landscape. Perhaps this is what Carl Beam meant when he said that "all landscape is internal."[40]

The issue of displacement—of removal from ancestral lands, of literal and spiritual homelessness—is a recurring theme in contemporary Native American art. Richard Ray Whitman's 1985 photographic series *Street Chiefs* was an early and unflinching look at the predicament of homeless Indian men. Recently, both Zig Jackson and Hulleah Tsinhnahjinnie have addressed the issue of relocation in their respective works, *Entering Zig's Indian Reservation* (1998) and *Urban Survival* (1998). While it is tempting to interpret these works as disparaging statements lamenting the isolation of Native people in the city, Tsinhnahjinnie claims that her image of a feather lying on the pavement of San Francisco's Embarcadero "is about making home anywhere—it is all Indian land."[41]

The effort on the part of contemporary Native American artists to affirm that the ground underfoot is Native land has perhaps nowhere been as successful as in the case of the *Native Hosts* series by Cheyenne-Arapaho artist Hachivi Edgar Heap of Birds. In the late 1980s and early 1990s, Heap of Birds erected aluminum signs in major cities across the United States and Canada, informing the residents of each city who the original inhabitants were. Significantly, the statements were written in the present tense ("New York—Today Your Host Is Shinnecock") affirming an ongoing Native presence. In 1989, in the midst of his home state's celebration of the Oklahoma Land Run Centennial, Heap of Birds erected five billboards in Oklahoma City. These read: "Sooners Run Over Indian Nations Apartheid Oklahoma." Though certainly not landscapes, both *Native Hosts* and *Apartheid Oklahoma* are expressions of the artist's concerns regarding the land; both are powerful indictments of the dispossession of Native peoples.

Heap of Birds's utilization of the forms of mass media, such as advertising, road signs, T-shirts, and even the Times Square electronic billboard, has led the artist to be criticized for letting the message in his works take precedence over the visual qualities of the art. One critic wrote: "While there are political artists . . . who go to some trouble to make their work visually compelling, there are others for whom the visual character of the work seems hardly to matter. They are not using art to get a message across, rather, the getting across of the message is their art. . . . Hachivi Edgar Heap of Birds belongs to that growing body of artists for whom the message is the medium." This critic conveniently avoided Heap of Birds's abstract paintings when pronouncing his judgment; however, careful reading of the abstract works reveals that they, too, are embedded with "insurgent messages" about the land. Consider, for instance, Heap of Birds's installation in the National Gallery of Canada's *Land, Spirit, Power* show of 1992. One of those works, *American Policy* (1986–89), is illustrative of the artist's hallmark style—it is caustic, sardonic, and dense with meaning; word fragments such as "Moving against Earth," "Road Kill," and "Bombs Island Scar" are scrawled in pastel across each of thirty-two sheets of rag paper. Adjacent to *American Policy* are four abstract, color-field paintings, which constitute a series entitled *Neuf* (1991–92). In their repetition and juxtaposition of discrete, colorful fragments, the *Neuf* paintings echo the formal qualities of *American Policy;* however, as is the case with all abstract paintings, the content is more deeply encoded.[42]

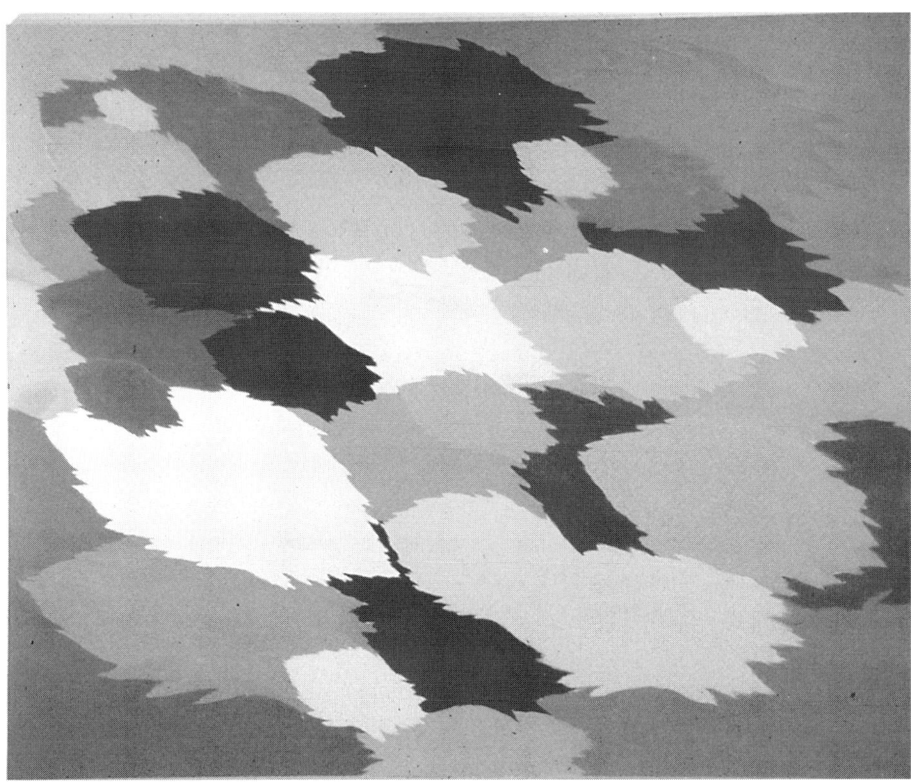

At first glance, differences among the four large (56 in. x 72 in.) *Neuf* paintings are nearly imperceptible (fig. 9.2); however, subtle variations in the number and size of the individual color blocks contribute to a sense of rhythm that resonates from the canvases. This sense of rhythm and vibrancy, the leaflike shapes of the color fragments, and the overall number of panels suggest the four seasons, despite the fact that the palette remains constant across the series. The title of the series, which means "four times" in the Cheyenne language, may serve to reinforce the notion of the changing seasons.[43] At the same time, *Neuf* evokes the four sacred colors and the four directions, as do other works in *Land, Spirit, Power.*[44] In the exhibition catalog, Heap of Birds stated that "[these] paintings have come from the old home-place in Oklahoma. Over many years of walking and watching in the out-of-doors, the images of movement, colour, pulse, and celebration have become an evolving visual language." In an interview with Abbott, Heap of Birds elaborated: "[The paintings] began from the canyon right outside the house. The earth color is very red here, so that came into it; and another part of the imagery is the break of the earth, how the earth washes." Certainly the movement, color, and pulse of the canyon that Heap of Birds describes are effectively conveyed in the *Neuf* series.[45]

The message of the *Neuf* paintings lies embedded in the formal qualities of the works, particularly in those aspects that are expressive of the artist's unique position in relation to the landscape. With the utterance of a single phrase—"old home-place"— the artist identifies himself as an insider, like Lavadour, irrefutably distinct from the majority of European landscape painters. Even when addressing a viewer who has never been to his reservation, Heap of Birds endeavors to convey that insider's perspective. "These four painted works seek to project the understanding that the world, as witnessed from the sage, cedar, and red canyon, is a lively and replenishing place." To a certain extent, then, the *Neuf* paintings can be regarded as invitational; the artist invites the viewer to share an experience, even a worldview. Nevertheless, the viewer is denied physical entrance into the landscape, as a result of the artist's choice of abstraction over perspectival illusionism as an expressive style.[46]

Standing in front of the *Neuf* paintings, the viewer finds herself fixed in a liminal space, neither fully within nor outside of the landscape. This position, familiar to anyone who has encountered Lavadour's vortex or WalkingStick's Minotaur is not an entirely disempowered one. According to one landscape theorist: "To the eye that has been properly educated a landscape presents itself as a spectacle, a deportment which in turn creates the position of the spectator. A landscape situates its spectator in an Olympian position." Given that this statement refers to the eye "properly educated" in the tradition of European landscape paintings, one would assume that the Native American artists discussed thus far would be reluctant to allow the spectator this "Olympian" position. Heap of Birds has voiced his concern: "It is wrongly accepted that we should all share the vantage point of the Euromale. This historical legacy is to be the focal point of human experience, just as once the sun was thought to revolve around the earth. As we have all chosen to stand on different points of this earth, we must be allowed to choose our own distinct priorities and references."[47]

For these artists, emancipation from the rigid confines of the subject-object relationship is to be achieved through the staking of claim to reference points distinctly different from those of the European landscape painters. By claiming their status as insiders, by personalizing events of nature, and by drawing analogies between their bodies and the landscape, Lavadour, WalkingStick, and Heap of Birds have done just that. Most important, they have chosen not to obscure their own agency. Pratt found that "the emissaries of the European states . . . positioned themselves in their discourse as neither ruler nor ruled, neither actor nor acted upon, but as invisible, passive, and personally innocent conduits for information." At the other end of the spectrum, Native American artists have endeavored to make themselves as visible and as effectual as possible. "We [must] challenge the white man through our use of the mass media [in art]. . . . The survival of our people is based upon our use of expressive forms of modern communication. The insurgent messages within these forms must serve as our present-day combative tactics."[48]

Despite this invocation, Quick-to-See Smith has noted, it is "more rare to find political content [in Native references to land] than not." Lucy Lippard agreed, writing alongside Quick-to-See Smith in the catalog for *Our Land/Ourselves*: "The bitterly satirical vein of Indian humor is for the most part absent from the work in this show. Most of these artists concentrate on the positive aspects of an unthreatened land. . . . This constitutes a form of prayerful thinking." While these authors are undeniably correct in their characterization of the works in the *Our Land/Ourselves* exhibit, and while the works of Lavadour and WalkingStick seem to support this generalization, there are notable exceptions to the rule that the "bitterly satirical vein of Indian humor" is absent from the genre of Native American landscape painting.[49]

George Longfish's triptych *The End of the Innocence* (1991–1992, plate 13), which covered nearly twenty-five horizontal feet of wall space at the *Indigena: Contemporary Native Perspectives in Canadian Art* exhibit in 1992, takes as its subject nothing less than the Indian condition on the eve of the Columbian quincentennial. In keeping with its size and subject, the painting is striking in its execution; vibrant colors and slashing brush strokes contrast with carefully stenciled words and photographic images seemingly frozen in time. Textual ambiguities abound as well: the Pawnee leader Pitaresaru shares the pictorial space with four Teenage Mutant Ninja Turtles and a Harley-Davidson emblem, while Medicine Crow and a golf ball flank the words "Sacred Land." All is not chaos, however. *The End of the Innocence* is closely governed by compositional rules of balance and symmetry. For instance, the central panel, which Longfish painted first, is also the most stable. All the elements in the panel are centered on the vertical axis, while horizontal stability is maintained by the zigzag line forming the upper border. In the flanking panels, the myriad words and colors increase in visual complexity; nonetheless, the zigzag lines angle in toward the center, and the outer boundaries of the triptych are defined by the two seated figures, each with his knees turned inward to close the composition.

A fine example of the style that Longfish refers to as "narrative abstraction," *The End of the Innocence* can be read as a series of landscapes. In each panel there is a horizon line; in the central panel, the area below the horizon is predominantly green, with patches of yellow and rust that clump like prairie grasses. In this panel, the underbelly of the leaping horse delineates red hills in the distance, above the horse is the night sky. In the left panel, the area below the horizon line is again the color of grass, and the inclusion of a golf ball to the right suggests a more specific—and more literal—reading of the "green." Jutting up from the horizon are eight blue streaks, diminishing into the perspectival distance like the poplars in van Gogh's painting of the same name. Above the horizon the sky is ablaze with color, and the jagged line, far less precisely drawn than in the central panel, may be read as lightning. Finally, in the right panel, an interior environment is represented—the grass has given way to a tiled space inhabited by cartoon heroes, and the chair of Pitaresaru rests solidly on the flowered rug of the photography studio in which he sits. Again, the sky is ablaze.[50]

When read in the context of landscape, many of the stenciled words on the painting support the narrative. For instance, in all three panels, the area under the horizon is designated "Land," "Sacred" or otherwise. In the left panel, all but one of the words in the green field relate to the physical land: "Mineral Rights," "Toxic Waste," and even, "Reservations." By contrast, the words above the horizon represent concepts, such as "Self-Determination" and "Self-Sufficiency." "Appropriate Goods" and "Inappropriate Goods" inhabit this space as well. According to Longfish, the "Appropriate Goods" include "Navajo Electronics," "Blackfeet Pencil Co.," and "Apache Ski Resort," while "Bingo," "Cut Rate Cigarettes," and "Gambling" are "Inappropriate Goods."[51] In Longfish's critical view, the word "Spiritual" floats above these lists, as if it too has been commodified. Below, "Sacred Land" has been turned into a golf course. Repeating words from the composition, Longfish has titled the whole panel "Appropriate Goods."

The right panel, which is titled, "History Repeating Itself," is even more disheartening than the left panel. This one juxtaposes Native land (the word "Land" appears surrounded by the names of Indian tribes) with "Reservations," "Termination," "Acculturation," and "Assimilation." In the extreme right, the number of "Broken Treaties" seems to have been tallied: "389." The massacre of more than two hundred unarmed Sioux men, women, and children by federal soldiers at "Wounded Knee 1872" is commemorated, as is the American Indian Movement's firefight with U.S. soldiers on the same site more than eighty years later ("Wounded Knee 1973"). With the single word "Rainforest," Longfish reminds the viewer that the kinds of destruction visited on indigenous peoples and the land are not unique to North America.[52]

For the most part, Longfish's assessment of the Native landscape on the eve of the Columbian quincentennial is not a positive one. Nevertheless, an element of Lippard's "prayerful thinking" may be embedded here after all. In contrast to the flanking panels—where commercialism, spirituality, and history collide, and where the land-scape is transformed by chaotic eruptions of word and color—the central panel exhibits an iconological and formal sense of balance. This panel, which Longfish entitled "Owning Your Cultural Information," depicts an inviolate "Land" bounded top and bottom by the "Spiritual." As the title avers, the stability of the panel is owed to the recognition, and application, of cultural knowledge. Longfish wrote in his statement for the *Indigena* show: "The more we are able to own our religious, spiri-tual, and survival information, and even language, the less we can be controlled. . . . The greatest lesson we can learn is that we can bring our spirituality and warrior information from the past and use it in the present and see that it still works."[53]

In effect, what Longfish demonstrates in *The End of the Innocence* is that only the exercise of true sovereignty—control over access to resources, information, and knowledge—will restore balance to the Native landscape. The artist provides a final painted testimony in this regard: the seemingly enigmatic numeral "1" that appears in the center of "Owning Your Cultural Information" memorializes the Royal Canadian Mounted Police officer who was killed during the Mohawk uprising at the Quebec town of Oka in 1990. At issue was the destruction of a sacred pine grove by developers intent on expanding a nearby golf course; this aspect of the struggle is referenced by the golf ball on sacred land in the "Appropriate Goods" panel. Longfish's placement of the "1" at the very heart of *The End of the Innocence* reiterates his conviction "that we do have this warrior information and that one of the things we will defend is land." Both formally and ideologically, then, *The End of the Innocence* is the antithesis of the European landscape painting. Whereas the European paintings have for centuries functioned in the service of colonialism, the works of Native American painters such as Longfish, Lavadour, WalkingStick, and Heap of Birds proclaim an end to this process.[54]

Notes

1. Jaune Quick-to-See Smith, ed., *Our Land/Ourselves: American Indian Contemporary Artists* (Albany: State University of New York at Albany, University Art Gallery, 1990), vi.

2. James Duncan, "Sites of Representation: Place, Time, and the Discourse of the Other," in *Place/Culture/Representation,* ed. James Duncan and David Ley (New York: Routledge, 1993), 40–41. This understanding of the development of linear perspective did not originate with Duncan, of course. *Gardner's Art Through the Ages* describes it thus: "The discovery of perspective by the artists of the Renaissance reflects the emergence of science itself, which is, put simply, the mathematical ordering of our observations of the physical world"; ed. Horst de la Croix and Richard Tansey, 8th ed. (New York: Harcourt Brace Jovanovich, 1986), 556.

3. Simon Schama, *Landscape and Memory* (New York: Vintage Books, 1995), 61, 6. W. J. T. Mitchell, ed., *Landscape and Power* (Chicago: University of Chicago Press, 1994), 15. The term "social hieroglyphs" is borrowed from Karl Marx.

4. These artists were instructed to "draw to life one of each kind of thing that is strange to us in England . . . all strange birds beasts fishes plants herbs Trees and fruits . . . also the figures and shapes of men and women in their apparel as also their manner of weapons in every place as you shall find them differing"; instructions to Thomas Bavin, artist on Sir Humphrey Gilbert's voyage to "exploit land in North America," in 1582. Quoted in Paul Hulton, *America, 1585: The Complete Drawings of John White* (London: British Museum Publications, 1984), 9. *An Account of the Voyages Undertaken by the Order of His Present Majesty for Making Discoveries in the Southern Hemisphere* was published in three volumes in London in 1773. Enormously well received, the *Account* was published in French, American, English, and German versions by 1774; four subsequent editions, including supplemental volumes of Cook's second and third voyages (1772–79), were in print by the first decade of the nineteenth century. See John Lawrence Abbot, *John Hawkesworth: Eighteenth-Century Man of Letters* (Madison: University of Wisconsin Press, 1982). *Les Sauvages de la Mer Pacifique,* a twenty-panel scenic wallpaper produced by Dufour and Leroy in 1804, is a continuous landscape pastiche culled from the engravings of Cook's encounters in Tahiti, Hawaii, New Zealand, Prince William Sound, Easter Island, and the Marquesas. This subject matter was equally popular at panoramic theaters in London, New York, and Paris, in the early nineteenth century. See Odile Nouvel-Kammerer, *Papiers Peints Panoramiques* (Flammarion, France: Musée des Arts Decoratifs, 1990); also, Stephan Oetterman, *The Panorama: History of a Mass Medium* (New York: Zone Books, 1997).

5. "Landscape is a marketable commodity to be presented and re-presented in 'packaged tours,' an object to be purchased, consumed, and even brought home in the form of souvenirs such as postcards and photo albums. In its double role as commodity and potent cultural symbol, landscape is the object of fetishistic practices involving the limitless repetition of identical photographs taken on identical spots by tourists with interchangeable emotions"; Mitchell, *Landscape and Power,* 15. Mitchell goes on to suggest that the endless reproduction of eighteenth- and nineteenth-century landscapes irrevocably consigned them to the realm of kitsch, leading to a decline in their popularity, 20.

6. Elizabeth Helsinger, "Turner and the Representation of England," in Mitchell, *Landscape and Power,* 105.

7. See Ann Bermingham, *Landscape and Ideology: The English Rustic Tradition, 1740–1860* (Berkeley: University of California Press, 1986), 9–10.

8. Mitchell, *Landscape and Power,* 9.

9. The most famous demonstration of the picture plane reimagined as a window onto the painted world is Rene Magritte's painting *La Condition Humaine* (1933), in which an easel propped in front of an open window supports a painting of the view that is exactly aligned with that view. See Schama, *Landscape and Memory,* 12. Bermingham, *Landscape and Ideology,* 119–20; Helsinger, "Turner and the Representation of England," 108–9; Bermingham, *Landscape and Ideology,* 35.

10. Mary Louise Pratt, "Scratches on the Face of the Country; or What Mr. Barrow Saw in the Land of the Bushmen," in *"Race," Writing, and Difference,* ed. H. L. Gates (Chicago: University of Chicago Press, 1986), 142.

11. Duncan, "Sites of Representation," 50. Excellent examples of this kind of visual representation can be found in J. W. Buel, *Heroes of the Dark Continent and How Stanley Found Emin Pasha: Complete History of all the Great Explorations and Discoveries in Africa, from the Earliest Ages to the Present Time* (San Francisco: History Company, 1890).

12. George French Angas, *Savage Life and Scenes in Australia and New Zealand: Being an Artist's Impression of Countries and People at the Antipodes,* in two volumes (London: Smith, Elder, 1827), 2:121; quoted in Paul Shepard, *English Reaction to the New Zealand Landscape before 1850* (Wellington: Pacific Viewpoint Monograph No. 4, 1969), 36.

13. Pratt, "Scratches on the Face of the Country," 143–45; paraphrased by Duncan, "Sites of Representation," 50.

14. Schama, *Landscape and Memory*, 197.

15. Harrison seems simply to be confirming the already-established fact that landscape is a human construct, rather than a naturally occurring phenomenon. He continues, "The genre is a resource for the symbolization of an already represented world, which is inescapably the world of human concepts and values"; Charles Harrison, "The Effects of Landscape," in Mitchell, *Landscape and Power*, 216. Schama, *Landscape and Memory*, 10. See also John Brinkerhoff Jackson, *Discovering the Vernacular Landscape* (New Haven: Yale University Press, 1984).

16. Mitchell reminds us that "empires move outward in space as a way of moving forward in time"; Mitchell, *Landscape and Power*, 17. John Hanning Speke, *What Led to the Discovery of the Source of the Nile* (Edinburgh, 1864), 307; quoted in Pratt, "Scratches on the Face of the Country," 145; *Webster's New Twentieth-Century Dictionary*, 2d ed., s.v. "prospect."

17. Joel Snyder, "Territorial Photography," in Mitchell, *Landscape and Power*, 187. Snyder is ultimately unable to reach any kind of resolve concerning the intention in Watkins's works. In a single paragraph, Snyder remarks, "I don't mean to suggest that Watkins was a self-conscious propagandist for mining or railroad interests, but only that the evolving character of photographic practice and reception allowed him to think of himself as an entrepreneur whose job was to record preexisting scenes in a thoroughly disinterested manner"; and "he was a champion of development and, like most American businessmen of his time, was devoted to the idea of progress—understood in terms of ownership and industrial development of the land and its resources," 188.

The rationale for discussing Watkins's photographs as analogous to contemporaneous landscape painting is provided by Joel Snyder: "These photographs did not escape landscape conventions; they adopted and reformulated them. This is clear not only from comparing photographs like those made by Watkins to drawings, prints, and paintings by Keith and Bierstadt but from the critical literature of the period, which continually commends photographers for having achieved pictures faithful to nature that coincidentally share specific compositional and pictorial features with landscapes wrought in other media," 185.

18. J. J. Brody and Rina Swentzell, *To Touch the Past: The Painted Pottery of the Mimbres People* (New York: Hudson Hills Press, 1996), 11.

19. Quoted in Diana Nemiroff, ed., *Land, Spirit, Power: First Nations at the National Gallery of Canada* (Ottawa: National Gallery of Canada, 1992), 177.

20. Quoted in Tracy Smith, "Review: James Lavadour at PDX," *Art in America* 85, no. 3 (March 1997): 111; Lyn Smallwood, "Review: James Lavadour at Cliff Michel," *ARTnews* 90, no. 1 (January 1991): 168; quoted in Nemiroff, *Land, Spirit, Power*, 177.

21. Durham and Lowe quoted in Nemiroff, *Land, Spirit, Power*, 145, 185; Beam quoted in Shelagh Young, *Carl Beam: The Columbus Project, Phase I* (Peterborough, Ontario: Artspace and the Art Gallery of Peterborough, 1989), 8.

22. Ron Glowen, "Review: James Lavadour at Cliff Michel," *Art in America* 78 (December 1990): 177.

23. Lavadour quoted in Nemiroff, *Land, Spirit, Power*, 177.

24. A propagandist for a New Zealand land holding company wrote: "The plains are certainly, at first sight, monotonous, but they improve as you know them. The beautiful views, the magnificent range and files of mountains, can hardly be equaled; and the rapid growth of homesteads over the plains, with their necessary accompaniments—plantations, hedgerows, gardens, and trees of every description, which are being planted universally—will so alter the face of the country, that four years hence it will hardly be known, and will effectually do away with any objection on the score of monotony"; Edward Brown Fitton, *New Zealand: its present condition, prospects and resources; being*

a description of the country and general mode of life among New Zealand colonists, for the information of intending emigrants (London: Edward Stanford, 1856), 272. Quoted in Shepard, *English Reaction,* 29.

25. Barbara Novak, "The Double-Edged Axe," *Art in America* 64, no. 1 (January–February 1976): 48, 50.

26. "To me 'apocalyptic' has a prophetic Christian connotation relating to the end of the world or some such thing that seems against nature. I am not a Christian and do not accept the popular concepts of doom and damnation, the chosen few, the only way, or whatever is generally associated with such terms"; Lavadour quoted in Nemiroff, *Land, Spirit, Power,* 177.

27. Quoted in Anne Barclay Morgan, "Kay WalkingStick: Interview," *Art Papers* 19, no. 6 (November–December 1995): 12.

28. Quoted in Lawrence Abbott, *I Stand in the Center of the Good* (Lincoln: University of Nebraska Press, 1994), 273.

29. WalkingStick reference to "imagistic," quoted in Morgan, "Kay WalkingStick: Interview," 12; other WalkingStick quotations in this paragraph in Abbott, *I Stand in the Center of the Good,* 273, 274.

30. Robert Houle, "Kay WalkingStick," in Nemiroff, *Land, Spirit, Power,* 218. The first page of WalkingStick's book reads, "You're an Indian! I should have known with those cheekbones!" On the last page, WalkingStick asserts: "I am the grandmother. I am Kay WalkingStick. Of the people, Cherokee!" "Enough," she says, "eligwa!" See Erin Valentino, "Mistaken Identity: Between Death and Pleasure in the Art of Kay WalkingStick," *Third Text* 26 (spring 1994): 61–73; for more complete text, see also, Kay WalkingStick, artist's statement, in Sara Bates, *Indian Humor* (San Francisco: American Indian Contemporary Arts, 1995), 94–95.

31. Quoted in Abbott, *I Stand in the Center of the Good,* 269.

32. Kay WalkingStick, "Native American Art in the Postmodern Era," *Art Journal* 51, no. 3 (fall 1992): 16–17.

33. Quoted in Abbott, *I Stand in the Center of the Good,* 277.

34. WalkingStick, "Native American Art in the Postmodern Era," 17.

35. Ibid.

36. Quoted in Abbott, *I Stand in the Center of the Good,* 274, 275, 279.

37. Quoted in Morgan, "Kay WalkingStick: Interview," 13.

38. WalkingStick quoted in Abbott, *I Stand in the Center of the Good,* 273.

39. Quoted in Morgan, "Kay WalkingStick: Interview," 12–13.

40. WalkingStick, "Native American Art in the Postmodern Era," 16. The figure in *Il Minotauro* is painted bright, neon green, analogous in form to laser or cyber imagery. Durham quoted in Nemiroff, *Land, Spirit, Power,* 146.

41. Hulleah Tsinhnahjinnie, conversation with the author, University of California at Davis, June 7, 1998. Jackson would concur. In the series *Entering Zig's Indian Reservation,* the artist is posed, wearing blue jeans and a feather headdress, against a variety of urban backdrops, under a sign proclaiming that the land is both a reservation and "private property." A recent exhibit of these works at the Carl Gorman Museum at the University of California at Davis (1998) was entitled *Photographs from Indian Country.*

42. Meyer Raphael Rubinstein, "Review: Hachivi Edgar Heap of Birds at Exit Art," *Flash Art* 23, no. 155 (November–December 1990): 156–57. The date of these paintings is given as 1991–92 in the *Land, Spirit, Power* catalog; however, at least two of the canvases were exhibited in 1990 in New York's *Decade Show.* In the *Decade Show* catalog, the panels are dated 1989.

43. Abbott, *I Stand in the Center of the Good,* 39.

44. See James Luna's installation *The Sacred Colors* (1992) in Nemiroff, *Land, Spirit, Power,* 190–95.

45. Quoted in Nemiroff, *Land, Spirit, Power,* 149; quoted in Abbott, *I Stand in the Center of the Good,* 39.

46. Echoing Heap of Birds's statement that the paintings come from "years of walking and watching in the out-of-doors," Lavadour has remarked, "I don't make sketches, I begin by hiking"; quoted in Smallwood, "Review: James Lavadour at Cliff Michel," 168. Heap of Birds quoted in Nemiroff, *Land, Spirit, Power,* 159.

47. Jonathan Smith, "The Lie That Binds: Destabilizing the Text of Landscape," in Duncan and Ley, *Place/Culture/Representation,* 78; Heap of Birds quoted in Nemiroff, *Land, Spirit, Power,* 148.

48. Pratt, "Scratches on the Face of the Country," 145; Heap of Birds, "My Past, My People," in *Sharp Rocks*; reprinted in *Blasted Allegories,* ed. Brian Walis (New York: New Museum of Contemporary Art, 1987), 171.

49. Quick-to-See Smith, *Our Land/Ourselves,* vi; Lucy Lippard, "The Color of the Wind," in Quick-to-See Smith, *Our Land/Ourselves,* 10.

50. Longfish described the photograph of Pitaresaru to Abbott: "I found a photograph of a Pawnee who appeared in Washington, oh, I guess in the 1800s. He just appeared there. They didn't know why he was there. . . . He basically came and said, 'Okay, I did my job. Where's our agreement? Where's my pay?' And they didn't know about the agreement. They just took his picture"; quoted in Abbott, *I Stand in the Center of the Good,* 165. This same photograph is reproduced in Roger Echo-Hawk and Walter Echo-Hawk, *Battlefields and Burial Grounds: The Indian Struggle to Protect Ancestral Graves in the United States* (Minneapolis: Lerner Publications, 1994), 56. The sitter is identified as Pitaresaru, Man Chief, a Chaui Pawnee chief.

51. Longfish quoted in Abbott, *I Stand in the Center of the Good,* 166.

52. The Wounded Knee massacre actually occurred on December 29, 1890. The artist's inclusion of the term, "Rainforest" also evokes the temporal aspect of the title of the panel: "Our biggest Indian problem is not going to be in the United States but in South America, with the rainforest and the annihilation of indigenous people. In a sense, I'm saying, history always repeats itself, and we're always the ones that get done to"; Longfish quoted in Sandy Corley, "In Our Language: Native American Art," *Art Papers* 17, no. 5 (September–October 1993): 29.

53. Quoted in Gerald McMaster and Lee-Ann Martin, *Indigena: Contemporary Native Perspectives in Canadian Art* (New York: STBA, 1992), 163.

54. Quoted in Corley, "In Our Language," 29.

Chapter 10

Rock Art and the Shape of Landscape

H. DENISE SMITH

*R*ock art is that rare medium where art historians can deconstruct, then reconstruct, art's complex, multilayered relationship within its context. This is possible because the art was conceived as an integral part of a cultural landscape, and it usually remains in its original location, not being easily portable or collectible. Rock art—images painted or carved on rocks—is a product of human social and cognitive behaviors and can now be analyzed in situ with the new tools available with geographic information systems (GIS) software. With this new tool, analysis of rock art in its landscape takes a quantum leap ahead of earlier, more intuitive methods. As J. J. Brody writes, such analysis is necessary, as "pictorial images and the surfaces on which they are made are interdependent, rather than independent of each other. Classification of artistic images alone can be of little interpretive value, because in the end, observation of the ways that artists use their chosen pictorial spaces is necessary to refine an understanding of how images and the locations where they occur serve any people." By analyzing the landscape context, the researcher can observe certain clues revealing the functions of such images.[1]

This chapter explores meaningful patterns of cultural interaction recorded in the rock art of Abo Pueblo, located within the old Spanish province of Salinas, and the surrounding physical landscape (fig. 10.1). The rock art recorded for this study is only a fraction of the total number of images present in the pass region. More rock art awaits recording at Tenabo, throughout the Canyon Saladito, and along both sides of Abo Wash through the pass. For the purposes of this study, only the images within the boundaries of the Abo unit of the Salinas Pueblo Missions National Monument were

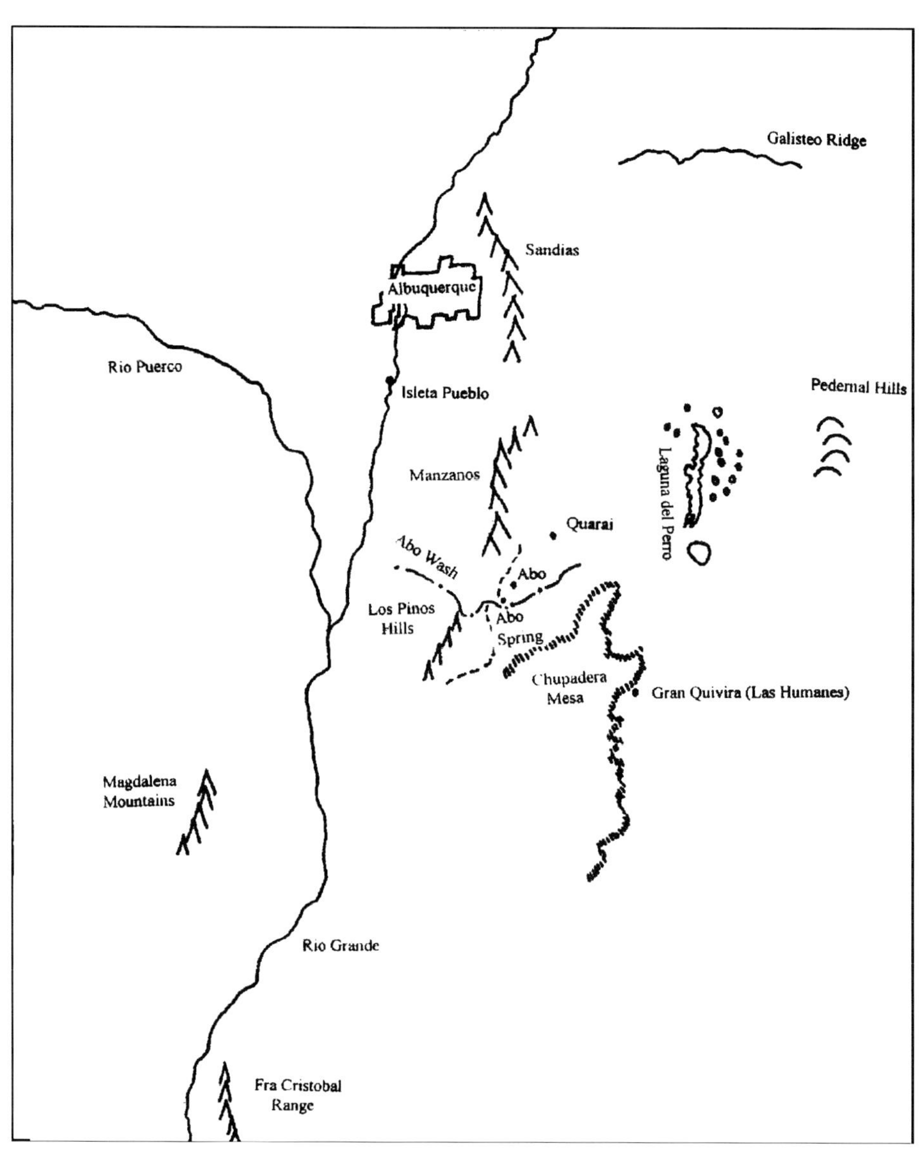

FIGURE 10.1

Map of Abo Pueblo and Vicinity.

recorded. The site of Abo was selected for a rock art study for four reasons: (1) the site is well documented by several archaeological investigations throughout the twentieth century; (2) the rock art and archaeological resources possess a relative integrity; (3) the sheer number of images present at the site promises a detectable variability of cultural patterns throughout time; and (4) the site is located within a mountain pass, a physical point in the landscape for cultural interface.

Less complex studies of rock art precede this work. In his studies of petroglyphs in southeastern Alaska, E. L. Keithahn noted that petroglyphs on Prince of Wales Island were found by the mouths of rivers, facing the ocean rather than the inhabited villages, and placed where they could be easily seen by incoming salmon. Linking the evidence of physical context to oral literature, Keithahn suggested that the rock art was created to communicate with the salmon spirits. This is but one simple example of how analysis of landscape can inform the interpretation of rock art's function.[2]

More complex questions may be asked with GIS software about how the cultural landscape was shaped by rock art, how the rock art was defined by its physical space, and if that dynamic interplay shifted over time. The ultimate goal of the following investigation of rock art at Abo is to illustrate and expand what is already known or hypothesized about Pueblo culture and its interaction with southern Plains dwellers. Rock art is frequently a record of a place created by humans in a historical landscape. This art form is specific to culture and to historical time and thus can be deciphered like an environmental text. Rock art studies to this point have only occasionally and tentatively examined the relationship between the images and the surrounding landscape, and then only on an intimate, intuitive level.[3] What is needed is a more articulate study of this relationship between landscape and art, focusing on a larger scale than earlier studies. To examine the relationship between art and landscape, how the land shapes art must first be shown, then how rock art is used to create a place, center, or boundary. After a brief discussion about landscape theory, a short description of the site's history follows, and then an analysis of specific patterns detected during a recent study of the rock art of Abo Pueblo.

Space, Place, Center, and Boundary

In the western European tradition, landscape is often incorrectly equated with space. Within this space are cities, villages, roads, churches, and other man-made structures, in addition to natural sites that have come to hold special meaning for people. These living or visitation sites have been called places or centers. But what is a precise definition of these terms: space, place, and center? Maps are commonly drawn with solid lines denoting boundaries between political, cultural, and economic units. But what constitutes a boundary? Does a boundary have a specific role in each enclosed society?

Such questions have been addressed by many cultural geographers in the formulation of a general theory of space. While it has proven to be as difficult for geographers to precisely define space as for art historians to define art, some characteristics of space, place, center, and boundary have been established.[4] According to Aristotle, space was only one category for naming and classifying the evidence of the senses. As explained by Albert Einstein, this earlier concept of space was shaped by the psychologically simpler concept of place. All places were identified as material objects. Space, then, was a collection of these material objects. To conceive of empty space, devoid of material objects, was logically impossible. This Aristotelian sense of space dominated western European thought until the seventeenth century, when Descartes proposed that space was absolute; space *contained* all senses and all material objects. Space then became container. To speak of empty space-as-container is to speak of that which is devoid of objects, but the void itself still exists.[5]

Space-as-container holds objects referencing ideas specifically defined by culture. Each culture creates—or in Henri Lefebvre's words, produces—its own space, filling the container with unique objects in a culturally defined manner. The distinction that the production of space is a cultural process is important here, because "an already produced space can be decoded, can be *read.*" Unique codes exist in each specific historical period. Lefebvre would describe Abo and other rock art sites as "representational spaces." He writes, "Redolent with imaginary and symbolic elements, they have their source in history—in the history of a people as well as in the history of each individual belonging to that people." History, then, is inscribed in representational space. But this "representational space" is also always a *present* space, an immediate whole, complete in every historical period. Thus in each historical period, the space can be read as a complete text.[6]

Lefebvre's representational spaces contain what he terms "affective centers," such as churches and graveyards. Place is a locus of emotion, action, and history.[7] History is recorded by objects and their functions in place. Places are emotional or social loci that are not easily translatable to outside cultural groups. Following this line of reasoning, a place as defined by Archaic traders is different from that which is inhabited by later Puebloan peoples, even though they occupy the same point in geographical space. Such loci could be built environments such as villages or rock art sites, or natural foci such as mountain passes.

Places are created in a cultural context. According to Yi-Fu Tuan, "place" is that locus where a culture organizes the forces of nature and society, assigning them specific locations in the landscape, "thus transforming space . . . into place." Culture creates the perception of important objects in space, but "certain objects, both natural and man-made, persist as places through eons of time, outliving the patronage of particular cultures." The rock art of Abo creates such a place. From the Archaic images to modern graffiti, Abo persists as a place "outliving the patronage" of subsequent cultures.[8]

Art can serve at least two functions in the definition of place: it can intensify the human experience by serving as a point of orientation, or it can mark a place as having been the site of intense human experience. Art can make space into place. Citing a sculpture by Henry Moore as an example, Tuan writes: "The sculpture creates a place, a center of meaning, by creating an apt image of human feeling; a stone figure takes on the illusory power of life and draws the surrounding space to itself." In a later article, he reiterates this point when he discusses how art gives the viewer clues as to the cultural complexity of landscape; art causes a fusion of disparate personal, and perhaps even cultural, perspectives. Kent Ryden would agree, although he cites examples like colossal fiberglass ears of corn. Art focuses attention and distinguishes part of the landscape.[9]

Visibility can also create place. According to Tuan, both art and architecture seek visibility.[10] Paleolithic cave paintings, for example, are but another dimension of the built environment.[11] Rock art shapes space in ways that are similar to architecture. In the rock shelters of Abo, art transforms rock formations, reinforcing the identity of this place. While physical features of the landscape affect the production of art, other factors—what Jack Steinbring terms phenomenal attributes—may also play a role. Phenomenal attributes may at least contribute to the selection of a place for the creation of rock art. In his investigations of Canadian rock art sites, Steinbring observed that phenomenal attributes may not be critical in initial site selection, but many sites do exhibit at least one. He writes: "Phenomenal attributes, while unquestionably conditioned by numerous cultural influences, exceed the merely pragmatic by stimulating visual, auditory, and aesthetic responses."[12] Such attributes would be

1. Prominence—view towards and away from
2. Caves or rock shelters—size and shape, location near water or remoteness, orientation, rock type
3. Sound or resonance—echo chambers or resonances when rock is struck
4. Effigy forms—human or animal forms in rocks
5. Presence—"special surroundings" composed by nature, e.g., the Grand Canyon
6. Environmental extremes—water holes in the desert, volcanic lava tubes.[13]

Another power-producing phenomenal attribute would seem to be inaccessibility of place, certainly for the Zuni of western New Mexico.[14] High places are associated by Tewa people of the Rio Grande Valley with access points to other levels of existence.[15] More subtle features in the landscape may shape the rock art of Abo, but any suggestions made here are only tentative, intended to provoke thought and discussion.

While Tuan and Ryden use examples of Western art, rock art also transforms space into place. In places such as Abo, generations of artists have left their marks to record experience, to express deeper meaning, and to focus viewer attention. The challenge is to separate and examine the many layers. As M. Jane Young and Polly Schaafsma—among others—have discussed, rock art can focus the observer's attention on particular features of the landscape. As Schaafsma explains, petroglyphs and pictographs have "the distinction of being art forms that have remained through the centuries in their original settings and in which settings they had certain specific functions. Even though meanings and the symbolic import of the many motifs may be lost to the modern viewer, the mere presence of imagery within the natural scene inevitably conveys a sense of significance and heightens the sense of place." Rock art not only heightens the sense of place but may also function to create—or at least emphasize—a locally important center. In the appropriate environmental context, multiple images can dominate the local landscape, denoting a center. A "center" is a special kind of place. All centers are places but not all places are centers. It is important to consider how a place becomes a center. In his book *The Sacred and the Profane,* Mircea Eliade discusses how humans orient themselves in their environment by establishing sacred centers.[16]

Carole Crumley, an archaeologist working in the Burgundy region of France, defines "center" in relation to boundaries and to analytical scale. She reiterates frequently that scale is a key concept in the identification of a place as a center. Most archaeological work focuses on the community scale, reconstructing only one aggregation of dwellings. So, on this intimate scale, the community is a center for the people who built and lived in it, and certainly for the archaeologist attempting to reconstruct those lives. To consider the relationship of the subject community to nearby sites is to consider culture on a larger scale. However, a community or place—a center in the smaller scale—could lose that special status in the larger scale, perhaps even becoming a boundary place between larger centers. There is no diagnostic set of variables for identifying center versus boundary or in-between place. As Crumley points out, "cities may . . . mediate varieties of custom, . . . serving a function also served by some boundary areas. Some centers and . . . boundaries are sparsely populated, yet charged with meaning, e.g., . . . 'ceremonial center' "; some teem with human mental and physical activity, e.g., "gateway cities." Careful examination of environmental and cultural context is crucial in determining whether a place is a center.[17]

Often, a center is defined by its relationship to other places. History is encoded in places and the relationships between them.[18] Places are connected throughout a geographic region, while paths and places exist at all levels of space. On the physical level, they manifest as buildings, roads, and vistas. On the mythic level, paths can lead to other worlds; places can be sites of mythical events. Such an example would be the Zuni path of deformed boulders thought to have been warped by the supernatural figure Old Salt Woman in her angry retreat from the Pueblo.[19]

In her earlier work, Crumley suggests that centers and the relationships between them are based on economic models. A "functional center" would be "any spot/place/site/location which serves a function or functions not equally available elsewhere." Such single-function centers could develop into commercial, multifunctional sites based on trade. When a place becomes a center for one function, such as the provision of water in an otherwise sparsely watered environment, it could rapidly become a multifunction center, acquiring greater economic importance, and later political, cultural, perhaps even religious functions. In addition to providing water for travelers, Abo could have acted as an intermediate trading stop between the Rio Grande Valley and the higher eastern Plains. The growth of the Pueblo after the eleventh century may point to increasing trade and a desire on the part of Puebloan people to reduce the cost of trade goods flowing through their country.[20]

Crumley defines the social network of relationships between functional centers as a "functional lattice." She gives two examples of such functional lattices: farmers' markets (or short-range relationships) and trade fairs (or long-range relationships). On the local scale, Abo may have acted as a market for local farmers. On the larger scale, trade fairs would have attracted long-range travelers such as traders from the river valley and hunters from the Plains. While there are no records of trade fairs at Abo, the Spanish did describe such activities occurring at nearby Gran Quivira Pueblo (Las Humanes).[21]

Trade fairs often occur in smaller centers located on boundaries between two cultural groups. But what defines a boundary? Any definition is problematic, since it must always be linked to a specific cultural context, disallowing any universal statements. Due to this interdependence, boundaries will shift as the scale changes.[22] What is a center on a community scale may be a boundary on the regional scale. In terms of art, boundaries are often defined by changes in the way certain objects are created or simply by how the same objects are used differently.[23] Kent Ryden, a social geographer writing about the folk sense of place, discusses the roles boundaries play and some aspects of their nature:

Boundaries—not those drawn by surveyors and cartographers and marked by fences and signs, but those superimposed on the land and inscribed in the mind through the daily experience of inhabiting a locality; not those erected fiercely from without, but those pushed out gently from within—are frequently an important component of people's lived sense of place. . . . Such regions, self-consciously known and defined by the people within them, may or may not correspond with prominent and visible features on the landscape or with conventional political division; what is important is that the people themselves know and can point out the boundaries of their regions—the regions are accurately defined only from within, not without.[24]

Humans tend to erect markers on boundaries, thus making a record of the role the division plays. Ryden observes that these marks can be read rather like an environmental text. Through historical custom, boundaries may be inherited by successive inhabitants of an area, particularly if the border is defined in relationship to the physiognomy of the landscape, such as a mountain pass. Through time, people create many signs and markers on the boundary, creating "a palimpsest: a layered accumulation, with each new layer erasing and obscuring the last, of man-made frontier—announcing artifacts, of implied landscapes, of attitudes toward travel, of the unremarkable everyday history of this spot on the border." This is precisely what occurred at Abo.[25]

Rock art can denote a center in the landscape but can—at the same time—mark boundaries between regions. As has been pointed out by Schaafsma and other scholars, rock art serves multiple functions. Imagery can not only strengthen the connection between religious society members and their sacred past by identifying sacred locations, as well as honoring supernatural forces, but also serve the secondary function of defining tribal boundaries, "as certain shrines may be 'owned' by particular social groups." Young mentions the use of rock art for boundary markers by both Hopi and Zuni people. The Hopi are known to have used boundary stones engraved with clan symbols. This may also be the case at Zuni, but not every petroglyph is a clan symbol. Deduced solely from its geographical location on the eastern slopes of the Manzanos Mountains, Abo may have served as a boundary between the Rio Grande Valley and the eastern Plains. The rock art, in at least the historic period, seems to have reinforced cultural as well as physical boundaries.[26]

Landscape is, and probably has always been, integral to rock art. In addition, unusual rock formations are linked to ancient stories about catastrophic floods, sacrificial children, or the anger of Old Salt Woman. Context is so important to some Zuni people that decontextualized images drawn on index cards could not be identified by one man because he had never visited the site. As Young summarizes: "The importance of context was also revealed by those Zunis who came with me to rock art sites. They not only looked closely at the carved and painted figures on rock surfaces, but carefully observed the features of the landscape within which the rock was located, paying particular attention to varieties of plants, sources of water when available, bird nests, and animal tracks." Landscape is a medium in which humans encode cultural meaning and history. Abo's rock art is a palimpsest recording different cultural styles and time periods. The art is visual evidence of changing histories in the landscape, of changing cultural landscapes through history. The landscape itself is a cultural narrative.[27]

To analyze the cultural patterns in Abo's rock art, a computer model was created using GIS software. To develop the model certain assumptions and limitations had to be made. The model assumes that the arroyos were a focus for travel, therefore ancient roads may have existed along the banks of Abo Wash and its tributaries (fig. 10.1). Virtually all rock art sites reported in the pass by various field-workers are located along the length of three drainages. Several limitations must also be acknowledged for this model. The first is the size of the site recorded for the current study. In response to legal and logistical constraints, the 1994 fieldwork was confined to the arbitrary boundaries of the Abo unit of the Salinas Pueblo Missions National Monument. Rock art, primarily petroglyphs, has been reported at thirty-four other locations in the Abo Pass region. The rock art recorded for this study is estimated to be approximately one-tenth of the total. Therefore, any conclusions stated here must be considered tentative because of the small sample size, statistically speaking, and are subject to revision once more rock art has been recorded and analyzed.

Because of the intimate scale of this study, certain factors have already been determined, whereas at a regional scale there would have been more variables. For instance, virtually all Abo's rock art faces toward either Arroyo Espinoso or Abo Wash, hence toward hypothetical roads. A physical reason for such a phenomenon is that the most suitable rock surfaces in this geographic area are located on bedrock exposed in arroyo banks. A cultural reason may have also existed for the connection between the rock art and the arroyos, such as the use of images to define frontiers or boundaries. To my knowledge, the fieldwork accomplished for this study represents the first full recording of all rock art, including more than 2,300 images, found within the Abo unit's boundaries. Four Laboratory of Anthropology sites were recorded, totaling 163 loci with 343 panels. To simplify the discussion, these sites will be referred to as the north site (LA 33127), the mask site (LA 44066), the west site (LA 44065), and the south site (LA 8989; see fig. 10.2).

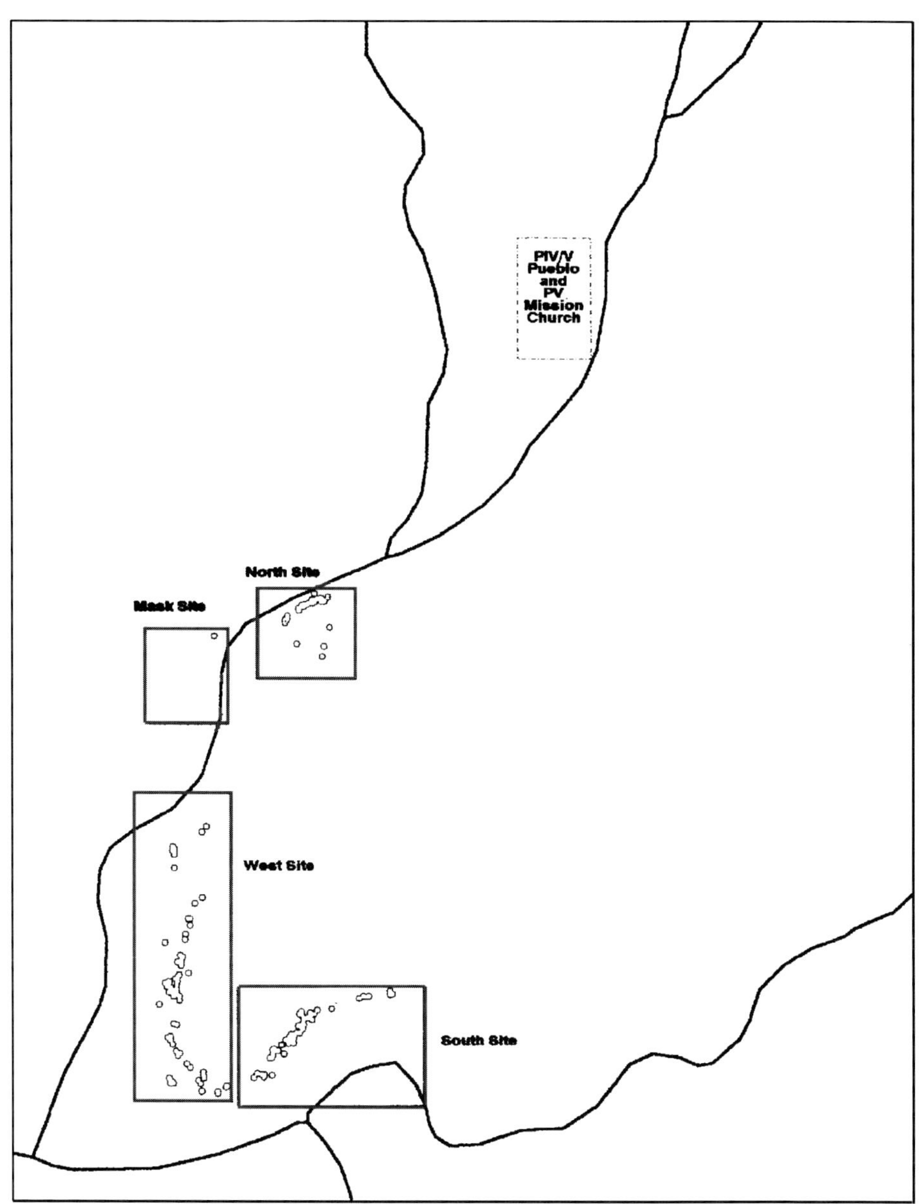

PIV/V
Pueblo
and
PV
Mission
Church
North Site
Mask Site
West Site
South Site

Figure 10.2
Map Showing All Loci Recorded at Abo Pueblo.

A Brief Cultural History of Abo Pueblo

Stretching from the Paleo-Indian era to contemporary twentieth-century habitation, Abo's history can only be partially reconstructed from archaeological investigations and historical documents written by Spanish and American observers. The history of this region is generally organized into several time periods, corresponding mainly to the Pecos sequence but also including phenomena unique to Abo Pueblo. No single chronological sequence has been established for the Abo region, nor have any of the proposed sequences been adhered to by the many scholars who have worked on this site.[28] The time depth of cultural interaction recorded in rock at this site extends well beyond the chronological parameters of the associated Pueblo ruins. Following is the chronology used here:

PREHISTORIC
>Paleo-Indian 10,000–6,000 B.C.E.
>Archaic (for Abo region) 6,000 B.C.E.–1,000 C.E.

EARLY PUEBLOAN
>Pueblo I 700–900 C.E.
>Pueblo II 900–1100 C.E.
>Pueblo III 1100–1300 C.E.

LATE PUEBLOAN
>Pueblo IV 1300–1600 C.E.

HISTORIC
>Pueblo V 1600–ca. 1672 C.E.
>Abandonment of Abo 1671–73 C.E.
>Pueblo Revolt 1680–92 C.E.
>Post-Revolt Presence 1692–1800 C.E.
>Hispanic and American Presence 1800–present

No Paleolithic sites have been found in the immediate region of Abo Pass. Tantalizing Archaic remnants have been found, which has led some scholars to date certain rock art panels at Abo to this period. A more detailed chronology concerning these earlier periods appears elsewhere.[29]

Several investigators have reported on excavations at Abo, dating several room blocks to the Pueblo III period (1100–1300 C.E.). Abo is a large complex of room blocks organized around plazas and located on both sides of Arroyo Espinoso. Two mounds have received the most archaeological attention, because they are located immediately adjacent to the historic Spanish colonial mission church. Scholars such as Adolf Bandelier, Joseph Toulouse, Bertha Dutton, and Stuart Baldwin have surveyed or excavated these mounds.

Much of the information available regarding the Pueblo IV, or Late Puebloan, period in the Abo Pass is derived from two sources: Spanish historical documents and the archaeological record. During the Pueblo IV period, three Spanish expeditions documented their visits to the highland Tompiro, inhabitants of Abo Pueblo.[30] Trade relations between the Tompiro and Plains groups are documented in the archaeology but also primarily through Spanish observations in the late Pueblo IV period. In 1583 Espejo recorded: "The Maguas [Tompiro] province borders on the land of the so-called Cibola cattle [bison]. The natives clothe themselves with the hides of these animals, cotton blankets, and chamois skins."[31] Spanish observers document trade fairs among the Tompiro in the sixteenth century. They list meat, hides and hide products, tallow, and bone products from bison as trade items. Drawing on Spanish observations and biological studies of bison, Baldwin suggests that such trade fairs probably took place in July, late November, and early December. The presence of Abo-area glazewares in Rio Grande Valley sites dating after 1500 C.E. suggests that the western Tompiro maintained trade relationships with the lowland Pueblos. Logistically, the western Tompiro are the middlemen between the eastern frontier Pueblos and the lowland dwellers, providing a link between the Great Plains and the Rio Grande Valley.[32] Products for trade could have included salt, buffalo hides, jerked meat, tallow, and piñon nuts. The riverine Pueblos may have traded surplus agricultural goods, raw cotton, turkey feather items, tobacco, and obsidian to the Tompiro.

Sweeping changes in Tompiro material culture are reflected in the rock art during the Pueblo V era (1600–ca. 1672 C.E.). Influenced by the Spanish colonization and Franciscan missionary efforts, the Tompiro adapted new forms in architecture, pottery, and agricultural food crops. Much of the documentation from this period is derived from historical Spanish records but also from the archaeological investigations conducted by Toulouse, Dutton, Ivey, and Baldwin. Franciscan documents provide evidence that Abo Pueblo was abandoned well before the Pueblo Revolt of 1680.[33]

In 1692, at the end of the Pueblo Revolt, Don Diego de Vargas brought back one hundred Native refugees from El Paso.[34] There is a distinct possibility that Tompiro people were included in this group. Governor Vargas used Pueblo auxiliaries—which may have included some Tompiro warriors—in his campaigns against the Faraon Apaches in the Sandia Mountains in 1704. This practice was followed later by Gov. Velez Cachupin during his first term in office, 1751 to 1754, and perhaps in his second term, 1762 to 1767.[35] Spanish documents establish a Puebloan presence in the Salinas area, particularly in the pass regions, which served as entrances for raiders into the Rio

Grande Valley. Given Abo's proximity to one of the most heavily traveled passes from the valley to the Plains, it is logical to conclude that these Pueblo auxiliaries did patrol in the entire Abo area, possibly camping in the Pueblo ruins as did later American soldiers. Toulouse notes the presence of Puname Polychrome and Acoma Polychrome sherds in his excavations of San Gregario de Abo, which indicated to him an eighteenth-century presence of Pueblo people.[36] Whether any of the Pueblo auxiliaries were descendants from Tompiro refugees is impossible to prove. Pueblo people, particularly warriors, were present in the Abo region in the mid-eighteenth century. It is at least possible that they were responsible for much of the warrior iconography in rock art panels located close to the modern highway.

Another warrior group may also have made their mark at Abo. Scholars have long assumed that the Tompiro of Abo abandoned the area to the Apache, who then maintained a presence in the pass region until they were expelled by Spanish homesteaders in the nineteenth century. Baldwin records an Apache presence in the archaeological sites of Abo and Tenabo, but such remains are tenuous. Dated broadly from 1675 to 1850 C.E., "Apache" buildings are described as rock shelters with drywall structures, two stone circles, and one rock-lined cache.[37]

Shortly after 1800 Hispanic homesteaders and ranchers began to exploit the resources of the Salinas area. In 1819 Bartolome Baca received the Torreon Grant, which included the ruins of Abo.[38] A rancher, he employed some twenty-seven hundred herders to shepherd forty thousand sheep, three hundred mares, and nine hundred cattle on pastures in the Manzanos Mountains. Due to its proximity to the Manzanos pastures and the presence of a perennial stream running near the Pueblo ruins, Abo may have been visited by these shepherds, some of whom were Pueblo people. This is a tenuous supposition, but there is a possibility that Pueblo people were in the Abo area in the early nineteenth century. Certainly there were Spanish shepherds, and Christian motifs are to be found in the rock art of Abo. Shepherds continued to visit the water sources at Abo through the 1830s.[39]

People have been camping or living at Abo since the Archaic period. Hunters and travelers may have left their marks upon the landscape, but certainly the farmers of the Early Puebloan periods were responsible for the increase in numbers and the change in iconography of rock art images at Abo. During the Late Puebloan periods, Abo reached its greatest population level, so it is logical that much of the rock art dates from this time period. Even after the abandonment of the region, Pueblo people continued to foray into the pass, perhaps leaving images on the rocks to record their understanding of the boundaries. Athapaskans, too, lived and camped in the area, and may have left their marks.

The Rock Art of Abo Pueblo

Abo has the advantage of possessing two rock art media, paintings and carvings, facilitating comparisons between them and between rock art and other works of art. Brody (1991) was the first to make an extended comparison between rock art and kiva murals, discussing them in terms of material, technique, iconography, and structure. His insights inspire this research and thus are briefly summarized here.

During the Pueblo IV period, rock art underwent tremendous changes in style. Brody traces a decline in the number of pictographs in this period, while petroglyphs greatly increase. Subject matter also changes, seemingly linked more closely to kachina figures than in previous periods; in fact, Brody notes a lack of iconographic continuities from earlier periods of paintings or rock art. Rock art in the Pueblo IV period becomes more tightly organized, coming closer to the structure of wall murals, while the murals become more loosely organized, comparable to rock art.[40] Brody also suggests that the function of rock art can be glimpsed through the analysis of rock art iconography in the context of ethnographic analogy. In his comparisons between wall murals and pictographs, for example, Brody finds that the images differed only in matter of degree in color, material, technique, and composition. "Open air sites" may have served—or have continued to serve—various purposes, such as being "a historically important place, a boundary marker, a shrine, a ceremonial site such as an 'outdoor kiva,' or a shelter for bored hunters and shepherds."[41] But identification of a rock art site as a shrine or ceremonial site cannot be based exclusively on the iconography, for many sites known to be secular in function contain sacred images. For example, some sheep corrals contain pictographs of identifiable kachina masks. Brody cautions: "Imagery alone can never tell us why art is made or what uses are made of an art site." Brody further warns that the past use of a place often differs from the present use and the latter may give no clues whatever to the former. Therefore, the purpose of rock art often relates to how places were used and what meaning was attached to that place by the originating audience, but reconstruction of that purpose and meaning must depend on ethnographic context as well as formal interpretation.[42]

Brody has also suggested that, at Abo, there may be different functions for each of the media found in the rock art there. Many of the paintings are clearly visible from the modern road and therefore were probably also visible from the prehistoric trail that may have existed near the banks of Abo Wash, whereas most of the nearby petroglyphs are placed on surfaces invisible from the same vantage point. This indicates a possible distinction made by the artists between public and private art. Polly Schaafsma also discusses public versus private functions in rock art, focusing on rock art located a distance from a living or public space, remote and inaccessible, which is then interpreted to mean that such a place could have been the locus for ritual activities of a private or restrictive nature. Abo's rock art does not qualify as a truly remote or inaccessible location because all the rock art recorded for this study is found between the public road and the Pueblo. Some images seem to be intended for viewing while others are more hidden. This seeming connection between public paintings and private petroglyphs is attenuated, however, upon consideration of the rock art along the Arroyo Espinoso. The only pictograph found was a tiny mask or face within a small rock shelter on the mask site, a painting too small to be seen except at a close distance. However, some petroglyph panels are visible from the banks of the arroyo. Brody's cautions regarding linking iconography to purpose also apply to medium and function. To avoid overdetermining what the function of each image or even medium may have been, more evidence is necessary.[43]

Within a medium, formal differences may indicate more than one cultural group of artists. One such formal distinction is the different white pigments used in many of the pictographs. At least two different values of white were observed in the 1994 fieldwork: the first was a slightly pinkish white; the second, a thick cream-colored pigment. Quite possibly the slightly pinkish white is a gypsum base with some reddish contamination. This slightly pink white is used consistently throughout the more complex pictographs in both rock shelters on the south site. The only exceptions are whole figures painted in the thick cream pigment, which is much more heavily applied than the pinkish white, therefore indicating a completely different batch of paint. Due to differences in pigment and application technique, I suggest there may have been two different groups of artists.[44]

In several pictograph panels on the south site, earlier paintings have been covered with layers of white—or in one case, green—which then serve as the base for new paintings. One possible explanation for the layering of pictographs at Abo may be that they were perceived as very similar to kiva paintings, thus subject to the same renewal process. Young offers other possibilities from her work on Zuni rock art. She found superimposed paintings to be common in the areas around Zuni. Interpreters often commented that the later layers of paintings were enhanced by the power of those that were earlier, or were a means of taking power away from older images. Young found this to be especially true in areas where more than one culture group coexisted, as would have been the case at Abo in the seventeenth through nineteenth centuries.[45]

Pueblo warriors may have taken the opportunity to add to the palimpsest of images near the abandoned Pueblo where they apparently encamped. After the abandonment of the village by its inhabitants, Pueblo people continued to return sporadically to Abo, most notably military patrols stationed to guard the pass from Apache incursion during the eighteenth and early nineteenth centuries. But a few non-Puebloan images are also painted in the rock shelters near the Pueblo pictographs. Polly Schaafsma has suggested that Athapaskans considered painted rock shelters as sacred, often creating their own images over earlier Pueblo pictographs or even incorporating them. Young recorded superimposed paintings in her survey of Zuni rock art. When questioned, her Zuni friends described a process by which the later paintings could be enhanced by absorbing, or possibly stealing, the power of the earlier paintings. This process operates in reverse as well; the Zuni are also known to appropriate images in the landscape even if they were not originally created by a Zuni artist.[46] Subject matter and structural elements are also used to distinguish style. I define four major styles in the rock art of Abo: (1) Geometric, (2) Early Puebloan, (3) Late Puebloan, and (4) the White Figure style.[47]

With many reservations, I suggest that the White Figure style may be of Athapaskan origin. There are too few paintings at Abo to make any convincing arguments; however, several provocative details might support this hypothesis. First, the White Figure style is dated relatively later than the Puebloan styles due to superimposition. After the Tompiro abandoned Abo in the early 1670s, the Spanish frequently reported that the "Apaches" were hunting and camping in the Salinas area.[48] Later Spanish and American documents indicate that the Mescalero Apache were living in the dry lands between the Rio Grande Valley and the Pecos River during the seventeenth through nineteenth centuries. As Schaafsma points out, however, little is known about these groups and even less of their rock art. Hueco Tanks, near El Paso, Texas, is one site where a relatively large concentration of pictographs have been tentatively identified as Mescalero in origin.[49] As at Abo, some figures in the Hueco Tanks panels belong to an art tradition identifiable as non-Puebloan. Most of the pictographs are created with thick, white paint. The figures are often linear or geometric. There are far too few figures at Abo to make any conclusive comparisons, so the discussion must be left in this tentative state. Perhaps further investigation of the rock art in the Abo Pass will reveal more examples of the White Figure style, thus providing more data for comparison. Athapaskan peoples, as they came into areas previously inhabited by Pueblo people, may have respected the rock art, rarely painting over earlier pictographs but often leaving some small contribution to the overall composition. This may have been the case at Abo as well. This raises the intriguing possibility that Pueblo people were aware of Athapaskan paintings at Abo and may have created some of the Late Puebloan paintings in response to serve as boundary markers or cultural signposts. The most prominently displayed paintings may have been created for this very purpose. Unfortunately, such interesting speculations must await objective date analysis of the paint components of the Abo pictographs.

For contextual analysis, chronological periods were mapped across the landscape of Abo with the intent of discerning cultural patterns on the landscape and whether they have changed through time. To accomplish this, GIS software was used, specifically the Environmental Planning and Programming Language. A geographic information system is a bundle of programs designed to analyze data organized around thematic layers. Layers represent different data, that is, site hydrology, archaeological sites, or rock art panels divided into chronological categories. These layers can be "analyzed individually, combined, or overlaid to reveal patterns in data values or relationships among variables." For this study, the base layer is the hydrology of the Abo site; the remaining are the five different chronological periods: the Early Puebloan, Late Puebloan, Late or Historic Puebloan, Historic Puebloan, and Historic Athapaskan periods. The primary advantage to using GIS is that a researcher can accurately map a specific feature as small as one meter on the larger landscape and can create models to relate such features to others. For example, it is possible to map elements within a certain distance, perhaps one-quarter mile from a physical feature such as a stream or road. With the visual results, it is then possible to make tentative interpretations regarding the relationships between images and significant landscape features.[50]

The disadvantage of GIS is a human one. It is too easy to read meaning into patterns on the landscape that may be truly random or to define a border where in fact one never existed. The data are useful only in creating another analytical tool, but they should not be taken as a greater authority than they are. Ultimately, after all the analysis and modeling are finished, one must acknowledge that rock art was created by humans for their idiosyncratic purposes and these can only be partially glimpsed, even with the most sophisticated of methods and tools. GIS software is useful as a visual method of studying rock art in its physical context. Such models provide one way to analyze the changing relationships between art and landscape.

The rock art panels dated to the Early Puebloan period are evenly spread throughout the site but do occur in slightly higher concentrations on the west and south sites (fig. 10.3). Two physical factors may account for this: visibility to and from the roadways along the arroyos and exposure of large, smooth rock surfaces. Exclusively petroglyphs, the images on the west and south sites include paw prints of various shapes, bird tracks, dot-style masks/faces, and many unidentifiable or indescribable forms. The cluster of loci on the west site are focused along an exposure of enormous vertical cylindroid boulders breaking away from a bedrock layer of Abo sandstone. A wide variety of petroglyphs occur on both the stream and top faces of these boulders; thus they face the sky as often as the arroyo. There is a concentration of Early Puebloan panels on the north site, but they are scattered along the bedrock face rather than occurring in significant clusters. Interspersed with these panels are a roughly

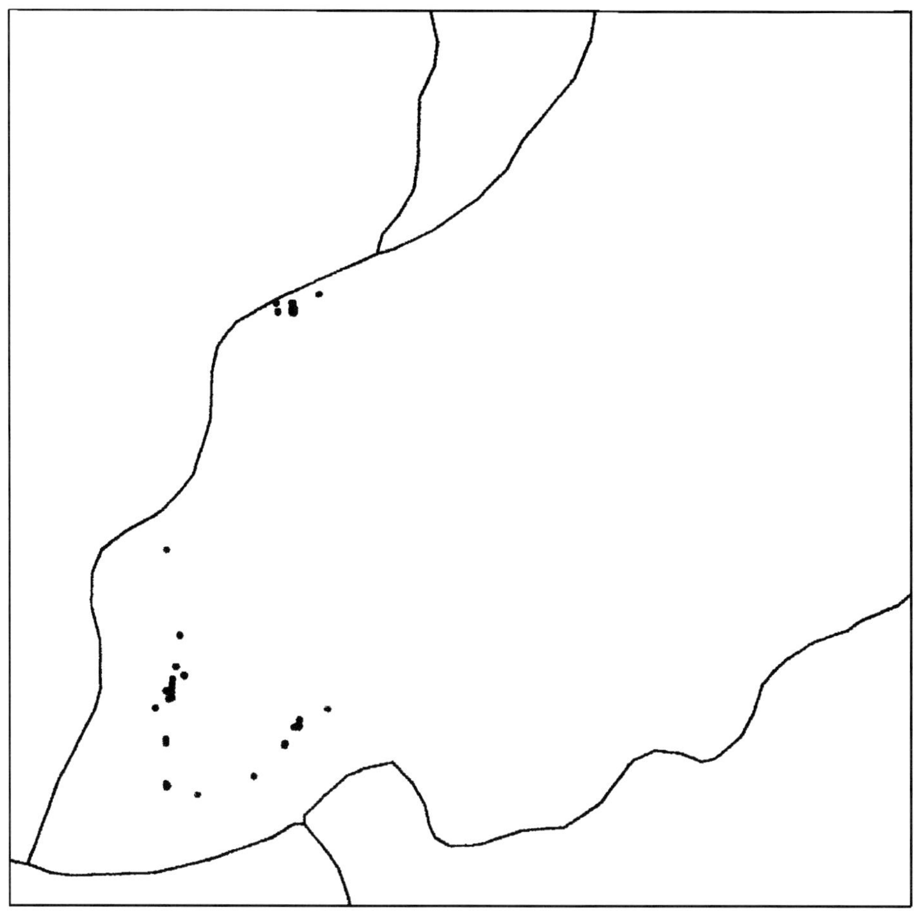

FIGURE 10.3

Early Puebloan Rock Art Loci, Abo.

equal number of Late Puebloan panels, although the two styles are freely inter-mingled. The iconography is similar to that discussed on the west and south sites. The more rapid accumulation of rock art during the Early Puebloan period would seem to indicate that Abo changed from an Archaic place to a Puebloan center.

The Late Puebloan period was a time of great construction and expansion at Abo Pueblo, which is taken to reflect a growth in population and perhaps also in trade. Not surprisingly, the majority of rock art panels are dated to this period (figs. 10.4, 10.5). However, separating precontact (Pueblo IV) from postcontact (Pueblo V) figures in the Late Puebloan style is difficult, particularly in the pictographs. There is a

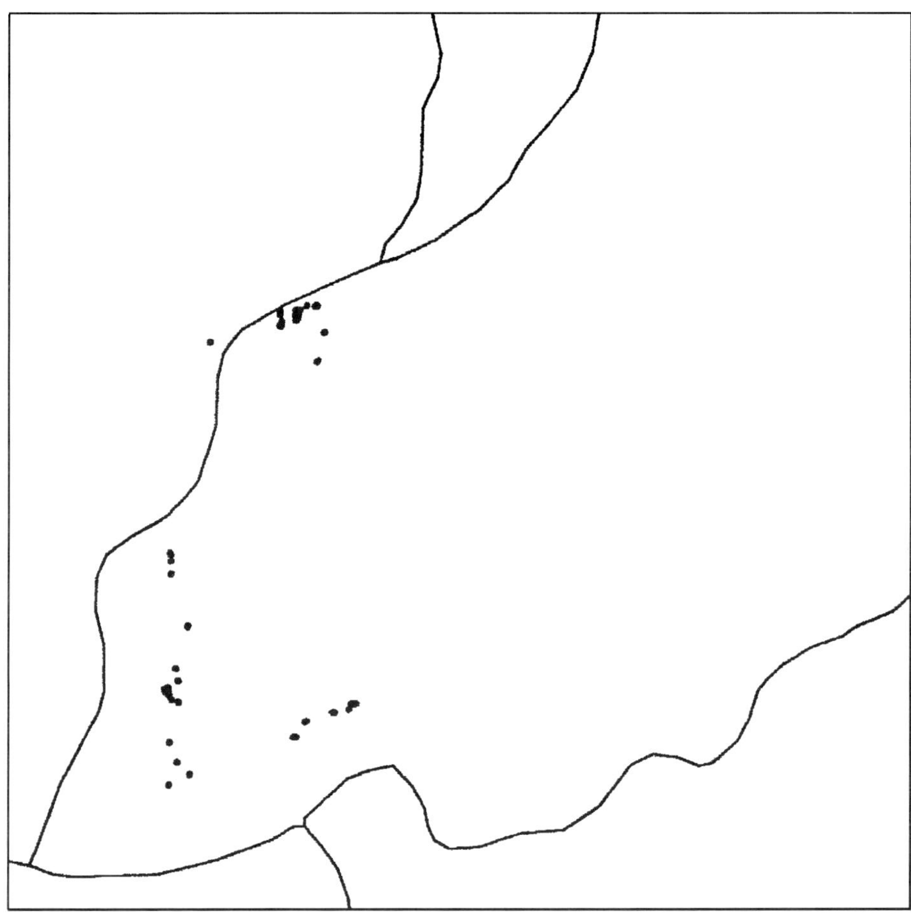

large concentration of Late Puebloan loci on the north site, which would have been easily visible from the Pueblo, whereas the other loci are widely scattered down the west site and throughout the southern shelters. The mask site, located across the Arroyo Espinoso due west of the north site, is also dated to the Late Puebloan period. The shallow cave at this site contains the only pictograph outside the south site. All the remaining mapped loci on the east bank of Arroyo Espinoso within the park boundaries are petroglyphs also dated to the Late Puebloan period. The continuing accumulation of images during this period indicates that Abo remains a center, at least in the scale of this initial study.

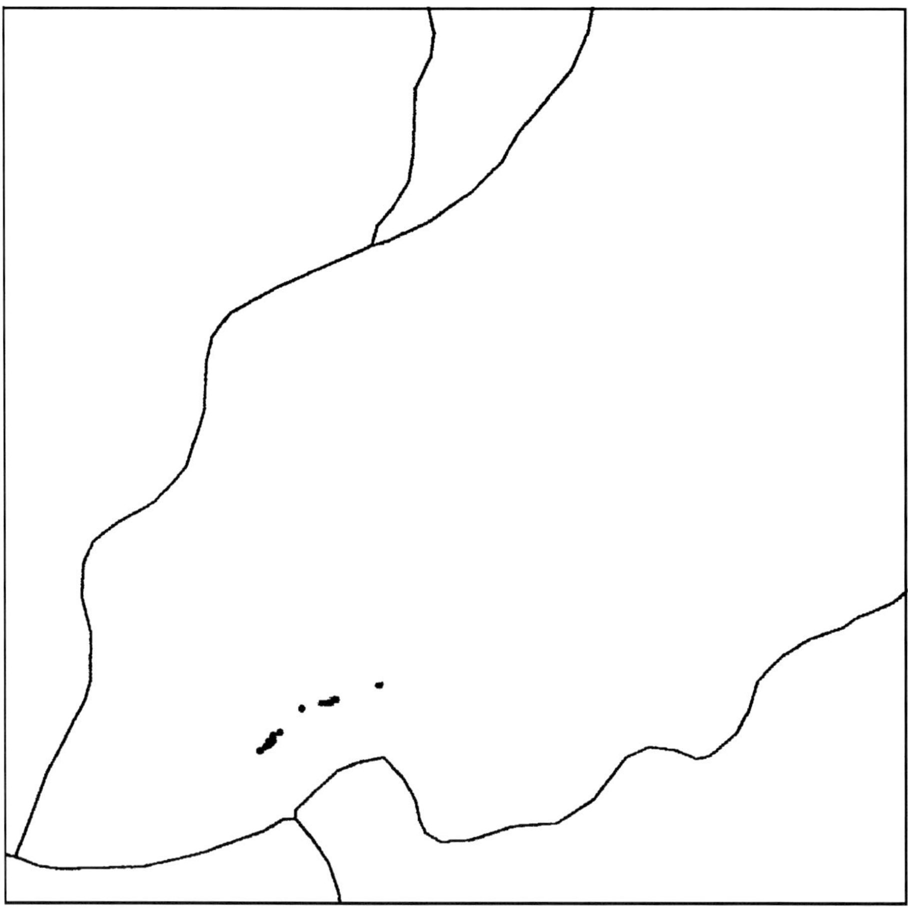

As detailed and visually interesting as the Late Puebloan images are, some figures categorized within this style appear more historical in nature. Several panels in both shelters contain elaborately painted, detailed images that could date either before or after European contact. Without empirical data, it is impossible to be more specific about the chronology of these images. Some of the pictographs are clearly visible from the arroyo banks; others are carefully hidden. This attribute of visibility seems to be a factor in the function of the rock art and the site.

Historic panels would have been painted by Pueblo people returning to the area well after Abo Pueblo was abandoned. An ephemeral Pueblo presence in the Abo area

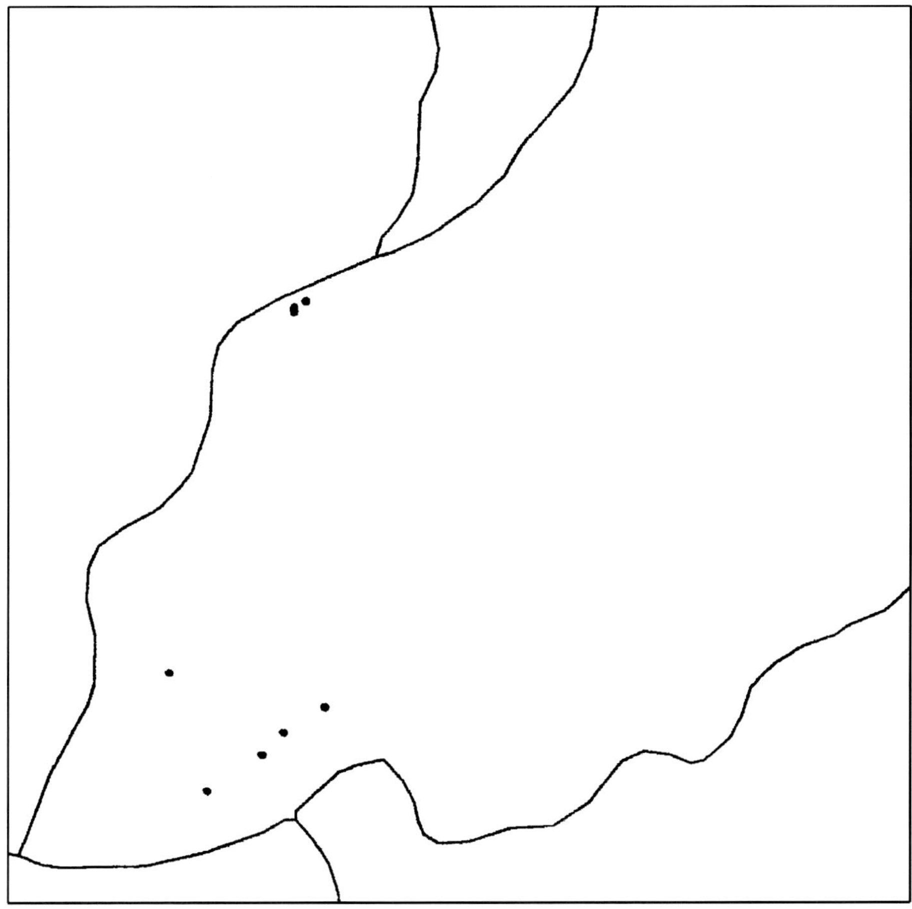

FIGURE 10.6
Historic Rock Art Loci, Abo.

during the eighteenth and early nineteenth centuries is supported by potsherds found by Toulouse. Spanish documents also record the assignment of Pueblo military auxiliaries to Quarai to patrol the entire Abo pass region during the early 1750s. There is a probability that these Pueblo warriors used the ancient roads along the arroyo banks and camped in the abandoned village, leaving the sherds Toulouse reported from his 1940 excavations. After 1819 Puebloan and Hispanic shepherds working for Bartolome Baca may also have encamped in the ruins and created rock art on nearby boulders.[51]

Abo has only nine clearly dated Historic Puebloan panels (fig. 10.6). These few

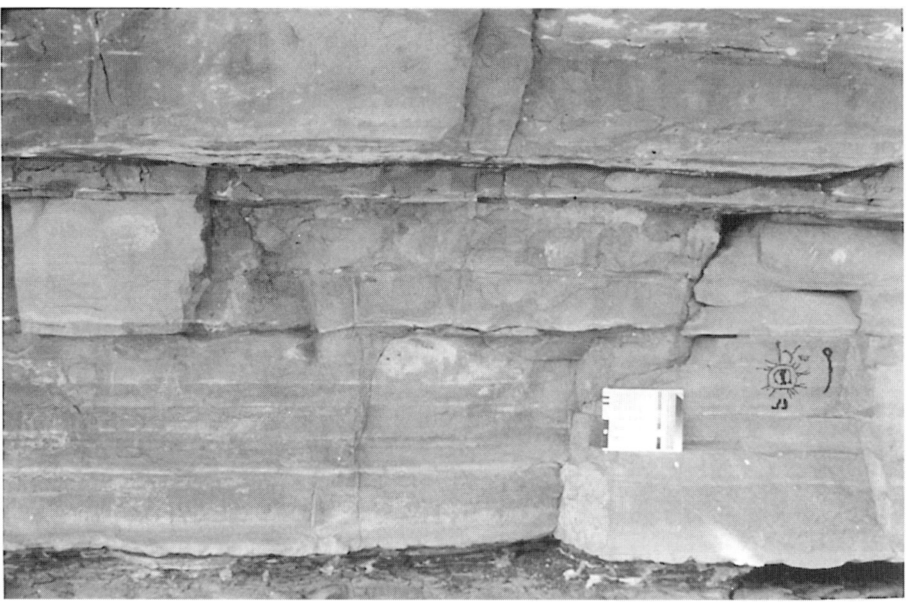

FIGURE 10.7
Locus ET4 (computer enhanced).

panels are divided between the north site and the south site. Although few in number, these images pose very interesting questions. For example, figure 10.7 is dated to the Historic Period due to the depiction of an apparently European-style saber painted with the same pigment as the shield bearer to the left. This particular panel is easily visible from the banks of the Abo Wash where the aboriginal route is presumed to lie. But not all the images are so clearly visible because they are either turned away from the road or they are on a very small scale. Their subject matter also differs. The pictographs in figure 10.7 are related to warrior iconography, but the loci visible from the Arroyo Espinoso have a very different content.[52] The iconography of the images in figure 10.8 on the west site seems more metaphorical, not quite so clearly connected to war as are shield bearers and swords. This panel displays what is clearly a flying eagle in the upper portion of a tall, narrow panel. Below is an unmistakable rendering of a rattlesnake, complete with triangular head, forked tongue, and enlarged rattles. A small, simple circle and a paw print complete the composition. Schaafsma has clearly linked eagles and rattlesnakes to the Pueblo war complex, but these particular images could just as easily represent completely different concepts; ethnographic context is crucial to making any distinction. This panel is dated to the Historic Period because

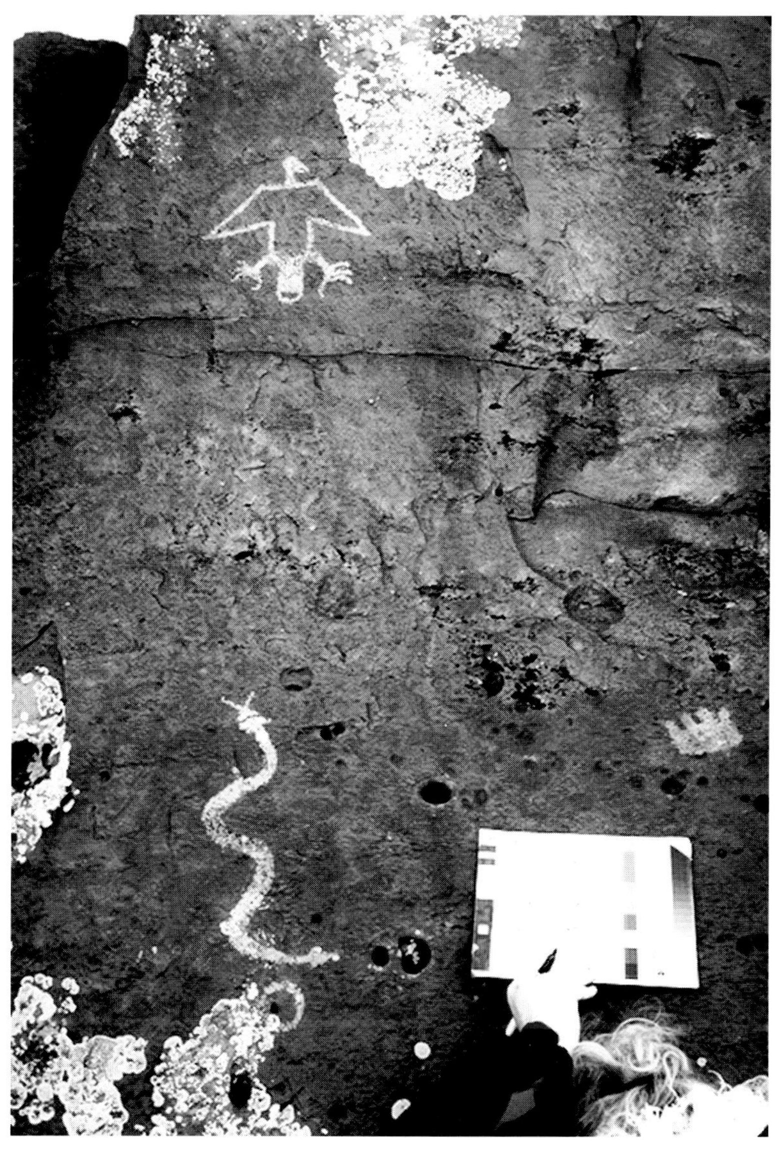

FIGURE 10.8
Locus AL (computer enhanced).

of the lack of patina on the petroglyphs and the more refined draftsmanship. The north site panels contain an enormous variety of images, including paw prints, quadrupeds, one split-hoofed bovine, and a possible rider mounted on a fantastic creature. None of these images are easily interpreted, but their haphazard composition appears to be an accretion of images over time, suggesting highly idiosyncratic content and function. Such change in iconography between the sites may be explained by different functions or audiences. Panels located on the south site face foreign travelers and invaders who may have entered the region along the east-west route, whereas the north-south arroyos may have supported less foreign and more local traffic; therefore the rock art may have served a different audience. A dual function could be hypothesized for some of these panels. The more private panels may have been created for a variety of purposes, including continuing to indicate that Abo was still an important center; the more public panels may have been intended to serve as boundary markers. There is the intriguing possibility that there may be a link between the eighteenth-century Pueblo warriors and the pictographs of shield bearers and weapons clearly visible to travelers on the banks of the Abo Wash.

Some of the foreign travelers along the arroyos would have been Athapaskan or other Plains dwellers who also left their marks on the landscape. As many as fifteen panels in the southern shelters contain possible Athapaskan, or at least non-Puebloan, paintings (fig. 10.9). However, this rock art is difficult to definitively identify and date. So the sparsity of mapped loci reflects more the difficulties of relative dating than a lack of Athapaskan participation in the creation of rock art. All the loci plotted on figure 10.9 are found in the two shelters of the south site and consist entirely of pictographs. However, these images often occur on or near Late Puebloan images, suggesting an aggressive relationship between the two artistic traditions. As the Athapaskan images often superimpose or juxtapose Puebloan images, this may be a case of co-opting the site or the power of the earlier paintings for political, religious reasons. Such a relationship may indicate that both cultures were using these images to mark a cultural boundary on the landscape.

When selected periods are plotted on the same map, interesting clusters appear (fig. 10.10). Most of the later rock art loci cluster on the north and south sites. One faces the Pueblo; the other is oriented toward the east-west road possibly used by both local and long-distance traffic. Another possible explanation for clusters in these two regions could be phenomenal attributes. Both the north and south sites possess several of the attributes that Steinbring considers equal to iconography in importance in rock art. Both possess prominent rock surfaces and shelters. Both sites are associated with environmental extremes, facing onto perennial streams in an otherwise arid environment. Both places are higher than surrounding surfaces and seek visibility,

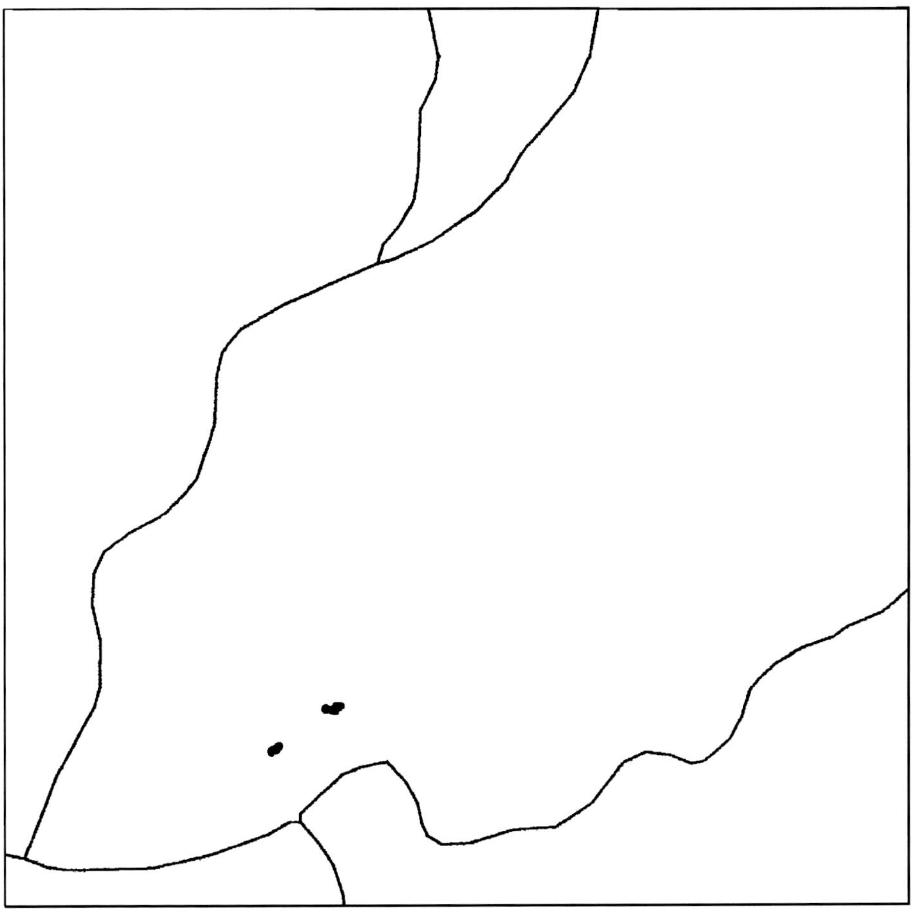

both away from and toward their exposures. This would coincide with modern Pueblo thought regarding Native emphasis on high and visible places.

In addition to the iconography, such visibility may also be a clue to the role of rock art in shaping landscape. There may be a link between iconography, medium, and visibility that may indicate the function of certain images. Some panels seem to have been created with the intent of being visible to passersby, while others are quite hidden. Brody has suggested that there may be a discernible difference between the paintings usually being more public, while the petroglyphs are commonly invisible at a distance and, therefore, perhaps created for more private reasons. It is true that on

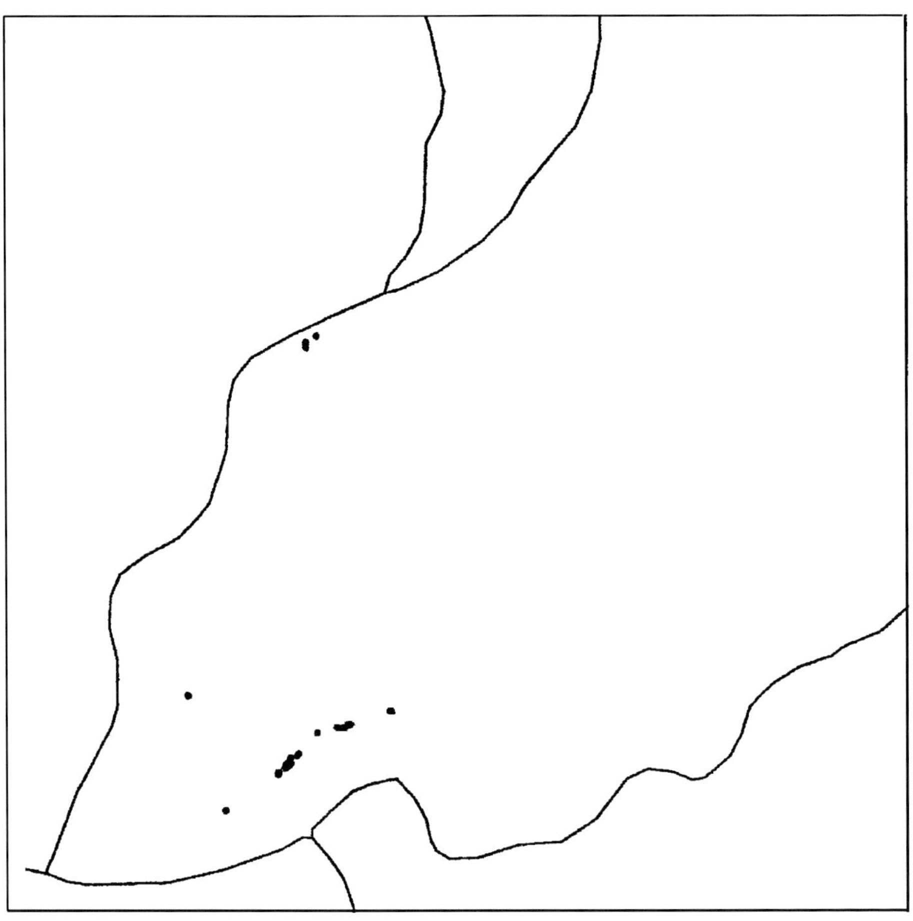

the south site, the images most visible from the arroyo are the pictographs, but this does not hold true for any other site. On the north and west sites, the rock carvings seek visibility. I suggest that different iconography and media served the same functions at different times.

What has been accomplished in this chapter is only the beginning. In considering the relationship between rock art and the landscape, there are many more possibilities to explore when analyzing rock art with GIS software. Rock art is a trace on the landscape, a manifestation of a cognitive concept or template. It is the visual evidence of how the landscape was perceived, whether in marking a place, a center, or a boundary; the images function in all these roles. Place is marked by rock art to record or intensify human experience, to express a deeper meaning, but also to hold the viewer's attention, a focus for human passion or need. Rock art is used to shape space, comparable to architecture.

Rock art is not a mute record of human passages. As Young has so eloquently described, sometimes the images are metonyms of narrative, calling to the mind of a knowledgeable person stories, myths, parables, history. This history is inscribed in space, what Lefebvre would term representational space, through the petroglyphs and pictographs. Each culture, each period, has its own unique code to inscribe upon the landscape and the rock faces. This space is a complete text in every time period; new images enrich and embellish it. They not only create a deeper, richer texture of visual stimuli but also serve as symbols of oral histories to be told and retold.

Notes

1. J. J. Brody, "Site Use, Pictorial Space, and Subject Matter in Late Prehistoric and Early Historic Rio Grande Pueblo Art," *Journal of Anthropological Research* 45 (1989): 16.

2. E. L. Keithahn, "The Petroglyphs of Southeastern Alaska," *American Antiquity* 2 (1940): 128–32.

3. I refer here to the growing body of literature linking specific rock art images to movements of light and shadow across a rock surface or the link between an "abstract" petroglyph and the landscape view beyond. An example would be John M. Rafter, "More Sunlight/Petroglyph Interaction at Counsel Rocks," in *Rock Art Papers,* San Diego Museum Papers 27 (1991): 65–74. See also the American Rock Art Research Association's series of papers for a sample of recent work along these lines.

4. For a more in-depth discussion of these terms, see H. Denise Smith, "The Rock Art of Abo Pueblo: Analyzing a Cultural Palimpsest," Ph.D. diss., University of New Mexico, 1998, or the publications by Yi-Fu Tuan referenced herein.

5. Henri Lefebvre, *The Production of Space,* trans. Donald Nicholson-Smith (Oxford: Blackwell, 1991), 1; Albert Einstein, foreword, in *Concepts of Space,* ed. Max Jammer (1954; reprint, New York: Harper and Brothers, 1960), xv.

6. Lefebvre, *The Production of Space,* 17, 47, 39, 41–42, 37.

7. Ibid., 41–42.

8. Yi-Fu Tuan, *Space and Place: The Perspective of Experience* (Minneapolis: University of Minnesota Press, 1977), 91, 93, 162–63. Specific Puebloan groups at Santa Ana, Hopi, and the Tewa villages are cited as examples of cultures who create place through the designation of landmarks in space.

9. Yi-Fu Tuan, "Place: An Experiential Perspective," *Geographical Review* 65 (1975): 161, paraphrasing Susanne Langer, *Feeling and Form* (New York: Scribner's, 1953), 91; Yi-Fu Tuan, "Thought and Landscape: The Eye and the Mind's Eye," in *The Interpretation of Ordinary Landscapes: Geographic Essays,* ed. D. W. Meinig (New York: Oxford University Press, 1979), 96–97; Kent C. Ryden, *Mapping the Invisible Landscape: Folklore, Writing, and the Sense of Place* (Iowa City: University of Iowa Press, 1993), 27.

10. Tuan, *Space and Place,* 164.

11. Margaret W. Conkey, "To Find Ourselves: Art and Social Geography of Prehistoric Hunter-Gatherers," in *Past and Present,* Hunter-Gatherer Studies, ed. C. Schrire (Orlando: Academic Press, 1984), 269.

12. Jack Steinbring, "Phenomenal Attributes: Site Selection Factors in Rock Art," *American Indian Rock Art* 17 (1992): 102.

13. Steinbring, "Phenomenal Attributes," 102–8.

14. M. Jane Young, *Signs from the Ancestors: Zuni Cultural Symbolism and Perceptions of Rock Art* (Albuquerque: University of New Mexico Press, 1988), 174.

15. Alfonso Ortiz, *The Tewa World: Space, Time, Being, and Becoming in a Pueblo Society* (Chicago: University of Chicago Press, 1969), 15–19.

16. Polly Schaafsma, "Rock Art: Ideas in Time and Space," in *Marks in Place: Contemporary Responses to Rock Art* (Albuquerque: University of New Mexico Press, 1988), 1; Mircea Eliade, *The Sacred and the Profane* (New York: Harper Torchbook, 1961), 20–22.

17. Carole L. Crumley and William H. Marquardt, eds., *Regional Dynamics: Burgundian Landscapes in Historical Perspective* (San Diego: Academic Press, 1987), 2, 13.

18. Lefebvre, *The Production of Space,* 41–42.

19. Edward Relph, *Place and Placelessness* (London: Pion, 1976), 21–22; Young, *Signs from the Ancestors,* 148.

20. Carole L. Crumley, "Toward a Locational Definition of State Systems of Settlement," *American Anthropologist* 78 (1976): 67.

21. See Stuart J. Baldwin, "Tompiro Culture, Subsistence, and Trade," Ph.D. diss., University of Calgary, 1988.

22. John Justeson and Steve Hampson, "Closed Models of Open Systems: Boundary Considerations," in *The Archaeology of Frontiers and Boundaries,* ed. Stanton Green and Stephen Perlman (Orlando: Academic Press, 1985), 17.

23. Ian Hodder discusses this process in his seminal study of West African cultures. Hodder, "Boundaries as Strategies: An Ethnoarchaeological Study," in *The Archaeology of Frontiers and Boundaries, (Orlando: Academic Press, 1985)* 141–59.

24. Ryden, *Mapping the Invisible Landscape,* 127.

25. Ibid., 130, 34. Ryden is describing the border on Route 101 between Connecticut and Rhode Island with all the signs and markers posted by government agencies, but signs are made by many cultures to serve very similar purposes.

26. Schaafsma, "Rock Art," 3; Young, *Signs from the Ancestors,* 182.

27. Young, *Signs from the Ancestors,* 148, 176.

28. The Pecos sequence was a historical time line created at the first conference at Pecos Pueblo in 1927. With some adjustments, this chronology is still the main framework for Anasazi studies. Joseph Tainter and Frances Levine, *Cultural Resources Overview of Central New Mexico* (Santa Fe and Albuquerque: Bureau of Land Management and U.S. Forest Service, 1987), 75.

29. H. Denise Smith, "The Rock Art of Abo Pueblo," 118–21; the detailed chronology is in chap. 3.

30. Ibid., 41.

31. Stuart J. Baldwin, "Piro and Tompiro Ethnography: First Draft" (Santa Fe: Laboratory of Anthropology, 1981), 23.

32. Baldwin, "Tompiro Culture," 164, 185, 229–30.

33. James Ivey, *In the Midst of a Loneliness: The Architectural History of the Salinas Missions,* Salinas Pueblo Missions National Monument Historic Structure Report, Professional Papers 15 (Santa Fe: Division of History, Southwest Cultural Resources Center, 1988), 232; Wesley R. Hurt,

The 1939–1940 Excavation Project at Quarai Pueblo and Mission Buildings: Salinas Pueblo Missions National Monument, New Mexico (Santa Fe: Division of History and Division of Anthropology, National Park Service, 1990), 4.

34. Oakah L. Jones, *Pueblo Warriors and Spanish Conquest* (Norman: University of Oklahoma Press, 1966), 38.

35. Ibid., 128–29; Ivey, *In the Midst of a Loneliness,* 236. Ivey assumes this is the case although Jones clearly does not imply that Cachupin followed the practices of his first term in office in his second.

36. Joseph H. Toulouse, Jr., "The Mission of San Gregorio de Abo," *School of American Research Monograph 13* (Albuquerque: University of New Mexico Press, 1949), 100. He posits an eighteenth-century reoccupation of Abo by Pueblo people based on these sherds, but it is much more likely that they were left by Pueblo people camping temporarily at the site.

37. Stuart J. Baldwin, "A Tentative Occupation Sequence for Abó Pass, Central New Mexico." Manuscript on file at Salinas Pueblo Missions National Monument, Mountanair, NM, 1983." 3, 17–18.

38. Ivey, *In the Midst of a Loneliness,* 241.

39. Tainter and Levine, *Cultural Resources Overview,* III, 241.

40. J. J. Brody, *Anasazi and Pueblo Painting* (Albuquerque: University of New Mexico Press, 1991), 81, 105–12.

41. Brody, *Anasazi,* 130, 132. An example he cites is a comparison between the Willow Springs and West Mesa sites located in Arizona and New Mexico, respectively. Both sites contain similar images, yet Willow Springs is a record of clan visits, whereas the West Mesa petroglyphs were apparently created in homage to the spirits of dead ancestors; cultural context is crucial to the interpretation of these petroglyphs.

42. Brody, *Anasazi,* 132–33, 129.

43. Brody, personal communication, December 5, 1997; Schaafsma, "Rock Art," 4.

44. I have observed that the gypsum sands of White Sands National Monument in the southwestern portion of New Mexico have a slight pinkish cast, so the "contamination" in the pigment used at Abo may be a natural occurrence.

45. Young, *Signs from the Ancestors,* 185.

46. Schaafsma, "Rock Art," 3; Young, *Signs from the Ancestors,* 234.

47. The Early Puebloan style coincides with Schaafsma's Rio Grande style, which in my opinion was coined during Schaafsma's formulations regarding the origins of kachina imagery in Puebloan rock art. In publication and in presentations, she has stated that Hopi and Zuni examples would be included in this style. The name "Rio Grande" reflects her biases regarding the rock art she knows best, as well as the origin and spread of kachinas from east to west. To avoid these pitfalls, the term "Puebloan" is used here since I believe this to be what Schaafsma really means.

48. The Spanish did not distinguish between many of the raiding groups, lumping them all together under the generic term "Apache." Since the actual tribal affiliation of these raiders is beyond the scope of this essay, they are here designated as Athapaskans, thus incorporating many of the newly arrived hunter-raiders in the Southwest by the seventeenth century.

49. Morris E. Opler, "Mescalero Apache," *Handbook of North American Indians,* ed. William C. Sturtevant, vol. 10 (Washington, D.C.: Smithsonian Institution, 1983), 419; Polly Schaafsma, *Indian Rock Art of the Southwest* (Albuquerque: University of New Mexico, 1980), 334; W. W. Newcomb, Jr. and Forest Kirkland, *The Rock Art of Texas Indians* (Austin: University of Texas Press, 1967), 199–201.

50. Mary Ann Cunningham, David Arbeit, and Jed Becher, *User Manual Version 3.0: The*

EPPL7 Geographic Information System (Saint Paul: State of Minnesota, Land Management Information Center and Minnesota Planning, 1997), 1–2.

51. Toulouse, "The Mission of San Gregorio de Abo," 100; Ivey, *In the Midst of a Loneliness,* 241.

52. For a discussion of warrior iconography, see H. Denise Smith, "The Rock Art of Abo Pueblo," chap. 5.

Chapter 11

Chief Blankets on the Middle Missouri

Navajo Artists and Their Patrons

GRETA J. MURPHY

*I*mages ranging from Cheyenne ledger drawings to American expeditionary photographs illustrate the extent to which nineteenth-century Plains Indians readily embraced objects produced by culturally and geographically distant peoples. Lakota, Arapaho, and other middlemen acquired a variety of articles, from horses to items of personal adornment, through an important and complex system of exchange extending throughout the trans-Mississippian West. Among the most striking of the trade objects were Navajo chief blankets, which had, by the mid-nineteenth century, become a costly and prestigious element of central Plains attire. Curiously, these wearing blankets were a significant departure from other styles of Navajo weavings and were not often worn by the Navajos themselves.[1] The Navajos, known for their remarkable ability to adapt to new cultural influences and economic demands, purposely created a distinctive blanket style that would appeal to the aesthetic sensibilities of the Plains Indians with whom they bartered through an ancient and complex trade network.

Collectors and historians consider nineteenth-century chief blankets to be among the most accomplished of all Navajo weavings. They were expertly woven (so tightly woven, in fact, that they actually shed water) using costly yarns and indigo dyes and thus commanded a relatively high price. The blankets did not indicate the wearer's political status, as the name suggests, although they were undoubtedly symbolic of wealth and prestige.

Costly materials and superior craftsmanship alone cannot fully account for the high regard in which these blankets were, and are, held. That the blankets were traded far from Dinétah and worn as emblems of status indicates that they were also valued for other qualities. Significantly, and not coincidentally, most chief blankets in collections today were taken from among central Plains Indians. Evidence suggests that the Navajos, familiar with Plains artwork through objects of trade, deliberately courted Plains patronage by emulating their aesthetic tastes.

Given the dearth of concrete evidence to support this premise, other elements from the historic record need to be explored. A description of early weaving traditions illustrates how chief blankets developed and how they differed from other Navajo blankets. A brief account of Navajo silver and its relationship to Plains silver ornamentation follows, in order to confirm that the Navajos had access to at least one Plains Indian aesthetic form and to demonstrate the possibility of access to others. Comparison of buffalo hide robes, cradles, and other Plains art forms to chief blankets illustrates how the blankets might have satisfied Plains aesthetic sensibilities. Finally, a chronicle of the trade networks by which chief blankets reached the Plains is provided.

Early Navajo Weaving

The Navajos have long been recognized for their ability to selectively adapt and assimilate those properties of other cultures that in some way enhance their own quality of life. Unlike their nomadic Apache relatives and neighbors, the Navajos showed a readiness to adopt a new way of life when the Spaniards introduced sheep into the Southwest. Often the tendency to borrow from other cultures took aesthetic forms that added beauty to Navajo life and ultimately became important sources of economic stability.

Most scholars believe that Pueblo people taught the Navajos to weave, perhaps before the Pueblo Revolt of 1680 but certainly by the Spanish Reconquest of 1692 when many Puebloans fled persecution to live among neighboring Navajo. According to Kate Peck Kent, "the Navajos adopted the textile types of their Pueblo neighbors at the time they learned to weave on Pueblo-type upright looms, probably before 1700. For about a hundred years, Navajo and Pueblo textiles were almost identical in technique, form, function, materials, and many aspects of design. Both groups wove wider-than-long mantas." Textiles woven according to the old Pueblo dimensions ("wider than long") were worn on the body as they appeared on the loom, with stripes enfolding the body horizontally.[2]

Navajo weavers eagerly experiment with new compositions, and it is a testament to their pronounced creativity that they can borrow artistic forms and elements without producing objects that are simply derivative. Kluckhohn, Hill, and Kluckhohn make the following observation: "The Navajos are notably acquisitive, and momentum for change has usually been derived from the outside. Sources have varied through time. . . . Not that the Navajo accepted blindly anything that was offered: there is ample evidence for selectivity and there is also evidence that the Navajo modified borrowed elements to conform them to prevailing Navajo patterns." Creativity of design and technical experimentation increased the quality and desirability of Navajo weaving during the eighteenth century. Textile proportions began to change as blankets were increasingly woven "longer than wide" so that vertical compositions were wrapped horizontally around the body. Early records indicate that Navajo blankets were commonly traded to Spanish and Pueblo people as early as 1706.[3] Although the Navajos were enjoying some economic success with their weavings, which probably stimulated an increase in production, there is little to suggest that Navajo women experimented with designs for any reason other than their own gratification; new motifs and patterns developed from the earliest Puebloan prototypes.

The nineteenth century was a period of even greater experimentation. Mexican serapes imported into the northern Rio Grande Valley and the influence of new dyes and yarns inspired Navajo weavers to create increasingly complex design fields. The textile trade was expanded to include the Apaches, Comanches, Mexicans, and, with the opening of the Santa Fe Trail in 1821, Anglos.[4] Chief blankets, popular among the Utes and other Plains peoples to the north, deviated from the simple striped blankets of the eighteenth century and Mexican Saltillo-like patterns of the nineteenth. These blankets were not a simple restatement of Puebloan, Mexican, Spanish, or Anglo textile influences, as is generally assumed. Rather, they incorporated elements derived from the art of Cheyenne, Lakota, and other Plains peoples. Typically, during the nineteenth century, only chief blankets and women's mantas were woven in the ancient Pueblo proportions of wider than long.

Cultural Pathways: Navajo and Plains Indian Silver

The history of Navajo silver illustrates that Navajo silversmiths not only had access to Plains artwork but also quickly adapted that art to their own needs. By 1830 Plains people were commonly wearing silver bracelets, rings, brooches, earrings, and hair ornaments. According to Arthur Woodward, "the Dakota, Crow, Cheyenne, Kiowa, Comanche, Ute . . . wore these round discs and oval ornaments . . . fastened to leather belts. The women of the Plains favored such belts and at first glance one might easily mistake one . . . for an early Navajo belt of similar pattern." Woodward not only suggests that Plains Indians created prototypes of the first Navajo *concha* belts but also asserts that Navajo silver evolved from a few primary forms borrowed from Delaware and Anglo silver. According to Woodward, these forms "spread from the Plains area to the Navajo country." The primary concha form, having originated among northeastern Indians, was traded to the Utes, Kiowas, Comanches, Sioux, Crows, and Cheyennes by traders and trappers between 1820 and 1840. Woodward speculates that the Navajos could also have obtained the concha and crescent-shaped *naja* from horse bridles plundered in the aftermath of battles with their Ute, Comanche, and Kiowa enemies before the Navajo incarceration at the Bosque Redondo in 1863. However, the most convincing explanation is that the Navajos traded for silver ornaments with the Utes, who had in turn obtained them from the Kiowas.[5]

John Adair both supports and disputes various aspects of Woodward's suppositions. He observes that "Woodward has conclusively demonstrated that the Navajo derived the concha from the Plains Indians." Adair also asserts that the Navajos obtained silver ornaments in battles with southern Plains tribes but credits the forms of Navajo conchas to those found on Mexican headstalls. In any case, clearly the Navajos borrowed freely from Plains Indian art, and Adair's premise that the Navajo also borrowed from Mexican silver does not dilute the importance of this point. Neither is it of any consequence that the Navajos created ornaments for their own use and according to their own aesthetic preferences after their return to Dinétah from the Bosque Redondo in 1868. Only a few years later Navajo silversmiths would show their willingness to oblige an outside market when, in 1899, the Fred Harvey Company began to custom order Navajo silver to accommodate the tastes of Anglo tourists.[6] It is also well-known that J. B. Moore and Juan Lorenzo Hubbell at Ganado and Crystal trading posts, respectively, forever changed the direction of Navajo weaving when they began to impose their own notions of beauty, quality, and tradition on that art form.

Clearly Navajo artists were quite able and willing to satisfy the aesthetic requirements of outsiders, and a comparison of Navajo chief blankets and Plains Indian art further illustrates this point. The relationship of artist and patron that existed between Navajo weavers and Plains peoples may have made the later successes of the trading posts and tourism industry possible.

Chief Blankets: Style and Development

Early striped mantas are commonly believed to be prototypes of the first chief blankets. Early mantas are characterized by alternating narrow stripes of white and black or brown and are woven wider than long. When worn, the stripes enfold the body horizontally. This characteristic differs from typical Navajo *moqui* blankets, which are woven longer than wide so that stripes are worn vertically. It is generally believed that moqui patterns reflect seventeenth-century Spanish, Pueblo, and Mexican weaving influences.[7]

Early striped mantas were largely limited to the natural colors of the churro wool from which they were woven on simple upright looms. These blacks, browns, and whites could be carded together to make grays. The Spanish introduced indigo dye in the 1630s, and weavers would sometimes mix this with a yellow dye made from rabbit brush to create green.[8] For the most part, early striped mantas were woven according to the Navajos' own aesthetic preferences and use, although some of these blankets have been collected elsewhere in the Southwest and on the Plains, indicating that some trade may have occurred.

Chief blankets are classified into three phases, with a fourth transitional phase developing during the years following the Navajos' incarceration at the Bosque Redondo. The use of the term "phase" is misleading, however, because these styles probably developed somewhat simultaneously rather than in some linear progression as the term implies. The fourth blanket phase seems to have developed from a conflation of influences largely outside the scope of this study.[9] The fluorescence of the first-phase chief blanket occurred between 1800 and 1850 (fig. 11.1). It is characterized by a pattern of wide, alternating black or brown and white stripes, two slightly wider border stripes, and a double-wide center band. The band and borders sometimes include narrow indigo stripes, a style that was particularly favored by the Utes.[10] These areas often have the addition of thin red lines.

The second-phase blanket developed between 1800 and 1870 (fig. 11.2). These are characterized by twelve red bars or rectangles introduced into the central band and borders. These red threads were from unraveled wool trade cloth, or *bayeta,* which bayeta became increasingly popular with Navajo weavers during the nineteenth century. Bayeta complemented stripes of indigo, natural brown, and white homespun yarns.[11] There are stripes of equal width in the second-phase blankets but those at the warp edges are often double-wide. Always, the center band consists of double-wide stripes that, like the border stripes, are frequently woven with strongly contrasting colors. For example, the "body" of the blanket is generally woven in alternating brown and white stripes, while the borders and center are woven in red and blue. Often the tension between these areas creates the illusion that the red and blue areas are, in fact, applied onto, as opposed to woven into, the blanket. The tension is controlled by the stability of the blanket's quadrilaterally symmetrical form.

The third and last phase considered in this analysis developed between 1860 and 1880. It is distinguished by nine geometric elements replacing the twelve bars of the second phase. Typically a terraced diamond is woven in the center of the blanket's

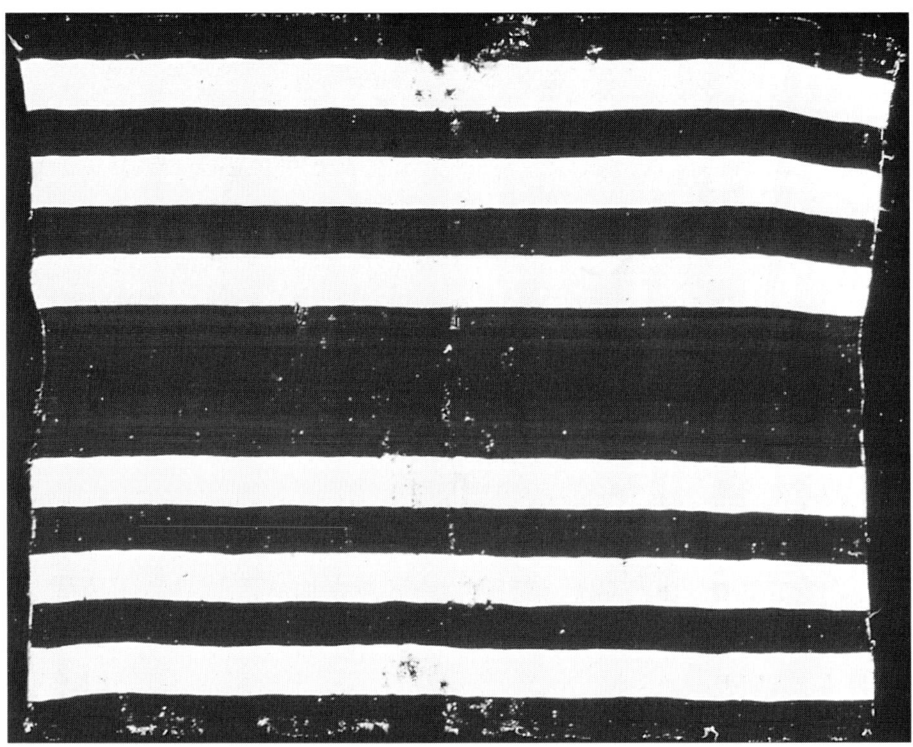

wide middle band. Half-diamonds interrupt the end of this band as well as the center of the warp-edge bands. The four blanket corners are marked with one-quarter terraced diamonds. Together these elements create a bilaterally symmetrical design field, and, like the previous blankets, the field is horizontal. When worn, the elements on the central vertical axis articulate the wearer's spine as they do in the second phase (fig. 11.3). Significantly, the two half-diamonds on the weft edges of the center band form a complete diamond when the blanket enfolds the body.

Plains Aesthetics

An extensive network of intertribal trade played an important role in the economy of the Great Plains and beyond. Many kinds of objects were bartered from one tribal

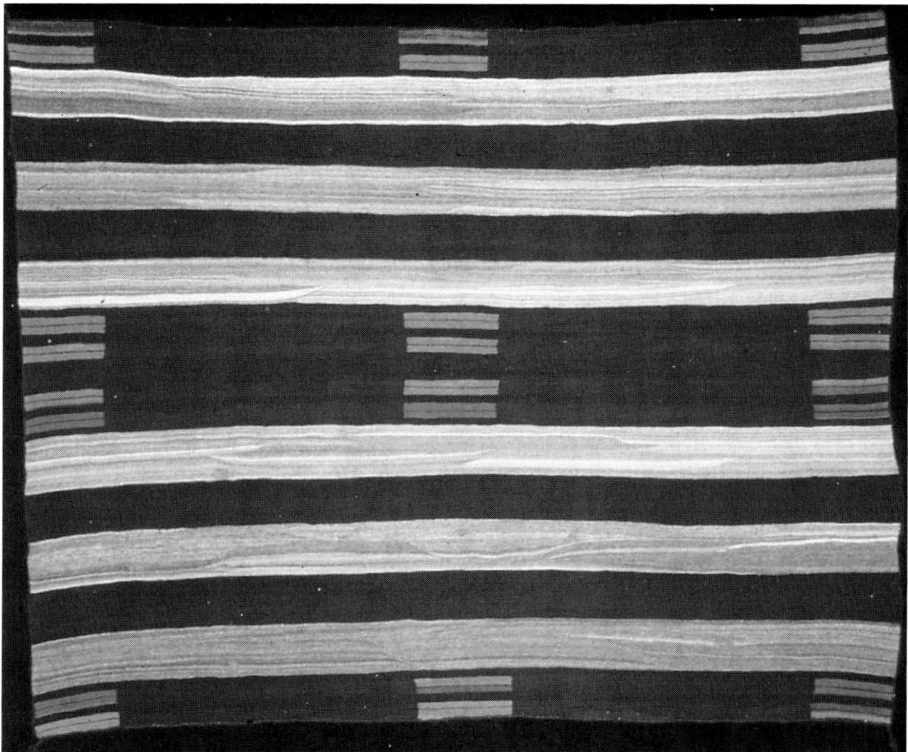

group to the next, throwing a glimmer of doubt on the provenance of even the most carefully documented objects collected before the reservation era. Due in part to these exchanges and the aesthetic influences that were a by-product of them, distinctive tribal styles are difficult to determine. However, many of the basic design elements, compositions, and forms found throughout this culture area are shared with those Plateau and Great Basin tribes that had, by the nineteenth century, assimilated facets of Plains Indian culture. By no means does this analysis intend to suggest that tribal and individual variations do not exist. In fact, great artistic diversity is found on the Plains but it usually occurs within established aesthetic parameters. The scope of Plains art is tremendous, and so this analysis must necessarily be limited to general forms that were universally created and that shared fundamental similarities of design.

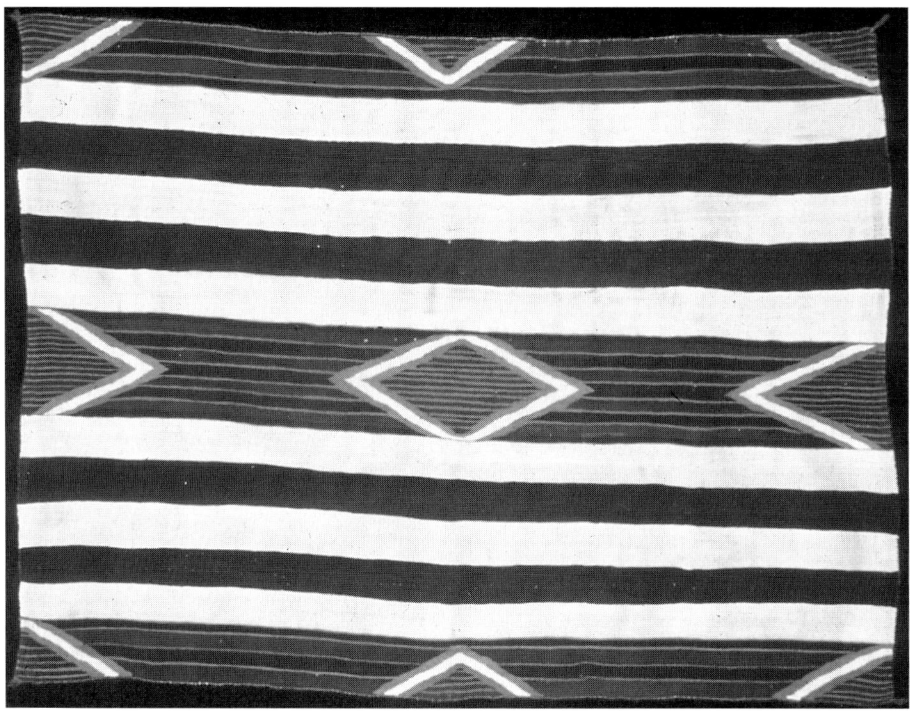

One such ubiquitous form was the buffalo robe. Commonly, when buffalo fell during the hunt their skin could only be removed by being slit into two pieces along the spine. If the skin was to be worn as a robe, the slit would be mended and the seam concealed with a quilled or beaded strip. The robe was worn with its greatest dimension wrapped around the body, and, consequently, the blanket strip also encircled the wearer in this direction. So favored was this horizontal emphasis that Plains people also used embroidered strips to decorate cloth trade blankets (fig. 11.4). This practice occurred independently of any need to conceal seams, for when two blankets were sewn together, the seam ran vertically. The blanket strip, however, continued to be applied horizontally. The device of horizontal stripes punctuated with vertically aligned spots of color could be found on a tremendous number of quilled, beaded, and painted surfaces throughout the Plains. Quilled dew cloths or tipi liners, beaded or quilled saddle blankets, and painted backrests are but a few of these objects.

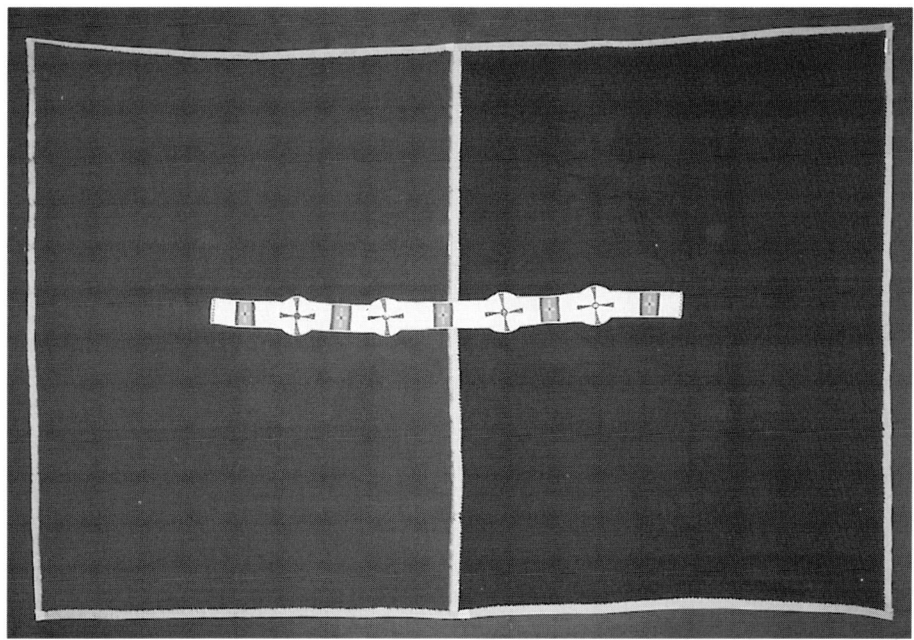

Rawhide containers called *parfleche* were widely used after the introduction of the horse and the subsequent rise of nomadism. This art form spread from the Plains to the Plateau and Intermontane until it was made and used by more than fifty tribes. Parfleche were used to store and transport a wide range of items from food to clothing, and while they are often photographed as if they are longer than wide, parfleche were actually attached to saddles in such a way that they were seen as horizontal fields (fig. 11.5).[12]

Aesthetic Meeting Grounds

Chief blankets often exhibit striking similarities to the decorated robes so ubiquitous on the Plains. While the striping on first-phase blankets may only superficially resemble embroidered strips found on robes, this particular blanket style conceptually integrated key elements of classic striped mantas and buffalo robes. Like the blanket, robes were worn so that their greatest dimensions enfolded the body horizontally, with the robe's decorated strip corresponding to the emphasized wide middle area of

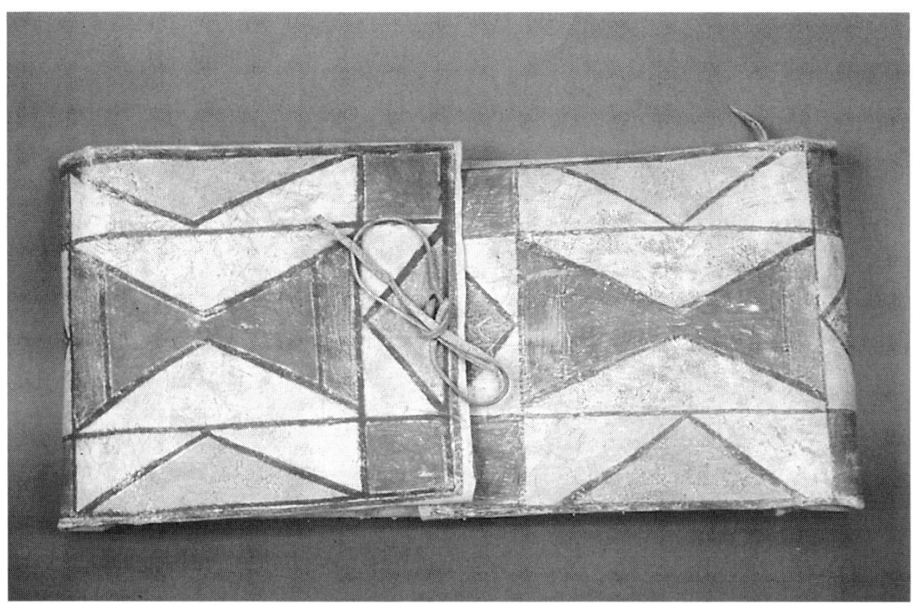

the chief blanket. A first-phase blanket collected from the Brulé Sioux bears witness to the presence of such a relationship. Porcupine quill-wrapped thongs, tin cone tinklers, and red horsehair are suspended from the buttons. These decorative elements are commonly found on hide robes, but wear patterns suggest the Brulé also added a quilled or beaded blanket strip to the wide center band of this blanket.[13]

Second-phase chief blankets also bear a strong resemblance to objects used on the Plains. *Possible bags,* so named because of their versatility, were used to carry clothing and small household objects. They are decorated with red quilled or beaded stripes across the front of their horizontal fields, intersected by vertical rows of red fluff feathers, quills, or beads that visually correspond to the red rectangles of the second-phase blankets. The unbeaded background, or negative space, similarly compares to the neutral-colored areas of the chief blankets. Notably, the tension created between the different blanket areas gives the illusion that the blue and red areas are applied, much like bead and quillwork. Another important resemblance is that blankets and possible bags are both created in quadrilaterally symmetrical fields. Beaded shirt

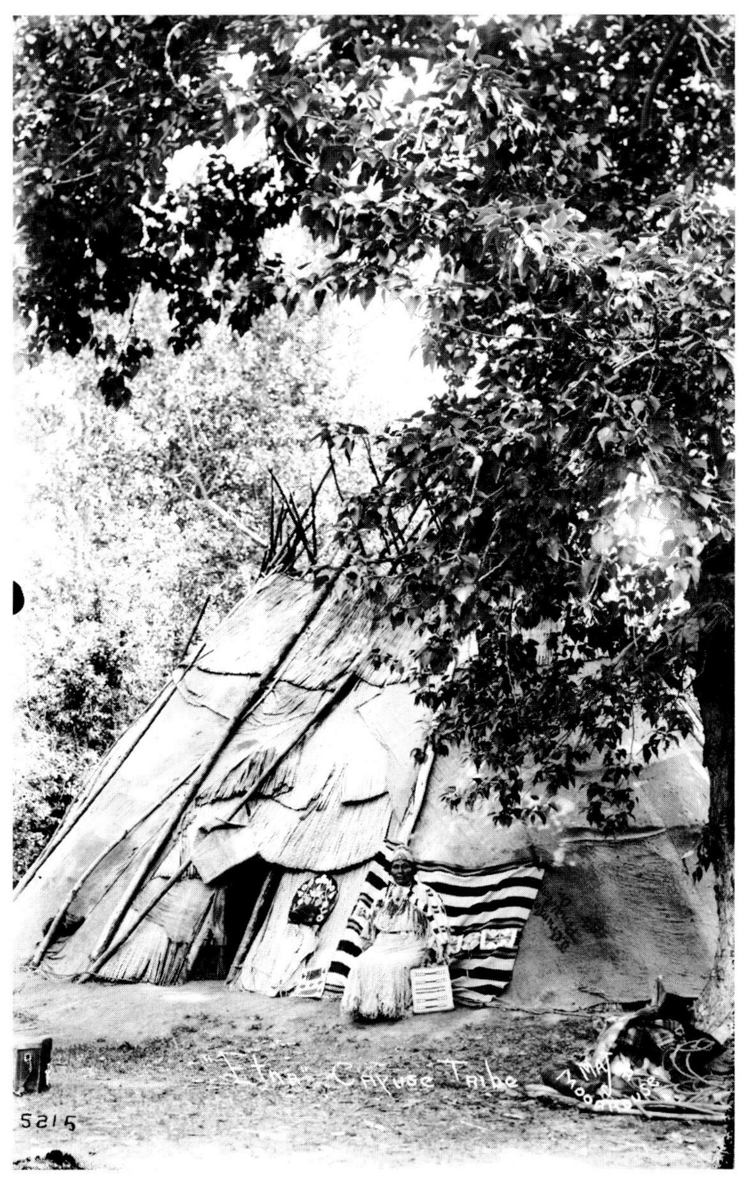

F I G U R E 1 1 . 6
Edna Kash Kash (Cayuse-Umatilla) and a Navajo
First-Phase Chief Blanket to which an intermontane-
style blanket strip was added. Photograph by Lee
Moorhouse, ca. 1895. Collection of the University of
Oregon Knight Library, Special Collections, Lee
Moorhouse Collection, neg. no. 5215.

yokes, pipe bags, cradles, and many other examples of Plains artwork exhibit these similarities. These art objects would have been well known to anyone visiting a Plains Indian camp. Even items that occupied private spaces such as dew cloths and backrests would have been known to camp guests, due in part to the hospitality and ceremonial visits that were often an important part of intertribal trade.

Second-phase blankets also bear some resemblance to decorated robes. In *Plains Indian Painting,* John Ewers asserted that robes painted with horizontal stripes were common among the Sarsi and Blackfoot, while robes decorated with horizontally quilled or beaded stripes were found throughout the northern and central Plains. Vertical accents were common to these robes and persisted well into the reservation period. Again, both second-phase chief blankets and robes were worn with the horizontal stripes punctuated by small vertical elements. That robes and blankets have obvious visual similarities, serve the same function, and are contemporaneous indicates that they either shared a common origin or one inspired the other. Due to the fragile nature of organic materials, few eighteenth-century robes and blankets survive with which to positively date and analyze the fluorescence of each. However, historical accounts of both Navajo weavings and intertribal trade suggest that striped robes predate striped blankets, and so the former most likely informed the latter.[14]

The bilateral symmetry inherent in third-phase chief blankets results in an intriguing characteristic: when folded like a parfleche, all the elements come together at different points to form complete diamonds.[15] J. J. Brody recalls once seeing judges at the Indian Exhibit Building of the New Mexico State Fair around 1968 fold chief blankets in this manner as a method of determining the unity of design. Charles Amsden makes a similar observation: "Thus when the blanket was folded to bring the corners together, the four quarter-figures matched to form one whole. The two ends and the two sides could each be brought together to match their half-figures. This layout therefore required a precision in size and spacing which was a supreme test of the weaver's eye."[16]

Parfleche designs reveal other chief blanket similarities. A central stripe commonly bisects the middle of the two flaps, dividing the field horizontally into two symmetrical panels. This coincides with the wide center band of the blankets. Cheyenne parfleche, especially noted for their emphasized vertical axis, influenced those of the Utes and Arapaho. Also common to parfleche design are framing bands at top and bottom borders that compare to the blanket's warp-end bands.[17]

The Crows, whose art influenced that of the Intermontane and Plateau tribes, often favored large central diamonds that were formed by the closing of the two flaps of the parfleche.[18] When folded, two half-diamonds come together on the front of the parfleche to form a whole, as they do in the third-phase blankets. The Crows and

Wind River Shoshonis often painted solid rectangles on the four corners that have a visual equivalent in the second-phase blankets.[19] Quilled and beaded objects from the Plains also resemble third-phase blankets. Again, design elements commonly found on embroidered objects distributed throughout the Plains might have inspired Navajo weavers to further expand their chief blanket patterns. Beaded possible bags from the central Plains display design characteristics similar to many modified third-phase blanket patterns. The striped horizontal fields of these possible bags and blankets are accented with crosses that intersect on a vertical axis. While the number of crosses decorating the possible bags varies, the general effect resembles this modified third-phase pattern. Other storage bags offer visual similarities to the more common third-phase diamond patterns, although, again, the number of geometric elements does not necessarily correspond.

Lines punctuated with stepped or terraced diamonds decorate some Plains cradles in a manner reminiscent of third-phase blankets.[20] Triangles are also a part of the cradle designs, but these can be seen as half-diamonds that are completed on the other side of the cradle much the same way they are completed in parfleche designs and folded blankets. Diamonds and half-diamonds arranged in similar fashion are also found on items such as moccasins and pipe bags. It is also worth noting that in the third phase the tension between the two grounds is so great that the geometric units seem all the more applied. As with the first two phases, its resemblance to robe design is readily apparent.

One would expect to find similar color choices if the Navajos were, indeed, trying to appeal to the Plains' artistic sensibilities. In fact, the red, white, and blue color scheme was also common in mid-nineteenth century Plains, Plateau, and Great Basin beadwork. Although Navajo weavers are notably flexible in their ability to accommodate an outside market, there is no reason to believe they ever abandoned their own notions of beauty.[21]

Navajo-Plains Trade Network

Centuries before European contact, a complex trade network now termed the Middle Missouri system connected Indians of the Great Plains with countless diverse cultures on both sides of the Mississippi River (fig. 11.7). This network changed little from the first Spanish contacts in the sixteenth century until well into the nineteenth. Trade across the Plains since Paleolithic times is evidenced by Knife River flint found in an archaeological site in southeastern Colorado that establishes the existence of trade contact there eight thousand years ago.[22] The Middle Missouri system was comprised of both permanent trade centers and rendezvous points. Although these were the two

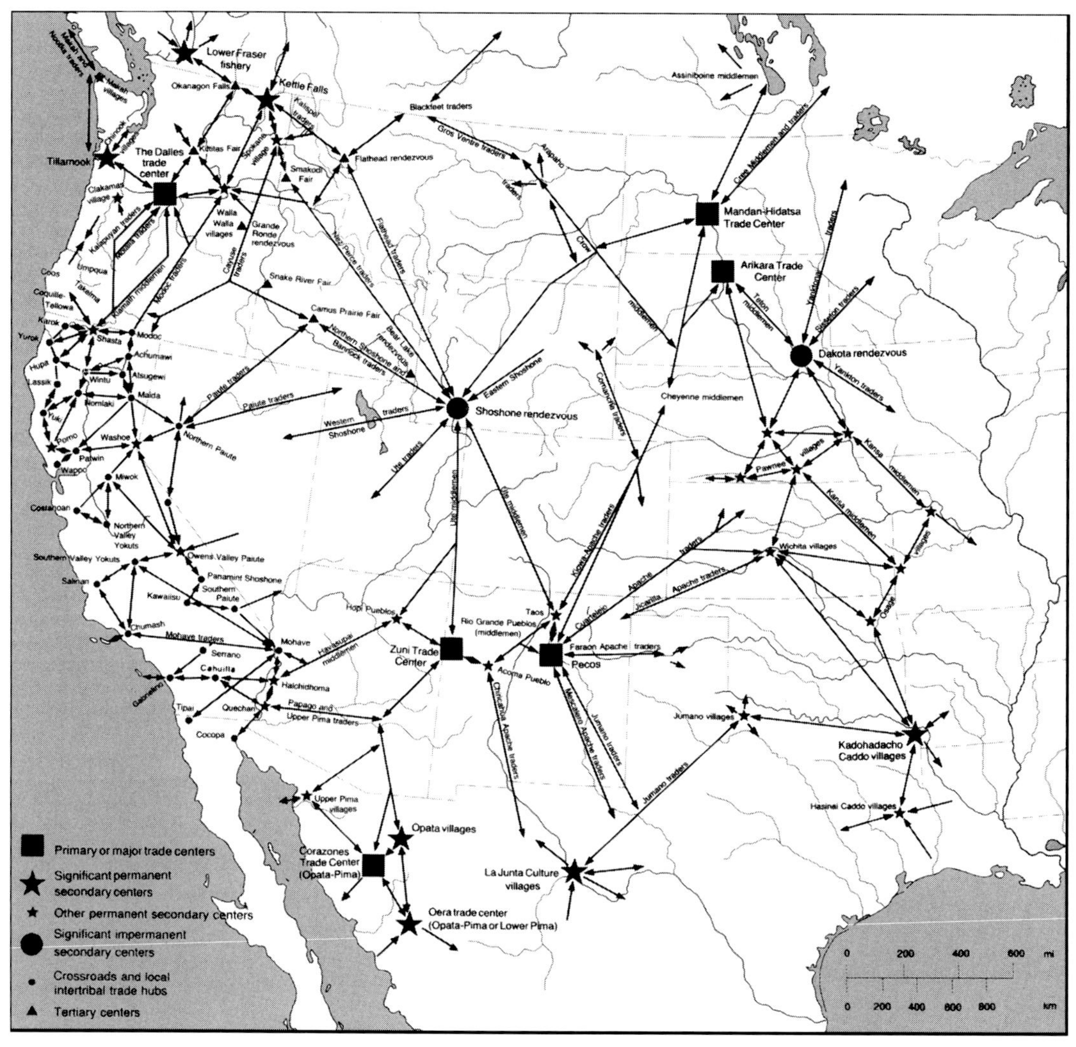

FIGURE 11.7

Map Showing the Protohistoric Middle Missouri, Pacific-Plateau, and Southwest Trade Systems. Published in William R. Swagerty, "Indian Trade in the Trans-Mississippi West to 1870," in *Handbook of the North American Indians,* ed. William C. Sturtevant, vol. 4 (Washington, D.C.: Smithsonian Institution, 1983).

general patterns of intertribal trade, informal exchanges and impromptu trade fairs occurred whenever disparate groups came together.

The sedentary Mandan, Hidatsa, and Arikara hosted trade fairs at their agricultural villages along the Missouri River. By creating surplus-abundant economies based on agricultural goods, these villagers readily exploited their geographical advantage to become important middlemen. Assiniboin and Plains Cree traders came from the north; Cheyenne, Arapaho, Comanche, Kiowa, and Kiowa-Apache traders, from the south; and Crow traders, from the west. They brought "dried meat, deer hides, bison robes, mountain sheep bows, and other leather goods" to exchange for agricultural produce and Knife River flint.[23] Early European observers reported seeing "dressed skins, trimmed and ornamented with plumage and porcupine quills, painted in various colors" traded along the Missouri.[24]

The diffusion of the horse illustrates the two major routes by which trade goods traveled from the Southwest. Horses were a relatively new commodity, but Ewers asserts that the pattern of horse trade would have necessarily followed preexisting trade routes in order to assure that transactions were both peaceful and successful, for the exchange was not only of horses but of the knowledge of horse handling. Distribution of the horse from the Southwest was a complex matter. According to Ewers, the Kiowas and Kiowa-Apaches, who probably traded or stole horses from the Spanish, transported them from the Southwest to the Arikara villages on the Middle Missouri. From there, the Arikaras traded them to Lakotas and eastern Dakotas.[25]

Major trails leading to agricultural villages were linked to secondary trade centers or rendezvous. Unlike the symbiotic trade relationship that existed between nomads and agriculturists at permanent villages, these seasonal rendezvous occurred only at prearranged times and places as a means for hunting and gathering people to exchange commodities among themselves.[26] Two important rendezvous points, the Dakota and Shoshoni, linked the Missouri River villages to the Spanish Southwest. Indian traders at the Shoshoni rendezvous indirectly connected the Dalles, a third rendezvous site located in present-day Oregon, to the Missouri. The Dakota rendezvous, a favorite of the Lakota, Yankton, and Sisseton, was located on the James River in South Dakota. There, the people would gather each spring to barter for objects as foreign as those acquired from North West Company traders on the Saint Peter and Des Moines Rivers. The Lakotas bartered commodities such as lodge covers, buffalo robes, shirts, leggings, and horses for walnut bows, red stone pipes, and European goods from their Dakota relatives.[27]

Jean-Baptiste Truteau, a trader with the Company of Explorers of the Upper Missouri, gave the first written record of the Dakota rendezvous.[28] Truteau worked the Missouri as far north as the Arikara from 1794 to 1796.[29] Lewis and Clark were aware of this rendezvous and considered it vitally important in their efforts to secure trade agreements with the Missouri villagers. They believed the rendezvous allowed the Lakotas to remain independent of the Missouri River traders and hostile toward the traders' efforts to establish a trade agreement with the agricultural villagers. This rendezvous was an active trade fair at least as early as 1700, when it was located farther east on the Minnesota River before the Lakotas expanded westward onto the Plains.[30]

The Shoshoni rendezvous located in what is now southwest Wyoming connected the Plateau and Great Basin trading systems with the Missouri villagers via Crow and Shoshoni middlemen. Generally, the Crows acted as brokers between the Missouri and the Shoshoni rendezvous; the Utes mediated between the rendezvous and the Southwest. Nez Perce and Flathead traders came from the Plateau.[31] The Shoshoni rendezvous was a major center for the distribution of horses and items of Spanish, French, and English origin. Interestingly, this occurred years before actual contact with these outsiders.[32] Here, Lewis and Clark observed the Shoshonis with "Spanish riding gear and branded mules" and Crow Indians trading for bridle bits and blankets.[33] The explorers also reported seeing similar objects among the Mandans.[34] The Utes brought horses to this rendezvous site, and Shoshoni brokers then traded them to the Flathead, Nez Perce, and Crow. The latter group took horses as far as the Mandan and Hidatsa villages where they were exchanged for double their original purchase value in European goods. The horses were eventually resold to the Assiniboin, Plains Cree, and Plains Ojibwa. Notably, the Shoshonis and Nez Perce traded "thick, striped blankets, possibly of Spanish or Navajo weave" to the Crows, who in turn traded them at the Missouri River villages.[35]

A third major rendezvous site was indirectly linked to the Middle Missouri trade. Located at the Dalles of the Columbia River, it was the major hub of the Pacific-Plateau trade network that reached from the Pacific to the Nez Perce tribe and ultimately to the Missouri villages by way of the Shoshoni rendezvous. The Yakama, Tenino, Umatilla, Walula, and Nez Perce were among the many peoples trading there. The Nez Perce brought skin clothing, horses, and buffalo meat to exchange for metal objects and beads of European manufacture.[36] Plains traders took pipestone, buffalo bone beads, feather headdresses, parfleche, and buffalo robes to exchange there.[37]

Trade fairs, a third type of exchange, happened whenever people came together. These somewhat informal gatherings must have been a frequent occurrence as bands from various friendly tribes often camped together. One such fair took place in 1815 when the Cheyennes, who often camped with the Sioux on the Cheyenne River, traveled to the North Platte where they were joined by some Kiowa and Arapaho bands. The Kiowas, afraid to venture to the Cheyenne River for fear of the Sioux, sponsored this particular fair on the Platte. Unfortunately, the Cheyenne brought along a band of Sioux in what might have been an attempt to establish peaceful relations between those two tribes. This meeting resulted in a quarrel in which a Brulé war club ended a Kiowa man's life. After this episode, the Arapaho, Cheyennes, and Kiowas traveled down to the Red River where they met some Comanches and Apaches. Continuing to travel north and south on the Plains, the Kiowas and Cheyennes reportedly gathered once again on the Platte in 1821. Here they joined some Crows hoping to recover captured women and children.[38] These incidents illustrate the complexity of informal trade relationships among the nomadic peoples of the Plains.

Navajo Trade Networks

The Navajos, too, played an important role, however indirect, in Plains commerce. Long before their incarceration at the Bosque Redondo in 1863, the Navajos traded extensively in wearing and saddle blankets, sash belts, garters, saddle cinches, dresses, and "knitted" socks and leggings. In 1744 a dispatch sent to the viceroy governor of New Spain from Don Joachin Codallos y Rabal, governor and captain general of New Mexico, spoke of events and conditions in New Mexico during the years 1706 to 1743. Included were details of Navajo social, political, and economic conditions. Rabal estimated the Navajo population to be as many as four thousand and declared that they had become relatively prosperous from their new livestock industry. Sheep and goats were central to this enterprise. Governor Rabal described Navajo women's clothing as being constructed of black wool like those worn by Pueblo women. Navajo men wore buckskin clothing. Both genders wore the woolen blankets that had by 1706 become highly favored in the Southwest. This is the earliest known mention of Navajo weaving in historical documents.[39]

Although the Spanish and Navajos lived in relative peace during most of this period, hostile raids by Utes and Comanches pushed the Navajos into lands occupied by Spanish settlers. Years of hostilities ensued. In 1804–5 the Spanish embarked on a punitive expedition that culminated in the killing of a Navajo band in what is now known as the Massacre Cave of Canyon del Muerto, Arizona. It is from weavings found in this cave that knowledge about early Navajo textiles originates.[40]

Throughout the eighteenth century, Navajo trading partners included Pueblos, Utes, Apaches, Comanches, and Spaniards.[41] However, Navajos dealt primarily with Ute and Pueblo peoples. Navajos knew their ceremonial calendars and, therefore, when large gatherings of people were available to engage in trade. Pueblo trade goods included turquoise, white shell beads, buckskin, ceramics, corn, piki bread, and chili. The Utes traded buckskin clothing, buffalo skin clothing and robes, elk hides and storage bags, horses, saddle bags, bandoliers, beaded bags, and some ceremonial items.[42]

The Utes coveted chief blankets above all Navajo trade items. In fact, W. W. Hill asserts that chief blankets were made exclusively for trade, particularly to the Utes. While these blankets were still relatively rare, a chief blanket was worth five buckskins, a dressed buffalo robe, or one good mare, but with the increase in their production they gradually became worth as little as one buckskin. According to Hildegard Wetherill, the wife of trader Richard Wetherill, "the Navajos traded chief blankets for Ute buckskins and baskets. The Utes did not weave. The Navajos stopped making baskets years before. The Navajos wanted only their own pattern in baskets and the Utes wanted their own pattern in blankets, with slight variations to tell them apart. The blankets were made for tall or short men by order and were such a fine weave as to make them pliable for a garment."[43] During the seventeenth and eighteenth centuries, Ute men commonly married captured Cheyenne and Arapaho women, and by the nineteenth century the Utes and their Shoshoni neighbors had become very Plains-like.[44] Thus "their own patterns" conformed to Cheyenne and Arapaho sensibilities.

Notably, people engaging in trade networks typically purchased nonperishable items during times of plenty to be "banked" until they needed to trade them for food.[45] Perhaps the Utes, intending to exploit their middleman status at the Shoshoni rendezvous, encouraged an increase in chief blanket production. Charles Bent estimated that in 1846 the Navajos owned approximately five hundred thousand sheep, enough wool to create a commodity of trade blankets, perhaps in response to market demands at these trade fairs.[46]

Nineteenth-century ledger drawings, winter counts, and photographs verify that chief blankets were important symbols of status among Indians of the Plains. Few early written documents discuss Navajo weaving in the context of intertribal commerce, but an inquiry into trade networks and comparative aesthetics offers evidence that chief blankets were purposely created to appeal to a general Plains concept of the beautiful. In fact, to use the word *trade* is to undermine the Navajos' economic and artistic sophistication, for they and their buyers participated in a complex patronage system not unlike that which existed among European artists and their patrons. The Navajos have a long history of cultural adaptations necessitated by economic demands as clearly demonstrated by the aesthetic adjustments they made under the auspices of the trading posts. One might conclude that the trading posts' success was rooted in the Navajos' gift for borrowing elements and making them uniquely their own while simultaneously appealing to outside tastes. Their skillful accommodation to new market demands was accomplished largely because these adaptations provided an important means of survival as well as creative inspiration. The high esteem in which the Sioux, Cheyenne, Ute, and Arapaho held the chief blankets they so avidly collected was perhaps the greatest testament to the Navajos' creative and economic genius.

Notes

I express my gratitude to the late Douglas George, Associate Professor of Art History, University of New Mexico, for sharing his enthusiasm for New Mexico, its people, and its arts. Thanks, Snoop.

1. W. W. Hill, "Navajo Trading and Trading Ritual: A Study of Cultural Dynamics," *Southwestern Journal of Anthropology* 4, no. 4 (winter 1948): 380.

2. Kate Peck Kent, *Navajo Weaving* (Santa Fe: School of American Research, 1985), 8, 49.

Historically, weaving has been a gender-specific activity in the Southwest: Navajo weavers are female and Pueblo weavers male, with a few notable exceptions. This gender delineation raises some interesting questions concerning the origin of Navajo weaving. How, and why, might Pueblo men have taught Navajo women to weave? Historians typically answer that Navajo women learned to weave from their Zuni neighbors where it is the women, and not the men, who weave.

According to Kaufman and Selser, a manta is a "woman's shawl or cape, woven wider than long, produced by both Navajo and Pueblo weavers"; Alice Kaufman and Christopher Selser, *The Navajo Weaving Tradition, 1650 to the Present* (New York: Dutton, 1985), 144.

3. Clyde Kluckhohn, W. W. Hill, and Lucy Wales Kluckhohn, *Navajo Material Culture* (Cambridge: Harvard University Press, 1971), 448; Kaufman and Selser, *The Navajo Weaving Tradition,* 17; Hill, "Navajo Trading and Trading Ritual," 371–96. A useful description of trade routes is beyond the scope of this essay; fortunately, there are many thorough and engaging accounts, beginning with those of the Lewis and Clark expedition.

4. Kent, *Navajo Weaving,* 10–11.

5. Arthur Woodward, *Navajo Silver* (Flagstaff: Northland, 1974) 5–8, 26–27, 45–48. Following years of conflict with Hispanic and American settlers, approximately eight thousand Navajos were rounded up for what would be called the "Long Walk" to the Bosque Redondo, where they were imprisoned from 1863 until 1868 in an effort to solve the "Navajo problem."

6. John Adair, *Navajo and Pueblo Silversmiths* (Norman: University of Oklahoma Press, 1989), 29, 30–31, 25–26.

7. Kent, *Navajo Weaving,* 52; Kaufman and Selser, *Navajo Weaving Tradition,* 42, 10. *Moqui* is defined as "a blue, brown, and sometimes with white banded background blanket style, influenced by striped Rio Grande blankets, and often elaborated on by the Navajos with the introduction of terraced or serrate design in red"; Kaufman and Selser, *Navajo Weaving Tradition,* 144. Also spelled *moki.* Kent, *Navajo Weaving,* page 42, plate 3 (SAR T.109) provides an excellent example of a Navajo moqui-patterned blanket.

8. Kaufman and Selser, *Navajo Weaving Tradition,* 10.

9. These blankets are dated from the post-Bosque Redondo period, during which time Navajo weavers were responding to different aesthetic demands.

10. Kaufman and Selser, *Navajo Weaving Tradition,* 17.

11. Ibid. 17–18.

12. See Gaylord Torrence, *Native American Parfleche,* (Kansas City: Kansas City Art Institute, 1984).

13. Chief blankets and robes were also conceptually related among Plateau tribes. A late

nineteenth-century photograph by Lee Moorhouse shows a Cayuse-Umatilla woman with a first-phase blanket to which an Intermontane-style beaded strip was added to its wide center band (fig. 11.8).

Kathleen E. Ash-Milby, caption Plate 128, in *Woven by the Grandmothers: Nineteenth-Century Navajo Textiles from the National Museum of the American Indian,* ed. Eulalie H. Bonar (Washington D.C.: Smithsonian Institution Press, 1996).

14. John Ewers, *Plains Indian Painting* (Stanford: Stanford University Press, 1939), 14.

15. Barbara A. Hail, *Hau Kola! The Plains Indian Collection of the Haffenrefer Museum of Anthropology* (Providence: Haffenrefer Museum of Anthropology, Brown University, 1980) provides a diagram illustrating the manner by which parfleche are typically folded (fig. 159).

16. J. J. Brody, personal communication; Charles Avery Amsden, *Navaho Weaving: Its Technique and History* (Santa Ana: Fine Arts Press, 1934; reprint, Salt Lake City: Peregrine Smith, 1975), 100.

17. Torrence, *Native American Parfleche.*

18. Ibid.

19. Robert H. Lowie, *Indians of the Plains* (Lincoln: University of Nebraska Press, 1982), 138.

20. See, for example, the Cheyenne cradle in the Detroit Institute of Arts collection (DIA 81.778), published in David W. Penney, ed., *Art of the American Indian Frontier* (Detroit: Detroit Institute of Arts, 1992), catalog no. 107, p. 180.

21. Unfortunately, a meaningful discussion of Navajo aesthetics is outside the scope of this essay. Simply stated, beauty is understood as the manifestation of cosmic balance. This concept is apparent in the symmetry found in Navajo textiles.

22. Raymond Wood, "Plains Trade in Prehistoric and Protohistoric Intertribal Relations," in *Anthropology on the Great Plains,* ed. Margot Liberty (Lincoln: University of Nebraska Press, 1980), 107.

23. William R. Swagerty, "Indian Trade in the Trans-Mississippi West to 1870," in *Handbook of the North American Indians,* ed. William C. Sturtevant, vol. 4 (Washington, D.C.: Smithsonian Institution Press, 1983), 351, 353.

24. John C. Ewers, *Indian Life on the Upper Missouri* (Norman: University of Oklahoma Press, 1988), 18.

25. John C. Ewers, *The Horse in Blackfoot Culture* (Washington, D.C.: Smithsonian Institution Press, 1969), 9–12.

26. Swagerty, "Indian Trade," 353.

27. Ewers, *Indian Life,* 17; Ewers, *The Horse,* 10.

28. Ewers, *Indian life,* 17.

29. James P. Ronda, *Lewis and Clark among the Indians* (Lincoln: University of Nebraska Press, 1988), 12.

30. Ewers, *Indian Life,* 18.

31. Wood, "Plains Trade in Prehistoric and Protohistoric Intertribal Relations," 103.

32. Swagerty, "Indian Trade," 353.

33. Ewers, *The Horse,* 6.

34. Meriwether Lewis and William Clark, *History of the Lewis and Clark Expedition* (1893; reprint, New York: Dover, n.d.), 198–99.

35. Ewers, *The Horse,* 7, 10–12; the quotation is in Ewers, *Indian Life,* 26.

36. Ronda, *Lewis and Clark among the Indians,* 170.

37. Swagerty, "Indian Trade," 353.

38. George C. Hyde, *Red Cloud's Folk* (Norman: University of Oklahoma Press, 1976), 33.

39. W. W. Hill, "Some Navajo Culture Changes during Two Centuries (with a Translation of the Early Eighteenth-Century Rabel Manuscript)," *Essays in Historical Anthropology of North Amer-*

ica, Smithsonian Miscellaneous Collections (Washington, D.C.: Smithsonian Institution, 1940), 395–98.

40. Kent, *Navajo Weaving,* 10.

41. Ibid.

42. Hill, "Navajo Trading and Trading Ritual," 375–82; Richard I. Ford, "Inter-Indian Exchange in the Southwest," in *Handbook of the North American Indians,* ed. William C. Sturtevant, vol. 10 (Washington, D.C.: Smithsonian Institution Press, 1983), 711.

43. Hill, "Navajo Trading and Trading Ritual," 380; Jan Pettit, *Utes: The Mountain People* (Boulder: Johnson, 1990), 100.

44. Charles S. Marsh, *People of the Shining Mountains* (Boulder: Pruett, 1982), 139.

45. Ford, "Inter-Indian Exchange in the Southwest," 711.

46. Frank McNitt, *Indian Traders* (Norman: University of Oklahoma Press, 1963), 33.

"WALKING IN STRANGE GARDENS"

Early Floral Design in the Columbia River Plateau

STEVEN LEROY GRAFE

*I*f one were to inventory those aspects of Native American art often overlooked by academicians, it would be difficult to find two more neglected topics than the study of Columbia Plateau art forms or the study of Native North American floral designs. Little has been published about Plateau art in part because the culture area is often seen as a transitional zone between the Plains and the Northwest Coast. Some texts have addressed the region in tandem with the Plains or Great Basin; others have ignored its presence entirely. The basis for the bias against floral design can be more easily identified. Writing in the autumn 1997 issue of *American Indian Art Magazine,* Andrew Hunter Whiteford noted, in part: "In spite of the Indians' enthusiasm for floral designs, floral beadwork has generally been held in low regard by most curators and serious collectors of Indian art, who have shown a preference for geometric designs. . . . Because many collectors tend to be antiquarians, they believe that older is better, and art from the past is superior to art produced in more recent times. Floral designs are usually held in low esteem compared with woven geometric designs that are regarded as earlier . . . and purer examples of unsullied Indian aesthetics."[1]

Early studies of North American floral design were often concerned with whether flower motifs were an indigenous invention, were introduced at some late date and reflected Euro-American, mixed-blood influences, or both. Frank G. Speck's 1914 "Double-Curve Motive in Eastern Algonkian Art" argued that floral designs in at least a portion of the aboriginal Northeast were derived from indigenous double-curve motifs.[2] This idea was subsequently challenged by Marius Barbeau, who wrote:

The floral patterns of our northern tribes . . . belong, one and all, to the French *renaissance* and peasant art, and were adapted at an early date by the Indians to suit their fancies. The evolution of this spurious American art can easily be traced through all its stages. Sewing and embroidery, as well as other domestic arts, were taught systematically to Indian girls of Algonkin and Iroquois, even of Eastern Eskimo, extraction by the nuns in the ancient colonial missions and schools. . . . In such published compilations as Speck's "Double-curve Motive", possibly not a single design can be traced back to prehistory. They are derived from rococo figures and ornaments of the Francis I period as transplanted to Canada.[3]

Much of the academic discussion that has since addressed the indigenous use of floral motifs has aligned itself with one or another of these viewpoints or sought to occupy a middle ground that acknowledged the merits of both arguments. In the early 1990s, however, two essays appeared that offered interpretive insights into the cultural implications of the floral design phenomenon. The first of these, Ruth Phillips's "Moccasins into Slippers," considered the transformation of several northeastern Woodlands objects as their meaning and form changed during the course of the nineteenth century. In each instance, items originally manufactured for Native use and adorned with indigenous patterns—hats, shoes, and bags—came to be remade with floral decoration for the express purpose of sale to Euro-American tourists. Phillips determined that these articles thus provided an opportunity for an important cross-cultural dialogue. Prototypical objects passed from Euro-Americans to Native communities where Native artists modified them and returned them to the dominant culture for sale as souvenirs. This production and marketing phenomenon was determined to be an important strategy in the Native American quest for cultural survival in the face of government extermination and acculturation policies.[4]

David Penney also discussed the role of floral design in the arts of nineteenth-century Great Lakes peoples. In describing the Huron of Lorette, the Chippewa and Ottawa of Michigan Territory, and the Red River Métis, he observed that floral designs were used by each group to promote the preservation of Indian identity while simultaneously signifying progress and civilization to the white buyers of their handicrafts. Penney suggested that the Great Lakes floral style had developed as a subversive exercise, whereby a civilizing art (mission school-taught embroidery) was recontextualized. Rather than providing evidence of assimilation, floral designs were reinterpreted by Native artists to become symbols of ethnic identity and cultural resistance.[5]

Stylistic Influences

In light of these two essays, provocative questions are raised about the social contexts and symbolism associated with the genesis of Plateau floral embroidery. It is now generally accepted that throughout Native North America, floral decoration began as a by-product of white contact. The Plateau has been held as an exception to this rule, and scholars have for some years hypothesized that the new iconographic system was inspired by Indian-to-Indian interaction. An Iroquois, Huron, and Woodlands influence has been argued on the assumption that "these adventuring warriors obviously brought with them westward the clothing and paraphernalia of their tribal background." The double-curve motif is here seen as providing inspiration for all early Plateau contour-beaded bags, and the initial Plateau floral designs are thought to represent a local simplification of the "delicate French embroidered elegance seen on much early Huron and Iroquois beadwork."[6]

Plateau floral motifs have also been interpreted as being produced in response to the mid-nineteenth-century beadwork of some Subarctic and Great Lakes peoples. This argument credits Ojibwa, Cree, and Métis fur trade employees and their wives with introducing floral motifs to Pacific Northwest artisans. Firebags and shot pouches are specifically cited as providing much of the necessary inspiration for the new style, and the assumption has been that "between the 1840s and some point late in the century Plateau beadworkers were copying Ojibwa prototypes of floral design."[7]

One or two hundred eastern Indians and their descendants were indeed present in the Plateau after 1810. Few new Iroquois entered the region after 1830, however, and those few Métis and affiliated peoples resident in the region were being actively absorbed into the surrounding white population by 1845. If regional floral embroidery was not being produced by this time it would seem likely that local artists were not inspired to produce floral patterns as a result of intrusive Native objects and instruction. American emigration and settlement occurred in earnest after the opening of the Oregon Trail and more than sixty thousand Americans and their material culture followed the route west between 1843 and 1860. If the Plateau floral style had its origins during or after this time period, it may be assumed that white contact provided much of the stylistic and symbolic impetus for the style.

A review of mid-nineteenth-century Euro-American decorative arts reveals that floral motifs were the most memorable feature of the period's design style. Flowers frequently appeared in textiles, on clothing, and in home furnishings, whether commercially manufactured or homemade. Floral designs had appeared on the printed cotton cloth and ready-made clothing that were standards of the fur trade enterprise after 1810. By the late 1830s local Protestant missionaries had also discovered that calico dresses and shirts were valuable trade items. The experience of the Oregon Trail emigrants confirmed the value of these garments, and the historic record is rife with references describing Plateau men and women wearing calico clothing.

During the first half of the nineteenth century, transfer-printed earthenwares were the ceramics most commonly used for Euro-American table and toiletry needs. As with printed textiles, floral decoration was the standard for these ceramics. As early as 1814 the North West Company had included "Canton Plates" among the gifts it gave prominent Indian leaders, and by the 1820s the Hudson's Bay Company had begun shipping quantities of earthenware to the Columbia Department. The officers at Fort Vancouver regularly ate from a large set of "elegant Queen's ware." Company officers at satellite posts also enjoyed the use of the ceramics, and by the 1830s hundreds of pieces of earthenware were being sold annually through the Hudson's Bay Company's stores. These were some of the first items acquired by incoming missionaries and emigrants.

Victorian floral opulence was also apparent in the wallpapers in use in a variety of burgeoning Plateau settlements after 1860. By 1857 announcements in the *Portland Oregonian* were noting the availability of large quantities of French and American paper hangings. French paper manufacturers of the period were said to arrange "flowers in stripes, in spotted patterns, or in meandering masses. They strung them out in leafy lines to form the borders for panels dividing a wall into a series of vertical rectangles. They showed flowers growing artfully on imitation trellises and pillars. They entwined flowers with scrollwork in endless variations—a favorite theme for the American market . . . Machine-printed American derivations from the French florals were less beguiling, but sold in larger numbers because they were cheaper."[8] Floral wallpapers appear to have been a standard of the Portland market, and that city was the commercial hub that supplied the interior Columbia River region. By 1861 paper-hanging services were being advertised in the Walla Walla, Washington, newspaper. Portland businesses purchased advertisements in these same papers with the promise that "all orders from the interior [will be] filled with care and dispatch."[9]

Due to the space and weight guidelines that informed the baggage selection of the Oregon Trail emigrants, many heirloom textiles made the overland trip. Quilts and woven coverlets were light, functionally necessary, and, in many cases, imbued with great sentimental value. Such textiles were desired trade items, and many found their way into Indian hands. One emigrant described the 1849 Indian-white trade situation in Oregon's Grande Ronde Valley with the comment, "the articles which [the Indians] wished for most, were cows, blankets, shirts, and knives."[10]

The thirty-year period that gave rise to the heaviest traffic on the Oregon Trail (1840–70) was squarely in the middle of the period when quilt-making was considered an American "rage."[11] The same three decades also coincided with the golden age

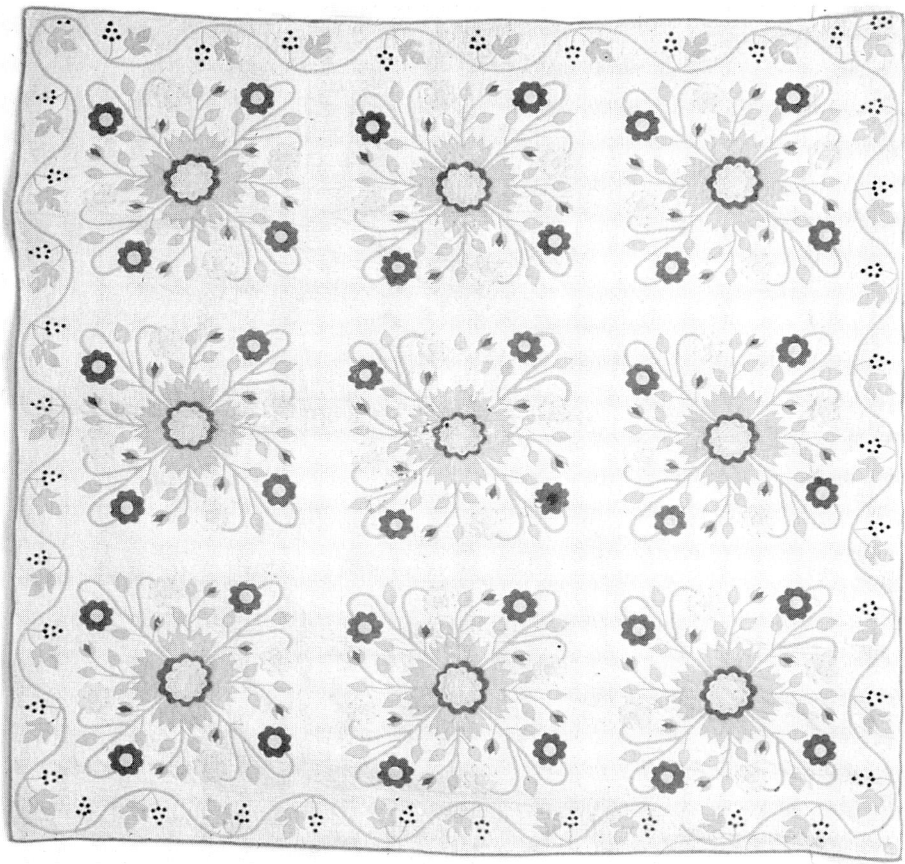

of classic floral quilt construction. According to quilt historian Ricky Clark, "classic" floral quilts were generally appliquéd using a predominantly red and green color scheme on a white ground. They contained repeated blocks surrounded by a related border, utilized conventionalized botanical motifs, and had a red or green binding. Their blossoms were "conventionalized: simplified, flat, and two-dimensional, yet still recognizably floral. They cannot confidently be identified as a particular flower but instead are generic."[12] The "Oregon Rose" quilt shown in figure 12.1 displays many of these conventions. It was made in Indiana in 1851 as a gift for a family that was preparing to travel overland to Oregon during the following year.

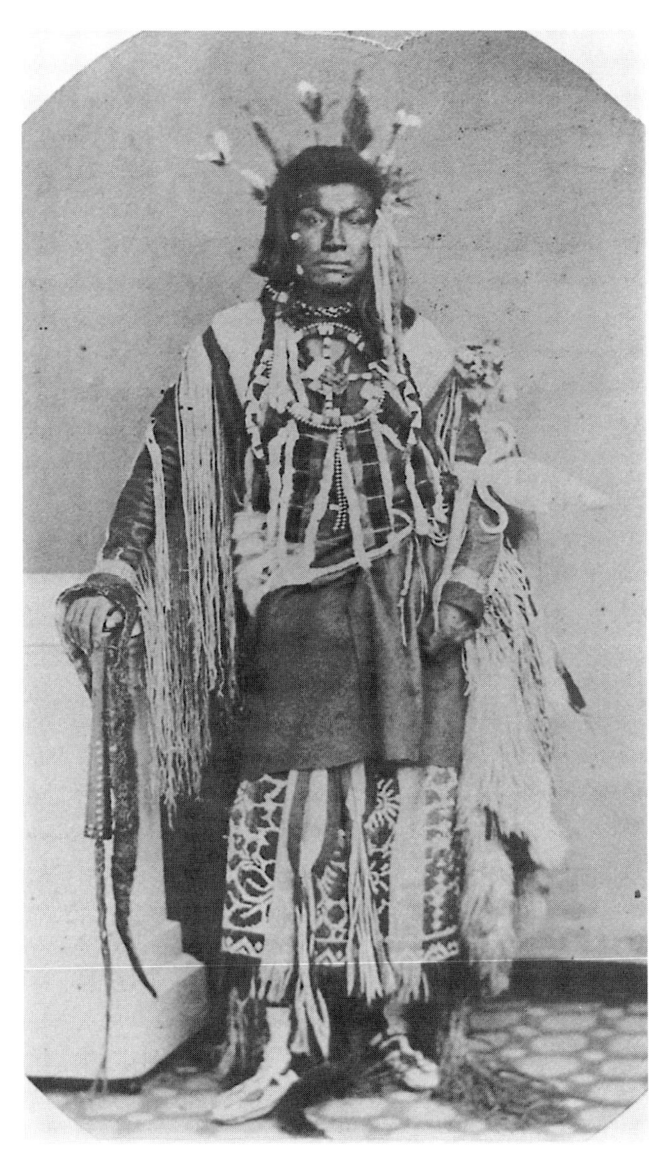

FIGURE 12.2
Tish Kamiakin, wearing a woven coverlet, ca. 1864.
Historical Photograph Collection, Washington
State University Libraries, neg. no. 91–108.

Jacquard woven coverlets likewise contained bold and simplified floral motifs. By the 1830s many of the European craftspeople who were the prime coverlet producers had settled in the midwestern states, which yielded the highest percentages of overland emigrants. As the decades that coincided with the heaviest activity on the Oregon Trail also spawned the greatest production of quilts created in classic floral patterns, so did this same time span give rise to the weaving of the most complex and ornate coverlet designs (fig. 12.2). The woven format of coverlets required both a moderately simplified rendition of given motifs and a bilaterally symmetrical arrangement of designs. "Looking at the designs of these coverlets is like walking in strange gardens. Here flits the Bird of Paradise, here bloom thistles, roses, lilies, and clematis, and the wild cactus shows both flower and fruit; here are flower and leaf conventionalized beyond recognition, and in the coverlet's border you will find things as interesting and mysterious as the hieroglyphics of Egypt. History, politics, and masonry jostle each other; there are churches and dwellings . . . palm trees and pine trees, an American eagle and a ridiculous jackanapes."[13]

Plateau Floral Design: The Prototypes

A systematic examination of the surviving ethnographic material record offers considerable insight into the origins of Plateau floral design. This study was restricted to embroidered objects with a documented history and included items were evaluated on the basis of their association with known dates, known collectors, known contexts, or all three. The relevant objects do not necessarily represent a scientific cross-section of all Plateau items created before 1880, but their manufacture dates and places of origins can be assumed to be fairly accurate. The chronology outlined by this material is fairly defensible and provides a reasonably accurate base from which to assess the impact of diverse regional design influences.

The initial documented example of Plateau floral design appears in a photograph made in 1860 or 1861 by members of the British North American Boundary Commission (fig. 12.3). Entitled *Half-Breed Child in Cradle, with Indian Ornamental Trappings,* the photograph was probably taken at the boundary commission's winter quarters near present-day Marcus, Washington, or at the nearby Hudson's Bay Company's Fort Colvile. Of interest in the image are a beaded Nez Perce-style cradleboard, a crupper, and a horse collar. Both the internal and external evidence suggest that the items in the photograph belonged to Catherine McDonald, the wife of Fort Colvile's chief trader, Angus McDonald. Catherine was the daughter of a French-Mohawk fur trapper and a Nez Perce mother. In her youth she had attended various of the Rocky Mountain fur trade rendezvous and accompanied her father on extended trapping

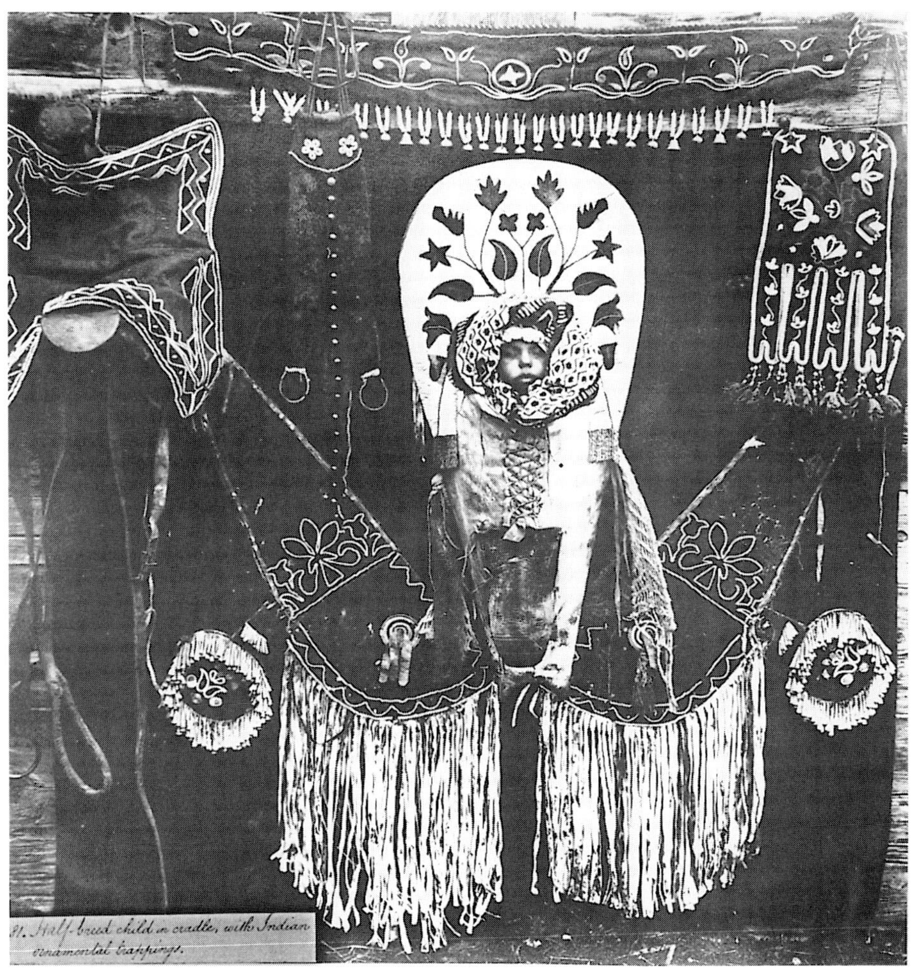

FIGURE 12.3
*Half-breed Child in Cradle with Indian Ornamental
Trappings,* 1860–61. Courtesy Royal Engineers
Library, Chatham, Kent, England.

expeditions. She married Angus McDonald at Fort Hall, Idaho, in 1842. The pair
lived at Fort Colvile for much of the time between 1852 and 1871, although their
extended regional travels were noted in contemporary accounts.[14]

The cradle shown here is remarkable in its appearance. Beaded objects with an
allover light ground and naturalistic figures do not generally appear in the visual and
material record of the Plateau until after 1880. The bilaterally symmetrical outlined

figures on the crupper and martingale are likewise the prototypes of this regional design style, although they predate subsequent examples by less than a decade. These three items may be considered the earliest known examples of Plateau floral embroidery. Catherine McDonald's unique social and economic situation may explain the archetypal quality of her belongings. By virtue of her birth she was linked to a prominent Nez Perce family and was related to various important tribal leaders. By virtue of her marriage to a Hudson's Bay Company officer she had unusual access to beads and other trade goods. She further lived in a household that was unusually well furnished with British goods. During her residence there, Fort Colvile served as the social and commercial hub of the upper Columbia River region.

Catherine McDonald was acquainted with contemporary European and American decorative trends. Transfer-printed English earthenwares were daily used by the few company officers in residence at Fort Colvile; they were also used at many of the social events hosted by the fort. Current British publications circulated with some regularity through the post, enough so that, despite his remote station, Angus McDonald was considered to be "well up in the politics of the day." It is, of course, impossible to guess the range of factors that influenced the beadwork on the cradleboard, but the appearance of a symmetrical floral arrangement on a light ground follows the formula used on many Spode/Copeland earthenwares. These same ceramics also employed foliate arrangements whereby leaves on the same bough appeared in frontal, three-quarter, profile view, or all three. The light-on-dark beaded outlines present on the crupper and horse collar mimic the decorative braiding patterns that appeared in contemporary women's magazines such as *Godey's Lady's Book.* Although executed in reverse when actually created with fabric, the printed patterns were published in white lines on a dark ground. The motifs on the crupper, particularly the tulip designs, bear a marked resemblance to this mid-Victorian decorative tradition.[15]

A miniature double saddlebag collected on the Nez Perce reservation between 1866 and 1869 displays a very similar floral or protofloral outline (fig. 12.4). This diminutive object was accompanied by a toy cradle, a toy saddle and saddle blanket, and a toy drum in a shipment of ethnographic items sent to the Army Medical Museum in Washington, D.C., in 1869. The items were collected by Acting Assistant (Contract) Surgeon Edward Storror. In May 1864 Storror had crossed the Plains to California while serving as the medical attendant to an emigrant escort. He served at several military posts in Oregon and Washington before signing a November 1866 contract to become post surgeon at Fort Lapwai, Idaho Territory. During the next three years, Storror attended to the medical needs of both the local military and Indian communities. According to a contemporary military assessment, he was "one

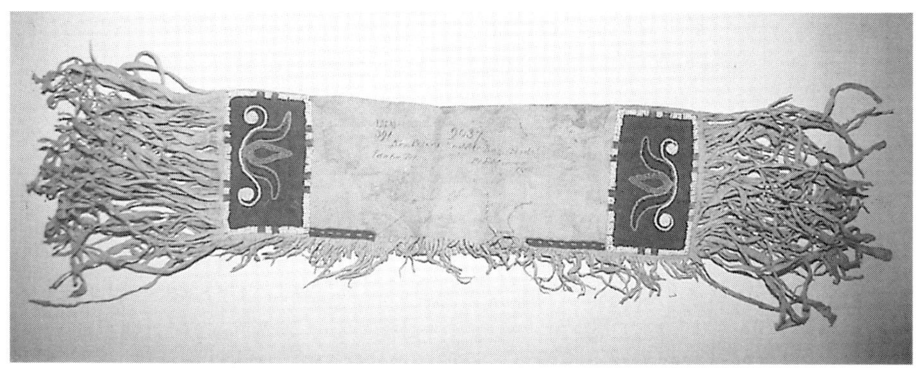

FIGURE 12.4
Nez Perce Miniature Double Saddlebag, collected
1866–69. Department of Anthropology,
Smithsonian Institution, cat. no. E9037.
Photo by author.

of the best doctors in [the] whole country. He went down to the Agency daily. The Indians loved him."[16]

The miniature saddlebag (and accompanying cradle and saddle blanket) are decorated with red wool and seed beads. While the blanket has one edge covered with a series of diamond shapes, either end of the saddlebag is adorned with what seem to be the profile outlines of flowers. These rest on tendril-like bases worked in a curvilinear design. Given their eventual donation to the Army Medical Museum, Dr. Storror may have commissioned the miniatures as representations of full-size pieces.

The next Plateau object to contain floral or protofloral motifs is a rather unusual double saddlebag from the Yakama reservation (plate 14). This item was forwarded to the Smithsonian for inclusion in the 1876 Centennial Exposition by Yakama Indian agent James H. Wilbur. The shipment was reportedly a gratuitous contribution of articles donated by reservation residents. It included antique objects such as a side-fringed rawhide bag, a wooden mortar and stone pestle, and an unadorned and fully perforated man's shirt. These were accompanied by three items that were apparently made expressly for the exposition: this double saddlebag and several pieces of tooled leather saddlery that had been produced by Indian men trained in the reservation's vocational school.

This second group of items appear to represent the Yakama as Wilbur wished them to be seen, as having "made great advancement in agriculture and other civilized arts."[17] The saddlebag is in pristine condition and, again, its design may have been influenced by the context surrounding its creation. Its construction and shape are unusual. At least one of its two faces is decorated in what can be considered abstract floral designs. Here, three black-and-yellow figures are worked in a loose tripartite arrangement. Three complementary black-and-blue figures also appear on the predominantly white-and-blue contour-beaded ground. Red cloth, pony beads, and a commercial blue black fringe edge the entire piece.

Additional Plateau floral items were obtained by Army Asst. Surgeon George Martin Kober during 1877 and 1878. When fighting broke out between nontreaty Nez Perce and the U.S. military in the summer of 1877, Kober was assigned to a force of the 1st U.S. Cavalry that was sent to Kamiah, Idaho, to reinforce the troops of Gen. O. O. Howard. Some of these mounted soldiers accompanied Howard in his pursuit of the Nez Perce; others remained in Idaho to protect the local population against the anticipated return of the nontreaties. Kober was subsequently stationed at Camp McBeth, near Kamiah, between July 29 and October 1, 1877. During this time, his autobiography reports:

> From some of the friendly Indians, especially Archie and his brother James Lawyer, we learned of the hasty flight of Chief Joseph and his warriors after the [Clearwater] battle, and how they had abandoned their lodges, filled with their effects like blankets, buffalo robes, and even some provisions, such as jerked beef, venison, and flour. The civilian scouts and packers, who knew the Indians' customs, had gone over the ground and found many "caches" where the Indians had buried their greatest treasures in expectation of return. From these caches beautiful beaded ceremonial robes, belts, moccasins, rugs, and trinkets were taken and sold to the officers. A sister of Chief "Archie," who in her younger years had helped to make and decorate a ceremonial buckskin suit for Chief Joseph, was awarded this treasure. I am glad that she yielded to my request to let me have it on the promise that I would present it to the National Museum in Washington.[18]

The suit Kober acquired consisted of a coat and pants fashioned after the Euro-American style. The coat is made of fringed buckskin lined with plaid woolen fabric (fig. 12.5). Its collar and shoulders are decorated in two sets of stylized floral embroidery executed in silk thread. The motifs are individually asymmetrical but symmetrically opposed when viewed as a set. Each lapel has a vertical arrangement of four generic beaded flower blossoms. The pants are also constructed of fringed buckskin and are decorated with strips of red woolen trim that extends along the outside of each pant leg. Matching vertical arrangements of abstract flowers worked in beads appear on each strip.[19]

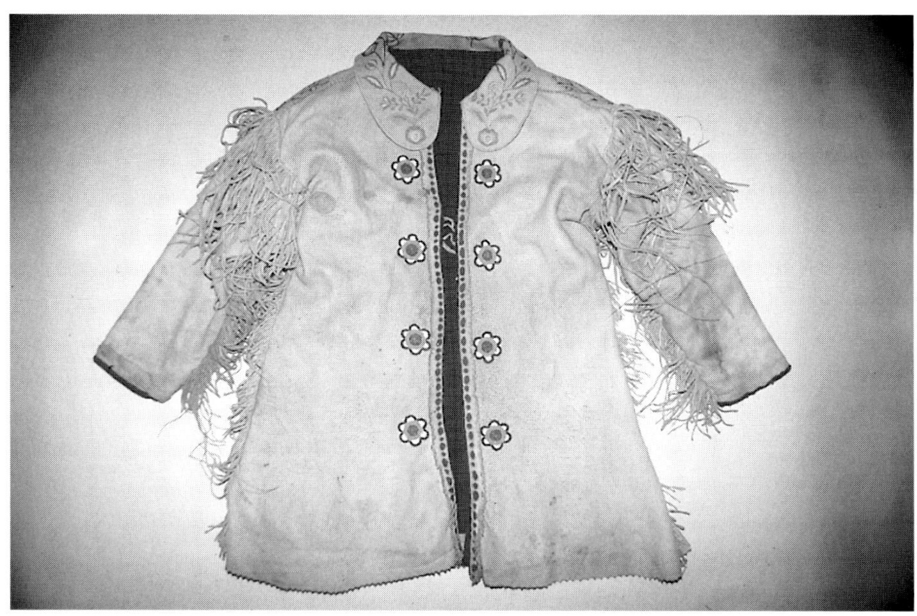

George Kober was not a witness to the aftermath of the Battle of Clearwater, as he arrived on the Nez Perce reservation fully two weeks after the fighting there had concluded. These two garments appear to be of contemporary Nez Perce origin although their association with any nontreaty caches or Chief Joseph is doubtful. The "sister of Chief 'Archie,' who . . . had helped to make and decorate" this outfit and who subsequently yielded to Kober's request for it was Lucy Lawyer. When Agent John Monteith was collecting material for the Centennial Exposition during 1876, the majority of the large Nez Perce items he purchased came from this same Lucy Lawyer. In monetary terms, the five objects obtained from her totaled nearly two-thirds of Monteith's total expenditure. The European cut of the garments and the silk-thread decorative embroidery they display do suggest that the coat and pants may indeed have been made by members of the Christian Nez Perce community, as was represented to Kober. Whether members of that faction would have fashioned a special suit for a leader of the nontreaty bands is open to dispute, however. During the 1870s the two groups were in marked opposition, and Lucy Lawyer's father was numbered among the harsh critics of the nontreaty element.

Leaving Camp McBeth in October 1877, George Kober traveled to the Presidio in San Francisco but returned to Fort Lapwai three weeks later. He was then sent to help establish Camp Coeur d'Alene (Fort Sherman) on the shores of Lake Coeur d'Alene, Idaho. He remained at that post until November 1879, when he was reassigned to Fort Klamath, Oregon. During this interlude he collected a pair of embroidered gloves that he identified as having had a Colville origin (plate 15). The silk-thread decoration on the gloves is similar to that which appears on the coat described above. The gloves' overall design and pristine condition suggest they were probably manufactured specifically for sale.

The final two objects to be considered here are in the collection of the American Museum of Natural History. Both items probably date to the mid- or late 1860s but thus far cannot be proven to predate their 1883 donation to the museum. The first of these is a pair of Nez Perce woman's leggings collected by James Terry. Terry was a Hartford, Connecticut, businessman who was interested in anthropology. He acquired a number of archaeological and ethnographic specimens during the 1870s and 1880s. In 1890 the American Museum of Natural History purchased his collection of North American archaeology. Terry was appointed curator of the Department of Anthropology at the museum in that same year and served in the post through 1893. The woman's leggings are constructed of wool cloth and decorated with seed beads (fig. 12.6). The beaded designs on this set of leggings are floral in their conception. Taken together, the motifs are symmetrically arranged. Color is applied in concentric rows and a series of tendrils proceed from the main figures. Small horse heads appear on each legging; these represent an early appearance of a figurative motif that became popular during later decades.[20]

A Nez Perce cradle now in the collection of the American Museum of Natural History was acquired by Maj. Sewall Truax before 1883 (fig. 12.7). In June 1863 Truax arrived at Fort Lapwai, Idaho. He commanded the post until late in 1864, when he resigned his commission. He remained at or near the fort until 1870, serving as post sutler for much of that time. At one point during this period he was apparently promised the job of Indian agent but did not receive the appointment. In 1870 Truax moved to Walla Walla. He relocated to an isolated region along the Snake River in 1877 before moving on to Spokane several years later. The cradle Truax collected could have been secured at any time after 1863. As the beadwork that adorns its surface follows the Transmontane style, it may have been made for Native use before being obtained by the collector. It may also have been commissioned or made specifically as a gift for the Truax family. Three or perhaps four Truax children were born during the family's tenure on the Nez Perce reservation.[21]

Two protofloral motifs are incorporated into the cradle's beaded design: a sym-

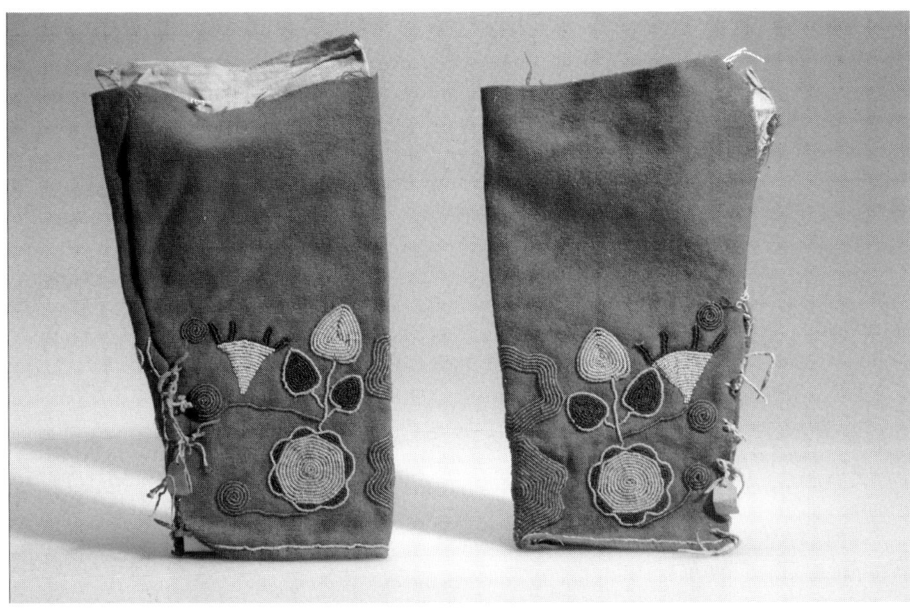

metrical leaf and petal arrangement appears in profile on its foot, and a simplified frontal view of a blossom appears on its hood. The combination of lozenge with outlining serrations evident in the foot motif closely resembles the upper portion of the central figures on the woman's leggings in the Terry collection. The simplified blossoms on the hood mirror the construction of the lower portions of the central figures on these same leggings. This suggests that the cradle and leggings were made by the same person, that they came from the same circle of artists, or that they were produced during an analogous time period.

New Designs and New Messages

Based on the available evidence, Plateau floral design apparently dates to the 1860–75 time period. The genesis of the art form thus seems temporally unrelated to any supposed Iroquois influences from the 1810–30 time span or to pre-1845 Cree-Ojibwa-Métis artistic expressions. As occurred elsewhere in North America, indigenous floral design appeared in the Plateau in the wake of white expansion and not as a

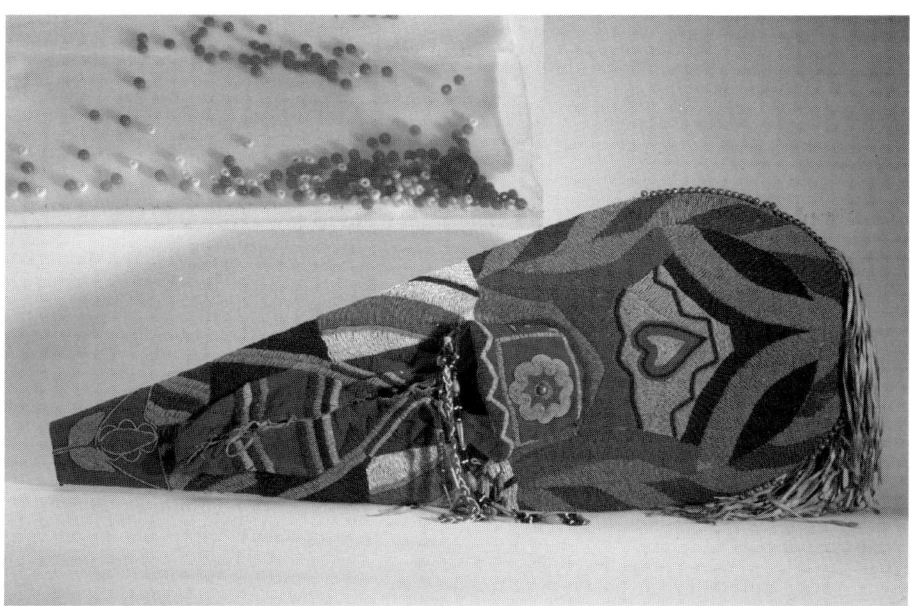

response to Indian-to-Indian contact. The relatively late appearance of the design style in the inland Northwest may partially relate to the geographic isolation of the interior Columbia River region. It may also be linked to the late date at which the white population came to recognize the economic opportunities the local landscape offered.

By the 1870s a diversity of floral styles were simultaneously developing in the Plateau. Symmetrical and asymmetrical compositions seem to have appeared at much the same time. Simplified and realistic designs appeared coincidentally and even together on the same object. Together, this would suggest that individual innovation was developing within a larger tradition and that diverse sources were serving as inspiration for the new motifs. In general terms, the earliest floral objects produced in the region can be linked to local traders, Indian agents, or military personnel. Although it could be argued that the gatherings of such persons would be the ones most likely to appear in modern museum collections, items retrieved from other contexts reveal a markedly different iconographic system. Those traditionally designed and contemporaneous objects such as dresses, shirts, leggings, blanket strips, bandoliers, and guncases that were recovered as war souvenirs are free of floral figures. Items of this type associated with the 1860–75 time period are instead decorated with geometric Transmontane motifs. Floral designs appear conversely on a coat and pair of trousers cut in the European style, on a pair of gloves, and on an unusual saddlebag—items that are nontraditional and introduced. Early floral motifs also appear on a miniature saddlebag and a full-size cradle, both of which may have been produced for a white patron. In all, it seems that the earliest manifestations of the design style were freely applied to those classes of objects associated with the white community and that, in most cases, a premeditated economic exchange may have influenced the creation of the items.

The decorative devices of the newly dominant culture were first adopted and reproduced within reservation communities. By doing so, reservation residents appear to have been signaling an awareness of the fact that their lives had begun to straddle two worlds: Indian and white. The creation of floral motifs in beads and on leather was representative of a middle ground. The new designs were foreign, and in some cases the objects being created and decorated were introduced. Nonetheless, the materials and mediums were familiar and linked with established artistic traditions. The new style was subsequently accessible and familiar to members of both ethnic communities. It represented a common ground where all could find comfort and meaning.

Notes

This essay summarizes data contained in Steven LeRoy Grafe, "The Origins of Floral-Design Beadwork in the Southern Columbia River Plateau," Ph.D. diss., University of New Mexico, 1999. I thank my dissertation committee—Joyce Szabo, Jerry Brody, Bill Holm, and the late Douglas George—for their advice and assistance during the course of this study. My wife, Christina, also contributed significantly to the project.

1. Andrew Hunter Whiteford, "Floral Beadwork of the Western Great Lakes," *American Indian Art Magazine* 22, no. 4 (autumn 1997): 78.

2. Frank G. Speck, "The Double-Curve Motive in Eastern Algonkian Art," *Canada Department of Mines, Geological Survey, Anthropological Series* no. 1, memoir 42 (1914): 1–17.

3. Marius Barbeau, "The Origin of Floral and Other Designs among the Canadian and Neighboring Indians," *Proceedings of the Twenty-Third International Congress of Americanists* (New York, 1930), 512.

4. Ruth B. Phillips, "Moccasins into Slippers: Woodlands Indian Hats, Bags, and Shoes in Tradition and Transformation," *Northeast Indian Quarterly* 7, no. 4 (winter 1990): 26–36.

5. David W. Penney, "Floral Decoration and Culture Change: An Historical Interpretation of Motivation," *American Indian Culture and Research Journal* 15, no. 1 (1991): 53–77.

6. John Gogol, "Columbia River/Plateau Indian Beadwork. Part 1: Yakima, Warm Springs, Umatilla, Nez Perce," *American Indian Basketry and Other Native Arts* 5, no. 2 (1985): 6, 13.

7. Kate C. Duncan, "Beadwork on the Plateau," *A Time of Gathering: Native Heritage in Washington State,* ed. Robin K. Wright (Seattle: University of Washington Press, 1991), 191; Richard Conn, "Floral Design in Native North America," *Native American Art from the Permanent Collection,* ed. Kay Koeninger and Joanne M. Mack (Claremont: Claremont Colleges, 1980), 78.

8. Catherine Lynn, *Wallpaper in America, From the Seventeenth Century to World War I* (New York: W. W. Norton, 1980), 338.

9. *Washington Statesman,* December 20, 1861.

10. William J. Watson, *Journal of an Overland Journey to Oregon Made in the Year 1849* (1851; reprint, Fairfield, Wash.: Ye Galleon Press, 1985), 40. In contemporary nomenclature, "blanket" was the term generally used to describe quilts and comforters.

11. Patsy Orlofsky and Myron Orlofsky, *Quilts in America* (New York: Abbeville Press, 1992), 60.

12. Ricky Clark, *Quilted Gardens: Floral Quilts of the Nineteenth Century* (Nashville: Rutledge Hill Press, 1994), 3–4, 21. For a brief history of the "Oregon Rose" quilt, see Mary Bywater Cross, *Treasures in the Trunk: Quilts of the Oregon Trail* (Nashville: Rutledge Hill Press, 1993), 64.

13. Eliza Calvert Hall, *The Book of Handwoven Coverlets* (New York: Dover Publications, 1988), 47.

14. For a broad general history of the McDonald family, see James Hunter, *Scottish Highlanders, Indian Peoples: Thirty Generations of a Montana Family* (Helena: Montana Historical Society Press, 1996).

15. Twenty-five distinct designs, most of them floral, were present in the Spode/Copeland earthenwares excavated from the site of Fort Colvile. Lynne Sussman, *Spode/Copeland Transfer-Printed Patterns Found at Twenty Hudson's Bay Company Sites,* Canadian Historic Sites, Occasional Papers in Archaeology and History 22 (Hull, Quebec: Canadian Government Publishing Centre, 1979), 12–19.

The quotation is from Hunter, *Scottish Highlanders, Indian Peoples,* 137. Remnants of an issue of *Punch* were recovered during excavations at Fort Nez Perces, and illustrations torn from copies of *Punch* and the *London Illustrated News* served as wall decorations in the quarters of at least one member of the British Boundary Commission. Thomas R. Garth, "Archaeological Excavations at Fort Walla Walla," *Pacific Northwest Quarterly* 43, no. 1 (January 1952): 47; Charles Wilson, *Mapping the Frontier: Charles Wilson's Diary of the Survey of the 49th Parallel, 1858–1862, While Secretary of the British Boundary Commission,* ed. George F. G. Stanley (Seattle: University of Washington Press, 1970), 135.

The use of a light ground is in direct contrast to most contemporary Subarctic and Great Lakes floral beadwork, where dark woolen backgrounds were the norm, as illustrated by the octopus bag in the upper right-hand corner of the photo.

16. Erwin N. Thompson, *Spalding Area, Nez Perce National Historic Park, Idaho,* Historic Resource Study (Denver: National Park Service, 1972), 34.

17. James H. Wilbur, "Report of Agents in Washington Territory, Yakama Indian Agency," *Annual Report of the Commissioner of Indian Affairs to the Secretary of the Interior for the Year 1875* (Washington, D.C.: Government Printing Office, 1875), 367.

18. George Martin Kober, *Reminiscences of George Martin Kober, M.D., LL.D.,* vol. 1 (Washington, D.C.: Kober Foundation of Georgetown University, 1930), 362.

19. A photograph of this garment appears in Steven L. Grafe, "Nez Perce Decorative Art of the 1870s: Scientific and Souvenir Collections," *American Indian Art Magazine* 24, no. 4 (autumn 1999): 69.

20. One implicit and one explicit reference have thus far been found documenting Terry's activity in the Plateau. In his *Sculptured Anthropoid Ape Heads Found In or Near the Valley of the John Day River* (New York: J. J. Little, 1891), Terry makes reference to his presence in the Columbia River

region during 1882. He states that, at that time, he had already gained experience with the Nez Perce, Yakima, and Warm Springs peoples. Clark Wissler became curator of anthropology at the American Museum in 1905, seven years before Terry's death. In his 1916 "Costumes of the Plains Indians," Wissler used an illustration of a Nez Perce shirt as the essay's initial figure. The shirt was among the Nez Perce items collected by Terry, and Wissler's caption calls it "a Nez Perce shirt. Collected about 1865."

21. The Transmontane style refers to the geometric beadwork designs produced by the residents of the southern and eastern Plateau after about 1860. The nomenclature recognizes the fact that the style was practiced contemporaneously by both Plateau and Crow beadworkers.

Bibliography

PRIMARY SOURCES

Barton, John R. Papers. State Historical Society, Madison, Wisc.

Boyce, George. Papers. Collection of Oleta Boyce. Santa Fe, N.M.

Curry, John Steuart. Papers. Archives of American Art, Smithsonian Institution, Washington, D.C.

Dorsey, G. A., and Cleaver Warden. Arapaho Notes. Anthropology Archives, Field Museum of Natural History, Chicago.

Force, Roland, and James Smith, Stan Steiner, William Stiles, and Douglas Latimer. Miscellaneous Correspondence, 1979. National Museum of the American Indian, Registration Files, Cultural Resources Center, Suitland, Md.

Frazier, Bernard. Letter to Wa Wa Chaw, June 23, 1947, with handwritten response from Wa Wa Chaw. Archives, Philbrook Museum of Art, Tulsa, Okla.

Goddard, Pliny Earle. Catalog of specimens purchased on the Sarcee Reserve, July and August, 1905, Accession File, 1905–44, American Museum of Natural History.

"Indian Artist Receives Honor in His Own Land." Unattributed newspaper article, Jackson County History Room, Black River Falls (Wisconsin) Public Library.

Institute of American Indian Arts Archives. Santa Fe, N.M.

Museum of the American Indian. Benefit auction list, January 29, 1975.

Nuñez, Bonita Wa Wa Calachaw. Biographical information form, n.d. [after 1946]. Archives, Philbrook Museum of Art, Tulsa, Okla.

——. "The Indian Game." *The Indian: The Magazine of the Mission Indian Federation* (August 1992): cover. Arthur and Shifra Silberman Collection, National Cowboy Hall of Fame, Research Center.

——. Letter to Jeanne Snodgrass, October 9, 1957. Archives, Philbrook Museum of Art, Tulsa, Okla.

——. Letter to Jeanne Snodgrass, April 15, 1963. Native American Artists Resource Collection, Heard Museum, Phoenix.

——. Response, written on letter from Bernard Frazier, 1947. Archives, Philbrook Museum of Art, Tulsa, Okla.

Pino, Juan I. Letters to Jessie Hall, March 31, September 9, December 5, and December 19, 1926. Collection of Edward T. Hall, Santa Fe, N.M.

Pratt, Richard H. Papers. Western Americana Collections, Beinecke Rare Book and Manuscript Library, Yale University.

Rockefeller Foundation Archives. Rockefeller Archive Center. Pocantico Hills, North Tarrytown, New York.

Rush, Olive. Block printed Christmas card sent by Charles Kassler from Paris, 1929. OR-AAA, reel 1628, no f. no. Archives of America Art, Washington, D.C.

——. Diary entry, Thursday, August 17, 1932. OR-AAA, reel 1629, f. 1195. Archives of American Art, Washington, D.C.

School of American Research, Indian Arts Research Center. Anonymous, undated note attached to catalog card number 2937a and b.

Snodgrass, Jeanne. Letter to Wa Wa Chaw, October 25, 1957. Archives, Philbrook Museum of Art, Tulsa, Okla.

Williamson, Leslie. Condition reports, 1997. Conservation Department, National Museum of the American Indian, Cultural Resources Center, Suitland, Md.

Wissler, Clark. Letter to Franz Boas, 3 August, 1902, Accession File, 1902–72, American Museum of Natural History.

Wyckoff, Lydia L. Letter to Charles Putney, October 24, 1994. Archives, Philbrook Museum of Art, Tulsa, Okla.

SECONDARY SOURCES

Abbott, John Lawrence. *John Hawkesworth: Eighteenth-Century Man of Letters.* Madison: University of Wisconsin Press, 1982.

Abbott, Lawrence. *I Stand in the Center of the Good, Interviews with Contemporary Native American Artists.* Lincoln: University of Nebraska Press, 1994.

Adair, John. *The Navajo and Pueblo Silversmiths.* Norman: University of Oklahoma Press, 1944.

Adams, Clinton. *Printmaking in New Mexico, 1880–1990.* Albuquerque: University of New Mexico Press, 1991.

"All-American Art." *Art Digest,* January 1, 1941, 17.

American Indian Performing Arts Exhibition. Washington, D.C.: U. S. Department of the Interior, 1964.

American Magazine of Art. November 1925.

Amsden, Charles Avery. *Navaho Weaving: Its Technique and History.* Santa Ana: Fine Arts Press, 1934. Reprint, Salt Lake City: Peregrine Smith, 1975.

Anderson, Jeffrey Dale. "Northern Arapaho Knowledge and Life Movement." Ph.D. diss., University of Chicago, 1994.

"April Exhibits." *El Palacio* 20 (May 1, 1926): 185–86.

Archuleta, Margaret, and Rennard Strickland, eds. *Shared Visions: Native American Painters and Sculptors in the Twentieth Century.* Phoenix: Heard Museum, 1991.

Arts. (March 1927): cover and table of contents.

Ash-Milby, Kathleen E. Caption Plate 128. In *Woven by the Grandmothers: Nineteenth-Century Navajo Textiles from the National Museum of the American Indian,* ed. Eulalie H. Bonar. Washington D.C.: Smithsonian Institution Press, 1996.

"At Work on Taos and Rito Pictures." *El Palacio* 6 (January 1919): 18, 47.

Bal, Mieke, and Norman Bryson. "Semiotics and Art History." *Art Bulletin* 73 (June 1991): 174–208.

Baldwin, Stuart J. "Piro and Tompiro Ethnography: First Draft." Laboratory of Anthropology, Santa Fe, 1981.

——. "Tompiro Culture, Subsistence, and Trade." Ph.D. diss., University of Calgary, 1988.

Bancroft-Hunt, Norman. *The Indians of the Great Plains.* Norman: University of Oklahoma Press, 1981.

Barbeau, Marius. "The Origin of Floral and Other Designs among the Canadian and Neighboring Indians." *Proceedings of the Twenty-Third International Congress of Americanists* (New York, 1930): 512.

Barker, Garry G. *The Handcraft Revival in Southern Appalachia, 1930–1990.* Knoxville: University of Tennessee Press, 1991.

Barker, Ruth Laughlin. "John Sloan Reviews the Indian Tribal Arts." *Creative Arts* 9 (December 1931): 445–49.

Barry, John W. *American Indian Pottery: An Identification and Value Guide.* Florence, Ala.: Books Americana, 1984.

Barton, John R. *Rural Artists of Wisconsin.* Madison: University of Wisconsin Press, 1948.

Bataille, Gretchen M., ed. *Native American Women: A Biographical Directory.* New York: Garland, 1993.

Bates, Sara. *Indian Humor.* San Francisco: American Indian Contemporary Arts, 1995.

Batteau, Allen W. *The Invention of Appalachia.* Tucson: University of Arizona Press, 1990.

Bean, Lowell John, and Florence Shipek. "Luiseño." In *Handbook of North American Indians,* ed. William C. Sturtevant, 550–63. Vol. 8. Washington, D.C.: Smithsonian Institution Press, 1978.

Becker, Jane S. *Selling Tradition: Appalachia and the Construction of an American Folk, 1930–1940.* Chapel Hill: University of North Carolina Press, 1998.

Benjamin, Walter. "Unpacking My Library: A Talk about Book Collecting." In *Illuminations.* Trans. Harry Zohn. Ed. Hannah Arendt. New York: Harcourt, Brace and World, 1968.

"Berg Jewelry Displaying Monegar Pictures." *Black River Falls (Wisconsin) Banner-Journal,* January 29, 1964.

Berlo, Janet Catherine, ed. *Plains Indian Drawings, 1865–1935: Pages from a Visual History.* New York: Harry N. Abrams in association with the American Federation of Arts and the Drawing Center, 1996.

Bermingham, Ann. *Landscape and Ideology: The English Rustic Tradition, 1740–1860.* Berkeley: University of California Press, 1986.

Berthrong, Donald. *The Southern Cheyennes.* Norman: University of Oklahoma Press, 1963.

Betterton, Rosemary. "Mother Figures: The Maternal Nude in the Work of Käthe Kollwitz and Paula Modersohn-Becker." In *An Intimate Distance: Women, Artists, and the Body,* 20–45. New York: Routledge, 1996.

Bhabha, Homi. *Location of Culture.* New York: Routledge, 1994.

Bighead, Kate. "She Watched Custer's Last Battle." In *The Custer Reader,* ed. Paul A. Hutton, 363–77. Lincoln: University of Nebraska Press, 1992.

Biolsi, Thomas. "The Anthropological Construction of 'Indians': Haviland Scudder Mekeel and the Search for the Primitive in Lakota Country." In *Indians and Anthropologists: Vine Deloria Jr. and the Critique of Anthropology,* ed. Thomas Biolsi and Larry J. Zimmerman, 133–59. Tucson: University of Arizona Press, 1997.

Bird, S. Elizabeth. "Introduction: Constructing the Indian, 1830s–1990s." In *Dressing in Feathers,* ed. S. Elizabeth Bird, 1–12. Boulder, Colo.: Westview Press, 1996.

Blessing, Fred. "The Woodland Indian–Conservationist." In *Outdoor Horizons,* ed. L. Brings, 148–54. Minneapolis: T. S. Denison, 1957.

"Block Prints by Juan Pino." *El Palacio* 18 (June 1, 1925): 237–40.

Boehme, Sarah E., et al. *Powerful Images: Portrayals of Native America.* Seattle: Museums West in association with the University of Washington Press, 1998.

Bol, Marsha C. "Collecting Symbolism among the Arapaho: George A. Dorsey and C. Warden, Indian." In *The Great Southwest of the Fred Harvey Company and the Santa Fe Railway,* ed. Marta Weigle and Barbara A. Babcock, 110–24. Phoenix: Heard Museum, 1996.

——. "Lakota Women's Artistic Strategies in Support of the Social System." *American Indian Culture and Research Journal* 9, no. 1 (1985): 33–51.

Boyd, Maurice. *Kiowa Voices.* Vol. 1. Fort Worth: Texas Christian University Press, 1981.

Brant, Charles S. "Peyotism among the Kiowa-Apache and Neighboring Tribes." *Southwestern Journal of Anthropology* 6, no. 2 (1950): 212–22.

Brasser, Ted. "The Tipi as an Element in the Emergence of Historic Plains Indian Nomadism." *Plains Anthropologist* 27 (1982): 309–21.

Braun, Barbara. "Art from the Land of the Savages, or Surrealists in the New World." *Boston Review* 13, nos. 5–6 (1988).

——. *Pre-Columbian Art and the Post-Columbian World: Ancient American Sources of Modern Art.* New York: Harry N. Abrams, 1993.

Brody, J. J. *Anasazi and Pueblo Painting.* Albuquerque: University of New Mexico Press, 1991.

——. *Indian Painters and White Patrons.* Albuquerque: University of New Mexico Press, 1971.

——. *Pueblo Indian Painting: Tradition and Modernism in New Mexico, 1900–1930.* Santa Fe: School of American Research Press, 1997.

——. "Site Use, Pictorial Space, and Subject Matter in Late Prehistoric and Early Historic Rio Grande Pueblo Art." *Journal of Anthropological Research* 45 (1989): 15–28.

Brody, J. J., and Rina Swentzell. *To Touch the Past: The Painted Pottery of the Mimbres People.* New York: Hudson Hills Press, 1996.

Brooks, Van Wyck. *John Sloan: A Painter's Life.* New York: E. P. Dutton, 1955.

Buel, J. W. *Heroes of the Dark Continent and How Stanley Found Emin Pasha: Complete History of All the Great Explorations and Discoveries in Africa, from the Earliest Ages to the Present Time.* San Francisco: History Company, 1890.

Bunn, David. "Our Wattled Cot: Mercantile and Domestic Space in Thomas Pringle's African Landscapes." In *Landscape and Power,* ed. W. J. T. Mitchell, 127–73. Chicago: University of Chicago Press, 1994.

Callahan, Alice Ann. *The Osage Ceremonial Dance I'n-Lon-Schka.* Norman: University of Oklahoma Press, 1990.

Caudill, Harry M. *Night Comes to the Cumberlands: A Biography of a Depressed Area.* New York: Little, Brown, 1963.

Chadwick, Whitney. *Women, Art, and Society.* London: Thames and Hudson, 1990.

Charlot, Jean. "All-American." *Nation* 152, no. 6 (1941), 165.

Clark, Kenneth. *The Nude: A Study in Ideal Form.* Princeton: Princeton University Press, 1956.

Clark, Ricky. *Quilted Gardens: Floral Quilts of the Nineteenth Century.* Nashville: Rutledge Hill Press, 1994.

Coe, Ralph T. "Native American Craft." In *Revivals! Diverse Traditions, 1920–1945: The History of Twentieth-Century American Craft,* ed. Janet Kardon, 65–83. New York: Harry N. Abrams in association with the American Craft Museum, 1994.

Conkey, Margaret W. "To Find Ourselves: Art and Social Geography of Prehistoric Hunter-Gatherers." In *Past and Present in Hunter-Gatherer Studies,* ed. C. Schrire, 253–76. Orlando: Academic Press, 1984.

Conklin, Abe. "Origin of the Powwow: The Ponca He-Thus-Ka Society Dance." *Native Americas Special Edition: Native American Expressive Culture* 11, nos. 3 and 4 (1994): 17–21.

Conn, Richard. *Circles of the World: Traditional Art of the Plains Indians.* Denver: Denver Art Museum, 1989.

———. "Floral Design in Native North America." In *Native American Art from the Permanent Collection,* ed. Kay Koeninger and Joanne M. Mack, 78–81. Claremont: Claremont Colleges, 1980.

———. *Native American Art in the Denver Art Museum.* Denver: Denver Art Museum. 1979.

Corley, Sandy. "In Our Language: Native American Art." *Art Papers* 17, no. 5 (September–October 1993): 27–32.

Cowling, Elizabeth. "The Eskimos, the American Indians, and the Surrealists." *Art History* 1, no. 4 (1978): 484–500.

Crafts in the Southern Highlands. Asheville: Southern Highland Handicraft Guild, 1958.

Craig, T. L., and Anne Powell. "Florida Bullfight with Redskin Matadors." *Times Journal Magazine* (October 1, 1967).

Craven, Thomas. *Modern Art.* New York: Simon and Schuster, 1934.

Cross, Mary Bywater. *Treasures in the Trunk: Quilts of the Oregon Trail.* Nashville: Rutledge Hill Press, 1993.

Crumley, Carole L. "Toward a Locational Definition of State Systems of Settlement." *American Anthropologist* 78 (1976): 59–73.

Crumley, Carole L., and William H. Marquardt, eds. *Regional Dynamics: Burgundian Landscapes in Historical Perspective.* San Diego: Academic Press, 1972. Saint Paul: State of Minnesota, Land Management Information Center and Minnesota Planning, 1987.

Cuba, Stanley L. *Olive Rush: A Hoosier Artist in New Mexico.* Muncie, Ind.: Minnetrista Cultural Foundation, 1992.

Cunningham, Mary Ann, David Arbeit, and Jed Becher. *User Manual Version 3.0: The EPPL7 Geographic Information System.* Saint Paul: State of Minnesota, Land Management Information Center and Minnesota Planning, 1997.

"Curry of Kansas." *Newsweek,* November 15, 1943, 80.

Curtis, Edward S. *The North American Indian.* Vol. 6. 1911. Reprint, New York: Johnson Reprint, 1970.

——— *The North American Indian.* Vol. 18. 1928. Reprint, New York: Johnson Reprint, 1970.

Darrah, William C. *Cartes de Visite in Nineteenth Century Photography.* Gettysburg, Pa.: William C. Darrah, 1981.

Deitrich, Margretta S. "Their Culture Survives." *New Mexico Magazine* 4 (February 1936).

Deloria, Philip J. *Playing Indian.* New Haven and London: Yale University Press, 1998.

Deloria, Vine, Jr. *Custer Died for Your Sins: An Indian Manifesto.* New York: Macmillan, 1969.

Dobkins, Rebecca J. *Memory and Imagination: The Legacy of Maidu Indian Artist Frank Day.* Oakland: Oakland Museum of California, 1997.

——. "The Work and Influence of Maidu Painter Frank Day." *American Indian Art Magazine* 23 (autumn 1998): 54–67.

Dockstader, Frederick J. *Directions in Indian Art.* Proceedings of a conference held at the University of Arizona, March 20–21, 1959. Tucson: University of Arizona Press, 1959.

——. *Great North American Indians: Profiles in Life and Leadership.* New York: Van Nostrand Reinhold, 1977.

Dorsey, George A., and Alfred L. Kroeber. *Traditions of the Arapaho.* Field Columbian Museum Anthropological Series, vol. 5, no. 81. Chicago: Field Columbian Museum, 1903.

Douglas, Frederick H., and Rene d'Harnoncourt. *Indian Art of the United States.* New York: Museum of Modern Art, 1941.

Dubin, Margaret. "Sanctioned Scribes: How Critics and Historians Write the Native American Art World." In *Native American Art in the Twentieth Century,* ed. W. Jackson Rushing III, 149–166. London and New York: Routledge, 1999.

Duncan, James. "Sites of Representation: Place, Time, and the Discourse of the Other." In *Place/Culture/Representation,* ed. James Duncan and David Ley, 39–56. New York: Routledge, 1993.

Duncan, James, and David Ley, eds. *Place/Culture/Representation.* New York: Routledge, 1993.

Duncan, Kate C. "Beadwork on the Plateau." In *A Time of Gathering: Native Heritage in Washington State,* ed. Robin K. Wright, 189–96. Seattle: University of Washington Press, 1991.

Dunn, Dorothy. *American Indian Painting of the Southwest and Plains Areas.* Albuquerque: University of New Mexico Press, 1968.

Eaton, Allen. *Handicrafts of the Southern Highlands.* New York: Russell Sage Foundation, 1937. Reprint, New York: Dover, 1973.

Echo-Hawk, Roger, and Walter Echo-Hawk. *Battlefields and Burial Grounds: The Indian Struggle to Protect Ancestral Graves in the United States.* Minneapolis: Lerner Publications, 1994.

Echo-Hawk, Walter. "Loopholes in Religious Liberty: The Need for a Federal Law to Protect Freedom of Worship for Native People." *American Indian Religions: An Interdisciplinary Journal* 1, no. 1 (winter 1994): 5–16.

1877 Plains Indian Sketch Books of Zo-Tom and Howling Wolf. Intro. Dorothy Dunn. Flagstaff: Northland Press, 1969.

Einstein, Albert. Foreword. In *Concepts of Space,* ed. Max Jammer xii-xvi. 1954. Reprint, New York: Harper and Brothers, 1960.

Eldredge, Charles C. *Pacific Parallels: Artists and Landscape in New Zealand.* Seattle: University of Washington Press, 1991.

——. "Prairie Prodigal: John Steuart Curry and Kansas." In *John Steuart Curry: Inventing the Middle West,* ed. P. Junker, 89–109. New York: Hudson Hills Press, 1998.

Eliade, Mircea. *The Sacred and the Profane.* New York: Harper Torchbook, 1961.

Erikson, Erik. *Childhood and Society.* New York and London: W. W. Norton, 1950.

Evans, C. Scott. *The "Northern Traditional Dancer."* Denison, Tex.: Crazy Crow Trading Post, 1990.

Ewers, John C. *The Horse in Blackfoot Culture.* Washington, D.C.: Smithsonian Institution Press, 1969.

——. *Indian Life on the Upper Missouri.* Norman: University of Oklahoma Press, 1988.

——. *Murals in the Round: Painted Tipis of the Kiowa and Kiowa-Apache Indians.* Washington, D.C.: Smithsonian Institution Press, 1978.

——. "Plains Indian Artists and Anthropologists: A Fruitful Collaboration." *American Indian Art Magazine* 9 (winter 1983): 39–49.

——. *Plains Indian Painting.* Stanford: Stanford University Press, 1939.

"Exhibit by Charles Kassler." *El Palacio* 18 (March 16, 1925): 125.

"Exhibit by Charles M. Kassler, Jr." *El Palacio* 18 (June 1, 1925): 235–36.

Exposition of Indian Tribal Arts. *Catalogue: The Exposition of Indian Tribal Arts, Inc., Grand Central Galleries, December 1–24.* New York: Exposition of Indian Tribal Arts, 1931.

Fagin, Nancy L. "The James Mooney Collection of Cheyenne Tipi Models at Field Museum of Natural History." *Plains Anthropologist* 33 (1988): 261–78.

Fawcett, David M., and Lee A. Callander. *Native American Painting: Selections from the Museum of the American Indian.* New York: Museum of the American Indian, 1982.

"The Fiesta of 1925 as Viewed by One Observer." *El Palacio* 21 (July 1, 1926): 2–20.

Fine American Indian Art. Sotheby's Auction Catalog. Sale 6783, 1995.

Fleming, Dan. *Powerplay: Toys as Popular Culture.* Manchester and New York: Manchester University Press, 1996.

Fletcher, Alice C. "The Elk Mystery or Festival, Ogallala Sioux." *Sixteenth and Seventeenth Annual Reports of the Trustees of the Peabody Museum of American Archaeology and Ethnology* 3 (1884): 276–88.

Fletcher, Alice C., and Francis La Flesche. "The Omaha Tribe." In *Bureau of American Ethnology Twenty-Seventh Annual Report, 1905–1906.* Washington, D.C.: Government Printing Office, 1911.

Flint, Jennifer Jean. " 'A Woman's Experience: From the Collection of Bonita Wa Wa Calachaw Nuñez.' An Exhibit Design." Master's thesis, Oklahoma State University, 1998.

Ford, Richard I. "Inter-Indian Exchange in the Southwest." In *Handbook of the North American Indians,* ed. William C. Sturtevant, 711–22. Vol. 10. Washington, D.C.: Smithsonian Institution Press, 1983.

Foster, Morris W. *Being Comanche: A Social History of an American Indian Community.* Tucson: University of Arizona Press, 1991.

Foucault, Michel. *Discipline and Punish: The Birth of the Prison.* New York: Vintage Books, 1977.

——. *History of Sexuality.* New York: Vintage Books, 1985.

——. *Power/Knowledge: Selected Interviews and Other Writings, 1972–1977.* New York: Vintage Books, 1980.

Fowler, Loretta. *Arapaho Politics, 1851–1978: Symbols in Crises of Authority.* Lincoln: University of Nebraska Press, 1982.

———. "Oral Historian or Ethnologist?: The Career of Bill Shakespeare." In *American Indian Intellectuals,* ed. Margot Liberty, 226–40. Saint Paul: West Publishing, 1978.

Frost, William Goodell. "Our Contemporary Ancestors in the Southern Mountains." *Atlantic Monthly,* March 1899, 311–19.

Fry, Aaron. "The Northern Traditional Powwow Clothing Style and the United States Postal Service: A Study in Conflicting Meanings." Master's thesis, University of New Mexico, 1999.

Garth, Thomas R. "Archaeological Excavations at Fort Walla Walla." *Pacific Northwest Quarterly* 43, no. 1 (January 1952): 27–50.

Gilman, Carolyn, and Mary Jane Schneider. *The Way to Independence: Memories of a Hidatsa Indian Family.* Saint Paul: Minneapolis Historical Society Press, 1987.

Glowen, Ron. "Review: James Lavadour at Cliff Michel." *Art in America* 78 (December 1990): 177.

Gogol, John. "Columbia River/Plateau Indian Beadwork. Part 1: Yakima, Warm Springs, Umatilla, Nez Perce." *American Indian Basketry and Other Native Arts* 5, no. 2 (1985).

Goodrich, Frances Louis. *Mountain Homespun.* 1931. Reprint, Knoxville: University of Tennessee Press, 1989.

Gordon, Beverly. "The Souvenir: Messenger of the Extraordinary." *Journal of Popular Culture* 20 no. 3 (1986): 135–46.

Grafe, Steven LeRoy. "Nez Perce Decorative Art of the 1870s: Scientific and Souvenir Collections" *American Indian Art Magazine* 24, no. 4 (autumn 1999): 60–71.

———. "The Origins of Floral-Design Beadwork in the Southern Columbia River Plateau," Ph.D. diss., University of New Mexico, 1999.

Graham. H. W. "The Fireside Industries of Kentucky." *Craftsman,* January 1902, 45–48.

Graham, John D., ed. *Systems and Dialectics of Art.* London and New York: Delphic Studios, 1937.

Gray, Gary G. *Wildlife and People.* Urbana and Chicago: University of Illinois Press, 1993.

Green, Harvey. "Culture and Crisis: Americans and the Craft Revival." In *Revivals! Diverse Traditions, 1920–1945: The History of Twentieth-Century American Craft,* ed. Jane Kardon, 31–54. New York: Harry N. Abrams in association with the American Craft Museum, 1994.

Green, Rayna. Introduction to the Dover Edition. In *Handicrafts of the Southern Highlands,* Allen Eaton, xix–xxi. New York: Russell Sage Foundation, 1937. Reprint, New York: Dover, 1973.

Greene, Candace S., and Thomas D. Drescher. "The Tipi with Battle Pictures: The Kiowa Tradition of Intangible Property Rights." *Trademark Reporter* 84 (1994): 418–33.

Grinnell, George Bird. *The Cheyenne Indians: Their History and Ways of Life.* 2 vols. 1923. Reprint, Lincoln: University of Nebraska Press, 1972.

———. *The Fighting Cheyennes.* New York: Charles Scribner's Sons, 1915. Reprint, Norman: University of Oklahoma Press, 1956.

Gritton, Joy. *The Institute of American Indian Arts: Modernism and U.S. Indian Policy.* Albuquerque: University of New Mexico Press, 2000.

Hail, Barbara A. *Hau Kola! The Plains Indian Collection of the Haffenrefer Museum of Anthropology.* Providence: Haffenrefer Museum of Anthropology, Brown University, 1980.

Hall, Edward T. *An Anthropology of Everyday Life.* New York: Doubleday, 1992.

Hall, Eliza Calvert. *The Book of Handwoven Coverlets.* New York: Dover Publications, 1988.

Hallpike, C. R. "Social Hair." In *Reader in Comparative Religion,* ed. William A. Lessa and Evon Z. Vogt, 99–105. New York: Harper Collins, 1979.

Hammond, Nicholas. *Modern Wildlife Painting.* New Haven and London: Yale University Press, 1999.

Harris, Ann Sutherland, and Linda Nochlin. *Women Artists, 1550–1950.* New York: Knopf and Los Angeles County Museum of Art, 1976.

Harris, Moira. *Between Two Cultures: Kiowa Art from Fort Marion.* Saint Paul: Pogo Press, 1989.

Harrison, Charles. "The Effects of Landscape." In *Landscape and Power,* ed. W. J. T. Mitchell, 203–39. Chicago: University of Chicago Press, 1994.

Hawkes, Terence. *Structuralism and Semiotics.* London: Methuen, 1977.

Hays, Robert G. *A Race at Bay: New York Times Editorials on "the Indian Problem," 1860–1900.* Carbondale and Edwardsville: Southern Illinois University Press, 1997.

Helsinger, Elizabeth. "Turner and the Representation of England." In *Landscape and Power,* ed. W. J. T. Mitchell, 103–25. Chicago: University of Chicago Press, 1994.

Henkes, Robert. *Native American Painters of the Twentieth Century: The Works of Sixty-one Artists.* Jefferson, N.C.: McFarland, 1995.

Heth, Charlotte. "American Indian Dance: A Celebration of Survival and Adaptation." In *Native American Dance: Ceremonies and Social Traditions,* ed. Charlotte Heth, 1–17. Washington, D.C.: National Museum of the American Indian with Starwood Publishing, 1992.

Hilger, Sister M. Inez. *Arapaho Child Life and Its Cultural Background.* Smithsonian Institution, Bureau of American Ethnology Bulletin 148. Washington, D.C.: Government Printing Office, 1952.

Hill, Jennie Lester. "Fireside Industries in the Kentucky Mountains." *Southern Workman* 32 (April 1903): 208–13.

Hill, W. W. "Navajo Trading and Trading Ritual: A Study of Cultural Dynamics." *Southwestern Journal of Anthropology* 4, no. 4 (winter 1948): 371–96.

——. "Some Navaho Culture Changes during Two Centuries (with a Translation of the Early Eighteenth-Century Rabel Manuscript)." *Essays in Historical Anthropology of North America.* Smithsonian Miscellaneous Collections. Washington, D.C.: Smithsonian Institution, 1940.

Hirschfelder, Arlene B. "Association on American Indian Affairs." In *Native America in the Twentieth Century: An Encyclopedia,* ed. Mary Davis, 64–66. New York: Garland, 1994.

Hobsbawm, Eric, and Terence Ranger, eds. *The Invention of Tradition.* Cambridge: Cambridge University Press, 1986.

Hodder, Ian. "Boundaries as Strategies: An Ethnoarchaeological Study." In *The Archaeology of Frontiers and Boundaries,* ed. Stanton W. Green and Stephen W. Perlman, 141–59. Orlando: Academic Press, 1985.

Hoebel, E. Adamson, and Karen Daniels Petersen, commentary. *A Cheyenne Sketchbook by Cohoe.* Norman: University of Oklahoma Press, 1964.

Hogue, Alexandre. "Picturesque Games and Ceremonial[s] of Indians." *El Palacio* 26 (March 2–23, 1929): 177–83. Reprinted from the *Dallas Times Herald.*

——. "Pueblo Tribes Aesthetic Giants, Indian Art Reveals." *El Palacio* 24 (March 24, 1928): 214–17.

Horse Capture, George P. *Powwow.* Cody, Wyo.: Buffalo Bill Historical Center, 1989.

Houle, Robert. "Kay WalkingStick." In *Land, Spirit, Power: First Nations at the National Gallery of Canada,* ed. Diana Nemiroff, 43–73. Ottawa: National Gallery of Canada, 1992.

Howard, James H. "The Pan-Indian Culture of Oklahoma." *Scientific Monthly* 18, no. 5 (1955): 215–20.

Howard, Kathleen L., and Diana F. Pardue. *Inventing the Southwest: The Fred Harvey Company and Native American Art.* Phoenix: Heard Museum, 1996.

Huenemann, Lynn F. "Northern Plains Dance." In *Native American Dance: Ceremonies and Social Traditions,* ed. Charlotte Heth, 125–47. Washington, D.C.: National Museum of the American Indian with Starwood Publishing, 1992.

Hulton, Paul. *America, 1585: The Complete Drawings of John White.* London: British Museum Publications, 1984.

Hunter, James. *Scottish Highlanders, Indian Peoples: Thirty Generations of a Montana Family.* Helena: Montana Historical Society Press, 1996.

Hurley, Dave. "Honor the Earth." *Native Peoples* 8, no. 4 (summer 1995): 64–69.

Hursthouse, Charles. *New Zealand, or Zealandia, the Britain of the South.* London: Edward Stanford, 1857.

Hurt, Wesley R. *The 1930–1940 Excavation Project at Quarai Pueblo and Mission Buildings: Salinas Pueblo Missions National Monument, New Mexico.* Santa Fe: Division of History and Division of Anthropology, National Park Service, 1990.

Hyde, George. *Life of George Bent Written from His Letters,* ed. Savoie Lottinville. Norman: University of Oklahoma Press, 1967.

———. *Red Cloud's Folk.* Norman: University of Oklahoma Press, 1976.

Indian Art in the United States and Alaska: A Pictorial Record of the Indian Exhibition at the Golden Gate International Exposition. Prepared by the Indian Arts and Crafts Board of the U.S. Department of the Interior at the Federal Building on Treasure Island, San Francisco, 1939. Ann Arbor: University Microfilms.

"Indian Monegar's Art on Display." *Black River Falls (Wisconsin) Banner-Journal,* July 9, 1969.

Indian Notes and Monographs. 9, no. 3 (summer 1973). New York: Museum of the American Indian.

Irwin, Lee. *The Dream Seekers: Native American Visionary Traditions of the Great Plains.* Norman: University of Oklahoma Press, 1994.

Iverson, Peter. *Carlos Montezuma and the Changing World of American Indians.* Albuquerque: University of New Mexico Press, 1982.

Ivey, James. *In the Midst of a Loneliness: The Architectural History of the Salinas Missions.* Salinas Pueblo Missions National Monument Report. Professional Papers 15. Santa Fe: Division of History, Southwest Cultural Resources Center (1988).

Jackson, John Brinkerhoff. *Discovering the Vernacular Landscape.* New Haven: Yale University Press, 1984.

Jewell, Edward Alden. "The American Indian Exhibition: A Tradition Lives On." *New York Times,* December 6, 1931.

Jonaitis, Aldona. "Creations of Mystics and Philosophers: The White Man's Perceptions of Northwest Coast Indian Art from the 1930s to the Present." *American Indian Culture and Research Journal* 5, no. 1 (1981): 1–45.

Jones, Oakah L. *Pueblo Warriors and Spanish Conquest.* Norman: University of Oklahoma Press, 1966.

Justeson, John, and Steve Hampson. "Closed Models of Open Systems: Boundary Considerations." In *The Archaeology of Frontiers and Boundaries,* ed. Stanton Green and Stephen Perlman, 15–30. Orlando: Academic Press, 1985.

"Kassler in Santa Fe." *El Palacio* 18 (April 1, 1925): 150–51.

Kaufman, Alice, and Christopher Selser. *The Navajo Weaving Tradition, 1650 to the Present.* New York: E. P. Dutton, 1985.

Kavanaugh, Thomas W. "Southern Plains Dance: Tradition and Dynamics." In *Native American Dance: Ceremonies and Social Traditions,* ed. Charlotte Heth, 105–23. Washington, D.C.: National Museum of the American Indian with Starwood Publishing, 1992.

Keithahn, E. L. "The Petroglyphs of Southeastern Alaska." *American Antiquity* 2 (1940): 128–32.

Kelly, Lawrence. *The Assault on Assimilation: John Collier and the Origins of Indian Policy Reform.* Albuquerque: University of New Mexico Press, 1983.

Kent, Kate Peck. "From Blanket to Rug: The Evolution of Navajo Weaving after 1880." *Plateau* 52, no. 4 (1981): 10–21.

———. *Navajo Weaving.* Santa Fe: School of American Research Press, 1985.

Kephart, Horace. *Our Southern Highlanders: A Narrative of Adventure in the Southern Appalachians and a Study of Life among the Mountaineers.* 1913. Reprint, Knoxville: University of Tennessee Press, 1976.

Kessler, Jane. "From Mission to Market: Craft in the Southern Appalachians." In *Revivals! Diverse Traditions, 1920–1945: The History of Twentieth-Century American Craft,* ed. Jane Kardon, 122–33. New York: Harry N. Abrams in association with the American Craft Museum, 1994.

Key, Donald. "His Art Overcame Tragic Life and Jail." *Milwaukee Journal,* July 6, 1969.

Kleeblatt, Norman L. "MASTER NARRATIVES/minority artists." *Art Journal* 57 (fall 1998) no. 3, 29–35.

Kluckhohn, Clyde, W. W. Hill, and Lucy Wales Kluckhohn. *Navajo Material Culture.* Cambridge: Harvard University Press, 1971.

Kober, George Martin. *Reminiscences of George Martin Kober, M.D., LL.D.* Vol. 1. Washington, D.C.: Kober Foundation of Georgetown University, 1930.

Kroeber, Alfred L. *The Arapaho.* 1902, 1904, 1907. Reprint (3 parts in 1), Lincoln: University of Nebraska Press, 1983.

Lawin, Tom. "Fame Game Comes a Bit Late for Jackson Artist." *Eau Claire (Wisconsin) Leader and Daily Telegram,* November 21, 1969.

Leckie, William H. *The Military Conquest of the Southern Plains.* Norman: University of Oklahoma Press, 1963.

Lefebvre, Henri. *The Production of Space.* Trans. Donald Nicholson-Smith. Oxford: Blackwell, 1991.

Leopold, Aldo. *Sand County Almanac.* 1949. Reprint, Oxford: Oxford University Press, 1987.

Lester, Patrick. *The Biographical Directory of Native American Painters.* Tulsa: Servant Education and Research Foundation, 1995.

Levi-Strauss, Claude. *The Savage Mind.* Chicago: University of Chicago Press, 1966.

Lewis, Meriwether, and William Clark. *History of the Lewis and Clark Expedition.* 1893. Reprint, New York: Dover, n.d.

Libhart, Miles, and Rosemary Ellison. *Painted Tipis by Contemporary Plains Indian Artists.* Anadarko, Okla.: Oklahoma Indian Arts and Crafts Cooperative, 1973.

Liles, Joe. "Powwow Tales: The Jingle Dress." *News from Indian Country* 10, no. 2 (late January 1996).

Lincoln, Louise. "The Social Construction of Plains Art, 1875–1915." In *Visions of the People: A Pictorial History of Plains Indian Life.* In Evan Maurer, 51–52. Minneapolis: Minneapolis Institute of Arts, 1992.

Linderman, Frank B. *Pretty Shield, Medicine Woman of the Crows.* 1932. Reprint, Lincoln: University of Nebraska Press, 1972.

Lippard, Lucy. "The Color of the Wind." In *Our Land/Ourselves: American Indian Contemporary Artists,* ed. Jaune Quick-to-See Smith, 7–15. Albany: State University of New York at Albany, University Art Gallery, 1990.

Lowie, Robert H. *Indians of the Plains.* Lincoln: University of Nebraska Press, 1982.

Lynn, Catherine. *Wallpaper in America, From the Seventeenth Century to World War I.* New York: W. W. Norton, 1980.

M.A.C. "Art Works of Tesukue Indians to Be Shown in Linoleum Print Blocks at Chappell House: Dealer in Pinon Wood Displays His Ability When Given Opportunity." *Denver Rocky Mountain News,* May 3, 1925.

M.A.C. "Wood Block Exhibition Is Worth Study." *Denver Rocky Mountain News,* June 12, 1927.

MacCannell, Dean. *The Tourist: A New Theory of the Leisure Class.* New York: Schocken Books, 1976. Reprint, 1989.

"March Exhibits." *El Palacio* 18 (March 16, 1925): 124.

Marriott, Alice. "The Trade Guild of the Southern Cheyenne Women." *Bulletin of the Oklahoma Anthropological Society* 4 (April 1956): 19–27.

Marsh, Charles S. *People of the Shining Mountains.* Boulder: Pruett, 1982.

Maurer, Evan. "Dada and Surrealism." In *"Primitivism" in Twentieth-Century Art,* ed. William Rubin, 541–84. Vol. 2. New York: Museum of Modern Art, 1984.

——. *Visions of the People: A Pictorial History of Plains Indian Life.* Minneapolis: Minneapolis Institute of Arts, 1992.

McEvilley, Thomas. "The Selfhood of the Other." In *Art and Otherness: Crisis in Cultural Identity,* 85–108. Kingston, N.Y.: McPherson, 1992.

McMaster, Gerald, and Lee-Ann Martin. *Indigena: Contemporary Native Perspectives in Canadian Art.* New York: STBS, Ltd. 1992.

McNitt, Frank. *Indian Traders.* Norman: University of Oklahoma Press, 1963.

Means, Russell, with Marvin J. Wolf. *Where White Men Fear to Tread.* New York: St. Martin's Press, 1995.

Mighetto, Lisa. *Wild Animals and American Environmental Ethics.* Tucson: University of Arizona Press, 1991.

Miller, Angela. *Empire of the Eye.* Ithaca and London: Cornell University Press, 1993.

Mitchell, W. J. T. *Landscape and Power.* Chicago: University of Chicago Press, 1994.

Mooney, James. "The Ghost Dance Religion and the Sioux Outbreak of 1890." In *Bureau of American Ethnology Fourteenth Annual Report, 1892–1893.* Part 2. Washington, D.C.: Government Printing Office, 1896.

Morgan, Anne Barclay. "Kay WalkingStick: Interview." *Art Papers* 19, no. 6 (November–December 1995): 12–15.

"Mountain Baskets." *American Magazine of Art* 26 (December 1933): 546–49.

Nabokov, Peter, and Robert Easton. *Native American Architecture.* Oxford: Oxford University Press, 1989.

Nagy, Imre. "'The Black Came Over the Sun . . .' Lame Bull's Spiritual Oeuvre." *Irodalom-és Müvészettörténeti Tanulmányok, Studia Historiae Literarum et Artium* 1 (Szeged: Móra Ferenc Müzeum, 1997): 59–93.

——. "Lame Bull, the Cheyenne Medicine Man." *American Indian Art Magazine* 23 (winter 1997): 70–83.

Nemiroff, Diana, ed. *Land, Spirit, Power: First Nations at the National Gallery of Canada.* Ottawa: National Gallery of Canada, 1992.

Nerburn, Kent. *The Wisdom of the Great Chiefs: The Classic Speeches of Chief Red Jacket, Chief Joseph, and Chief Seattle.* San Rafael: New World Library, 1994.

New, Lloyd. *Young Indian Painters from the Institute of American Indian Arts.* Santa Fe: Museum of New Mexico, 1966.

Newcomb. W. W., Jr., and Forest Kirkland. *The Rock Art of Texas Indians.* Austin: University of Texas Press, 1967.

Newman, Barnett. *Northwest Coast Indian Painting.* New York: Betty Parsons Gallery, 1946.

Ninepipe, Louie. "The Grass Dance." In *Gathering of Nations Powwow Program* 9 (1992): 20.

Nouvel-Kammerer, Odile. *Papiers Peints Panoramiques.* Flammarion, France: Musée des Arts Decoratifs, 1990.

Novak, Barbara. "The Double-Edged Axe." *Art in America* 64, no. 1 (January–February 1976): 45–50.

Nye, W. S. *Carbine and Lance, The Story of Old Fort Sill.* 3d ed., rev. and enl. Norman: University of Oklahoma Press, 1974.

Ockenga, Starr. *On Women and Friendship: A Collection of Victorian Keepsakes and Traditions.* New York: Stewart, Tabori, and Chang, 1993.

Oetterman, Stephan. *The Panorama: History of a Mass Medium.* New York: Zone Books, 1997.

Opler, Morris E. "Mescalero Apache." In *Handbook of North American Indians,* ed. William C. Sturtevant, 419–39. Vol. 10. Washington, D.C.: Smithsonian Institution Press, 1983.

Orlofsky, Patsy, and Myron Orlofsky. *Quilts in America.* New York: Abbeville Press, 1992.

Ortega y Gasset, José. *Meditations on Hunting.* New York: Charles Scribner's and Sons, 1972.

Ortiz, Alfonso. *The Tewa World: Space, Time, Being, and Becoming in a Pueblo Society.* Chicago: University of Chicago Press, 1969.

Pach, Walter. "The Indian Tribal Arts: A Critic's View of the Significance and Value of a Unique American Asset." *New York Times,* November 22, 1931.

Patrick, David L., et al., *Southwest Indian Art: A Report to the Rockefeller Foundation Covering the Activities of the First Exploratory Workshop in Art for Talented Younger Indians Held at the University of Arizona in the Summer of 1960.* Tucson: University of Arizona, 1960.

Penney, David W., ed. *Art of the American Indian Frontier.* Detroit: Detroit Institute of Arts, 1992.

——. "Floral Decoration and Culture Change: An Historical Interpretation of Motivation." *American Indian Culture and Research Journal* 15, no. 1 (1991): 53–77.

Petersen, Karen Daniels. *Plains Indian Art from Fort Marion.* Norman: University of Oklahoma Press, 1971.

Pettit, Jan. *Utes: The Mountain People*. Boulder: Johnson, 1990.

Phillips, Ruth B. "Great Lakes Textiles: Meaning and Value in Women's Art." In *On the Border: Native American Weaving Traditions of the Great Lakes and Prairie*. Moorhead, Minn.: Plains Art Museum, 1990, 4–10, 45–46.

——. "Moccasins into Slippers: Woodlands Indian Hats, Bags, and Shoes in Tradition and Transformation." *Northeast Indian Quarterly* 7, no. 4 (winter 1990): 26–36.

——. "Souvenirs from North America: The Miniature as Image of Woodlands Indian Life." *American Indian Art Magazine* 14 (summer 1989): 52–63, 78.

Philp, Kenneth. *John Collier's Crusade for Indian Reform, 1920–1954*. Tucson: University of Arizona Press, 1977.

PL 101–644. Summary of Text of Title I, Public Law 101–644 [104 Stat. 4662], Act of November 29, 1990, Indian Arts and Crafts Board, U.S. Department of the Interior.

Powers, William K. "The American Flag in Lakota Art: An Ecology of Signs." *Whispering Wind* 28, no. 2 (1996): 2–15.

——. "Contemporary Oglala Music and Dance: Pan-Indianism versus Pan-Tetonism." *Ethnomusicology* 12, no. 3 (1968): 352–72.

——. *War Dance: Plains Indian Musical Performance*. Tucson: University of Arizona Press, 1990.

Pratt, Mary Louise. "Scratches on the Face of the Country; or What Mr. Barrow Saw in the Land of the Bushmen." In *"Race," Writing, and Difference*, ed. H. L. Gates, 138–62. Chicago: University of Chicago Press, 1986.

Pratt, Richard H. *Battlefield and Classroom: Four Decades with the American Indian, 1867–1904*. Ed. Robert M. Utley. New Haven: Yale University Press, 1964.

"Premium List: Fourth Annual Southwest Indian Fair." *El Palacio* 18 (May 1, 1925): 202–11.

Quick-to-See Smith, Jaune, ed. *Our Land/Ourselves: American Indian Contemporary Artists*. Albany: State University of New York at Albany, University Art Gallery, 1990.

Raczka, Paul. "Minípoka: Children of Plenty." *American Indian Art Magazine* 4 (summer 1979): 63–67, 96.

Rafter, John M. "More Sunlight/Petroglyph Interaction at Counsel Rocks." *Rock Art Papers*. San Diego Museum Papers 27 (1991): 65–74.

Relph, Edward. *Place and Placelessness*. London: Pion, 1976.

Rickard, Jolene. "Sovereignty: A Line in the Sand." *Aperture* 139 (spring 1995): 51.

Riley, James Whitcomb. *All the Year Round with Twelve Illustrations Cut on Wood and Printed in Colors by Gustave Baumann*. Indianapolis: Bobbs Merrill, 1912.

Ronda, James P. *Lewis and Clark among the Indians*. Lincoln: University of Nebraska Press, 1988.

Rubinstein, Meyer Raphael. "Review: Hachivi Edgar Heap of Birds at Exit Art." *Flash Art* 23, no. 155 (November–December 1990): 156–57.

Rudisill, Richard. *Mirror Image: The Influence of the Daguerreotype on American Society*. Albuquerque: University of New Mexico Press, 1971.

"Rural Art." *Life*, March 31, 1941, 76–79.

Rushing, W. Jackson. "Marketing the Affinity of the Primitive and the Modern: Rene d'Harnoncourt and Indian Art of the United States." In *The Early Years of Native American Art History: The Politics of Scholarship and Collecting*, ed. Janet C. Berlo, 191–236. Seattle: University of Washington Press, 1992.

———. *Native American Art and the New York Avant-Garde: A History of Cultural Primitivism.* Austin: University of Texas Press, 1995.

Ryden, Kent C. *Mapping the Invisible Landscape: Folklore, Writing, and the Sense of Place.* Iowa City: University of Iowa Press, 1993.

Sandzen, Birger. *The Graphic Work of Birger Sandzen.* Lindsborg, Kans.: Birger Sandzen Memorial Foundation, 1957.

Sanford, Margaret. "Pan-Indianism, Acculturation, and the American Ideal." *Plains Anthropologist* 16, no. 53 (1971): 222–27.

Sapir, Edward. "Culture, Genuine and Spurious." *American Journal of Sociology* 29 (1924): 401–29.

Schaafsma, Polly. *Indian Rock Art of the Southwest.* Albuquerque: University of New Mexico Press, 1980.

———. "Rock Art: Ideas in Time and Space." In *Marks in Place: Contemporary Responses to Rock Art,* 1–5. Albuquerque: University of New Mexico Press, 1988.

Schama, Simon. *Landscape and Memory.* New York: Vintage Books, 1995.

Schrader, Robert. *The Indian Arts and Crafts Board: An Aspect of New Deal Indian Policy.* Albuquerque: University of New Mexico Press, 1983.

Scott, R. A. "Clarence Boyce Monegar . . . 1910–1968, Memorial Exhibition." Exhibition brochure, Charles Allis Art Library, Milwaukee, Wisc., July 8–31, 1969.

———. "Clarence Boyce Monegar—Wisconsin Artist." *Wisconsin Tales and Trails* 4 (November 1963): 26.

Seymour, Tryntje Van Ness. *When the Rainbow Touches Down.* Seattle: University of Washington Press, 1988.

Shapiro, Henry D. *Appalachia on Our Mind: The Southern Mountains in the American Consciousness, 1870–1920.* Chapel Hill: University of North Carolina Press, 1978.

Shared Visions: Native American Painters and Sculptors in the Twentieth Century. Proceedings of a conference held at the Heard Museum, May 8–11, 1991. Phoenix: Heard Museum, 1991.

Shepard, Paul. *English Reaction to the New Zealand Landscape before 1850.* Wellington: Pacific Viewpoint Monograph No. 4, 1969.

Shiff, Richard. "The Necessity of Jimmie Durham's Jokes." *Art Journal* 51, no. 3 (1992): 74–80.

Shipek, Florence C. "History of Southern California Mission Indians." In *Handbook of North American Indians,* ed. William C. Sturtevant, 610–18. Vol. 8. Washington, D.C.: Smithsonian Institution Press, 1978.

Sloan, John, and Oliver LaFarge. *Introduction to American Indian Art.* New York: Exposition of Indian Tribal Arts, 1931.

Smallwood, Lyn. "Review: James Lavadour at Cliff Michel." *ARTnews* 90, no. 1 (January 1991): 168.

Smith, H. Denise. "The Rock Art of Abo Pueblo: Analyzing a Cultural Palimpsest." Ph.D. diss., University of New Mexico, 1998.

Smith, Jonathan. "The Lie That Binds: Destabilizing the Text of Landscape." In *Place/Culture/Representation,* ed. James Duncan and David Ley, 78–92. New York: Routledge, 1993.

Smith, Tracy. "Review: James Lavadour at PDX." *Art in America* 85, no. 3 (March 1997): 111.

Snodgrass, Jeanne. *American Indian Painters: A Biographical Directory.* New York: Museum of the American Indian, 1968.

Snyder, Joel. "Territorial Photography." In *Landscape and Power,* ed. W. J. T. Mitchell 175–201. Chicago: University of Chicago Press, 1994.

Speck, Frank G. "The Double-Curve Motive in Eastern Algonkian Art." *Canada Department of Mines, Geological Survey, Anthropological Series* no. 1, memoir 42 (1914): 1–17.

Speke, John Hanning. *What Led to the Discovery of the Source of the Nile.* Edinburgh: Blackwood, 1864.

Stahl, Harvey. "Recent Exhibitions." *Arts Magazine* 40, no. 4 (1966): 52–54.

Steinbring, Jack. "Phenomenal Attributes: Site Selection Factors in Rock Art." *American Indian Rock Art* 17 (1992): 102–13.

Steiner, Stan, ed. *Spirit Woman: The Diaries and Paintings of Bonita Wa Wa Calachaw Nuñez, an American Indian.* San Francisco: Harper and Row, 1980.

Stevens, Bernice. "The Revival of Handicrafts." In *The Southern Appalachian Region: A Survey,* ed. Thomas R. Ford, 279–88. Lexington: University of Kentucky Press, 1962.

Stewart, Susan. *On Longing: Narratives of the Miniature, the Gigantic, the Souvenir, the Collection.* Durham: Duke University Press, 1993.

Stewart, Tyrone H., ed. "The Great Oklahoma Feather Bust: Some Concerned Opinions." *Indian America* 8, no. 7 (1974).

——. "Wotantin: Eagle Feather Bust—Oklahoma City." *American Indian Crafts and Culture* 8, no. 6 (1974): 18–19.

Strickland, Rennard. "The Silberman Collection." *Persimmon Hill* (winter 1996): 29–36.

Supree, Burton, with Ann Ross. *Bear's Heart: Scenes from the Life of a Cheyenne Artist of One Hundred Years Ago with Pictures by Himself.* Philadelphia: J. B. Lippincott, 1977.

Sussman, Lynne. *Spode/Copeland Transfer Printed Patterns Found at Twenty Hudson's Bay Company Sites.* Canadian Historic Sites, Occasional Papers in Archaeology and History 22. Hull, Quebec: Canadian Government Publishing Centre, 1979.

Swagerty, William R. "Indian Trade in the Trans-Mississippi West to 1870." In *Handbook of the North American Indians,* ed. William C. Sturtevant, 351–74. Vol. 4. Washington, D.C.: Smithsonian Institution Press, 1983.

Szabo, Joyce M. "Howling Wolf: An Autobiography of a Plains Warrior-Artist." *Allen Memorial Art Museum Bulletin* 46 (1994): 4–87.

——. *Howling Wolf and the History of Ledger Art.* Albuquerque: University of New Mexico Press, 1994.

Tainter, Joseph, and Frances Levine. *Cultural Resources Overview of Central New Mexico.* Santa Fe and Albuquerque: Bureau of Land Management and U.S. Forest Service, 1987.

Taylor, Charles. *Multiculturalism and "the Politics of Recognition."* Princeton: Princeton University Press, 1992.

Terry, James. *Sculpted Anthropoid Ape Heads Found In or Near the Valley of the John Day River, A Tributary of the Columbia River, Oregon.* New York: J. J. Little, 1891.

Thomas, Robert K. "Pan-Indianism." *Midcontinent American Studies Journal* 6, no. 2 (1965): 75–83.

Thompson, Erwin N. *Spalding Area, Nez Perce National Historic Park.* Historic Research Study. Denver: National Park Service, 1972.

Torrence, Gaylord. *Native American Parfleche.* Kansas City: Kansas City Art Institute, 1984.

Toulouse, Joseph H., Jr. "The Mission of San Gregorio de Abo." *School of American Research Monograph 13.* Albuquerque: University of New Mexico Press, 1949.

Tremblay, Gail. "Cultural Survival and Innovation: Native American Aesthetics." In *Revivals! Diverse Traditions, 1920–1945: The History of Twentieth-Century American Craft,* ed. Janet Kardon, 77–83. New York: Harry N. Abrams in association with the American Craft Museum, 1994.

Trenholm, Virginia Cole. *The Arapahoes, Our People.* Norman: University of Oklahoma Press, 1986.

Trouillot, Michel-Rolph. *Silencing the Past: Power and the Production of History.* Boston: Beacon Press, 1995.

Tuan, Yi-Fu. "Place: An Experiential Perspective." *Geographical Review* 65 (1975): 151–65.

——. *Space and Place: The Perspective of Experience.* Minneapolis: University of Minnesota Press, 1977.

——. "Thought and Landscape: The Eye and the Mind's Eye." In *The Interpretation of Ordinary Landscapes: Geographic Essays,* ed. D. W. Meinig, 89–102. New York: Oxford University Press, 1979.

Urry, John. *The Tourist Gaze.* London: Sage Publications, 1990.

Valentino, Erin. "Mistaken Identity: Between Death and Pleasure in the Art of Kay WalkingStick." *Third Text* 26 (spring 1994): 61–73.

Viola, Herman J. *Warrior Artists: Historic Cheyenne and Kiowa Indian Ledger Art Drawn by Making Medicine and Zotom.* Washington, D.C.: National Geographic Society, 1998.

Vizenor, Gerald. *Fugitive Poses: Native American Indian Scenes of Absence and Presence.* Lincoln and London: University of Nebraska Press, 1998.

Wade, Edwin L., ed. *The Arts of the North American Indian: Native Traditions in Evolution.* New York: Hudson Hills Press, 1986.

Wade, Edwin L., and Jacki Thompson Rand, "The Subtle Art of Resistance: Encounter and Accommodation in the Art of Fort Marion." In *Plains Indian Drawings, 1865–1935, Pages from a Visual History,* ed. Janet Catherine Berlo, 45–49. New York: Harry N. Abrams in association with the American Federation of Arts and the Drawing Center, 1966.

Walis, Brian, ed. *Blasted Allegories.* New York: New Museum of Contemporary Art, 1987.

WalkingStick, Kay. "Native American Art in the Postmodern Era." *Art Journal* 51, no. 3 (fall 1992): 15–17.

Wallace, Anthony F. C. "Revitalization Movements." In *Reader in Comparative Religion,* ed. William A. Lessa and Evon Z. Vogt, 421–29. New York: Harper Collins, 1979.

Wardwell, Allen, ed. *Native Paths: American Indian Art from the Collection of Charles and Valerie Diker.* New York: Metropolitan Museum of Art, 1998.

Warren, Alvin C. "Institute of American Indian Arts to Open at Santa Fe." In *Education for Cross-Cultural Enrichment: Selected Articles from Indian Education, 1952–1964,* ed. Hildegard Thompson, 139–41. Haskell, Kans.: Haskell Institute Press for the Bureau of Indian Affairs, U.S. Department of the Interior, 1964.

Washington Statesman. December 20, 1961.

Watson, William J. *Journal of an Overland Journey to Oregon Made in the Year 1849.* 1851. Reprint, Fairfield, Wash.: Ye Galleon Press, 1985.

Weatherford, W. D. Foreword. In *The Southern Appalachian Region: A Survey,* ed. Thomas R. Ford, v–vi. Lexington: University of Kentucky Press, 1962.

Whisnant, David E. *All That Is Native and Fine: The Politics of Culture in an American Region.* Chapel Hill: University of North Carolina Press, 1983.

Whiteford, Andrew Hunter. "Floral Beadwork of the Western Great Lakes." *American Indian Art Magazine* 22, no. 4 (autumn 1997): 68–79.

"Widely Known Artists Headed for a Divorce: Mrs. Charles Kassler Reported Preparing to File Suit." *Denver Post,* February 12, 1935.

Wilbur, James H. "Report of Agents in Washington Territory, Yakama Indian Agency." *Annual Report of the Commissioner of Indian Affairs to the Secretary of the Interior for the Year 1875.* Washington, D.C.: Government Printing Office, 1875.

Wilson, Charles. *Mapping the Frontier: Charles Wilson's Diary of the Survey of the Forty-ninth Parallel, 1858–1862, While Secretary of the British Boundary Commission.* Ed. George F. G. Stanley. Seattle: University of Washington Press, 1970.

Wissler, Clark. "Ceremonial Bundles of the Blackfoot Indians." *Anthropological Papers of the American Museum of Natural History* 7 (1912): 65–298.

——. "Costumes of the Plains Indians." *Anthropological Papers of the American Museum of Natural History* 17 (1915): 39–91.

Wood, W. Raymond. "Plains Trade in Prehistoric and Protohistoric Intertribal Relations." In *Anthropology on the Great Plains,* ed. Margot Liberty, 98–109. Lincoln: University of Nebraska Press, 1980.

"Wood Block Prints by Gustave Baumann." *El Palacio* 15 (January 18, 1925): 35–36.

Woodward, Arthur. *Navajo Silver.* Flagstaff: Northland Press, 1974.

Wyckoff, Lydia L., ed. *Visions and Voices: Native American Painting from the Philbrook Museum of Art.* Tulsa: Philbrook Museum of Art, 1996.

Young, Gloria. "Dance as Communication." *Native Americas Special Edition*: *Native American Expressive Culture* 11, nos. 3 and 4 (1994): 9–15.

Young, M. Jane. *Signs from the Ancestors: Zuni Cultural Symbolism and Perceptions of Rock Art.* Albuquerque: University of New Mexico Press, 1988.

Young, Shelagh. *Carl Beam: The Columbus Project, Phase I.* Peterborough: Artspace and the Art Gallery of Peterborough, 1989.

Young, Stella. *Navajo Native Dyes: Their Preparation and Use.* 1940. Reprint, Palmer Lake, Colo.: Filter Press, 1978.

Young American Indian Artists. New York: Riverside Museum, 1965.

Index

Page numbers in *italics* refer to illustrations; *pl* refers to plate numbers.

Abbott, Lawrence, 198
Abo Pueblo: area map of, *212*; cultural history of, 221–23, 238*n*28, 239*nn*35, 36; rock art (*see* rock art, Abo Pueblo); trade relationships, 217, 222
abstractionism, 175; in *The End of the Innocence* (Longfish), 203; in *Nest of Suns* (Lavadour), 194; in *Neuf* (Heap of Birds), 202; of WalkingStick, Kay, *196*, 196–99
Adair, John, 244
Albers, Anni, 176
Allanstand Cottage Industries, 168
American Indian Arts and Crafts Act (1990), 139*n*43
American Indian Movement (AIM), 80
American Policy (Heap of Birds), 200
Amsden, Charles, 252
Anderson, Jeffrey, 37, 43
Angas, George, 191
Anishnabe, 80–81, 89*n*9
anthropology field workers, gender bias of, 11, 44, 46*n*26
Apache, 223, 226, 239*n*48
Apartheid Oklahoma (Heap of Birds), 200
Appalachia: outsiders' images of, 166–67, 175; poverty of, 163–64
Appalachian arts, 6, 163–86 (*see also* Southwest Native arts); handcraft schools and cooperatives, 166, 167–69, 171; intervention in, compared to Southwest Native arts, 180–83; modern applications of traditional forms, 170–71; preservation vs. change, 171–72, 175–76; revival, motivations for, 164–65, 168; weaving revival, 166, 168–69, 170–71
Arapaho (*see also* Fire Wood, quillwork by): cradles, 40–43, *41*; elders, 34, 36–37, 40, 43, 45*n*3, 46*n*23; and the Grass Dance, 75, 76; kindred relations, 35–36, 45n5, 46*n*10; quillwork, four ritualized forms of, 34–35
Arts and Crafts movement, 166, 167
Ash-Milby, Kathleen E., 4, 5
assimilation policies: and education, 121; and pow-wows, 80–81; of Pratt, Richard H., 51–52, 54, 55
Athapaskan rock art, 226, 239*n*48
At Home (Buzzard), 59, *pl 3*
authentication of tribal identity, 133, 139*n*43
Awa Tsireh, 103, 104, 113

Baca, Bartolome, 223, 231
Bahti, Tom, 178
Bal, Mieke, 27
Baldwin, Stuart, 222, 223
Bandelier, Adolf, 222
Barbeau, Marius, 263–64
Barrow, John, 190–91
battle imagery: in Fort Marion drawings, 50, 59; miniature-tipi, 15–18, 29*nn*22, 29
Baumann, Gustave, 99, *108*, 109–10, *110*
beadwork (*see also* quillwork): Fancy Dance, 81; floral-designed, Columbia River Plateau, 269–73, *270*, *272*, 275, *276*; Ghost Dance, 78–79, 91*nn*35, 36; Lakota, 76–77, 91*nn*35, 36; on miniature tipis, 22–25, 28*n*7, 30*n*46; Transmontane style, 275, 278, 280*n*21
Beam, Carl, 194, 199

Bear's Heart, 59, 61, 62, 64, 70*n*32; *Courting Scene*, 51, *51*, 59; self-portrait, 59, *60*, *pl* 4

Becker, Jane S., 180

Bent, Charles, 258

Benton, Thomas Hart, 159

Berea College, 166

Bermingham, Ann, 190

Bertoia, Marta Lesta, 58, 69*n*23

Betty Parsons Gallery, 175

Bhabha, Homi, 158

biocentrism, 155

Bird's Head, 35, 36

Birth of a Baby (Nuñez), 123–24, *pl* 8

Bishop, Evelyn, 168–69

Blackfoot, 13

Blaustein, Richard, 182

Blue Ridge Weavers, 171

Bodmer, Karl, 84

Bol, Marsha C., 4, 76

Boyce, George, 163, 181

Brody, J. J.: career of, 2–4; on chief blankets, third-phase, 252; *Indian Painters and White Patrons*, 1; on landscape painting, indigenous, 193; on patron intervention in Native arts, 1, 165; on rock art, 211, 224, 225, 235; at the University of New Mexico, 1–2

Brulé, 250

Bryan, Nonabah, 169

Bryson, Norman, 27

Buck in the Snow (Monegar), *152*, 153

Buffalo, Charley, 15–16

buffalo robes and backrests: and chief blankets, 248, 249–50, 252, 259*n*13; quilled, by Fire Wood, 35–40, *37*, *38*, *39*

bustles: Fancy Dance style, 80, 81; Northern Traditional, 81–83, *82*, 84, 93*n*49, *pl* 6; original Crow Belt, 74–75, 77; reservation-era, 77, 80, 90*n*16, *pl* 5

Cannon, T. C., 163, 180, *pl* 11

Carlisle Indian School, 40, 45*n*1, 55

Carmonia-Nuñez, Manuel, *122*, 123

Cassidy, Gerald, 97

Caudill, Harry, 163–64, 181

Centennial Exposition (1876), 272, 274

ceramics, floral-designed, 266, 279*n*15

Charlot, Jean, 174–75

Cheyenne: at Fort Marion (*see* Fort Marion drawings); and the Grass Dance, 75, 76, 90*n*24; miniature tipis, 10, 13, 15, 22–23, *24*, 28*n*14, 29*n*22; *parfleche*, 252; at trade fair, 1815, 256–57; women's sewing guilds, 46*nn*12, 13

chief blankets, Navajo, 6, 241–61; blanket strips on,

248, 249–50, *251*; first-phase, 244, *246*, 249–50, *251*, 259*n*13; mantas, 242, 244, 245, 259*n*2; *moqui* blankets, 244–45, 259*n*7; second-phase, 244, *247*, 250, 252; third-phase, 244–45, *248*, 252–53; and trade networks, 243, 253–58; value of, 241, 258

Chief Runs Them All (Nuñez), 125

Chinle trading post, 169, 170

Christensen, Chris, 157

Clark, Ricky, 267

Cleland, Wayne, *85*

clothing, powwow. *See* powwow clothing, Northern Traditional

Codallos y Rabal, Joachin, 257

Cody, Cadzi, 20–22, 30*n*36

collectibles. *See* marketable art

colonialism, and landscape painting, 189–93, 195, 206*nn*4, 5, 9, 207*n*24

Colville gloves, 275, *pl* 15

Comanche, 76, 84, 90*n*26, 93*n*51

concha belts, 243–44

Courting Scene (Bear's Heart), 51, *51*, 59

coverlets, floral-designed, 266, *268*, 269

cradles: with chief blanket designs, 253; floral-designed, Columbia River Plateau, 269–71, *270*, 275–76, *277*; quilled, Arapaho, 40–43, *41*

Crafts in the Southern Highlands, 176, *177*

Craftsman magazine, 166, 169

Craven, Thomas, 157

Crow, 75, *250*, 252–53

Crumley, Carole, 216–17

Curry, John Steuart, 141, 144–45, 159, 160*n*8, 161*n*26

Dakota rendezvous, 255–56

Dalles rendezvous, 256

dance clothes. *See* powwow clothing, Northern Traditional

Day, Frank, 123

deer toe bells, *79*, 79–80

Denman, William and Leslie Van Ness, 114

Denver Art Museum, 97, 113

d'Harnoncourt, Rene, 173–74

Directions in Indian Art conference, 176, 178

displacement, in landscape painting, 199–202

Dockstader, Frederick, 119, 136

Douglas, Clementine, 171

Duggan, Mary, 120–21, 123, 132, 134

Duncan, James, 188, 191

Durham, Jimmie, 194, 199

Dutton, Bertha, 222

dyes, 81, 167, 169, 170, 245

Eagle feather controversy, 83–84, 92*n*46, 93*n*48

Eastern Association on Indian Affairs, 169–70

Eastern Woodlands tribes, floral design in, 264, 265
Eaton, Allen, 168, 175
Ela, Mary, 175
elders, Arapaho, 34, 36–37, 40, 43, 45*n*3, 46*n*23
Eldredge, Charles, 159
Eliade, Mircea, 216
elk dreamers, 23, 25
The End of the Innocence (Longfish), 203–5,
	209*nn*50, 52, *pl*13
Entering Zig's Indian Reservation (Jackson), 200,
	208*n*41
environmental consciousness, 1930s, 154–56, 160*n*16
Etahdleuh Doanmoe, 54, 64
Ewers, John, 10, 13, 252, 255
Exposition of Indian Tribal Arts (1931), 113, 114, 127,
	172–73
expressionism, 128

Fagin, Nancy, 10, 13
Fancy Dance style, 80, 81, 92*n*38
Feddersen, Joe, 193
Feeding Grouse (Monegar), 145, *145*
Fireside Industries, 166–67, 170
Fire Wood, quillwork by, 4, 33–47; buffalo robes and
	backrests, 35–40, *37, 38, 39*; cradles, 40–43, *41*;
	and elder women, role of, 34, 36–37, 40, 43,
	46*n*23; four ritualized forms of, 34–35; as protec-
	tion of kindred, 35–36, 38–39, 43–44, 46*n*25
First American Indian Performing Arts Festival (1964),
	179
floral design, Columbia River Plateau, 7, 263–80;
	ceramics, Western, 266, 279*n*15; coat and pants,
	273–74, *274*; Colville gloves, 275, *pl*15; cradles,
	269–71, *270*, 275–76, *277*; dark on light ground,
	271; influences on, 265–69, 277–78; leggings,
	275, *276*; light on dark ground, 271, 279*n*15;
	quilts and coverlets, 266–69, *267, 268*; sad-
	dlebags, 271–73, *272*, *pl*14; studies of, 263–64;
	through white contact, 265–66, 276–77; wall-
	papers, Western, 266
Fort Colvile, 269, 271
Fort Laramie Treaty (1851), 76, 90*n*26
Fort Marion: bullfights, 54, 68*n*14; Pratt's efforts at,
	49, 50–53, 54–55; tourism at, 53–56, 68*n*14
Fort Marion drawings, 4–5, 49–70, *51, 56, 60, 65*;
	Courting Scene (Bear's Heart), *51*, *51*, 59; dating
	of, 67*n*9; *At Home* (Buzzard), 59, *pl*3; *Indian
	Prisoners at Fort Marion Being Photographed*
	(Making Medicine), 55, *56*, 63; as personalized
	mementoes (autograph books), 57–62, 68*n*22; as
	political gifts, 50–53, 57–58; Pratt's role in, 49,
	50–53, 67*n*5; self-portraits, 59, *60*, 63–64, *65*,
	*pl*4; as souvenirs, 50, 53–57, 62, 67*n*4

Frost, William Goodell, 166
Fry, Aaron, 4, 5

Ghost Dance, 78–79, 90*n*24, 91*nn*31, 34–36
Giant Redwood Trees of California (Bierstadt), 192
Gilpin, Laura, 97
GIS (geographical information systems) software,
	211, 213, 219, 227
Glowen, Ron, 194
Goddard, Pliny Earle, 14–15, 29*n*20
Goodrich, Francis L., 168
Gordon, Beverly, 54
Grafe, Steven LeRoy, 4, 7
Graham, Hettie Wright, 166–67
Grass Dance, 73, 75–76, 77–78, 80, 90*n*26, 91*nn*28,
	31, 92*n*37
Great Lakes tribes, floral design in, 264, 265
Greenberg, Clement, 188
Gritton, Joy L., 4, 6

*Half-Breed Child in Cradle, with Indian Ornamental
	Trappings*, 269–71, *270*
Hall, Jessie G., 97, 112–13
Hallpike, C. R., 72
Handicrafts of the Southern Highlands (Eaton), 175
Handicrafts of the Southern Highlands exhibition
	(1933), 172
Harrison, Charles, 192
Harvesting Grain (Pino), 106, 109, *frontispiece*
Harvey, Fred, 169, 244
Hawkesworth, John, 189, 206*n*4
Hayes, Susan B., 167
Heap of Birds, Hachivi Edgar, 200–202, *201*
Heard, Marian, 175
Helsinger, Elizabeth, 190
Her Memory (Nuñez), 129–30, *130*, 132, 139*n*38
Herrera, Velino Shije, 102–3, *104*, 114
Hewett, Edgar Lee, 114
hide painting, 18, 20–21
hide scrapers, marks on, 36, 45*n*9
Hilger, Inez M., 42
Hill, Jennie Lester, 170
Hill, W. W., 242–43, 258
Hindman Settlement School, 167–68
Hopi, 218
horse trading, 255, 256
Howe, Oscar, 135
Howling Wolf, 57, 61, 68*n*17, 70*n*32
Hubbell, Juan Lorenzo, 169, 244
Huckabee, Mrs. F. D., 171
Huenemann, Lynn, 84
hunting imagery: on miniature tipis, 18–20, *19*; in
	Monegar's paintings, 149, 151, 155–56

Ickes, Harold, 175
illusionistic painting, 102, 103–4, 146, 187–88, 190,
     205*n*2, 206*n*9 (*see also* pan-Indian style)
Indian Art of the United States (1941), 127–28, 174–75
Indian Art of the United States and Alaska (1939),
     173–74
Indian Arts and Crafts Board, 173
Indian Painters and White Patrons (Brody), 1
Indian Prisoners at Fort Marion Being Photographed
     (Making Medicine), 55, *56*, 63
indian stereotypes, Vizenor's, 151, 153
Institute of American Indian Arts (IAIA), 163, 164,
     178–80
Ivey, James, 222

Jackson, Zig, 199–200, 208*n*41
Janvier, Alex, 193
Jewell, Edward Alden, 173
jingle dresses, 80–81, 89*n*9
John C. Campbell Folk School, 168
Joseph, chief of the Nez Perce, 273

Kabotie, Fred, 103, 104, 113
Kash Kash, Edna, *251*, 259*n*13
Kassler, Charles M., Jr., 97, 99, 101–2, *102*
Kavanaugh, Thomas, 84
Keithahn, E. L., 213
Kent, Kate Peck, 242
Kephart, Horace, 166
Kiowa: Fancy Dance style, 92*n*38; at Fort Marion
     (*see* Fort Marion drawings); and the Grass
     Dance, 76, 90*nn*23, 26; miniature tipis, 12–13,
     15–16, 28*n*14, 29*n*22; oak leaf motif, 73; shoulder
     fans, 84, 93*n*51
Kiowa Five, 111
Kluckhohn, Clyde, 242–43
Kluckhohn, Lucy Wales, 242–43
Kober, George Martin, 273, 274, 275
Koerner, W. H. D., 149, 160*n*7
Kollwitz, Käthe, 124, 128, *129*
Kootenai, 75
Kroeber, Alfred, 40

Lakota, 10, 76–77, 91*nn*35, 36
landscape, contemporary, 6, 187–209; Brody on,
     193; and colonialism, 189–93, 195, 206*nn*4, 5, 9,
     207*n*24; and displacement, 199–202; *The End
     of the Innocence* (Longfish), 203–5, 209*nn*50,
     52, *pl*13; fire motif, 195; human figures in, 190–
     92, 207*n*15; *Nest of Suns* (Lavadour), 193–96,
     208*n*26, *pl*12; *Neuf* (Heap of Birds), 200–202,
     201; perspectival illusionism in, 187–88, 190,
     205*n*2, 206*n*9; political content in, 203–5; sub-

jectivity of, 188–89; tree stump motif, 195; *Venere
     Alpina* (WalkingStick), 196, *196*, 198; of Walk-
     ingStick, Kay, 196–99, 208*n*30; Watkins's photo-
     graphs as, 192–93, 207*n*17
landscape theory, and rock art, 213–19 (*see also* rock
     art, Abo Pueblo)
LaNore, Ruth, 4, 5
Lavadour, James, 193–96, 208*n*26, 209*n*46, *pl*12
Lawyer, Lucy, 274
ledger art, 18, 20
Lefebvre, Henri, 214
Leopold, Aldo, 155, 156, 161*n*26
Lewis and Clark, 255–56
Linderman, Frank B., 9, 46*n*26
Lippard, Lucy, 203
Lippincott, Sallie, 170
Little Bluff, 15
Lodge, Sir Oliver, 132
Loloma, Charles, 178
Longfish, George, 203–5, 209*nn*50, 52
Lowe, Truman, 193, 194
Luiseño, 134

Made in Japan with Exception of One (Cannon), 163,
     *pl*11
Making Medicine, 52, 57–58, 64, 70*n*32; *Indian Pris-
     oners at Fort Marion Being Photographed*, 55, *56*,
     63
Man and Two Deer (Pino), *98*, 98–99, 109
Mandan, 17, 29*n*29
mantas, 242, 244, 245, 259*n*2
marketable art: chief blankets (*see* chief blankets,
     Navajo); at exhibitions, 174; exoticism of, 53–54;
     floral-designed, 264, 278; Fort Marion drawings
     as, 49–50, 53–57, 67*n*4; miniature tipis, 11, 20–
     22, *22*, 23, 25, 28*n*9, 31*n*49; by Monegar, Clar-
     ence (*see* Monegar, Clarence); by Nuñez, Bonita
     Wa Wa Calachaw (*see* Nuñez, Bonita Wa Wa
     Calachaw); pan-Indian (*see* pan-Indian style);
     patron intervention in, 165–66, 180–83 (*see also*
     Appalachian arts; Southwest Native arts); by
     Pino, Juan (*see* Pino, Juan); romantic stereotypes
     in (*see* romantic stereotypes); silver, 244; as sou-
     venirs, 22, 53, 67*n*4
Marsh, Reginald, 159
Martinez, Maria, 180, 181
Maurer, Evan, 19
McDonald, Angus, 269, 270, 271
McDonald, Catherine, 269–71
McGrath, Jim, 179
McSparron, L. H. (Cozy), 170
Mexican silver, 244
Mimbres, 193

Il Minotauro (WalkingStick), 199, 208*n*40

Mitchell, W. J. T., 188, 189, 190

modernism: in landscape painting (*see* landscape, contemporary); Native art as, 173–75, 179–80; and Nuñez, Bonita Wa Wa Calachaw, 127–28

Modersohn-Becker, Paula, 124

Monegar, Clarence, 5–6, 141–61; biographical sketch of, 143–46, 158, 161*n*24; *Buck in the Snow, 152, 153;* and Curry, John Steuart, 141, 144–45, 159, 160*n*8; *Feeding Grouse,* 145, *145;* hunting imagery of, 149, 151, 155–56; identity as Native artist, 158–59; and *indian* stereotypes, 151, 153–54, 158; landscape settings, 157–58; pan-Indian style of, 141, 143, 154–56; red arrowhead signature, 156, 158; *Running Deer,* 159, *pl* 10; at the Rural Arts Program, University of Wisconsin, 146, 157; sales of works, 145–46, 156, 157, 161*nn*19, 22; *Scout,* 149, *150;* Untitled (Indian hunter), 149, 151, *pl* 9; Untitled (warrior on horseback), *148,* 149, 153; and Van Gorden collection, 144, 146, *147,* 149, 153, 160*n*11; wildlife scenes, 144–45, 153–57, 158–59

Monteith, John, 274

Montezuma, Carlos, 124, 135, 139*n*48

Mooney (James) collection, 10, 11, 12–13, 15–16, 22–23, 28*nn*9, 14

Moore, J. B., 244

Mootza, Waldo, 123

moqui blankets, 244–45, 259*n*7

Morris, Kate, 4, 6

Morrison, George, 193

Murphy, Greta J., 4, 6

Museum of Fine Arts, Santa Fe, (N. M.), 97, 101, 109, 110, 112

Museum of Modern Art, 127, 174

Museum of the American Indian (MAI), 119, 125, 126, 136

Naja form, 244

Native Hosts (Heap of Birds), 200

Nauni, Haddon, 75

Navajo: adaptive abilities of, 241, 242; aesthetics, 253, 260*n*21; Bosque Redondo incarceration, 244, 259*n*5; chief blankets (*see* chief blankets, Navajo); *moqui* blankets, 244–45, 259*n*7; silver, 243–44; trade networks, 253–58, *254;* weaving, early, 242–43, 259*n*2; weaving revival, 169, 170–71

Nest of Suns (Lavadour), 193–96, 208*n*26, *pl* 12

Neuf (Heap of Birds), 200–202, *201*

New, Lloyd, 178, 179

Newman, Barnett, 175

Nez Perce: coat and pants, 273–74, *274;* cradle, 275–76, *277;* leggings, 275, *276;* miniature saddlebag, 271–72, *272;* at rendezvous, 256

nostalgia, reservation-era, 20, 50, 58, 59

Novak, Barbara, 195

nudes, maternal, 123–24, 138*n*15

Nuñez, Bonita Wa Wa Calachaw, 5, 119–40, *122;* as advocate for Indian rights, 128, 135; as an actress, 134–35; animal images by, 132–33; authenticity as Native artist, 126, 133–37; birth and childhood, 120–21, 123; *Birth of a Baby,* 123–24, *pl* 8; *Chief Runs Them All,* 125; children of, 123, 138*n*13; and the collective unconscious, 132; dating of works, 125, 137*n*3; *Her Memory,* 129–30, *130,* 132, 139*n*38; medical drawings by, 124; modernist influences on, 127–28; and the Museum of the American Indian, 119, 136; and Native American painting, exposure to, 127–28; in Philbrook Art Center Indian Annual, 124, 126, 135–36; portraiture by, 124; technique, oil-painting, 125; Untitled, (three men), 120, *120,* 125; Untitled, (two women), 130–32, *131;* Untitled, (village of spirits), 120, 132–33, *133,* 135, *pl* 7

Oheltoint, 64, 69*n*30, 70*n*34

Omaha Crow Belts, 74–75

Ortega y Gasset, José, 156

Osage, 76, 90*n*26

Our Land/Ourselves: American Indian Contemporary Artists, 187–88

Pach, Walter, 173

Palmer, Dixon, 16

pan-Indian style (*see also* illusionistic painting; marketable art; romantic stereotypes): as authentic tradition, 102–3, 113–14, 115, 126, 142; Bambi style, 159*n*3; and Monegar, Clarence, 141, 143, 154–56; and Nuñez, Bonita Wa Wa Calachaw, 135–36; of Pino, Juan, 96–98, 103, 104; powwow clothing, intertribalism of, 73–74, 77, 89*nn*9, 11; and Rush, Olive, 102–3; and Sloan, John, 111–12, 142; Southwest, or Studio style, 96, 103–4, 113–14, 115, 126–27, 139*n*29, 142

parfleche, 249, *250,* 252

Parkman, Francis, 58

Parsons (Betty) Gallery, 175

patron intervention in art, 1, 165–66, 180–83

Penney, David, 264

perspectival illusionism, 102, 103–4, 146, 187–88, 190, 205*n*2, 206*n*9

petroglyphs. *see* rock art, Abo Pueblo

Pettit, Katherine, 167

Philbrook Art Center, 125, 126, 135–36, 142

Phillips, Ruth, 22, 264

Pi Beta Phi Settlement School, 168–69

pictographs. *see* rock art, Abo Pueblo

Piegan, 13

Pine Burr Studio, 171

Pino, Joseph, 115, 117*n*38

Pino, Juan, 5, 95–117; animal figures of, 97; and
Baumann, Gustave, 99, 109–10; borders, decorative, 98, 99, 109; ceases printmaking, 114–15,
117*n*38; early prints, 96–104; exhibitions and
reviews of, 97, 98, 104, 112, 113; and the *Exposition of Indian Tribal Arts* (1931), 113, 114; and
Hall, Jessie, 97, 112–13; *Harvesting Grain*, 106,
109, *frontispiece*; human form, depictions of, 97,
98, 99, 104; influences on, 99–104; and Kassler,
Charles, 97, 99, 101–2, 115; later prints, 104–14;
Man and Two Deer, 98, 98–99, 109; pottery
painting of, 96, 99–101, *100*, 116*n*9; *Pueblo Scene
with Man in Overalls*, 106, *107*; *Pueblo Scene with
Two Burros and Walking Man*, *105*, 105–6; and
Rush, Olive, 102–3; and Sloan, John, 111–12

Pino, Lorencita, 99, *100*, 112

Plains Indians (*see also specific tribes*): aesthetic commonalities, 246–53; buffalo robes (*see* buffalo
robes and backrests); cradles, 40–43, *41*, 253; at
Fort Marion (*see* Fort Marion drawings); and
Navajo chief blankets (*see* chief blankets,
Navajo); *parfleche*, 249, *250*, 252; *possible bags*,
250, 253; powwow clothing (*see* powwow
clothing, Northern Traditional); silver, 243–44;
tipis (*see* tipis, miniature); trade networks, 253–
58, *254*

Polelonema, Otis, 103, 104, 113–14

Ponca, 76, 90*n*26, 92*n*38

possible bags, 250, 253

pottery, 96, 99–101, *100*, 116*n*9, 180–81

powwow clothing, Northern Traditional, 5, 71–93;
bustles (*see* bustles); deer toe bells, *79*, 79–80;
eagle feather controversy, 83–84, 92*n*46, 93*n*48;
Fancy Dance style, 80, 81, 92*n*38; the four styles
of, 89*n*9; gender differences in, 72, 89*n*9; Ghost
Dance, 78–79, 90*n*24, 91*nn*31, 34–36; Grass
Dance, 73, 75–76, 77–78, 80, 90*n*26, 91*nn*28, 31,
92*n*37; hair, significance of, 72; indigenization,
78–80, 81; jingle dresses, 80–81, 89*n*9; new Traditional style, 81; north-south distinctions, contemporary, 81, 92*n*43; pan-Indian (intertribal)
vs. tribal, 73–74, 77, 89*nn*9, 11; porcupine hair
roaches, *85*, 86, 93*n*52; as power through resistance, 72–73, 76, 77, 83–84, 88*n*7; shoulder fans,
84, *85*, 93*n*51; soldier hats, 84, 86, *87*; tradition,
defined, 72, 88*nn*3, 4

Pratt, Mary Louise, 190–91, 202–3

Pratt, Richard H., 49, 50–53, 54–55, 57, 58, 67*n*5, 121

Pretty Shield, 9, 28*n*2

Pueblos: Hopi, 218; in Pino's prints (*see* Pino, Juan);

pottery, 96, 99–101, *100*, 180–81; rock art (*see*
rock art, Abo Pueblo); Tewa, 216; weaving,
taught to Navajos, 242, 259*n*2; Zuni, 216, 217,
218–19, 225, 226, 259*n*2

Pueblo Scene with Man in Overalls (Pino), 106, *107*

Pueblo Scene with Two Burros and Walking Man
(Pino), *105*, 105–6

Quillwork: by Fire Wood (*see* Fire Wood, quillwork
by); four ritualized forms of, 34–35; on miniature
tipis, 22–25, 28*n*7, 30*n*46; perfection of, 42,
46*n*21

quilts, floral-designed, 266–67, *267*

Redding, Winogene B., 168

regional hegemony, 142–43, 157, 161*n*20

rendezvous, 255–56

rock art, Abo Pueblo, 6, 211–40; arroyos, role of,
219; Athapaskan, 226, 234, *235*, *236*, 239*n*48; as
boundary, 218, 234; Brody on, 211, 224, 225, 235;
chronology of, 221; Early Puebloan style, 226,
227, *228*, 239*n*47; functions of, 224–25; Geometric style, 226; GIS analysis of, 211, 213, 219,
227; Historic (Pueblo V), 222–23, 228, *230*, 230–
34, *231*, *232*, *233*, *236*; and landscape theory (*see*
rock art and landscape); Late Puebloan (Pueblo
IV), 222, 226, 228–30, *229*, *230*, 234, *236*, 239*n*41;
as palimpsest, 218, 225–26; phenomenal attributes of, 234–35; pictographs/petroglyphs, differences in, 224, 225, 235–36; pigments in, 225,
239*n*44; scope of, 211, 213, 219, *220*; White Figure
style, 226

rock art and landscape, 211–19; as boundary, 217–18;
at centers, 216–17, 218; and functional lattices,
217; multiple functions of, 218; as palimpsest,
218; phenomenal attributes, role of, 215–16, 234–
35; and place, defined, 214–16, 237*n*8; and space,
theory of, 214; studies of, 213, 237*n*3

Rockefeller Foundation, 175–76

romantic stereotypes (*see also* pan-Indian style): and
miniature tipis, 22, 25–27; in Monegar's paintings, 141–42, 151, 153–56; in Santa Fe, 96, 115

Rönnebeck, Arnold, 112, 113

Running Deer (Monegar), 159, *pl* 10

Rural Arts Exhibition (1937), 172

Rush, Olive, 102–3

Ryden, Kent, 215, 217–18

Ryder, Albert Pinkham, 127

The Sacrifice (Kollwitz), 128, *129*

saleable art. *See* marketable art

Sandzen, Birger, 109

Sanford, Margaret, 73–74, 89*n*13

Santa Fe, 96, 109–11, 115
Santa Fe Indian School, 103, 142
Santina, Andrianne A., 4, 5
Sarcee miniature tipi, *14*, 14–15, 29*n*20
Schaafsma, Polly, 216, 224, 226, 232
Schama, Simon, 188
Scout (Monegar), 149, *150*
Shakespeare, William (War Bonnet), 40, 46*n*15
Sherman, William Tecumseh, 53
Shields, George "Cricket," Jr., 86, 93*n*53
Shoshone, 20, 75, *250*, 253
Shoshone rendezvous, 255, 256
Shriver, Sargent, 163
silver, Navajo and Plains, 243–44
Sioux: blankets, *249*, 250; Brulé, 250; and the Grass
    Dance, 75; Lakota, 10, 76–77, 91*nn*35, 36, *249*;
    miniature tipis, 16–17, *17*, *21*, 21–22, 23, 25,
    30*n*40, *pl* 1–2; powwow clothing and dance,
    89*n*9; trade networks, 255–56, 257
Sleeping Bear, 15
Sloan, John, 111–12, 142, 172, 184*n*34
Smith, H. Denise, 4, 6
Smith, Jaune Quick-to-See, 187–88, 203
Smith, John Quincy, 52, 57–58
Smith, Lela, 157
Snyder, Joel, 192–93
Soaring Eagle, 57, 64
soldier hats, 84, 86, *87*
Southern Highland Handicraft Guild, 171, 172, 181
Southwest Indian Art Project, 164, 178
Southwest Native arts, 163–86 (*see also* Appalachian
    arts; Pino, Juan); Directions in Indian Art con-
    ference, 176, 178; Institute of American Indian
    Arts (IAIA), 163, 164, 178–80; intervention in,
    compared to Appalachian arts, 180–83; modern
    applications of traditional forms, 171; preserva-
    tion vs. change, 178–80; revival, motivations for,
    169, 170; Southwest Indian Art Project, 164, 178;
    Studio style painting, 96, 103–4, 113–14, 115,
    126–27, 139*n*29, 142, 159*n*3; University of New
    Mexico program, 2; weaving revival, Navajo,
    169, 170–71
souvenirs, 22, 53, 67*n*4 (*see also* marketable art)
space, theory of, 214
Spaniards, 222–23, 231, 245, 257
Speck, Frank G., 263, 264
Speke, John Hanning, 192
Spinning Wheel craft center, 171
Spybuck, Ernest, 126
Steinbring, Jack, 215–16, 234
Stevens, Bernice, 164–65, 181
Stewart, Susan, 11–12, 26, 57
Stickley, Gustave, 166

Stone, May, 167
Storror, Edward, 271–72
Street Chiefs (Whitman), 199
Studio style, 96, 103–4, 113–14, 115, 126–27, 139*n*29,
    142, 159*n*3
surrealism, 173
Szabo, Joyce M., 4–5, 20

Tahoma, Quincy, 126
Taylor, Charles, 151
Terry, James, 275, 279*n*20
Tesuque Pueblo pottery, 96, 99–101, *100*
Tewa, 216
tipis: construction of, 16, 29*nn*23, 26, 30; covers,
    dearth of, 9, 10, 28*n*1
tipis, miniature, 5, 9–31; battle imagery on, 15–18, *17*,
    29*nn*22, 29, *pl* 1; beaded or quilled, 11, 22–25, *24*,
    28*n*7, 30*n*46, *pl* 2; ceremonial scenes, 20–22,
    30*nn*35, 36, 40; as cultural specimens, 10–11, 12–
    14, 28*n*14, 29*n*20; hunting imagery on, 18–20,
    19; miniature vs. model, 11–12; numbers of, 9,
    28*n*1; as saleable collectibles, 11, 20–22, 23, 25,
    28*n*9, 31*n*49; as secondary documents, 10, 25–
    26; Tipi with Battle Pictures, 15, 16, 29*n*22; as
    toys, 9–10, 13, 28*n*6; with vision-inspired imag-
    ery, 12–15, *14*, 23, 25, 28*n*14, 29*n*20, *pl* 2
Tish Kamiakin, *268*
Tompiro, 222, 223
Toulouse, Joseph, 222, 223, 231, 239*n*36
tourism, at Fort Marion, 53–56, 68*n*14
toys: floral-designed, Columbia River Plateau, 271–
    72, *272*; miniature tipis, 9–10, 13, 28*n*6
trade fairs, 217, 255, 256–57
trade networks, Navajo/Plains, 243, 253–58
traditional Native art. *See* pan-Indian style
Transmontane style, 275, 278, 280*n*21
Tremblay, Gail, 180–81, 182
Truax, Sewall, 275
Truteau, Jean-Baptiste, 255
Tsinhnahjinnie, Hulleah, 199–200
Tuan, Yi-Fu, 214–15, 237*n*8

Udall, Stewart, 163, 179
University of New Mexico Native arts program, 1–2
University of Wisconsin Rural Arts Program, 146,
    157
Urban Survival (Tsinhnahjinnie), 199–200
Utes, 256, 258

Van Gorden, S. H. (Monegar), 146, *147*
Vargas, Diego de, 222
Velez Cachupin, Tomas, 222, 239*n*35
Venere Alpina (WalkingStick), 196, *196*, 198

Viola, Herman, 52
Vizenor, Gerald, 151

WalkingStick, Kay, *196*, 196–99, 208*n*30
Warden, Cleaver, 33, 40, 44, 45*n*1 (*see also* Fire
    Wood, quillwork by)
Warneke, Heinz, 97
Watkins, Carleton, 192–93, 207*n*17
Watson, Samuel E., III, 4, 5–6
Wa Wa Chaw. *See* Nuñez, Bonita Wa Wa Calachaw
Weaver, Emma, 176
weaving: Appalachian, revival of, 166, 168–69, 170–
    71; gender delineation in, Southwest, 259*n*2;
    Navajo, 169, 170–71, 242–43 (*see also* chief blan-
    kets, Navajo); trade networks, Navajo/Plains,
    243
Wetherill, Hildegard, 258
Weyhe (Erhard) Gallery, 112
Wheelwright, Mary Cabot, 169, 170

Whipple, Henry, 53, 55
Whisnant, David, 165, 180
White, Amelia, 172, 184*n*34
Whiteford, Andrew Hunter, 263
Whitehorse, Emmi, 193
Whitman, Richard Ray, 199
Wide Ruins trading post, 170
Wilbur, James H., 272
Wissler, Clark, 10–11
Wohaw, 64, *65*
Wolf, Ann, 42
Woodward, Arthur, 243–44

Yakama, 272–73, *pl* 14
Young, M. Jane, 216, 218, 219, 225, 226, 237

Zigrosser, Carl, 112
Zotom, 52, 57–58, 68*n*17
Zuni, 216, 217, 218–19, 225, 226, 259*n*2